Critical praise for this book

'The "Palestinian Question" is essentially about competing claims to land, within both the occupied territories and Israel itself. This carefully written and thoroughly researched study shows how Israel has succeeded, by means contrary to international human rights standards, in reserving 94 per cent of the land of Israel for the exclusive use of its Jewish population. The dispossession of the land of the Palestinians within Israel by discriminatory laws and practices is examined in the context of Palestinian history, Israeli law and international standards. This excellent study serves as a timely reminder that the "Palestine Question" is not only abou the occupied territories – it is also about the plight of Palestinians in Israel itself.'

John Dugard, Professor of International Law, University of Leiden; Special Rapporteur to the UN Commission on Human Rights on Violations of Human Rights in the Occupied Palestinian Territory

'In all settler colonies, control over land is at the heart of the conflict that will inevitably ensue between the natives and the settlers. Israel, being a settler colony, is no exception to this rule. Its protracted conflict with the Palestinians, whether refugees outside their homeland or internal refugees, is focused on the control of land. This carefully researched book is the definitive work on the various modalities Israel has devised and utilized to systematically colonize Palestinian land, to secure control thereof, and to frustrate any attempt by the Palestinians to reclaim their properties.'

Anis F. Kassim, Consulting Editor, *The Palestine Yearbook of International Law*

About the Authors

Hussein Abu Hussein is a Palestinian lawyer who practises in Um El Fahem, one of the largest Palestinian communities in Israel. He has been active in human rights and cultural organizations in the region for many years. He has handled many cases relating to land, discrimination, political prisoners and other issues affecting Palestinians who are citizens of Israel, including a number of test cases where he has invoked human rights arguments in the Israeli courts.

Fiona McKay is a British solicitor and international human rights lawyer. She worked with Palestinian human rights organizations in Israel from 1988 to 1991, focusing on land rights, other aspects of discrimination and the rights of the Palestinian unrecognized villages and of the Bedouin in the Naqab. She then worked in Jerusalem as director of a legal service organization operating in the West Bank. Since 1995 she has worked on broader human rights and international justice issues.

ACCESS DENIED
Palestinian land rights in Israel

HUSSEIN ABU HUSSEIN &
FIONA MCKAY

Zed Books
LONDON · NEW YORK

Access Denied: Palestinian land rights in Israel was first published by Zed Books Ltd, 7 Cynthia Street, London N1 9JF, UK and Room 400, 175 Fifth Avenue, New York, NY 10010, USA in 2003.

www.zedbooks.demon.co.uk

Cover designed by Andrew Corbett
Set in Monotype Dante by Ewan Smith, London
Printed and bound in Malta by Gutenberg Ltd

Distributed in the USA exclusively by Palgrave, a division of St Martin's Press, LLC, 175 Fifth Avenue, New York, NY 10010.

A catalogue record for this book is available from the British Library

Library of Congress Cataloging-in-Publication data: applied for

ISBN 1 84277 122 1 cased
ISBN 1 84277 123 X limp

Contents

Acknowledgements

In memory of Mansour Kardosh, a founder of the 'Al Ard' movement and tireless campaigner for the rights of Palestinian citizens of Israel, who was a source of inspiration for us both.

The research for this book was carried out under the auspices of the Galilee Centre for Social Research, Haifa, with a grant from the Ford Foundation. We would like to thank the Galilee Centre and the Ford Foundation for their generous support.

The authors would like to thank warmly the many individuals and organizations that contributed their expertise and input, by agreeing to be interviewed or providing materials or insights. We would like to express our special thanks to Hosne Abu Hussein, Jamil Dakwar, Mohammed Abu El Haija, Yaseen Garboni, Tewfiq Jabareen, Shafeek Nashaat Kassem, Anis Kasem, Ghazi Falah, Rasem Khamaysi, Oren Yiftahel, Ahmad Sobhi Jabareen, Ramez Jaraisy, Salman Abu Sitta, Maha Qupti, Hana Swed, Bruce Stanley, Sandy Kedar, Bill Bowring, Salim Wakeem and Mohammed Zeidan. This book could not have been written without their advice, help and support.

The cover photograph is by Michal Shwaty of Sabar Publications.

Tables

Glossary of Terms

ACRI	Association for Civil Rights in Israel
CEDAW	Convention on the Elimination of All Forms of Discrimination Against Women
CERD	Convention on the Elimination of All Forms of Racial Discrimination
CRC	Convention on the Rights of the Child
Dunam	Measurement of land used in the Ottoman Empire, use of which has continued in the region; 1 Turkish dunam was 919.3 square metres, and a metric dunam is 1,000 square metres or a quarter of an acre.
HC	The Israeli Supreme Court, sitting as the High Court of Justice
HCA	The Israeli Supreme Court, sitting as the highest Court of Appeal
ICCPR	International Covenant on Civil and Political Rights
ICESCR	International Covenant on Economic, Social and Cultural Rights
ICJ	International Court of Justice
IDP	Internally displaced person
ILA	Israel Lands Administration
ILC	Israel Lands Council
JA	Jewish Agency
JNF	Jewish National Fund
Knesset	The Israeli Parliament
LSI	Laws of the State of Israel, series of translations of Israeli statutes into English
PD	Piskei Dein, Reports of the High Court of Justice of Israel (in Hebrew)
Takdin	Series of Israeli Court decisions available on CD Rom
UDHR	Universal Declaration of Human Rights
WZO	World Zionist Organization

CHAPTER I

Introduction

§ THE conflict over land lies at the heart of the conflict between Zionism and the Palestinian national movement. This conflict dates back to the beginning of the twentieth century and over the last hundred years land has remained its central element. While international attention centres on the violent manifestations of that struggle in the West Bank and Gaza Strip, occupied by Israel since 1967, this book turns the spotlight on what has happened to the land that lies inside the State of Israel itself. What has happened to all the land belonging to the 750,000–800,000 Palestinian refugees created by the 1948 war, who, now numbering 4 million, remain the world's largest unresolved refugee problem? And what about the 150,000 Palestinians who remained and became citizens of Israel, largely forgotten by the outside world, who now number around one million, some 17 per cent of Israeli citizens, and are fighting their own struggle for access to land within the State of Israel?[1]

Land is perhaps the most important resource of all: humans rely on it for their very existence and it forms the basis for most human activity and development. In today's world, land distribution remains a major determinant of economic and social status as well as of political power. Systems of land allocation and regulation play a vital role in determining how alternative and competing claims over resources will be resolved (Ratcliffe 1976: 12). The role of the state is crucial; while the extent and manner of intervention varies, all states intervene to some extent in exercising control over access to land. Opportunity of access to land for citizens is therefore shaped by a government's land policy. An inequitable land policy, or one that fails to protect and guarantee access to land for all segments of society, will significantly restrict opportunities for minorities and other disempowered groups.

Two aspects of land policy can be identified as particularly significant in determining opportunity of access to land: ownership and administrative regulation such as planning control. Ownership refers to the system of rights and interests in land; those legal, contractual or customary arrangements whereby individuals or organizations gain access to economic or social opportunities through land (Ratcliffe 1976: 21). It is possible for several interests to exist in respect of the same piece of land, and for ownership to be conferred by a variety of means including actual possession and use. The second aspect of land policy having an important influence on access to land is administrative control of land distribution and use. This includes the exercise by the state of control over land owned by it, as well as the implementation of planning controls affecting all land. A key problem is how to prevent the state from operating systematically and consistently for the benefit of the dominant group at the expense of others (Bachrach and Baratz 1970: 43). A state has to take certain decisions concerning the form and extent of its intervention in controlling access to land. As regards ownership, for instance, should it take all, some or no land into public ownership? As regards regulation of land use, should it leave decisions as to where and how development takes place to the market and private initiative, or should it take some or all decisions that affect development? A major empirical study of land policies in different countries identified six categories of ways in which states exercise control over development (Lichfield and Darin-Drabkin 1980: 15).

Policy decisions of this type will be influenced by political, ideological and other factors. The United States, for instance, places great emphasis on protecting individual private property rights, which are regarded as among the most important civil rights.[2] At the opposite end of the spectrum, there are states that do not recognize private land rights at all and where all land is publicly owned. Policy choices might also change at different times. After the Second World War, for instance, serious consideration was given in Britain to taking all land into public ownership and converting all land tenures into fixed-term leases on the grounds that the interests of landowners must be subordinated to the public good.[3] Other states, such as Denmark, exercise a highly interventionist policy in the form of planning regulation. Many states implement a mixed system, with a degree of state landownership and some intervention in directing the development and supply of land for various purposes.

Israel chose a land policy that suited the goals of the Zionist movement, a system that comprises a high degree of state ownership and control, but falls short of nationalization of all land. More than 94.5 per cent of all land is administered directly by the state and owned either by the state or by Zionist bodies such as the Jewish National Fund (JNF) and the Jewish Agency (JA). The Zionist national institutions still play a major role in land policy and are given important public functions such as developing state land, even though they act in the interests of Jewish citizens only.[4] 'State' ownership of land has a rather special meaning in a context where that 'state' is defined as the state of the Jewish people, rather than as the state of all of its citizens, Palestinian Arabs as well as Jews. The implications of these factors will be explored during the course of this book. There is also a high degree of direct governmental regulation of land distribution, development and use in Israel.

How can the success of state land policies be measured? Whatever system a state adopts as regards ownership of and access to land, and whatever balance it strikes between private and public ownership of land, or as regards state intervention in access to land, it is obliged to respect certain principles. All states are bound to recognize historical rights and other principles well established in international law and practice including the right of individuals to return to lands from which they have been displaced or to choose compensation.[5] States must also respect the principle of equality, which means that whatever land system it adopts, a state must guarantee equality of opportunity for access to land to all citizens and groups within the state. Such an obligation arises from basic principles of administrative and constitutional law and of human rights law, as recognized internationally and in Israeli domestic law.[6] A number of prerequisites for equality can be identified based on principles of law and human rights. These include formal and actual equality before the law, prohibition of discrimination, equality of treatment (though not necessarily uniformity of treatment, since measures may be required to reflect legitimate differences or narrow gaps between previously unequal groups), a proper balance of competing interests, and a commitment to the provision of basic living standards for all citizens. Where there is a high degree of state ownership, a further factor comes into play. The state as owner of land has different duties and obligations in exercising its rights as owner than a private owner would have. While a private person can do anything with his or her land not prohibited by law, by contrast any action of a public body regarding land owned by it is subject to public law principles.[7] The public authority as landowner is exercising its discretion, governed by certain principles including that of equality.

Another crucial question is how equal access can be guaranteed. The choice of a land system might influence the capacity of a state to deliver equality of access, but will not be, by itself, the determining factor. State ownership of land does not, for instance, guarantee a more just and equal distribution of land any more than does the adoption of a completely privatized, mixed or any other type of system. And a system that is successfully implemented in one country might not work fairly in another. The key question is how the system operates in practice. Whatever land system a state adopts, it must find a way to ensure that it is able effectively to guarantee equal opportunity of access to land to all individuals and groups in society.

The historical context of the conflict over land in Palestine

Palestine, a part of the Ottoman Empire from the fifteenth century, was placed under a British Mandate following the First World War.[8] The British government had already committed itself, in the famous Balfour Declaration of 2 November 1917, to facilitating the establishment in Palestine of a national home for the Jewish people, and under its administration the Zionist colonization of the area, which had begun in 1882, increased. By 1948 the Jewish community owned some 6 per cent of the land of Mandate Palestine. During the different phases of the Arab–Israeli War of 1948, as many as 800,000 of the one million Arab inhabitants of Palestine were displaced, most of them ending up as refugees outside the area that became Israel.[9] Israel's responsibility for displacing the Palestinians from their land and creating the Palestinian refugees is beyond dispute, even if the extent to which the nature and scale of the operation was planned in advance is debated.[10] Whatever the causes of the mass movement of Palestinians from their land, the biggest factor in creating the dispossession of the Palestinians was the immediate steps taken by the Zionist leadership and settler community to ensure that the displaced did not return. The symbols as well as the manifestations of the indigenous community were systematically destroyed. Palestinian villages were flattened and settlements were built in their place with Hebrew names. Cities and districts were also given new names. Of 526 Palestinian towns and villages in the part of Palestine that became Israel, 418 were destroyed, or immediately settled by Jews.[11]

The United Nations immediately affirmed the right of the Palestinian refugees to return to their homes and property, in line with international law.[12] The UN General Assembly Resolution 194(III) of 1948

> Resolves that refugees wishing to return to their homes and live at peace with their neighbours should be permitted to do so at the earliest practicable date, and that compensation should be paid for the property of those choosing not to return and for loss of or damage to property which, under principles of international law or in equity, should be made good by the Governments or authorities responsible.

Instructs the Conciliation Commission to facilitate the repatriation, resettlement and economic and social rehabilitation of the refugees and the payment of compensation.[13]

The content of this resolution has been renewed by the General Assembly every year since 1948. It provides that the Palestinian refugees have a choice: either to return to their homes or to resettle elsewhere. But Israel flouted international law and the United Nations, and prevented the Palestinian refugees and the internally displaced from returning to their land and homes. Israel maintains that any Palestinian rights over land must be dealt with by payment of compensation (Benvenisti and Zamir 1995).[14]

Preventing the return of the refugees and the internally displaced was a crucial first step in pursuit of Israel's aspiration to take over and 'Judaize' the Palestinian land. This was a process carried out in several stages, each carefully given a veneer of legality. Initially, the land of the Palestinian refugees and the internally displaced was turned over to a 'Custodian of absentees' property'.[15] The refugees and internally displaced, in reality actively prevented from returning to reclaim their land, were simply treated as magically 'absent'. Far from taking care of the property on behalf of its owners, the Custodian straight away ploughed it into the intensive state-building exercise that was under way.[16] The next milestone came in 1953 when the Custodian formally transferred all land under his control to the state Development Authority.[17] The change in designation from private to state land was aimed at giving legal backing to the situation that prevailed already, which was that the land was put almost exclusively at the disposal of Jewish citizens of the state.[18] Thus not only the land's original owners, but all Palestinians are effectively excluded from it. The different ways in which Palestinian citizens of Israel are denied access to state land constitute the main theme of this book.

A further stage in the transformation of the Palestinian land under Israeli law is still ongoing. In recent years a vigorous debate has occurred in Israel as to whether or not to 'denationalize' part or all of the land owned by the state. If this step is taken, it would remove the land of Palestinian refugees and the internally displaced even further from its original owners. Jewish agriculturalists have lobbied for agricultural land in the state to be passed into the ownership of the kibbutzes and moshavs that have possessed it since 1948.[19] The Jewish national institutions and the Mizrahi (Eastern) Jews have also staked their claim, but the latter group is arguing that if the land is to be privatized it should be open to all on an equal basis.[20] Different interest groups within the Jewish community fight over who will gain the lion's share of the land from which the Palestinians were displaced, or at least for a large share in the profits when, as is increasingly occurring, its status is changed to development land. The Israeli Supreme Court dampened the hopes of the Jewish lessees of agricultural land when it ruled, in August 2002, that they are not entitled to benefit from the considerable increase in value of a piece of land that occurs when its status changes from agricultural to development land. But the longer-term question of whether or not agricultural land registered in the name of the state will be made transferable into private hands remains open. In so far as Israel has taken steps purporting to remove ownership of the land from the Palestinian refugees and displaced persons, they are clearly in violation of international law, and the issue of the refugees and their right of return remains to be resolved in the context of the political process.[21]

For more than fifty years, while Israel has busied itself with measures purporting to strip them of ownership of their former land and property, the Palestinian refugees and their descendants have lived in exile as refugees, the vast majority of them in camps in the West Bank, Gaza Strip and the surrounding Arab states, and others scattered around the world.[22] Surveys and reports show that the refugees overwhelmingly aspire to recognition of their right of return, and they still regard themselves, and are treated by the states hosting them, as in a temporary situation pending a permanent resolution of their plight.[23]

Palestinians who were displaced internally during the fighting were also prevented from returning to their land. Some 150,000 Palestinians remained in the area that was declared as the State of Israel on 14 May 1948, and an estimated one-quarter of this group were internally displaced in the course of the war of 1948. These internally displaced Palestinians were treated in the same way as the external refugees, since most have not been allowed to return to their land. Because of this they became known in the Palestinian community as the 'present absentees'. The experience of the Palestinian villages of Iqrit and Bir'im demonstrates both the intention to displace Palestinians permanently and the lengths to which successive Israeli governments, of all parties, have been prepared to go in order to ensure this state of affairs. Residents of Iqrit and Bir'im, Palestinian villages close to the Israeli border, were evacuated during the fighting in 1948 on the assurance of the Israeli army that the evacuation was temporary, lasting only until the fighting was over. The right of the villagers to return to their homes and land was even affirmed by the Israeli High Court in 1951, but nevertheless the army destroyed the villages, declared them closed areas and subsequently turned over their land to Jewish farming settlements. Subsequent Israeli administrations have been prepared to offer, at most, return to only a fraction of the land formerly belonging to the residents and compensation. Consistently, they have echoed the concerns expressed by Golda Meir in 1972, who refused to allow residents of the two villages to return because it would set a precedent for other displaced Palestinians.[24]

The Israeli project of taking over land for the purposes of building a Jewish state did not stop at taking the land of the Palestinian refugees and the internally displaced. Even those Palestinians who did not leave their land during the fighting and could not be classed as 'absentees' have had their land resources relentlessly chipped away by a series of laws and policies that have deprived them of ownership and possession of land and restricted their access to land that is theoretically 'state' land available for all, but is in reality allocated largely to Jewish citizens. As a result of more than fifty years of relentless chipping away at their land resources, Palestinian citizens of Israel have lost a majority of their land. While there has been no comprehensive survey to establish the precise extent of the loss across the whole community, it seems the average is at least 70 per cent of land lost.[25] More than 94.5 per cent of all land in the state is now directly administered by the state, the remaining area being privately owned by Palestinians or Jews.[26] The community is effectively barricaded within villages and towns that have hardly been allowed to expand since 1948, despite a six-fold increase in population. Whereas agriculture had been the main source of income and way of life of many Palestinians, the Palestinian community is now largely a population of wage labourers dependent on the Israeli economy, a transformation brought about largely as a result of the way in which Israel has exercised control over resources and development.[27] This book seeks to explain these laws and policies, and to demonstrate that they, and their implementation, are contrary to notions of justice and international standards such as those of due process. It will also reveal that the Israeli legal system, including the judiciary, has a disappointing record in protecting Palestinian citizens' rights in relation to land, and, on the contrary, has played a key role in facilitating the transfer of land from Palestinian hands.

Palestinian citizens of Israel today and their main challenges as regards land

Palestinians now live in three main geographic areas of the state (Statistical Abstract 2000: Table 2.7).[28] In the Northern District, including the Galilee, Palestinians make up a little over 50 per cent of the population; in the Haifa and Central Districts, including the Little Triangle alongside the Green Line which separates Israel from the West Bank, Palestinians comprise around 25 per cent and 10 per cent of the population respectively; and in the Naqab Desert in the south, Palestinians comprise around 19 per cent of the population.[29] Jewish and Arab citizens live largely separately; as many as 91 per cent of Palestinians in Israel live in all-Arab cities, towns and villages, of which there are a total of 123. The other 9 per cent of Palestinians live in mixed Jewish–Arab cities such as Haifa, Acre, Jaffa, Lod and Ramle. Some 7.5 per cent live in communities that are not legally recognized.[30]

The separation of Jews and Arabs is not only a matter of choice, although it is indeed the preference of both communities; it is also a matter of deliberate strategy. While Jewish citizens may choose to live in any part of the state and in a variety of types of settlement, whether tiny isolated rural communities, collective farms, towns or cities, Palestinians are effectively denied that choice. Astonishingly, not a single new Palestinian community has been established since 1948, other than a few concentration points for Bedouin. The Bedouin of the Naqab, in particular, have asked to be able to establish rural-style communities that would allow them the lifestyle and social organization they desire. The government has so far allowed them only one option, that is to live in urbanized townships, part of a policy that aims to evict them from the lands over which they claim ownership, to minimize the area of land they use, and to disconnect them from their rural lifestyle. In the north and centre of the country, the government for decades refused to recognize tens of smaller Palestinian communities, and has only in recent years, following a sustained and determined campaign by these communities, begun to grant some of them official recognition.[31] But even in the process of developing official plans for these communities, the Israel Lands Administration (ILA) and planning bodies seek to minimize their physical area. The established Palestinian towns and villages, prevented from expanding by the restrictive policies of the planning bodies and the ILA, have become uniformly urban and exceedingly overcrowded. With the acute shortage of building land in the Palestinian communities, a few Palestinians have applied to live in new communities developed with the intention of housing Jews. Several Palestinians denied permission to move into such areas took their cases to court and the High Court decision of 2000 in the case of Qa'dan that the state could not allocate land for the establishment of settlements intended for Jews only, was hailed by some as a landmark. We will argue that its significance is relatively limited, and has done little or nothing to relieve the chronic land and housing shortage that exists among the Palestinian community in Israel.

The physical segregation of Jews and Arabs in distinct communities is reinforced by the disconnection of Palestinian citizens from state goals and from political influence. Palestinian citizens of the state have never been recognized as a national minority, despite their self-identification as Palestinians. In Israel they tend to be referred to as 'Arabs', 'Israeli Arabs', 'non-Jews', 'minorities' or simply as Muslims, Christians or Druze. From 1948 until 1966, they were kept under military rule with severe restrictions on movement and other freedoms. Even after this was lifted, Palestinians have been viewed with suspicion as a potential 'fifth column' in the state. One Palestinian academic described their situation as follows: 'The Arab in the State of Israel today is in a blind spot where he is at one and the same time both citizen and alien; this spot is determined first by attitude, then by a range of legislation, policy and procedures, each of which sets out to humiliate, reject and subjugate him' (Zidani 1990: 3).

The objective of control has been nowhere more felt than in relation to land. Policies such as the establishment of 'look-out posts' on hills, settling Jews in all parts of the state ('Judaization') and breaking up areas densely populated with Palestinians, are all indications of the ongoing objective of control.

Palestinians face discrimination in every field of life. They have the lowest socio-economic status in the state: according to official statistics from March 2002, 52 per cent of Arab children in Israel live below the poverty line and seven of the ten poorest communities in Israel are Palestinian Bedouin towns (Central Bureau of Statistics 2002). The Arab sector receives a far lower proportion of public expenditure and investment than its proportion in the population, and far less than it needs. Few Palestinian towns and villages have significant local economies and most commute to work in Jewish commercial centres. The gaps between the two communities and the institutionalized discrimination which exists have been documented by the work of a number of Palestinian non-governmental organizations.[32]

Hardly surprisingly in this context, steadfastness (*sumud*, in Arabic) on the land has been the defining, dominant symbol for the Palestinians in Israel, consistently arousing passions and representing the sense that these Palestinians have of their own situation and their identity as Palestinians in the context of the wider Palestinian national struggle. Land expropriation, more than any other issue, has been the subject of bitter protest by the leadership of the Palestinian community in Israel to the Israeli government. Land expropriations have also been the major cause of popular protests by Palestinian citizens of the state ever since 1948. Every year, the community commemorates Land Day on 30 March, the date on which in 1976 six unarmed Palestinians were shot dead by Israeli security forces, including army and police, while protesting land expropriations in the Galilee. Each new wave of Jewish immigration to the state has had both a psychological and a harsh actual impact on Arab land holdings: the Arab fear of losing more land was the key issue in their opposition to the large-scale Jewish immigration from the Soviet Union from the late 1980s and early 1990s (Al Haj 1991: 250). In September 1998, Intifada-style clashes took place between Israeli police and security forces and local people in Um El Fahem, in which 500 young people were injured, following reports that areas of land in the vicinity closed off for military training would be expanded, and that the hidden objective was to secure land for building a new Jewish town.

It is not only the national significance of the land that has re-mained crucial to Palestinians. To the Palestinian community, land has a significance that goes far beyond its economic value. Similar to other communities in the world, land tenure is bound up with social structures, rights in land are not regarded as a commodity which can be easily given up, and any reform of the land system involves a transfer of status and power as well as of property (Dorner 1972: 40). Prior to 1948 the Palestinian community was overwhelmingly rural, and agriculture was the major source of livelihood. Each family was firmly rooted to its particular piece of land, handed down through generations, whether or not they held formal legal title, and regardless of whether they had access to the land as a family, tribe or in common with the entire village. Such attitudes survive to this day, and most Palestinians still define themselves according to the land where their family roots lie, even if they have been dispossessed. For instance, fifty years after the villagers of Iqrit were uprooted from their homes by the Israeli army, they still see themselves, and are viewed by those they live among, as 'from Iqrit'. Another example is the steadfastness of the tens of long-established Palestinian communities whose existence Israel refuses to recognize. The inhabitants of these 'unrecognized villages' refuse to leave their land despite being denied electricity and other infrastructure and basic services.

The land policies that Israel has pursued are not directed at taking land into public ownership and making it available to all citizens on an equal basis. This would be bad enough as it would be a denial of Palestinian historic rights. But this is not at all what has happened. Land once taken into 'national' ownership – now 94.5 per cent of all land in the state – becomes categorized as 'Israel Lands',[33] and is thus automatically of limited access to Palestinians because of the operation of a range of laws and policies described in this book. The Palestinian community's objection to the expropriation of privately owned land becomes even more understandable when viewed in a context where losing ownership of the family's land in many cases means losing all prospect of further access to it. Land expropriated by the state becomes land from which Palestinians are effectively excluded, and to which only Jews are allowed access. Palestinians are also limited to urban-style societies; Jews are free to choose where and how to live, while Palestinians are relegated to certain types of community and in designated areas only.

Those who follow the situation in the Occupied Territories will be familiar with Israeli policies and practices concerning land confiscation, house demolitions, destruction of crops and other violations of international law, particularly the Fourth Geneva Convention, in relation to those territories. Although this book does not deal with the situation of Palestinians living in the West Bank, including East Jerusalem, the Gaza Strip or the Golan Heights, occupied by Israel in 1967, there are many similarities between Israel's land policies in relation to these populations and the policies it has pursued within the Green Line.[34]

In many ways the situation of the Palestinian citizens of Israel lies at the core of the Zionist–Palestinian conflict. From the very beginning, this conflict has been about land. Of the global Palestinian community, it is the situation of the Palestinians in the Occupied Territories that has received most attention since 1967, and has been the subject of negotiations since 1990. The situation of the other two major Palestinian populations, the refugees in the Arab states and the Palestinians who remained in the state, has been ignored by most since 1948 and largely excluded from the negotiations.[35] The fact that at the core of both of these situations lies the question of access to land in Israel may help to explain this omission. The Palestinian community at large is demanding that the refugees' right of return be recognized as a precondition of any political agreement, and the peace process revived discussion, from a number of different perspectives, concerning what form this could take.[36] Ultimately, the 'Palestinian Question' as a political issue will not be resolved unless and until the fate of the Palestinian refugees, and with it the question of their land and property, is determined. As regards the status of the Palestinian citizens of the state, the question of access to land lies at the very heart of this issue also. At issue is the nature of Zionism and its product, the Israeli state, and its relationship with the Palestinians within its borders. Whether or not Israel can evolve into a state that accepts basic international and human rights norms will depend to a large extent on whether the state is willing to modify its fundamental systems regarding land and allow equality of access to land to all citizens. Since the start of the Al Aqsa Intifada in September 2000 and the ascendancy of right-wing governments in Israel, more and more strident calls have been heard from Israeli right-wingers for the expulsion of Palestinian citizens of the state, or for a population exchange, as part of any political solution.[37] At the same time, rising levels of tension and violence are occurring, and the scars created by the killing of thirteen Palestinian citizens by Israeli security forces in demonstrations connected to the start of the Al Aqsa Intifada in October 2000 will be slow to heal. And, because Israelis and Palestinians alike know that it is land which is at the core of the issue, so long as the question of access to land within Israel remains denied, the Zionist–Palestinian conflict will not be resolved.

Objectives, methodology and structure

What has happened to Palestinian land in Israel is the main subject of this book. There are three major imperatives for Palestinians as regards this land. The first is to address the question of the land of which Palestinians have been dispossessed, and to seek a solution based on international law and UN resolutions. Such a solution to these 'lost lands' would need to include justice for the 'present absentees', the Palestinians displaced internally who are citizens of Israel but have never had their land rights resolved, as well as recognition of the right of return of the Palestinian refugees. As Professor Nadim Rohana wrote on the one-year anniversary of the violence of October 2000: 'Many Palestinians are realizing that the basis of their relationship with the state of Israel is changing. Citizenship, the essence of this relationship, must be redefined in a way that takes their history and that of their people into account. Equal citizenship means nothing, if Israel does not face the issue of historic responsibility, injustice and past wrongs that continue to this day.'[38]

The second imperative is to avoid further dispossession of land; to halt the gradual erosion of the land holdings that remain in Palestinian hands. The third is to stop the discrimination in access to land that denies Palestinians, through processes such as planning and allocation of state land, the equal use of that land.

Focusing on the Israeli landownership system and the system for the regulation of land use, the book sets out to examine the law and practice relating to Palestinian access to land in Israel, its extent, and the means by which it is restricted. The hope is that by contributing to a better understanding and identification of these issues, we will facilitate these issues being addressed more effectively than has been the case to date. We seek to examine what legal provisions and mechanisms exist that could be drawn on to protect the land rights of Palestinian citizens of Israel, and how effectively such protections have fulfilled their function. We look at the body of domestic and international law that might offer protection, and the main institutional mechanisms that might operate to protect individuals and groups from interference with their rights, including checks and balances in legislation and methods of accountability for public bodies, officials and the judiciary. We look at how far these operate in practice to safeguard the land rights of the Palestinians in Israel. We examine the extent and the means by which Israeli land policy and state machinery operate to restrict access to land for Palestinian citizens within the 1948 boundaries of Israel, or the Green Line,[39] including the system of landownership, the acquisition and administration of public land, and control of land use through planning and housing regulation. We seek to shed light on the machinery of the Israeli land regime and the discriminatory laws and practices that operate to prevent equality of access to land and that result in scandalous situations such as the so-called 'unrecognized villages' or the denial of the land rights of Palestinians in the Naqab.

As to methodology, a wide range of primary and secondary source materials were reviewed, and a number of personal interviews were conducted. Materials reviewed include legislation of the Israeli and British Mandate periods, records of parliamentary debates, reports of government departments and ministries, reports of the Israel Land Administration, publications of the Jewish National Fund, the Land Use Research Institute and similar bodies, government statistical abstracts, and case pleadings and court judgments (some of them unreported). Persons interviewed included lawyers, heads of Arab local councils and community leaders. During the research period, preliminary findings were presented at local and international conferences, such as the Equality Conference held in Nazareth in December 1996, organized by the National Committee of Arab Mayors.

We begin by identifying a number of the structural and substantive safeguards, both domestic and international, that should operate to guarantee Palestinian access to land in Israel. Chapter 3 then describes the alienation of land from Palestinian ownership and possession: the process by which more than 94.5 per cent of land in Israel came under direct state control, a process that began before the establishment of Israel and continued afterwards. Chapter 4 looks at the process for determining rights in land, and analyses Bedouin land claims in the Naqab and Israel's refusal to recognize Bedouin rights over land possessed by this community for centuries. Chapter 5 examines the concept of 'Israel Lands', the introduction of the Israeli land regime and the ways in which it inherently excludes Palestinians from certain land. Chapter 6 looks at how administrative control over land owned by the state and the Jewish National Fund is exercised, and how it is operated so as to restrict Palestinian access to this land, focusing on the policies and activities of two key bodies, the Israel Lands Administration and the Jewish Agency. Chapter 7 focuses on regulation of land use, measuring discrimination in policy and practice in planning and housing regulations. Chapter 8 looks at the phenomenon of the 'unrecognized' Palestinian communities. In our final chapter, we seek to draw some conclusions about the nature of the Israeli land regime and its implications for the denial of access to land for the Palestinian community in Israel.

Notes

1. According to the Statistical Abstract of Israel (2000: Table 2.1), around 1.1 million, some 18.5 per cent of the Israeli population, is 'arab'. However, this figure includes around 200,000 Palestinians of East Jerusalem who are not Israeli citizens but were classed as permanent residents after Israel occupied and illegally annexed East Jerusalem in 1967. This population faces very serious encroachments on its land, not dealt with in this book, which focuses only on the situation within the 1948 borders of Israel. If the Palestinians of East Jerusalem are deducted from the statistics, non-Jewish citizens of Israel constitute just under 17 per cent of all Israeli citizens.

2. The Fifth Amendment to the US Constitution includes the following: 'nor shall private property be taken for public use, without just compensation'.

3. The Uthwatt Report, published in 1942.

4. The Jewish National Fund is a Zionist body given extensive functions relating to land by the state. See Chapter 5 for a discussion of the status of the Fund and the extent to which it should be considered a public body for the purposes of being accountable under administrative law.

5. These principles are expanded in Chapter 2.

6. The legal sources of the principle of equality are also expanded in Chapter 2.

7. See for example the UK case of R v. Somerset County Council, ex parte Fewings, discussed by F. Nardell in Nardell (1995: 27).

8. The British Mandate was agreed at the Versailles Peace Treaty in April 1920 and confirmed by the Council of the League of Nations on 24 July 1922.

9. During this early period, Palestinians were dispossessed from their land

in five waves: the first began in December 1947 and lasted to March 1948; the second took place during April and May 1948; the third during the fighting and first ceasefire (May to 8 July 1948); the fourth from July to December 1948; the fifth from January 1949 to the final cleansing of al-Majdal's population and the expulsion of Bedouin from the Naqab in October 1950. The debate over the total number of Palestinians displaced is highly charged, and a range of claims have been put forward. A report to the UN General Assembly on 5 April 1948 suggested that there were already 200,000 to 300,000 refugees. Early Israeli figures argue for between 350,000 and 450,000 as of 1 June 1948 (see the report of the Israel Defence Forces, on the emigration of the Arabs of Palestine in the period 1 December 1947 to 1 June 1948, as reported in Morris [1994: 83]). By 1949, estimates by British and American diplomats were in the range 700,000 to 800,000 (see the report from Mark Ethridge, American representative to the Palestine Conciliation Committee, to the Secretary of State, dated 28 March 1949). One Israeli official suggested in 1950 that the real figure was close to 800,000 (see Morris 1987). Subsequent estimates range from the 726,000 registered with UNRWA as of 1950 and supported by the UN Economic Survey Mission for the Middle East, to the Israeli Embassy in the USA arguing for 500,000 in its *Refugees in the Middle East: A Solution in Peace* issued in 1967. Benny Morris accepts the British formula of 1949 of 'between 600,000 and 760,000'. Today, the website of the Palestine Return Centre <www.prc.org.uk/english/palrights-eng.htm>, based on the work of Dr Salman Abu Sitta, puts forward a figure of 804,766 based on a reassessment of past documents (Abu Sitta 2000).

10. For over thirty years, Israeli scholarship on the causes of the Palestinian dispossession of 1948 presented the dominant narrative that Palestinian and Arab leaders were to blame for encouraging Palestinians to flee, and that there was no Israeli culpability for the creation of the refugee problem. However, starting in the 1980s, a group of Israeli scholars began to review the primary sources, and to question the assumptions and narratives presented about 1948 and Israel's role. One of these so-called 'revisionist historians', Benny Morris, makes the claim that, at the very least, Israel is to blame both for the 'atrocity factor' which set Palestinians fleeing in fear of their lives, and for a set of policies that were 'specifically designed to ensure the impossibility of a return' (Morris 1987: 291). Other authors such as Avi Schlim, Ilan Pappé and Nur Masalha go much further, finding premeditation, intentionality and consistency in Israel's destruction and ethnic cleansing of the Palestinians; see Masalha (1992). The popularity of the revisionist arguments has prompted numerous counterattacks, including that by Efraim Karsh in Karsh (1997).

11. Khalidi (1992) documents 418 destroyed or resettled villages. Dr Salman Abu Sitta argues for a revised number of 531 based on his research (website of the Palestine Return Centre, see note 9, above).

12. See Chapter 2 for an outline of international law.

13. Paragraph 11, Resolution 194(III). The resolution was adopted by the UN General Assembly on 11 December 1948 and has been renewed annually ever since.

14. Most Israeli commentators acknowledge the right of refugees to com-

pensation for their lost property, basing this on the general international law principle of protection of aliens' property. They favour a lump sum agreement, citing difficulties in identifying individual claims after such a long time. However, Arzt argues that since Palestinians were not citizens of the country that forced them to flee (Israel), Israel does not owe them compensation at all; Arzt (1997: 72).

15. Absentees' Property Law 1950; LSI, Vol. 4, p. 68.

16. In his 1969 study, Don Peretz finds that: 'The refugees left whole cities, including Jaffa, Acre, Lydda, Ramleh, Baysan, and Majdal; 388 towns and villages and large parts of 94 other cities and towns, containing nearly a quarter of all the buildings in Israel at the time. Ten thousand Arab shops, businesses and stores were left in Jewish hands' (Peretz 1969: 16). As already mentioned, hundreds of Palestinian villages were demolished or taken over. The first major 'benefit' was the summer agricultural crop. Benny Morris cites reports in the archives of the Arab Affairs Ministry that it was during this first harvest that Jewish settlements began to appeal to the Agricultural Ministry and the Jewish National Fund for 'permanent leaseholds and possession' of these lands (Morris 1994: 244). The decision to prevent the Palestinians from returning to harvest their crop was one of the results, and the new Israeli government took other policy decisions concerning returnees, harvesting and land acquisition that were related (Morris 1994: 249–55). Demolition was one aspect of claiming the land, both in the villages and in urban areas, and became a regular event after December 1947, part of a policy to demoralize and occupy. The policy intensified during 1948: for instance in Haifa Palestinian homes and businesses were demolished starting late July 1948 following the cleansing of the city's Palestinian population that started in April. The policy of demolition continued well into the 1950s: for instance Benny Morris documents the clearing of villages within the demilitarized zone with Syria or close to the borders, as 'part of the process of clearing areas for Jewish habitation or cultivation' (Morris 1987: 169).

17. The Development Authority (Transfer of Property) Law 1950; LSI, Vol. 4, p. 151.

18. According to Section 1 of the Basic Law: Israel Lands 1960, land owned by the state, the Development Authority and the Jewish National Fund are to be known as 'Israel Lands'. The means by which Palestinians are denied access to this land are explored in Chapters 5 and 6.

19. A draft bill was presented to the Knesset; see Chapter 5.

20. The Eastern Democratic Rainbow petitioned the High Court in January 2000, Petition no. 244/00, complaining that government policy was discriminatory and was benefiting only one small sector of the population, namely the kibbutzes. This case is discussed in Chapter 5.

21. The right of the Palestinian refugees to return to their land is argued in the following chapter. According to Article V of the Declaration of Principles on Interim Self-Government Arrangements of 13 September 1993, the question of the Palestinian refugees is one of the issues to be covered in permanent status negotiations.

22. According to UNHCR (2002), there are an estimated 4.25 million Pales-

tinian refugees worldwide. Of these, 3.9 million are covered by the mandate of UNRWA and a further 349,100 are outside UNRWA's area of operations.

23. See for example Daneels (2001), which includes an analysis of public opinion surveys of Palestinians in the West Bank and Gaza towards the refugee issues, and the Joint Paliamentary Council's Commission of Inquiry into the right of return of the Palestinian Refugees of 2001, which includes extensive interviews with Palestinian refugees in camps throughout the region.

24. This case is discussed in more detail in Chapter 3.

25. Abu Kishk compared landownership in thirty-eight Arab villages in 1945, 1962 and 1972, and found that by 1972 these villages had lost a total of 72 per cent of their original lands; Abu Kishk (1981: 128). As will be discussed in Chapter 4, the picture is complicated by the fact that Palestinians lost not only land to which they claimed private ownership rights, but also land to which they traditionally had right of access such as land surrounding villages.

26. ILA (2000: 163); ownership of settled land administered by the ILA.

27. See Haidar (1990: Ch. 2 and 130).

28. The statistics do not use the term 'Palestinians', but generally refer to 'Arabs and Others', and break this population down into Muslims, Christians and Druze.

29. According to the Statistical Abstract, the 'arab' population of the Naqab is 106,400, making them around 17 per cent of the population. However, a general note is included in the Statistical Abstract to the effect that the statistics regarding the Bedouin are incomplete. A Bedouin organization, the Regional Council for the Unrecognized Villages in the Naqab, estimates that the Bedouin population in the Naqab is around 120,000. This would make the Bedouin around 19 per cent of the population of the Naqab.

30. This figure is based not on official statistics, which record only 51,500 'population living outside localities' (Statistical Abstract 2000: Table 2.9), but on statistics from non-governmental organizations based within the Palestinian community which count some 60–70,000 Palestinians living in unrecognized communities in the Naqab and around 10,000 in the north.

31. This phenomenon of 'unrecognized villages' is addressed in detail in Chapter 8.

32. Examples of non-governmental organizations that have documented discrimination are Adalah: the Legal Center for Arab Minority Rights in Israel, the Arab Association for Human Rights, the Galilee Society for Health Research and Services, the Association of Forty and Sikkuy, the Association for the Advancement of Civil Equality. See for example the reports by the Arab Association for Human Rights (1998) and Adalah (2001).

33. Section 1, Basic Law: Israel Lands 1960.

34. See for example B'Tselem's report on land expropriation and planning in the Occupied Territories (B'Tselem 1995), Anthony Coon's 1992 report on town planning in the West Bank (Coon 1992) and Al Haq's 1986 report on planning as a strategy for Judaization in the Occupied Territories (Al Haq 1986).

35. According to Article V of the Declaration of Principles on Interim Self-Government Arrangements of 13 September 1993, the question of the

Palestinian refugees is one of the issues to be covered in permanent status negotiations. The situation of the Palestinian citizens of Israel has not been a subject of negotiation, though there have been calls by right-wingers in Israel for a transfer or exchange of populations involving Palestinian citizens to be part of any further peace talks.

36. See for example Abu-Sitta (2001) and Arzt (1997).

37. Israeli Tourism Minister Benny Elon of the far-right Moledet Party called for 'transfer' of Palestinians; Ben Lynfield, 'Israeli expulsion idea gains steam', *Christian Science Monitor*, 6 February 2001. According to an opinion poll conducted by the Jaffee Center for Strategic Studies in February 2002, 31 per cent of Israel's Jewish citizens favour transferring Israeli Arabs out of the country, while 60 per cent favoured encouraging them to leave the country; 'More Israeli Jews favor transfer of Palestinians, Israeli Arabs – poll finds', *Ha'aretz* (English edition), 12 March 2002. In March 2002 Adalah: the Legal Center for Arab Minority Rights in Israel, wrote to the Minister of the Interior following newspaper reports that he had prepared a list of Arab citizens of Israel whose citizenship he plans to revoke on the basis that they pose a potential security threat; *Adalah News Update*, 20 February 2002.

38. *Al-Ahram* (Arabic weekly newspaper), 5 October 2001, translated in *HRA Weekly Press Review*, no. 50, 9 October 2001, Nazareth.

39. The Green Line is actually the boundary agreed in July 1949 under the armistice agreements Israel signed with Jordan, Syria, Lebanon and Egypt, following the 1948 war.

CHAPTER 2

Palestinian Access to Land in Perspective

The nature of the State of Israel as a 'Jewish and democratic' state

The founding document of the State of Israel declares that Israel is 'the Jewish State'. The same document declares that the state will 'foster the development of the country for the benefit of all its inhabitants', and will 'ensure complete equality of social and political rights to all its inhabitants'.[1] This same approach is found in the Basic Law: Human Dignity and Liberty, enacted in 1992. Section 1A of this law states as follows: 'The purpose of this Basic Law is to protect human dignity and liberty, in order to anchor in a Basic Law the values of the State of Israel *as a Jewish and democratic state.*'[2]

The tension and fundamental contradiction between these two stated objectives of the Israeli state form the backdrop to the issues presented in this book. But at the outset it should be said that the relative weight given to the two principles is unequal. While the elements that make Israel the Jewish state are indeed deep-rooted and guarded with determination, the guarantees of full equality for non-Jews are shown to be shallower and more easily cast aside.

Israel's character as a Jewish ethnic state is written into constitutional and ordinary legislation. The Law of Return and the Citizenship Law give any Jew from anywhere in the world the right to come to Israel and acquire automatic Israeli citizenship.[3] No one may use the political process to change the Jewish and Zionist character of the state: no political party that denies the nature of the State of Israel as the Jewish state may stand in elections.[4] The Jewish national institutions that formed the backbone of the Zionist movement from the end of the nineteenth century and played a central role in nation-building and the colonization of Palestine still carry out this role and are given crucial functions, even though they continue to represent and serve Jews only.[5]

Turning to the second commitment expressed in Israel's constitutional documents, the declaration that Israel is a democratic state dedicated to ensuring 'complete equality of social and political rights' for all inhabitants, we find that the principle of equality for non-Jews does not have a comparable weight. It is true that equality and non-discrimination do have a legal status in Israel (Kretzmer 1990: 77). Equality is one of the principles that is supposed to guide the courts in interpreting legislation and determining the limits of administrative discretion (ibid., p. 8). It is a well-established principle of public law that public bodies have a duty not to discriminate on grounds such as race, sex, religion or national origin. Israel has also committed itself, through becoming party to a number of international human rights conventions, to safeguard these principles.[6]

However, the principle of equality has not been incorporated in the main constitutional document that purports to entrench fundamental rights in Israeli law, the Basic Law: Human Dignity and Liberty. Further, there are fundamental weaknesses in the mechanisms for protecting the principles of equality and non-discrimination in Israel, which will be discussed in the following section and the remainder of this book. At least in relation to land, there is neither the intention to allow equal access to land for Jews and Palestinians in Israel, nor the mechanisms for bringing it about. In practice neither Israeli governments nor the courts have adequately displayed the will to promote or protect the principle of equality for Palestinian citizens.

What does this situation indicate about the sort of democracy that Israel has committed itself to ensuring? Despite the image Israel likes to project of itself as 'the only democracy in the Middle East', Israel does not actually aim to be a Western-style liberal democracy, as this would necessitate a different approach to the presence of ethnic groups other than the dominant Jewish majority in the state.[7] Analysts disagree on how best to characterize the Israeli political system; for instance can Israel properly be described as an ethnic *democracy* in a situation where institutionalized dominance by the Jewish majority is so extreme, or is it merely an 'ethnocracy'?[8] Preference for Jewish citizens is endemic throughout the system and there is institutionalized discrimination against non-Jews in Israel.[9]

International human rights bodies have frequently criticized Israel for its discriminatory practices against Palestinians, and have not held back from pointing out the contradictions between the factors designed to make Israel the Jewish state on the one hand, and its international human rights obligations on the other. The United Nations Committee on Economic, Social and Cultural Rights, which monitors compliance with the International Covenant on Economic, Social and Cultural Rights, to which Israel is a party, in 1998 expressed concern 'that excessive emphasis upon the State as a "Jewish State" encourages discrimination and accords a second-class status to its non-Jewish citizens' (UNCESCR 1998). The Committee expressed grave concern at the fact that Jewish national institutions were allowed to control land in Israel and concluded that 'large-scale and systematic confiscation of Palestinian land and property by the State and the transfer of that property to these agencies constitute an institutionalized form of discrimination because these agencies by definition would deny the use of these properties to non-Jews. Thus, these practices constitute a breach of Israel's obligations under the Covenant.' The Committee also noted that, in its view, the Law of Return also discriminates against Palestinians in the diaspora, upon whom restrictive requirements are placed that make it almost impossible to return to their land of birth.

The far greater weight given to the fundamental goal of maintaining Israel as the Jewish state than to affording full equality to non-Jewish citizens is perhaps most starkly revealed in state land policies. In order to achieve their goal of building a 'national home' for the Jewish people in Palestine, the Zionist leaders of the nineteenth century set out to acquire land for colonization. Crucially for Palestinians, they decided it was not enough simply to conquer the land; Zionist planning from the very beginning included not only how to acquire the land, but also how to continue to control it in such a way that it would remain available for the exclusive use of the Jewish people.[10] All land that had been transferred into Jewish hands was viewed as 'redeemed'. One of the most obvious manifestations of the Jewish nature of the state today is the continuing role of Zionist agencies from the pre-state era. Special status and quasi-governmental functions are given by the state to these institutions – including a major role in land policy, landownership and development of new settlements, even though they are permitted to work for the benefit of Jewish citizens only. Other approaches that remain central tenets for all Israel's governments include the ongoing policy to 'Judaize' areas of the country where there is still a Palestinian majority, and to protect 'redeemed' land from encroachment by Palestinians.[11] Today, the drive to populate all parts of the state with Jews remains strong. The JNF is still actively involved in purchasing land, and still considers its main goal as 'redeeming' land.[12]

Against this background, the narrative about Palestinians that permeates both the state institutions and the Jewish national institutions sees them as encroachers, trespassers and illegal possessors of the land. For example, an interview given to *Globes* magazine by Shlomo Gravitz, head of the JNF Council, in October 2001 is extremely revealing. First, Gravitz makes the point that 'the lands of Israel belong to the people not to the state', an affirmation of the Zionist insistence on separation between state (which includes non-Jews) and the Jewish people, or ethnic nation. He then restates the Zionist approach to the Jewish acquisition of land in Palestine: 'We did not buy this land, it is our land and we should not purchase it but redeem it. 2.5 million dunams were redeemed by the people of Israel with the help of the JNF, on which 1,000 residential areas were built.' Gravitz goes on to lament the fact that the role of the JNF is under attack: 'The JNF is a national fund which spreads spirituality and contact between the people and their land. I am sorry to say that this nationalism has become unbeloved. The settlement of areas in the state has been perceived, mistakenly, as undemocratic and unequal, as has the aim of redeeming the land.' He also refers to recent attempts by a small group of members of the Knesset to enact a law 'against the JNF ... to prevent discrimination between Arabs and Jews on JNF land' which, fortunately in his view, had been defeated. He found solace in the fact that 'nowadays the public are returning to these values of the Jewish character and the importance of Jewish settlement on the land'. Gravitz stressed the importance of retaining the 'Jewish ownership' of state land, and the principle that 'Israel Lands are for the Jews'. As to the status of the Palestinians in the state, he told *Globes* that 'unsettled land is occupied by Bedouin in the Naqab as well as by Arabs in the Galilee', and confirmed that the JNF's tree-planting activities in all parts of the state, in addition to their environmental benefits, 'put facts on the ground and signals ownership in theory and in reality'. The fact that such attitudes still prevail among those at the top of perhaps the most influential land institution in the state does not bode well for the prospects of equality for non-Jews.

Some of the cases discussed in later chapters show the Israeli courts faced with the tension between the self-identification of Israel as at the same time a Jewish state and a democratic state. This is true just as much of recent cases raising issues of discrimination and equality in access to land, as of the cases in the early years of the state's existence when challenges to the land expropriation laws came before them. How Israel's legal system has resolved this tension has been crucial to all three of the key issues for Palestinians in relation to land, namely restitution of land already expropriated, preventing further dispossession and stopping discrimination in access to land.

Principles in the Israeli legal system relevant to the protection of Palestinian land rights

One important potential safeguard of fundamental rights is their constitutional entrenchment. Giving constitutional rights priority over ordinary legislation and allowing the courts to scrutinize legislation and acts of public bodies provides recourse in law to override political decisions that conflict with fundamental rights. Two Basic Laws enacted by the Knesset in 1992, the Basic Law: Human Dignity and Liberty, and the Basic Law: Freedom of Occupation, represent a first step towards entrenching certain fundamental rights and freedoms in Israel.[13] Prior to 1992 the Israeli High Court had developed what was known as Israel's judicial bill of rights.[14] Since the enactment of these two Basic Laws, the Israeli High Court has ruled that Basic Laws have constitutional force in that they give superior status to the provisions contained within them, including fundamental rights.[15]

A search for constitutional principles capable of protecting Palestinian land rights reveals that the right to property is one of the fundamental rights entrenched in the Basic Law: Human Dignity and Liberty, affording it constitutional status. Section 3 provides that 'There shall be no violation of the property of a person.' The constitutional entrenchment of property rights under section 3 of the Basic Law appears to offer a possible source of support for Palestinian property rights. In particular, it might offer support for Palestinians seeking restitution for the expropriation of their lands. However, the Basic Law cannot be used to challenge existing legislation[16] which, since the law was not introduced until 1992, by which time most Palestinian land had already been expropriated and taken into the ownership of the state or the JNF, significantly limits its potential usefulness. In relation to legislation prior to 1992, the Basic Law can be invoked only as a tool of interpretation.

Second, the Basic Law itself contains significant limitations. Section 8 provides: 'There shall be no violation of rights under this Basic Law except by a Law befitting the values of the State of Israel, enacted for a proper purpose, and to an extent no greater than is required.' It has already become clear that this provision will be used to legitimize laws that discriminate in favour of Jews. In the United Mizrahi Bank case, the first in which the Israeli High Court considered the validity of an ordinary law of the Knesset that allegedly contravened the Basic Law: Human Dignity and Liberty, Chief Justice Barak acknowledged that section 8 provided a basis for giving significant weight to the nature of Israel as a Jewish state and its goals, at the expense of the fundamental rights concerned.[17] Of section 8 in general, he said that it 'reflects the basic perception that human rights do not view the individual as an isolated island, but rather as a part of society with national goals'. Regarding the first part of the test set out in section 8, consistency with the values of the State of Israel, Barak stressed: 'Israel is different from other countries. It is not only a democratic State, but also a Jewish State.' Commenting on what might constitute a 'proper purpose', he said this test might be met 'if [the law in question] serves an important governmental objective'. From these pronouncements, it seems that at least in this first attempt at interpreting section 8 of the Basic Law: Human Dignity and Liberty, the High Court signalled its intention to give plenty of latitude to the legislature to enact legislation that preserves the character of Israel as the Jewish state, even if this comes at the expense of fundamental rights. In his critique of the Basic Law: Human Dignity and Liberty, Aeyal Gross contends that because of section 8, the constitutional protection of property rights, far from assisting Palestinians in establishing their rights over land, might actually serve to protect the property regime that is the result of major expropriations. In other words, it could be used to preserve the de facto reality that has been established, by protecting the outcome of the large-scale transfer of land from Palestinian to Jewish hands (Gross 1998: 103).[18]

Yet the introduction of the right to property in a Basic Law has had a positive impact in certain respects. Giving judgment in the United Mizrahi Bank case, Justice Shamgar, the former Chief Justice of Israel, stated that, as a constitutional right, the right to property in section 3 should be construed broadly and in a general way, and that its purpose was to prevent denial and reduction of an individual's right to property.[19] In the case of Kersek, the Israeli High Court relied on the introduction of the right to property in the Basic Law to find that, where an order has been made for the expropriation of a piece of land for public purposes, and the reason for the order ceases to exist, the land must be returned to its previous owner.[20] Whether or not this finding will be applied to expropriations carried out prior to the Court's ruling remains unresolved.[21] Clearly, if the ruling is applied to past expropriations, it could have a significant impact on the many declarations of expropriation of Arab land that were made without a specific purpose indicated, or where the nature of the 'public purpose' is changed after the initial declaration of expropriation. In Haltsman, the High Court relied on the Basic Law to raise the level of compensation payable to a person whose land had been expropriated for public purposes, and also to introduce the principle of proportionality.[22] These cases, none of which involves Palestinian land, suggest that the constitutional entrenchment of property rights is having an impact and has some potential for protecting Palestinian property rights.

A second constitutional principle that might be invoked in relation to Palestinian land rights is that of human dignity, a principle that is protected in sections 1, 2 and 4 of the Basic Law: Human Dignity and Liberty. Arguably, social and economic rights such as the right to housing violate the principle of human dignity, and have been interpreted as doing so in other countries.[23] The concept has been used internationally by groups making claims for recognition of their collective rights, as well as those claiming the right to choice in matters such as way of life.[24] While there has been little time for judicial interpretation of the right to human dignity in Israel, to date the judiciary has been reluctant to deduce specific human rights from the right to human dignity.[25]

The right to freedom of occupation is another right that has a bearing on Palestinian access to land. As described in Chapter 1, one of the key problems facing Palestinian citizens of Israel as a result of land expropriations and government policies has been the loss of the choice to live in a rural setting and make a living from agriculture, animal husbandry and similar pursuits. This is a choice that Jewish citizens do have. The contrast is particularly stark in the Naqab, where Palestinian Bedouin have so far been refused the option of establishing agricultural villages while numerous communities of this nature exist for Jews. Section 3 of the Basic Law: Freedom of Occupation establishes that '(E)very Israeli national or resident has the right to engage in any occupation, profession or trade.' This provision may only be violated, in accordance with section 4, 'by a law befitting the values of the State of Israel, enacted for a proper purpose, and to an extent no greater than is required'.

Another principle that has some constitutional status, though less strong than those previously discussed, is that of equality. This principle, particularly important in Palestinian attempts to halt ongoing expropriation of land and challenge discrimination in access to land, was omitted from the Basic Law: Human Dignity and Liberty. Instead, section 1 declares that human rights in Israel will be respected in the spirit of the principles enshrined in the Declaration of the Establishment of the State of Israel.[26] While included in the Declaration is the commitment to ensure equality to all inhabitants of the state, this indirect method of bringing in the principle is no substitute for a direct provision, and the question must be asked why this principle, which the Israeli High Court has said on a number of occasions is a fundamental principle of Israeli law, was omitted.

The question of how far the principle of equality in the Israeli legal system can be used effectively to protect Palestinian land rights remains somewhat open. While the Palestinians in Israel are accorded procedural equality before the law, individual civil rights (such as the right to vote and stand in elections), and a certain recognition as a group (separate schools, limited recognition of the Arabic language), to date there has been little recognition of the collective entitlement of the Palestinians, as a national minority, to redress for historical injustices, or to a proportional share of state resources, including land but also budgets, appointments to decision-making bodies and other resources.[27] An exception is the High Court's ruling in a case regarding state funding for religious cemeteries.[28] In that case it was held that the Minister of Religious Affairs must distribute funds for religious cemeteries equally to Jewish and Arab religious communities. The High Court had previously rejected a petition challenging the entire budget of the ministry, which had allocated less than 2 per cent to Arab religious communities, on the grounds of 'generality'.[29] The High Court's ruling in the case of Qa'dan, in which it found that the Israel Lands Administration had offended the principle of equality by allocating state land to a communal settlement that admitted Jews only, was cautiously welcomed by the Palestinian community, but the fact that the High Court failed to address the underlying issues such as the role and objectives of the Jewish Agency in developing communities exclusively for Jews provides a good illustration of the limitations on the application of the principle of equality to date in Israel.

While the entrenchment of fundamental rights in Israel in recent years is a positive development, constitutional entrenchment alone is not sufficient. Governmental action to implement these rights is also required, such as through the establishment of mechanisms to monitor and enforce rights guaranteed by law, and through effective access to justice. In Israel there are inadequate institutional mechanisms to guard against discrimination. There is no body charged with protecting against discrimination in the state that would operate to enforce the principle of non-discrimination in relation to Palestinians. Nor is there general anti-discrimination legislation in Israel. While legislation has been introduced to safeguard equal opportunities for women and the disabled, equal access to employment and representation for Arabs on the boards of public companies, there is no protection against discrimination for Palestinian Arabs in general.

If constitutional protections alone cannot be relied upon to protect Palestinian rights in relation to land, what is the situation as regards ordinary legislation? Ordinary legislation, for instance, could potentially provide accountability and a system of checks and balances designed to make public bodies and officials accountable in relation to principles such as equality and non-discrimination. In the process of examining law and practice in several spheres relevant to Palestinian access to land in Israel, we found that a central feature of the Israeli system of government, and one that has been enormously influential for Palestinians in relation to land, is the wide discretion that is given to the executive in various pieces of legislation. Ministers and other public officials are free to exercise powers in many areas without checks, and without clear guidelines being set out for criteria on which to base decisions such as allocation of resources. Professor Yitzhak Zamir, a former Supreme Court judge and Attorney General and leading authority on administrative law in Israel, criticizes the wide discretion given to the administrative authorities in Israel, and warns that such a situation endangers the rule of law, and in effect allows executive officials to be legislators (Zamir 1996: 233–8). To illustrate his point, Zamir refers to the Israel Lands Administration Law of 1960, which is the source of authority for the ILA to administer more than 90 per cent of land in the state. Despite its considerable role, the law contains no objectives to direct how the ILA should exercise its powers, no guidance as to how it should operate, no criteria to govern the leasing of land or its transfer without consideration. Even a small private company, Zamir argues, defines in its founding documents the objects and authorities of the company and its various components. Why, he wonders, did the legislature refrain from defining such crucial issues when it comes to the land of Israel?

The effect of the lack of a general prohibition on discrimination on Israeli law, coupled with the wide discretion given to the executive, is far-reaching. If a minister has funds to allocate, say, for alleviating problems in underprivileged communities, what is to stop him or her exercising his or her discretion so as to allocate first or exclusively to Jewish areas? Almost everywhere one looks, the evidence of discrimination is apparent. The Ministers of Finance and of Industry and Trade announce which areas of the country will be entitled to development grants and incentives, and select only or mainly Jewish areas.[30] The Israel Lands Administration awards reductions in the price of leasing property, but only in housing intended for Jews.[31] The Minister of Housing decides to give extensive grants for the acquisition of apartments in certain towns, but only those who buy in Jewish towns are given this entitlement.[32] While the Palestinian community has started to mount serious legal challenges to such decisions, and sometimes the threat or the initiation of legal proceedings succeeds in changing a certain decision, to date there have been few rulings that address the question of discrimination head-on.

The role of the judiciary in relation to the issue of equality between national groups in Israel One institution that should operate to protect citizens from abuse of their rights is the judiciary. The Israeli Supreme Court, acting as a High Court of Justice, supervises the implementation of the prohibition against discrimination by government or public bodies. The Israeli government has described its role as follows: 'The Supreme Court, seated in Jerusalem, has nationwide jurisdiction. It is the highest court of appeal on rulings of lower tribunals. In its capacity as High Court of Justice, the Supreme Court hears petitions in constitutional and administrative law issues against any government body or agent, and is a court of first and last instance' (State of Israel 1998b: para. 27).

As has already been mentioned, the High Court has an impressive record in developing a jurisprudence of rights in Israel before the constitutional entrenchment of certain fundamental rights in the basic laws of 1992. At the same time, however, it has an extraordinarily poor record when it comes to Israeli army practices in the Occupied Territories, and of responding to petitions brought by Palestinian citizens of Israel on issues such as equality and discrimination, a record aptly described by Aeyal Gross as the 'dark side' of the Israeli High Court's civil rights jurisprudence (Gross 1998: 86). This record includes avoiding redressing obvious discrimination and lack of equality while maintaining that these principles apply. A review of the judgments handed down in some of the leading cases brought by Palestinian citizens of Israel reveals some of the obstacles faced by applicants seeking to make such arguments.

One clear trend in the High Court's jurisprudence in cases brought by Palestinians is the tendency to give preference to reinforcing the Jewish nature of the state or national security interests, when they are presented as conflicting with fundamental rights such as the principle of equality.[33] A number of examples appear in this book. In the recent decision of Qa'dan, the High Court found itself once again forced to confront possible contradictions between the Jewish character of the state and other principles it is bound to uphold, such as the principle of equality.[34] The petition was brought by a Palestinian citizen of Israel whose application to join a new community built by the Jewish Agency was denied on the grounds that he was an Arab. In its judgment, the High Court acknowledged that the Jewish state incorporates the right to equality, and on this basis ruled that the Israel Lands Authority, as a state body, had acted unlawfully in allocating land to a body that discriminated on the grounds of religion or nationality. But the Court also took the opportunity to stress that the petition was not about whether settlement bodies could legitimately establish communities exclusively for Jews, and emphasized the importance of the historical mission of the Jewish Agency, which had a special statutory status and whose work was not yet complete. In other words, the Court was at pains to say that though the state in this individual case had erred, the legitimacy of the overall national programme that lay behind the particular incident, which was dedicated to developing the state for Jews specifically, including the role of the Jewish national institutions, was not in question. The Qa'dan case is also a good example of the High Court seeking to avoid a finding of collective discrimination on the basis of national origin. Unlike many of the other petitions brought by Palestinians, which have been framed as claims of national historical discrimination, the applicants in Qa'dan had framed the petition as an individual case, a fact that was noted by the High Court with approval.[35]

Another factor noticeable in the judgments of the Israeli High Court is its selective approach to the application of legal rights and principles. The Court has not always applied norms it has upheld in the Jewish sector in cases relating to Palestinians. The implementation of the Public Purposes Ordinance is one example. In the Kersek case, a Jewish landowner whose land had been expropriated for public purposes had his land returned to him by order of the Court, after it became clear that the original reason for the expropriation no longer existed. However, the case of Nusseibeh, a Palestinian landowner in East Jerusalem, with very similar facts, was also decided after the Basic Law, but the Court reached the opposite conclusion. In cases where there is a perceived national aspect, the High Court has been particularly reluctant to intervene. In the early years of the state's existence, the Court intervened rarely in decisions to expropriate Palestinian land and tended to defer to the executive.[36]

Another obstacle placed before applicants has been that the High Court has adopted legal tests that make it extremely difficult to establish discrimination. In a series of cases since the 1950s, Palestinian applicants have approached the High Court arguing that differences in treatment between Jewish and Arab citizens amount to unlawful discrimination, or presenting documented evidence of gaps in allocation of resources and benefits to Jewish and Arab citizens respectively, arguing that this difference between provision to the two national groups constitutes discrimination and is unlawful under Israeli law as it offends the principle of equality. Such challenges have reached the Court both before and after the enactment of the Basic Law: Human Dignity and Liberty in 1992. The response of the High Court has been varied, but it has only extremely rarely been prepared to accept such challenges.

In the early case of Nazareth Committee for the Defence of Expropriated Land v. Minister of Finance, decided by the High Court in 1955, the Court took the approach that in order to constitute discrimination that would justify its intervention, the administrative decision or action must be *intentionally* discriminatory, and furthermore it was for the petitioners to prove that it was the fact that they were Arabs that had been the determining factor in the decision.[37] The case concerned plans to expropriate land from Arab residents of Nazareth for the purpose of building government offices. In its judgment the Court stated:

> It was not enough that the Plaintiffs claimed that they were Arabs and that only Arab land was taken when it was possible to take the land of non-Arabs or to use government lands. *It would have to have been established that the fact that they were Arabs – that and not some other fact – was what motivated the Respondents to take their land and not someone else's.* This has not been proven. We have no basis for the assumption that the Respondents chose the Plaintiffs' lands, not for the declared public purpose or because these lands were the most suitable for their purposes, but in order to harm the Arab residents of the town.

In other cases also, the courts have been willing to look only at the *process* by which a decision has been made, not finding it sufficient that the *result* was discriminatory. Demonstrating a pattern of discriminatory effect alone has not tended to succeed; instead the courts have taken an excessively formal approach, finding that there has been no violation by the relevant minister or public body of the letter of the law, and that therefore there is no basis for it to interfere in decisions relating to allocation of resources, even though preference has been shown to Jewish over Palestinian citizens. A good example is the case brought in 1990 to challenge the fact that the Minister of Finance, when deciding which schools should be allocated extra resources for a longer school day in the first phase of a new policy aimed at improving educational standards in deprived areas, selected only Jewish schools even though there were many Palestinian areas with equal needs. The Court refused to make a finding of discrimination since it did not find a problem with the process of decision-making.[38] This approach of focusing only on the process and not on the result of a decision or policy certainly contradicts current international standards,[39] and has been criticized by legal scholars within Israel.[40] While there are indications that the Israeli courts now accept that the test of discrimination is one of result,[41] it remains unclear whether the Israeli courts would necessarily decide such cases differently today.

More recently, the courts have required evidence not only of disproportionate allocation of resources, but additionally of the needs of the different communities. In a case challenging differential allocations to cemeteries of different religions, the High Court agreed that there was *prima facie* discrimination, in that the 1998 budget of the Ministry of Religious Affairs allocated less than 2 per cent of its funding to Arab religious communities.[42] However, the Court refused to invalidate the relevant budget provision or to give a remedy to the petitioners, on the basis that the petition was too general to justify the provision of a specific and concrete remedy. Judge Heishin said that it was not enough to argue that the Arab community does not receive a portion of the budget of the ministry that was proportional to its percentage of the population. 'Even if this is the case,' Justice Heishin said, 'it does not mean that substantive inequality exists. To establish the existence of substantive inequality, it is necessary to examine the religious needs of each religious community. Only after such an examination can we conclude that substantive inequality exists.' This was despite the fact that the petitioners had submitted evidence of the monetary needs of the different Arab religious sects, evidence the Court dismissed as 'a work of magic'. Subsequently, the same public interest law group, Adalah, introduced another petition specifically challenging the lack of allocation in the ministry's budget to cemeteries of the Muslim, Christian and Druze communities. This time the challenge succeeded, and the High Court ordered that funds for cemeteries be spent on all religious groups on an equal basis.[43]

The High Court has also been called upon to deal with the question of whether some distinctions made between Jewish and Arab citizens might be legitimate, and therefore not constitute unlawful discrimination. Not every distinction in treatment between different groups will constitute discrimination, but the United Nations Human Rights Committee has said that in order to be lawful, a differentiation must be based on reasonable and objective criteria, and in order to achieve a purpose which is legitimate under the International Covenant on Civil and Political Rights.[44] In two cases the Court has been willing to recognize special historical factors as a basis for justifying discrimination in favour of Jews. In Wattad the Court held, in 1983, that the claim that child benefits had been paid to all Jews but not to most Arabs (the criteria were military service and studying in a Jewish religious institution) had not been proved, and in any event there was no discrimination because there was no distinction between equals; the Court noted that students in the Jewish religious institutions had a special place in Jewish history.[45] In the Bourkhan case, decided in 1978, the Court was ready to state more explicitly that certain distinctions may be considered to be legitimate and not to constitute discrimination, for instance if made for policy reasons.[46] In this case, Palestinians had attempted to challenge their exclusion from houses built in the Jewish quarter of the Old City of Jerusalem. The Court held that the reconstruction of the old Jewish quarter for Jews exclusively was a legitimate objective.

Finally, the Court has given relatively little weight to the principle of proportionality, which was introduced in relation to constitutionally protected fundamental rights in section 8 of the Basic Law: Human Dignity and Liberty, and has therefore been a constitutional principle in Israel at least since 1992.[47] Any harm to property rights must meet the test of proportionality. So, for example, any expropriation or other act affecting rights over land, such as under legislation authorizing expropriation of land for public purposes, must adhere strictly to the extent required for the relevant purpose only. In the Kersek case, the Court was influenced in its decision by the fact that the process by which land was expropriated must be proportional, and the same point was stressed by Judge Barak in the Haltsman case. The principle should be applied to any decision adversely affecting Palestinian land rights, not only expropriation of land but also the designation of military training areas and use of other emergency regulations, the current implementation of legislation enacted prior to 1992 such as the Absentees' Property Law, the conduct of the process of settlement of title and other aspects of Israeli land policy examined in this book.[48]

The approach taken by the Israeli High Court in cases raising discrimination against Palestinian citizens is broadly consistent with its role in politically sensitive cases generally, in which it prefers to defer to the legislature (Saban 1996: 541). So, for example, it has been argued that the role of the High Court in Israel has not been pivotal even in such changes as have occurred in the status of Palestinians in Israel, and that unlike the United States Supreme Court, which played a key role in the 1950s and 1960s in confronting institutional racism, the Israeli High Court has not been willing to criticize or depart from the prevailing regime and in particular, the state of ethnic relations in the country (ibid.). The Israeli High Court, fully aware that there is systematic discrimination against Palestinians in Israel, also knows that this is the result of deliberate policies and that the political will does not exist in government to take drastic steps towards giving equal rights to Palestinians. For it to force such steps would be to confront the political body, which it is not ready to do. Instead, there are indications, such as in the Qa'dan decision, that the Court sees any change as a process to be undertaken over time, and as not involving any questioning of historic injustices.[49]

International legal principles including the law of human rights

If domestic law in Israel offers only limited recognition and protection of Palestinian land rights, international law and practice provide a considerably stronger basis for protection. The language of human rights has considerable moral and legal force in today's world. There is an evolving rights-based approach that provides a yardstick for measuring a state's behaviour against internationally recognized standards. It permits an exception to the general rule that states do not intervene in another state's affairs. Human rights violations committed in one state are the concern of the international community as a whole. Sometimes, human rights law provides enforcement mechanisms such as international courts and tribunals, and UN human rights bodies that consider complaints. Israel has ratified many human rights treaties but has avoided making itself subject to the jurisdiction of complaints mechanisms such as those of the UN Human Rights Committee that monitors compliance with the International Covenant on Civil and Political Rights. However, it is obliged to report to a number of UN human rights monitoring bodies, and to have those reports examined, measured against international standards and commented upon. Such international human rights monitoring mechanisms may lack enforcement powers but can assert significant political pressure. Defining something as a violation of human rights based on international standards can play a key role in shaming states.

One example is Israel's response to being found in violation of human rights norms by the International Water Tribunal held in the Netherlands in 1992. Non-governmental organizations (NGOs) from the Palestinian community in Israel brought a case against the government of Israel, challenging its failure to supply drinking water to unrecognized Palestinian villages.[50] After the jury of experts found that the government of Israel had violated international law, including the Universal Declaration of Human Rights and the Stockholm Declaration on the Human Environment of 1972,[51] the government agreed to provide at least one central water tap to each unrecognized community. While the case did not bring about a fundamental change in government policy towards the unrecognized villages, it did arouse press coverage, elevate the profile of the villages as a political issue in Israel, and helped to relieve some of the worst problems suffered by these communities as a result of their unrecognized status (Kanaaneh et al. 1995: 203).

A second important advantage of a rights-based approach is that international human rights standards can be used to support submissions made in legal challenges in the Israeli courts. One example is the successful attempt to persuade the Israeli Supreme Court to agree with UN rights bodies that interrogation methods used by the Israeli General Security Services on Palestinian detainees amounted to torture.[52] To date, the Israeli courts have dismissed most cases dealing with the equal rights of Palestinian citizens of Israel (Adalah 1998: 11), but it is only very recently that the community has started to make greater use of international human rights standards in putting its arguments before the courts, and it remains to be seen whether this approach will have an impact.

Most importantly, the language of rights can be used as part of popular pressure to bring about change. Sometimes, it can help secure gains through the courts; more often, it can be used as part of a wider campaign for the introduction of new legislation or changes in government policy. Ultimately, the essence of a 'rights approach' is that it empowers people to participate in the struggle to achieve their rights, working through community-based organizations and NGOs: it equips them with legal tools and a framework for measuring government duties and policies, and legitimizes their campaigns (Abu Shakrah 1994: 6–7). Thus the step from saying that something is a need to defining it as a right is an important one.

Finally, human rights recognizes collective as well as individual rights, including the concepts of national minorities and indigenous peoples. Most importantly, the collective rights of the Palestinian people have already achieved international legitimacy through United Nations recognition of the Palestinian right to self-determination and the right of return. These two principles are crucial to recognition of Palestinian land rights.

International norms and standards relating to Palestinian land rights and to access to land generally The Universal Declaration of Human Rights (UDHR) of 1948, and the twin International Covenants of 1966 – on Civil and Political Rights (ICCPR), and on Economic, Social and Cultural Rights (ICESCR) – set out the broad range of human rights and still form the basis of human rights protection.[53] The Universal Declaration is widely regarded as reflecting customary international law and has been accepted as such in the Israeli courts (Lerner 1987: 7), while the two International Covenants were ratified by Israel on

3 October 1991. Article 17 of the UDHR provides that 'Everyone has the right to own property alone as well as in association with others.' The UDHR also protects procedural rights: Article 17.2 of the UDHR provides that 'No one shall be *arbitrarily* deprived of his property.' Similarly, under Article 5 of the International Convention on the Elimination of All Forms of Racial Discrimination, to which Israel is also a party: 'States Parties undertake to prohibit and to eliminate racial discrimination in all its forms and to guarantee the right of everyone, without distinction as to race, colour, or national or ethnic origin, to equality before the law, notably in the enjoyment of the following rights: ... (v) The right to own property alone as well as in association with others.'

International law, including the law of human rights, while not fettering the powers of states to carry out their political and economic agendas, such as nationalization or expropriation for public projects (Higgins 1982: Ch. V), places limitations on states intended to protect both individuals and groups in relation to their access to land. While the international human rights treaties such as the ICCPR and the ICESCR do not directly deal with the limitations on the rights of governments to expropriate property, they do guarantee certain important rights designed to protect citizens from the arbitrary use of such powers by the state. These include the right to peaceful use and enjoyment of one's property and the corresponding prohibition on arbitrary deprivation of property (found for instance in Protocol 1 of the European Convention on Human Rights); due process rights including the right to a fair and public hearing in the determination of rights and obligations (guaranteed *inter alia* in Article 14 of the ICCPR); and the right to equality before the law and to the guarantee of protection under law from discrimination in the implementation of such powers (found for instance in Article 26 of the ICCPR).

More specifically, regional human rights instruments and case law in national and international contexts have identified three main conditions limiting the freedom of states to deprive people of property:

1. The deprivation is in the public interest.
2. The process is in accordance with law.
3. Payment of just compensation.[54]

This formula is adopted, for instance, in Article 21 of the American Convention on Human Rights:

1. Everyone has the right to the use and enjoyment of his property. The law may subordinate such use and enjoyment to the interests of society.

2. No one shall be deprived of his property except upon payment of just compensation, for reasons of public utility or social interest, and in the cases and according to the forms established by law.

The European Court of Human Rights has laid down a 'fair balance' test, to balance the fundamental right of the individual to peaceful enjoyment of property against the power of the state to requisition and control property in the public interest. The test aims to protect against any arbitrary and disproportionate effects of the implementation of the law, and includes assessing the objectives of the interference with property rights, whether or not there is any alternative, whether or not adequate compensation has been paid, and other factors.[55]

The right of return and restitution of property There is considerable support in international law and practice for the right of the Palestinian refugees and internally displaced persons to return to their original land. The right of refugees displaced during conflict to return to their own country is well established, not only in human rights law but also in international humanitarian law and in international practice relating to refugees.[56] In human rights law, the right of return is based on Article 13 of the Universal Declaration of Human Rights – 'Everyone has the right to leave any country, including his own, and to return to his country' – and on Article 12.4 of the International Covenant on Civil and Political Rights: 'No one shall be arbitrarily deprived of the right to enter his own country.' On the meaning of the term one's 'own country', the Human Rights Committee has said it 'embraces, at the very least, an individual who, because of his or her special ties to or claims in relation to a given country, cannot be considered to be a mere alien. This would be the case, for example, of nationals of a country who have been stripped of their nationality in violation of international law, and of individuals whose country of nationality has been incorporated in or transferred to another national entity, whose nationality is being denied them' (UN Human Rights Committee 1999: para. 20). In other words, the fact that the Palestinian refugees do not hold Israeli nationality does not mean they are denied the right to return to their homes in Israel.[57] The right to return may be held not only by those who were actually exiled, but also by their descendants (ibid., para. 19).[58]

In international humanitarian law, the Geneva Conventions of 1949 make many references to the right of persons protected by the Conventions to repatriation, during or after cessation of hostilities.[59] Finally, although the Convention Relating to the Status of Refugees of 1951 does not address the issue, in international practice relating to refugees, the principle of voluntary repatriation has long been accepted as a general principle underlying its work by the Office of the UN High Commissioner for Refugees (UNHCR 1985). UN resolutions and peace agreements have reflected this in contexts such as the Balkans.[60]

The specific right of the Palestinian refugees to return, which is backed by the body of international law mentioned, has been affirmed in numerous resolutions of the UN General Assembly. Under UN Resolution 194 of 11 December 1948, the Palestinian refugees have a choice: they have a right to return to their homes, but if they choose not to return, they have a right to compensation. The right to return has also been affirmed by several UN bodies charged with monitoring states' compliance with international human rights treaties.[61]

The question then arises to what extent international law and practice provide a basis for 'undoing' the past fifty years, and give an individual right to Palestinian refugees to return to their original lands and homes, often now settled by Jewish citizens of Israel. While the human rights instruments support the right of return to one's 'country', UN Resolution 194 specifically says the Palestinian refugees have the right to return to 'their homes'.[62] There is also international practice along these lines. UN Security Council Resolution 876 on Abkhazia and Georgia of 1993 affirmed the right of refugees and displaced persons to return to their homes, and the Dayton Peace Agreement for Bosnia and Herzegovina of 1995 established the right of more than 2 million refugees and displaced persons to 'freely ... return to their homes of origin. They shall have the right to have restored to them property of which they were deprived in the course of hostilities since 1991 and to be compensated for any property that cannot be returned to them.'[63]

The European Court of Human Rights has also considered situations of deprivation of property and the continuing rights of its owners even decades later. In the case of Cyprus v. Turkey, the Court was called upon to consider whether the actions of the authorities of the self-proclaimed Turkish Republic of Northern Cyprus in refusing to allow Greek Cypriots displaced in 1974 to return to or even to visit their former homes was a violation of the European Convention on Human Rights.[64] Article 8 of the Convention provides as follows:

1. Everyone has the right to respect for his private and family life, his home and his correspondence.
2. There shall be no interference by a public authority with the exercise of this right except such as is in accordance with the law and is necessary in a democratic society in the interests of national security,

public safety or the economic well-being of the country, for the prevention of disorder or crime, for the protection of health or morals, or for the protection of the rights and freedoms of others.

Article 1 of Protocol 1 to the Convention provides:

Every natural or legal person is entitled to the peaceful enjoyment of his possessions. No one shall be deprived of his possessions except in the public interest and subject to the conditions provided for by law and by the general principles of international law. The preceding provisions shall not, however, in any way impair the right of a State to enforce such laws as it deems necessary to control the use of property in accordance with the general interest or to secure the payment of taxes or other contributions or penalties.

In its decision of 10 May 2001, the European Court held that there had been a continuing violation of Article 8 by reason of the refusal to allow the return of any Greek Cypriot displaced persons to their homes in Northern Cyprus, and, further, the continuing and total denial of access to their property is a clear interference with the right of the displaced Greek Cypriots to the peaceful enjoyment of possessions within the meaning of Article 1 of Protocol 1.[65] The Court added that the fact that the issue was pending agreement on an overall political solution through inter-communal talks could not be invoked in order to legitimate a violation of the Convention.[66] Furthermore, as the Court had already held in the earlier case of Loizidou, the fact that the so-called Turkish Republic of Northern Cyprus had purported to deprive Greek Cypriots of their title through the Constitution and legislation did not affect the rights of the displaced Greek Cypriots under the Convention.[67] In another case, Brumarescu v. Romania, the Court in 2001 ordered the government of Romania to return to the applicant a house that had been expropriated in 1950.[68] While Israel is not a party to the European Convention on Human Rights, this jurisprudence is interesting as an indication of international interpretation of property rights, and particularly in light of Israel's own constitutional protection of the right to property.

The right of people internally displaced during conflict to return to their homes also finds support in international law and practice. This is of particular relevance to the 'present absentees', the Palestinians who were displaced from their land but remained within the borders of Israel and became citizens. The UN Guiding Principles on Internal Displacement of 1998 provide, in Principle 28:

1. Competent authorities have the primary duty and responsibility to

establish conditions, as well as provide the means, to allow internally displaced persons to return voluntarily, in safety and with dignity, to their homes or places of habitual residence, or to resettle voluntarily in another part of the country. Such authorities shall endeavour to facilitate the reintegration of returned or resettled internally displaced persons.

2. Special efforts should be made to ensure the full participation of internally displaced persons in the planning and management of their return or resettlement and reintegration.[69]

The Principles define internally displaced persons (IDPs) as: 'persons or groups of persons who have been forced or obliged to flee or to leave their homes or places of habitual residence, in particular as a result of or in order to avoid the effects of armed conflict, situations of generalized violence, violations of human rights or natural or human-made disasters, and who have not crossed an internationally recognized State border'. The Palestinian 'present absentees' clearly fall within this definition. The Guiding Principles are not intended to establish new legal norms but to reflect existing international human rights law and international humanitarian law.[70] The document's wide acceptance since 1998 indicates that it has become the benchmark for states and others regarding internal displacement.

Collective and peoples' rights The notion of Palestinian collective rights has long permeated Palestinian discourse in relation to land. Individual legal title is not the only, or even the most important, basis of the Palestinian community's historical rights over land. Through the Ottoman and British Mandate times, though formally the sovereign had ultimate ownership of much land in the area, its title was merely nominal and it was recognized that the land actually belonged to Palestinian families or tribes through long use and possession, or was communal land held in trust for the inhabitants of the Arab villages and used by them for generations (Hadawi 1963: 18–23; Shehadi 1993: 21). Some 87.3 per cent of the land registered as state owned was situated in the Naqab Desert, where Palestinian Bedouin tribes laid claim to most of the cultivable land on the basis of customary arrangements. The broader approach to Palestinian ownership of land appeared to be accepted by the Palestine Conciliation Commission, entrusted by the United Nations General Assembly in 1950 with the task of making arrangements for the implementation of UN General Assembly Resolution 194.[71] In its global assessment of Palestinian refugee losses issued in 1951, the Commission encompassed all types of Palestinian rights over land, and estimated that the land abandoned by the Palestinian refugees amounted to 16,324 square kms (of a total area of 26,320 square kms that constituted Mandatory Palestine prior to 1948). However in its subsequent work to identify and value refugee property, published in its later report of 1964, the Commission took a different approach, including only individual rights in land based on British Mandate records such as registration and tax records.[72] Israel adopted an even more restrictive approach, refusing to recognize Palestinian rights over land other than those based on individual title. Further, upon taking over responsibility for land, Israel took a range of measures aimed at making it as difficult as possible for Palestinians to establish title, as will be described in particular in Chapter 4.

But the concept of Palestinian collective rights over land goes beyond such notions of acquisition of rights through long use, or communal rights over land surrounding the Palestinian villages. There is also the concept of the collective right of the Palestinians over the land as a people. Under this principle, it is not necessary for Palestinians to prove that they have legal title of specific pieces of land since they have collective rights as a people over the land of historical Palestine. Such an approach draws on the idea that peoples as such, and not only individuals, have rights.

Collective or peoples' rights, such as the right to self-determination, the right to permanent sovereignty over natural resources and the rights of indigenous peoples, are now accepted as a category in international law.[73] The right to self-determination was part of the rhetoric used by the major powers when the future of the different parts of the Ottoman Empire were being determined following the First World War. Palestinians had hoped for their own state on the dismantling of the Ottoman Empire, but instead had found themselves placed under a British Mandate. The concept of permanent sovereignty of nations over natural resources emerged as an articulation of self-determination on the part of developing countries upon decolonization. It was expressed in Article 1 of the UN General Assembly Resolution 1803(XVII) of 14 December 1962 on permanent sovereignty over natural resources, which declared: 'The right of peoples and nations to permanent sovereignty over their natural wealth and resources must be exercised in the interest of their national development and of the well-being of the people of the State concerned.'

The two International Covenants of 1966, on Civil and Political and on Economic, Social and Cultural Rights, both contain in Article 1.2 the following: 'All peoples may, for their own ends, freely dispose of their natural wealth and resources without prejudice to any obligations arising out of international economic co-operation, based upon the principle of mutual benefit and international law. In no case may a people be deprived of its own means of subsistence.' While the notion of permanent sovereignty has been used by states to assert complete rights over resources, the principle also operates to limit the power of national governments freely to dispose of the natural resources of the region without the consent, or against the wishes or contrary to the interests of, the people in question.[74] In the Palestinian context, these rights are obviously applicable to the Palestinian people as a whole, and not just to those who are citizens of Israel.

A separate body of international law has developed concerning the rights of indigenous populations. The development of separate standards is based on a recognition that indigenous populations have particular concerns which need to be addressed, particularly relating to land rights and respect of customs and traditions. The International Labour Organization, which led the development of international legal standards relating to indigenous peoples, has adopted two Conventions on indigenous and tribal peoples,[75] and a Draft Declaration on the Rights of Indigenous Peoples is currently going through the UN human rights machinery as a first step towards a UN Convention on this subject.[76]

The relationship to homelands is at the core of the identity of indigenous populations, and forms a fundamental part of the body of rights of indigenous peoples that is increasingly recognized at the national and international levels. This issue is considered so important that the UN Commission on Human Rights in 1997 commissioned a working paper on indigenous peoples and their relationship to land, with a view to suggesting practical measures to address ongoing problems.[77] In her report, UN Special Rapporteur Erica-Irene Daes identifies the following as among the principal problems: failure of states to acknowledge indigenous rights to land, discriminatory laws and policies, problems in regard to land claims, expropriation of indigenous lands for national interests, and removal and relocation.[78]

The following are the major provisions regarding land contained in ILO Conventions 107 and 169 and the UN Draft Declaration:

- All three documents recognize the rights of ownership and possession over lands traditionally occupied.[79] The ILO Convention emphasizes that this includes access to land used for traditional activities and states that particular attention is to be paid to nomadic peoples and shifting cultivators.
- Governments are called upon to take positive steps to identify lands

traditionally occupied, guarantee effective protection for the rights of the indigenous people to these lands, and establish procedures to resolve land claims.[80] There is an important difference between ILO Convention 169, which confers right of ownership over land that indigenous populations 'traditionally occupy', thus excluding land which they had occupied in the past but from which they had been expelled, and the Draft Declaration, which refers to land that indigenous peoples 'have traditionally owned or otherwise occupied or used'.

• Indigenous peoples are not to be forcibly removed from their lands, and relocation should only occur: with the 'free and informed consent' of those concerned; following legally established procedures providing the opportunity for effective representation; and agreement on just and fair compensation.[81] Wherever possible, relocation should be temporary; if not, compensation should take the form of land at least equal in quality, size and legal status unless otherwise agreed by those concerned.[82]

• Indigenous peoples are to be allowed to engage freely in their traditional and other economic activities, including, *inter alia*, herding and cultivation, and governments must accord them equal treatment in national agrarian programmes.[83]

The question whether or not the Palestinian citizens of Israel as a whole, or some part of them such as the Bedouin in the Naqab, constitute an indigenous people within the context of the international instruments described is discussed below. Although it has not been possible to reach consensus as regards a definition in the UN, key elements are original habitation prior to colonization, and a special relationship with the land and environment, such that it is essential for their survival as distinct peoples, to preserve their way of life and culture. At the same time, they share characteristics of other minorities, namely a language, religion and culture distinct from those of the rest of the population and a desire to preserve those characteristics. While people everywhere depend on access to land for a whole range of reasons, including for a livelihood (for agriculture, industry, etc.), and for residential purposes (for the establishment of communities including the full range of facilities and services), indigenous peoples give a spiritual, social, cultural, economic and political significance to their land and other natural resources, in such a way that their continued survival as communities depends on it (Daes 1999: para. 10).

Historic title and customary land tenure Redressing historic wrongs relating to dispossession of land by previous generations has become something of a trend in recent years, as states make arrangements with minorities or indigenous populations within their borders in order to make up for wrongs done in the past. This has occurred, for instance, in parts of Latin America and Eastern Europe, and in Canada and Australia.[84] In 1995 Queen Elizabeth II apologized to a Maori tribe in New Zealand for injustices suffered when the British colonial government confiscated their land and passed it to British settlers in the mid-nineteenth century, in breach of the Treaty of Waitangi of 1840.[85] While the situation of the Palestinians, the majority of whom are refugees, may not be strictly analogous, some of the principles that have emerged from the case law and practice are of relevance to the Palestinian situation.

One principle that has emerged is that a new sovereign power must respect pre-existing rights over land upon colonization; private property rights held under local law continue after the change of sovereignty unless expressly extinguished. This is known as the doctrine of continuity (McNeil 1989: 161). The contrary view, that conquered territory had no other lawful proprietor (*terra nullius*), was criticized in the International Court of Justice's Advisory Opinion in the case of Western Sahara in 1975, and is now generally rejected.[86] A sovereign power is permitted expressly to extinguish private property rights by expropriating land. However, in exercising its discretion to do so it is then bound by other duties such as the duty not to discriminate, to allow effective participation of those concerned, to follow proper procedures and to pay full and just compensation.

Second, it is widely accepted that forms of land tenure other than those of the conquerors should be recognized. In the landmark Mabo case decided in 1992, the Australian courts recognized Aboriginal title to the Torres Strait Islands.[87] The Australian High Court held that the pre-existing land rights of the Meriam people were not extinguished by the colonization of the area by Britain and must be recognized and protected, even if they were of a type not known to English law: 'The nature and incidents of native title must be ascertained as a matter of fact by reference to (traditional) laws and customs.'[88] The Supreme Court of Canada, in its 1997 decision in the case of Delgamuukw, affirmed that Aboriginal oral history was admissible as evidence in Aboriginal rights cases, in order to prove the required degree of use and occupation to make out a claim of ownership.[89]

Rights of minorities The UN has yet to adopt a treaty specifically on the human rights of minorities, though existing human rights treaties make some reference to minorities,[90] and in 1992 the UN Declaration on the Rights of Persons Belonging to National or Ethnic, Religious and Linguistic Minorities (the Declaration on Minority Rights) was adopted.[91] The Palestinian citizens of Israel clearly fall within its scope, being a national (Palestinian), ethnic (Arab), religious (Muslim, Christian and Druze) and linguistic (Arabic) minority in the State of Israel. Nevertheless, the application of international law relating to minorities to the Palestinian citizens of Israel is not unproblematic, given that Palestinians perceive themselves as part of the wider Palestinian population in the region. There are particular difficulties in regarding this population as a minority in relation to land, since this is a fundamental issue not only for Palestinians who are now citizens of Israel and a numerical minority in the state, but for those in the diaspora too who lost their land when forced to leave in 1948. Nevertheless, the Palestinian citizens of Israel are increasingly using the language of minority rights in order to claim equal rights with Jewish citizens of Israel in areas such as the application of the planning laws and allocation of public resources, while continuing to emphasize their historical and national rights as part of the Palestinian people as a whole.

The major theme of the Declaration on Minority Rights is the right to protection and promotion of the identity of minorities. Article 1.1 provides: 'States shall protect the existence and the national or ethnic, cultural, religious and linguistic identity of minorities within their respective territories, and shall encourage conditions for the promotion of that identity.' This duty was mentioned for the first time in Article 27 of the Covenant on Civil and Political Rights, albeit in a rather tentative and negative form: 'In those states in which ethnic, religious or linguistic minorities exist, persons belonging to such minorities shall not be denied the right, in community with other members of their group, to enjoy their own culture, to profess and practise their own religion, or to use their own language.' The concept of identity is not defined, but the requirement to protect and promote minority identity would be highly relevant to Palestinian access to land in Israel. For instance, the right to identity arguably includes the right to maintain traditional economic pursuits and way of life including traditional means of subsistence such as cultivation and herding, and special connection to traditional lands. While it is the instruments relating to indigenous peoples' rights which clearly protect rights over lands traditionally used, it has been suggested that the requirement in the Declaration on Minority Rights to encourage conditions for minority identity also implies respect for association with traditional lands where there is an intersection with culture and religion (Thornberry 1993: 21). This view is supported by the Human Rights Committee, which observes that cultural rights may include a particular way of life associated with the use of land resources, or traditional activities (UN Human Rights Committee 1994). The right to identity is therefore particularly relevant to the forced urbanization of Bedouin populations and the prevention of Bedouin and other Palestinians from engaging in agriculture or a rural way of life. The Israeli policies of obstructing the physical and economic development of Palestinian communities (described in Chapter 7), and their refusal to recognize some communities at all (described in Chapter 8), work against the existence and identity of this minority.

The Declaration on Minority Rights makes no specific reference to land. However, several of its provisions are highly relevant to the issue of access to land and other resources, including the duty to have regard to the interests of minorities, the right to participate effectively in decision-making, the right to participate in economic development, and the right to protection and promotion of identity, including traditional and chosen ways of life.

Article 5.1 of the Declaration provides that: 'National policies and programmes shall be planned and implemented with due regard for the legitimate interests of persons belonging to minorities.' This is relevant in the context of Israel's planning policies, which have disregarded the interests of the Palestinian communities.

Article 2 of the Declaration emphasizes the right of minorities to '*participate effectively*' in public life and in decisions that concern them or the regions in which they live. While the Declaration does not specify the form such participation should take, the term 'public life' probably includes both political and administrative life (Thornberry 1993: 22). Various models employed by states have included: advisory and decision-making bodies in which minorities are represented, elected bodies and assemblies for minority affairs, local and autonomous administration, self-administration in aspects concerning identity, and decentralized or local forms of government.[92] There will be many examples in this book of Israel's failure to consult with affected Palestinian communities or to allow their effective participation in planning, administration of public land and other matters relating to land. In a recent decision, the Israeli High Court seemed to acknowledge a duty to consult when it ordered that a small Palestinian community should have effective input in developing a local plan.[93] It remains to be seen whether this case will have a wider impact.

The Declaration on Minority Rights also includes a right to participate in economic development. According to Article 4.5: 'States should consider appropriate measures so that persons belonging to minorities may participate fully in the economic progress and development in their country.' This right is echoed in the UN Declaration on the Right to Development of 1986, which emphasizes both the right of all to participate in development (Articles 1 and 2) and the need for equality in development: Article 8.1 calls on states to ensure 'equality of opportunity for all in their access to basic resources'.

Despite the significant protections offered by minority rights, a comparison between the developing international standards outlined reveals a large gap between the standards relating to minorities on the one hand, and those relating to indigenous populations on the other, when it comes to land rights. If a group can be defined as an indigenous people, they qualify for extensive rights as regards land including ownership and possession of lands traditionally occupied; if they cannot be so defined, they are left to fall back on the standards relating to minorities, which are less specific as regards land. Inevitably, this leads to a situation where groups claiming a special relationship with the land are forced to seek to identify themselves as indigenous simply in order to take advantage of the greater protection than would then be available to them under emerging international law on indigenous peoples (Plant 1994: 7). This situation has already led commentators to question the justification for the differentiation.[94]

Attachment to particular territory has been put forward as one of the key reasons for special treatment of indigenous peoples. In a special report for the UN Sub-Commission on Prevention of Discrimination and Protection of Minorities, on indigenous people and their relationship to land, Erica-Irene Daes summarized the elements that are unique to indigenous peoples in terms of their relationship with lands:

1. A profound relationship between the indigenous people and their lands, territories and resources.
2. This relationship has various social, cultural, spiritual, economic and political dimensions and responsibilities.
3. The collective dimension of the relationship is significant.
4. The intergenerational aspect of the relationship is crucial to indigenous peoples' identity, survival and cultural viability. (Daes 1999: para. 18)

It is arguable that the Palestinian citizens of Israel, and particularly the Bedouin in the Naqab, share some of the characteristics of indigenous peoples. Certainly, in their tribal structures and strong traditional relationship with particular lands, the Palestinian Bedouin resemble indigenous peoples elsewhere. A number of the elements of indigenous peoples' relationship with land outlined in Mrs Daes's report (1999) apply to the Palestinians in Israel, and they share the principal problems relating to land that are faced by indigenous peoples as identified in the report: failure of the state to acknowledge their rights over land, discrimination in laws and policies, problems relating to land claims, expropriation of their land, and removal and relocation. It may be that some or all Palestinians may be entitled to benefit from the more extensive land rights afforded to indigenous peoples.[95]

Even if the Palestinians cannot properly be considered as indigenous peoples within the meaning of the international instruments, however, there are strong arguments for stronger and more specific rights relating to land, along the lines of those that have been developed within the scope of indigenous peoples' rights, to be applicable to minorities such as the Palestinians. While not all of the elements described as unique to indigenous peoples are present for all minorities, there are certainly many minorities for whom historical attachment to the land is extremely important. In Central and Eastern Europe, for instance, the victims of Stalin's forced deportations made huge efforts to return to their land (Aukerman 2000: 1038). The Palestinians in Israel have displayed tremendous and impassioned attachment to land, to the extent that tens of thousands are ready to live without basic utilities such as electricity and running water in order to preserve their ties to land they perceive as theirs.[96] They also share with many indigenous peoples the element of historic dispossession. Even if elements such as spiritual ties and collective ownership are not present, the historical attachment to place is strong and the relationship to land is bound up with powerful social, cultural, economic and political forces. In other words, as Miriam Aukerman convincingly argues, the important thing should be the underlying justification for the development of rights, rather than a simplified system of labelling groups (as either indigenous peoples or minorities) that might result in differential treatment being given to those that essentially have similar problems.[97] The United Nations Human Rights Committee, the monitoring body for the ICCPR, takes a more open approach. It its General Comment on Article 27 of the ICCPR, the Committee recognizes that it may not be exclusively indigenous peoples who have special ties to land giving rise to duties on the part of the state to enact positive legal measures of protection.[98]

Discrimination The prohibition on discrimination is one of the most fundamental and well established principles of human rights.[99] It is contained in both of the international human rights Covenants, and in other instruments, among them the international Convention on the

Elimination of All Forms of Racial Discrimination (CERD) of 1965, the Convention on the Elimination of All Forms of Discrimination Against Women of 1979 (CEDAW) and the Convention on the Rights of the Child of 1989 (CRC). All these instruments have been ratified by Israel. Prohibition of discrimination on the grounds of race and national origin is specifically included in the two Covenants and CERD.

The principle of non-discrimination means not just formal equality before the law, but a guarantee of protection from actual discrimination, and adherence to the principle of equal access to public resources. The concepts of equality in enjoyment of rights and non-discrimination contained in all human rights instruments are intended to ensure that *all* persons actually have access to these resources.

CERD defines racial discrimination as: 'any distinction, exclusion, restriction or preference based on race, colour, descent or national or ethnic origin which has the purpose or effect of nullifying or impairing the recognition, enjoyment or exercise, on an equal footing, of human rights and fundamental freedoms in the political, economic, social, cultural or any other field of public life'. This definition has been endorsed by the UN Human Rights Committee, which monitors compliance with the ICCPR, as applying also to the term discrimination as used in the ICCPR (UN Human Rights Committee 1989: 3). The use of the words 'purpose or effect' mean it is not only measures that are intentionally discriminatory that are prohibited; the prohibition also covers measures which may be neutral but in fact negatively affect a particular group.

Article 26 of the ICCPR sets out the duties of states as follows: 'All persons are equal before the law and are entitled without any discrimination to the equal protection of the law. In this respect, the law shall prohibit any discrimination and guarantee to all persons equal and effective protection against discrimination on any ground such as race, colour, sex, language, religion, political or other opinion, national or social origin, property, birth or other status.' The prohibition on discrimination applies to all substantive human rights. The scope of the protection against discrimination in Article 26 of the ICCPR is not limited to the specific rights contained in the Covenant; in the words of the UN Human Rights Committee (1989: 4), it prohibits discrimination in law or in fact in any field regulated and protected by public authorities, and all legislation must comply with its requirements.[100] Its protection would therefore certainly extend to legislation, policies or practices that involve discrimination in access to land. The right to equal access to land can therefore be inferred from this general right to equal treatment and the prohibition on discrimination that is contained in every human rights instrument.

CERD imposes heavy obligations on states to take measures to combat discrimination on the grounds of race, including amending discriminatory legislation, prohibiting discrimination by public authorities or 'by any persons, group or organisation', and amending governmental, national and local policies which have the effect of creating or perpetuating racial discrimination (Article 2). It calls on states to adopt such measures specifically for the purposes of eliminating discrimination in the enjoyment of specific rights, including the right to own property and the right to housing and other economic, social and cultural rights (Article 5). Non-discrimination is a duty that states must not delay in fulfilling; it must be implemented by states immediately and in full (Limburg 1987.: note 27).

Not every distinction in treatment between different groups will constitute discrimination, but the Human Rights Committee has said that in order to be lawful, a differentiation must be based on reasonable and objective criteria, and in order to achieve a purpose which is legitimate under the ICCPR (UN Human Rights Committee 1989: 4). Affirmative action in order to redress the effects of previous discrimination is explicitly endorsed by CERD; states are permitted to take 'special measures' in order to ensure equal enjoyment of rights for certain groups, which will not be considered contrary to the principle of equality, so long as they continue only until the objective is achieved (Article 1.4). The Human Rights Committee has also endorsed specific action under ICCPR to correct a situation where a certain group is not enjoying a certain right (UN Human Rights Committee 1989: 4).

The concept of a right to identity for members of a minority group raises a possible contradiction between the duty imposed on states to ensure equal enjoyment of human rights for every individual within the state, and the duty to take steps to promote the identity of certain groups. This potential problem was addressed by a member of the Sub-Commission on Prevention of Discrimination and Protection of Minorities, Asbjorn Eide, who proposed that societies 'must combine efforts to ensure equality in the common domain with acceptance of diversity in the separate domains' (Eide 1993: 12). In other words, while members of minorities must be treated equally in the larger society, they are additionally entitled to practise and develop their identity as a minority.

Eide's proposal does not entirely resolve the potential problem that special steps to promote the identity of one minority group may be taken to constitute discrimination against another group. The obvious example is South Africa under apartheid, where landownership was restricted by law to one ethnic group, the minority whites. In Israel, the right to a separate identity has been recognized only in the context of the right of the dominant Jewish majority to justify and maintain its dominance. Thus in the Bourkhan case, the Israeli High Court hinted that the desire for national uniqueness is not necessarily discriminatory.[101] The issue was whether it was legitimate to exclude Arabs from the rehabilitated Jewish Quarter of the Old City of Jerusalem, and the High Court held that it was.[102] In other words, in Bourkhan the right to be different was used to increase the dominance of the majority. International law relating to discrimination, on the other hand, calls for protection of the rights of the minority. As the Permanent Court of International Justice said in the case of Minority Schools in Albania in 1935, preferential treatment cannot be used in this way: 'The majority shall not be given a privileged situation as compared with the minority.'[103]

Domestic and international tribunals have attempted to determine whether legislation protecting or recognizing a group interest violates individual rights to equality or the prohibition on discrimination. Equality does not mean there can be no distinctions, but the question is what is acceptable and how to ensure an appropriate balance between the interests of different groups and individuals. There is a body of jurisprudence in the United States, for example, that distinguishes between discriminatory laws on the one hand, and protective measures for minorities on the other. According to this jurisprudence, the right to equality is not necessarily incompatible with measures designed to protect and advance the interests of a specific group. But laws dealing with specific groups must not be arbitrary or unjustified, must have a reasonable objective and legitimate aim, the means employed must be proportional to the aim and, once the object has been achieved, the distinction must be discontinued (Triggs 1992: 148).

There is further scope for confusion between measures to protect the identity of minorities and the provisions (such as in CERD) permitting affirmative action where the purpose is to redress discrimination. There is a difference between permanent preferential treatment for one ethnic group, and special measures designed to prevent or redress inequality, which are permitted to last only as long as required to achieve the objective. This is discussed in Chapter 8.

Housing rights The right to adequate housing is inextricably linked to the question of access to land, and one of its central elements. This is particularly so given the wide interpretation given to the right to housing, as meaning not merely a roof over one's head, but 'the right to live somewhere in security, peace and dignity' (UNCESCR 1991:

para. 7). The right to adequate housing has received considerable attention in the UN, largely due to an active international housing rights movement.[104] The right to adequate housing was first articulated in the UDHR,[105] was included in the CERD,[106] then in the ICESCR, which provides in Article 11.1: 'The States Parties to the present Covenant recognize the right of everyone to an adequate standard of living for himself and his family, including adequate food, clothing and housing, and to the continuous improvement of living conditions. The States Parties will take appropriate steps to ensure the realization of this right, recognizing to this effect the essential importance of international co-operation based on free consent.'[107]

The right to adequate housing has benefited from not only an active NGO movement, but also from the establishment of not one but several international institutions dedicated to its promotion. In addition to the UN Committee on Economic Social and Cultural Rights, which monitors states' compliance with the ICESCR, other UN human rights bodies, the UN Centre for Human Settlements (Habitat) and, since 1993, a UN Special Rapporteur on Housing have worked to articulate and define the right and to ensure its practical application.[108]

For instance, in its General Comment 4 of 1991, the UN Committee on Economic Social and Cultural Rights has identified seven aspects of the right to adequate housing:

- legal security of tenure
- availability of services, materials, facilities and infrastructure
- affordability
- habitability
- accessibility to all groups in society
- location that allows access to employment options and basic services
- cultural adequacy, enabling the expression of cultural identity and diversity of housing (UNCESCR 1991: para. 8)

States' obligations in relation to the right to adequate housing are set out in the ICESCR. According to Article 2.1: 'Each State Party to the present Covenant undertakes to take steps, individually and through international assistance and co-operation, especially economic and technical, to the maximum of its available resources, with a view to achieving progressively the full realization of the rights recognized in the present Covenant by all appropriate means, including particularly the adoption of legislative measures.'

The concrete state obligations imposed by this Article have been elucidated by the Committee on Economic Social and Cultural Rights.[109]

So for example 'undertakes to take steps ... by all appropriate means' is said to impose an immediate obligation; states must review their legislation and also administrative, judicial, economic, social and educational steps, in order to comply fully with the right to adequate housing. States should also develop a national housing strategy. The phrase 'to the maximum of its available resources' is not intended to allow lack of resources to be used as an excuse to do nothing; states are obliged to ensure respect for minimum subsistence rights for all, and should make equitable and effective use of available resources. Finally, 'to achieve progressively' means states must work continuously to achieve realization of the right to housing, and may not defer full realization indefinitely. It is also stressed that some obligations, such as that of non-discrimination in Article 2.2, require immediate implementation.

Israel has faced heavy criticism by several of the UN human rights treaty bodies for its failures to secure the right to adequate housing for all its citizens, and particularly Palestinian citizens, including its use of demolition of homes as a means of punishment (UN Human Rights Committee 1998: para. 24), the deterioration of Arab neighbourhoods in mixed cities and the continuing situation of the unrecognized villages which have no access to water, electricity, sanitation and roads (UNCESCR 1998: paras 23, 26). These examples and others will be discussed more fully in Chapters 7 and 8.

The series of UN-sponsored international conferences on human settlements ('Habitat') that have taken place since 1976 have also sought to detail the content and prerequisites for implementation of the right to housing. The Vancouver Declaration of 1976 included a detailed description of legal questions relating to housing, shelter and accompanying services. While not a binding treaty, the fact that 132 states participated in the conference indicates an international consensus (Leckie 1992: 15). The second Habitat Conference, in Istanbul in June 1996, focused on the themes of equal access and equal opportunity. The Istanbul Declaration contains many references to the need for equal access to land, housing and other resources, and includes the following:

> Equitable human settlements are those in which all people, without discrimination of any kind as to race, colour, sex, language, religion, political or other opinion, national or social origin, property, birth or other status, have equal access to housing infrastructure, health services, adequate food and water, education and open spaces. In addition, such human settlements provide equal opportunity for a productive and freely

chosen livelihood; equal access to economic resources, including the right to inheritance, the ownership of land and other property, credit, natural resources and appropriate technologies; equal opportunity for personal, spiritual, religious, cultural and social development; equal opportunity for participation in public decision-making; equal rights and obligations with regard to the conservation and use of natural and cultural resources; and equal access to mechanisms to ensure that rights are not violated. The empowerment of women and their full participation on the basis of equality in all spheres of society, whether rural or urban, are fundamental to sustainable human settlements development.[110]

After identifying these and other overall goals and principles, the Declaration goes on to specify actions that governments should take in different spheres. As regards access to land, for instance, the Declaration states that governments should take appropriate action in order to 'promote, protect and ensure the full and progressive realization of the right to adequate housing, including ... providing legal security of tenure and equal access to land for all, including women and those living in poverty, as well as effective protection from forced evictions that are contrary to the law, taking human rights into consideration and bearing in mind that homeless people should not be penalized for their status'.[111] As regards land use planning, the Declaration provides that governments should '(e)stablish, as appropriate, legal frameworks to facilitate the development and implementation, at the national, subnational and local levels, of public plans and policies for sustainable urban development and rehabilitation, land utilization, housing and the improved management of urban growth'.[112] Throughout the Declaration are references to the need for a participatory approach, respect for peoples' need for community and their own choices, and special attention to the most vulnerable in society.

Another important development that has taken place under the umbrella of the right to adequate housing has been increased attention to the question of forced evictions, which the UN Commission on Human Rights has stated 'constitutes a gross violation of human rights, in particular the right to adequate housing'.[113] The Economic, Social and Cultural Rights Committee has said that instances of forced eviction are *prima facie* incompatible with the Covenant, and can be justified only in the most exceptional circumstances, and in accordance with the relevant principles of international law (UNCESCR 1991: para. 18). In order to protect against forced evictions, states are urged to confer legal security of tenure on those threatened with forced eviction and to provide protection, based on effective participation, consultation and negotiation with those affected.[114] Israel's policies of forced evictions of Palestinians, still continuing today, will be covered extensively in Chapters 3, 4 and 8.

The status of human rights in Israeli law Israel, in ratifying most of the major international treaties on human rights, has taken upon itself a range of obligations under international human rights law. Israel is party to the International Covenant on Civil and Political Rights (ICCPR) of 1966, the International Covenant on Economic Social and Cultural Rights (ICESCR) of 1966, the Convention on the Elimination of All Forms of Racial Discrimination (CERD) of 1965, the Convention on the Elimination of All Forms of Discrimination Against Women of 1979 (CEDAW) and the Convention on the Rights of the Child (CRC) of 1989. The fact that Israel has become party to these treaties does not mean that they automatically have force of law in Israel, however. International treaties can only be incorporated into the body of Israeli law if a specific law to this effect is passed by the Knesset.[115]

A common feature of the human rights treaties mentioned is that they require states parties to take positive measures, including amending their law or taking administrative or judicial steps, to give effect to their provisions. Article 2.1(c) of CERD, for example, requires states parties to 'take effective measures to review governmental, national and local policies, and to amend, rescind or nullify any laws and regulations which have the effect of creating or perpetuating racial discrimination wherever it exists', while Article 2.2 of the ICCPR requires a state party to 'take the necessary steps, in accordance with its constitutional processes and with the provisions of the present Covenant, to adopt such legislative or other measures as may be necessary to give effect to the rights recognized in the present Covenant'. When reporting to the Human Rights Committee on its compliance with the ICCPR, Israel explained:

> International agreements are not, as such, part of Israeli internal law, and the Knesset generally does not legislate by way of direct reference to such agreements. Accordingly, the provisions of the Covenant have not been made a part of internal Israeli law by an enactment of the Knesset. However, the basic rights protected by the Covenant are to a very great extent already guaranteed by internal Israeli legislation or case law, and effective mechanisms exist for the assertion and enforcement of such rights, both in the courts and through other arms of government, as described under the other articles in this report. For this reason, among others, it has not been deemed necessary to enact

implementing legislation to give effect to the provisions of the Covenant. Thus, as a matter of domestic law, the Covenant does not, by itself, create private rights directly enforceable in Israeli courts. (State of Israel 1998: para. 42)

Israel argues, then, that its laws already protect human rights without the need for specific legislation, and that in any event human rights are safeguarded in Israel by the case law of the Supreme Court which, sitting as the High Court of Justice, hears petitions in constitutional and administrative law issues against any government body or agent. In its report, Israel cites examples of how recognition of basic rights, such as the right to equality, has come about through case law.

It is true that the lack of specific incorporating legislation does not mean that international human rights treaties have no status whatsoever in Israel: Chief Justice Barak has stated that local law must be interpreted wherever possible in accordance with the state's international obligations, and that only express, clear and unequivocal language in a local law which contradicts an international obligation will override an international obligation (Barak 1993: 20). As to the Universal Declaration on Human Rights, Israeli courts have specifically accepted it as reflecting customary law, and, according to Israeli domestic law, norms of customary international law will be applicable as long as they do not clash with positive laws of the Knesset (Lerner 1987: 7).

Nevertheless, the UN human rights treaty-monitoring bodies have consistently criticized Israel for failing to take appropriate measures, including enacting legislation, to meet the requirements of the human rights treaties and to make their provisions applicable in domestic law.[116] The mechanisms for enforcing these human rights standards to which Israel has committed itself on the international plane are sadly lacking. As already mentioned, two basic laws were enacted in 1992 in order to give constitutional force to certain fundamental human rights and freedoms. The Basic Law: Human Dignity and Liberty protects the rights to life, dignity, property, liberty, movement and privacy,[117] while the Basic Law: Freedom of Occupation aims to protect 'the right to engage in any occupation, profession or trade'.[118] However, these two laws do not cover the full range of human rights to which Israel has committed itself through ratifying international treaties, or which bind Israel under general international law. Particularly significant omissions are the right to equality, and economic social and cultural rights, such as the right to adequate housing.

In addition to the shortcomings of the constitutionally entrenched basic laws, there are inadequate mechanisms for enforcing human rights at the domestic level, whether through legislation or other means. The lack is particularly acute when it comes to safeguarding equality for Palestinian citizens of the state. They, of course, are most in need of protection because the political agenda in Israel, as already outlined, is to advance and prioritize the interests of Jewish citizens of the state. Israel has no general anti-discrimination legislation, no commission on equality, and no mechanism for ensuring that policy and practice are brought into line with international standards. However, concrete measures have been taken in particular sectors. The development of proactive measures to protect equality for women shows what can be done to safeguard equality in Israel, where the political will exists. As early as 1951, an Equal Rights for Women Law was enacted. Then in 1998 an Authority for the Advancement of the Status of Women was established, charged with suggesting policies to the government 'designed to advance women, promote gender equality, eliminate discrimination against women and prevent domestic violence targeted against women. In addition, the Authority supervises, *inter alia*, the gender policies of the different governmental bodies, monitors the implementation in Israel of the UN Convention on the Elimination of All Forms of Discrimination Against Women, promotes public awareness on the need to advance women and initiates legislative proposals and research' (State of Israel 2001: 22). These are precisely the sorts of measures that, if replicated with the aim of promoting equality of Palestinian citizens of the state, might go a long way to satisfy the requirement to give effect to the rights in the human rights treaties to which Israel is party, particularly the principle of non-discrimination contained in the two Covenants of 1966.

The language of rights does not, on the whole, permeate Israeli ordinary legislation either. For instance, there is no 'right to land' or housing in Israel despite the fact that so much land is state owned. Contrast the right given in section 3 of the Water Law 1959: 'Every person is entitled to receive and use water, subject to the provisions of this Law.' Although this right is qualified, and as a substantive right (as opposed to a procedural right) is difficult to enforce, it is given weight by the Israeli courts.[119] A comparable right to resources such as land and housing, if established, might help safeguard equal access in Israel. An international report on housing rights cites thirty examples of state constitutions that directly enshrine the right to housing in some form or another (Leckie 1992: 80–4).

In sum, while certain human rights have constitutionally entrenched status in Israel, or have achieved recognition by the High Court, Israel has failed to incorporate the full range of its international human rights obligations into domestic law, and has also fallen short of its international obligation to develop appropriate mechanisms to guarantee implementation of those rights. This situation creates particular difficulties for the safeguarding of rights of the Palestinian citizens of the state.

Notes

1. Declaration of the Establishment of the State of Israel, *Official Gazette*, no. 1, 14 May 1948.

2. Basic Law: Human Dignity and Liberty, passed by the Knesset on 17 March 1992, unofficial translation prepared by the Ministry of Justice, italics added by the authors.

3. Law of Return 1950; Citizenship Law 1952.

4. Basic Law: The Knesset, 1985.

5. The JA was given responsibility for immigrant absorption and rural settlement, and the JNF for land acquisition and development. See the World Zionist Organization–Jewish Agency (Status) Law 1952, the Memorandum and Articles of Association of the JNF of 1954, the Covenant between the State of Israel and the JNF of 1954, and the Covenant with the JA of 1958.

6. For instance, Israel has been a party to the UN Convention on the Elimination of All Forms of Racial Discrimination since 1979, and to the International Covenant on Civil and Political Rights and the International Covenant on Economic, Social and Cultural Rights since 1991, all of which prohibit discrimination.

7. Oren Yiftachel notes that majority–minority relations in a democracy differ from other regime types in that, in a democracy, elites are more disposed to make appreciable concessions to minority protest whereas authoritarian regimes are more likely to rely on repression, and minorities can expect to gain more from action under a democratic government (Yiftachel 1992: 18).

8. Academics have asserted various models for political systems in states divided along ethnic lines and the status of ethnic minorities within them, and applied them to the context of Israel. In 1980, Ian Lustick introduced the model of 'control', where one ethnic group takes over and controls the minority through isolating it, making it economically dependent and coopting the leaders (Lustick 1980). Sammy Smooha puts forward the model of 'ethnic democracy', which combines institutionalized dominance by one ethnic group with the granting of political and civil rights to minorities (Smooha 1999). Ilan Saban follows this model in his analysis of the influence of the Israeli High Court on the status of Arabs in Israel (Saban 1996: 541). Others disagree that Israel can properly be described as a democracy. Oren Yiftachel simply uses the term 'ethnocracy', see for example Yiftachel (1999a). Another model which is considered by these analysts but rejected as disconnected from current reality is the model of 'consociational democracy', in which minority ethnic groups are recognized and given separate communities, schools and media and language rights, and compromises are reached that are reflected in power-sharing, such as in Belgium or Canada.

9. David Kretzmer describes numerous examples in policy-making and administrative discretion that lead to what he terms institutionalized discrimination (Kretzmer 1990: 85). Kretzmer also analyses the different ways in which discrimination takes place: criteria are adopted in statutes or delegated legislation that intentionally lead to discrimination. For instance, welfare benefits and other grants and entitlements are often made dependent on the completion of military service, which automatically excludes most Arab citizens from benefiting since they do not serve in the army. Administrative discretion is exercised in a discriminatory manner in the allocation of budgets and other resources such as land and water. There is individual discrimination by public officials and private persons.

10. The original Memorandum and Articles of Association of the JNF of 1907 when it was registered in England provided that land owned by the JNF would be let to Jews only and would not be sold.

11. H. Law-Yone, 'Stuck in the Past', *Jerusalem Post*, 17 March 1994.

12. 'One hundred years of the JNF', interview with Shlomo Gravitz, head of the JNF Council, *Globes* (financial newspaper), 5 October 2001, p. 29 (in Hebrew).

13. Basic Laws form part of the evolving constitution of Israel, and eleven such laws have been adopted since 1948. The two laws enacted in 1992 represent the first attempt to entrench fundamental rights; previous Basic Laws had dealt with institutional aspects.

14. Examples of rights declared by the High Court to constitute fundamental rights in Israel include freedom of speech and equality (Gross 1998: 83–4).

15. Justices Shamgar and Barak in United Mizrahi Bank Ltd and Others v. Migdal Cooperative Village and Others, Civil Appeal 6821/93, PD 49(4), p. 221, judgment summarized in the Israeli *Yearbook on Human Rights*, Vol. 28 (1998), p. 217.

16. According to section 10, the validity of any law in force prior to the commencement of the Basic Law will not be affected.

17. See note 15, above. The Court was called upon to consider whether the Family Agricultural Sector Law 1992, aimed at assisting moshavs to pay off their debts, contravened section 3 of the Basic Law: Human Dignity and Liberty.

18. Gross's general thesis is that the primary effect of the Basic Law: Human Dignity and Liberty will not be progressive, but that it will be used to preserve existing distribution of wealth and entitlements.

19. Note 15 above, p. 221.

20. Judgment of 13 February 2001, Kersek and Others v. State of Israel, the ILA and Others, HC 2390/96, PD 55(2), p. 625. See further discussion of this case and its implications in Chapter 3.

21. The High Court asked the parties to submit further pleadings on this question and to suggest solutions as regards the implementation of the ruling. When further pleadings were not submitted, the Court postponed its consideration of the matter for a year.

22. Local Committee for Planning and Building of Kiryat Atta v. Hanah

Haltsman and Others, Civil Appeals 6417/97 and 5546/97, judgment of 12 June 2001, Takdin, HC 2001.

23. See for example the Indian Supreme Court case of Francis Mullin v. Delhi, All India Reporter 1981, SC 746, in which the Court found the constitutional right to life as meaning the right to live with human dignity, which encompassed 'the bare necessities of life, such as adequate nutrition, clothing and shelter over the head and facilities for reading, writing and expressing oneself in diverse forms'.

24. While it is difficult to find definitions of the term 'human dignity' in international instruments or national law, it appears frequently in international instruments, including the Preamble of the Charter of the United Nations, the Universal Declaration of Human Rights and the Helsinki Accords. Oscar Schachter suggests that it means respect for the intrinsic worth of every person, leading to the principle that individuals are not to be perceived or treated merely as instruments of the will of others. From this it follows that high priority should be accorded to individual choices in matters such as way of life. See Schachter (1983: 848) on human dignity.

25. See for example GILAT v. Minister of Education, HC 1554/95, 50(3) PD 2 (in Hebrew), cited in Hirschl (2000: 1087), in which the Court refused to find that the right to human dignity included the right to education.

26. Article 1a, added by the amendment of 9 March 1994.

27. According to Smooha, this is typical of ethnic democracies, in which minority groups are accorded certain individual and collective rights, but in an incomplete way falling short of full equality. Such systems are contrasted with consociational democracies, where accommodations are made with minority groups to ensure sharing of power, resources and state symbols (Smooha 1999).

28. Adalah v. Minister of Religious Affairs and Others, HC 1113/99, judgment of April 2000, reported in Adalah (2000: 75–6).

29. Adalah and Others v. Minister of Religious Affairs and Others, HC 240/98; Adalah (1999: 32–5). The Court had agreed that the 1998 budget of the Minister of Religious Affairs constituted *prima facie* discrimination, but declined to invalidate the relevant budget provision on the basis that the petition was too general to justify the provision of a specific and concrete remedy.

30. Encouragement of Investments Law, 1959; see Kretzmer (1990: 107).

31. This results from decisions of the Israel Lands Council and government decisions regarding national priority areas, see Chapter 6.

32. Housing Loans Law 1992; see Chapter 7.

33. Gross (1998: 86), cites Pnina Lahav: 'when a citizen comes before the Court to assert a right and the state objects for reasons related to national security or the welfare of the Jewish State qua Jewish State, the Court has tended to prefer the values embedded in the nation-state at the expense of those rooted in universal values' (Lahav 1993: 126).

34. 'Adil Qa'dan v. ILA and Others, HC 6698/95, judgment of 8 March 2000, PD 54(1), p. 258.

35. For commentary and analysis of the Qa'dan decision, see for example

Jamil Dakwar, 'Qa'dan, to what extent an achievement?', *Ha'aretz* (daily Hebrew newspaper), 15 March 2000; Eliakim Rubenstein, 'Not the End of the Fulfilment of Zionism', speech of the Attorney General before the Forum for Land Use Research, 2000; and several articles in *Adalah's Review* (Adalah 2000).

36. These cases will be examined in detail in Chapters 3 and 4.

37. The Nazareth Committee for the Defence of Expropriated Lands v. Ministry of Finance and Others, HC 30/55, PD 9(3), p. 1261. This case is discussed more fully in Chapter 3.

38. Mustafa Sabah Egbariah and Others v. Minister of Education, HC 3954/91, PD 45(5), p. 472 and Mustafa Sabah Egbariah and Others v. Minister of Education, HC 3491/90, PD 45(1), p. 224.

39. See section on Discrimination, later in this chapter.

40. See Kretzmer (1990: 79) and Shetreet (1988: 265).

41. For instance, the case of Dr Nbo v. Local Labour Court, HC 104/87, PD 44(4), p. 749.

42. Adalah and Others v. Minister of Religious Affairs and Others, HC 240/98, judgment of 3 December 1998; Adalah (1999: 32).

43. Adalah v. Minister of Religious Affairs and Others, HC 1113/99, judgment of April 2000; Adalah (2000: 75).

44. International law permits distinctions to be made in the treatment of different groups so long as there is no differentiation between equals and the differentiation is based on reasonable and objective criteria and in order to achieve a legitimate purpose. See for example General Comment 18 of the United Nations Human Rights Committee, discussed below under the subheading 'Discrimination', p. 47.

45. Wattad v. Minister of Finance, 1983, 38 PD(3), and see Kretzmer (1990: 106–7).

46. Bourkhan v. Minister of Finance, HC 114/78, PD 32(2), p. 800, and see Kretzmer (1990: 80–1).

47. Section 8 provides: 'There shall be no violation of rights under this Basic Law except by a Law befitting the values of the State of Israel, enacted for a proper purpose, and *to an extent no greater than is required*' (emphasis added).

48. The state's actual policies in relation to these issues are examined in Chapters 3 and 4.

49. The judgment includes the following: 'This petition looks ahead. The petitioners are not aiming to criticize the long-term policies of settlement bodies in establishing settlements including kibbutzim, moshavim and mitzpim for settling Jews only. Nor do the petitioners focus their claims on the legitimacy of the policies carried out in the period before the state's existence and the years since its establishment' (unofficial translation).

50. These are villages that have not been included in the state planning process and are officially illegal. See Chapter 8 for more detailed discussion of this status and its consequences.

51. Decision of the Jury of the International Water Tribunal, Amsterdam, 19 February 1992.

52. The Public Committee against Torture in Israel v. Government of Israel and Others, HC case 5100/94, and five other cases filed during 1995–97.

53. The Universal Declaration on Human Rights was proclaimed by the UN General Assembly Resolution 217A(III) of 10 December 1948, while the Covenants were adopted by Resolution 2200A(XXI) of 16 December 1966.

54. In the context of the right to peaceful enjoyment of property guaranteed in Protocol 1 to the European Convention on Human Rights, the right to compensation for non-aliens is not expressly included but the European Court of Human Rights has said that some compensation will be required in all but exceptional cases; Harris et al. (1995: 532).

55. Sporrong and Lonnroth v. Sweden, European Court of Human Rights, 1982, 5EHRR 35, pp. 52–4.

56. There is an increasing amount of writing on the basis of the Palestinian right to return in international law; see in particular Takkenberg (1998), Amnesty International (2001) and Quigley (1998: 171).

57. The International Court of Justice in its Advisory Opinion in the Nottebohm case (ICJ Reports, 1955, 1, judgment of 6 April 1955) said that, as a matter of international law, nationality would be judged not on the state's designation alone, but on objective principles including a genuine connection between an individual and a country.

58. The words 'enter his own country' in the ICCPR instead of 'return to one's country' indicate that the right might entitle a person to come to the country for the first time if he or she was born outside the country.

59. Articles 6, 36, 134 and 158 of the Fourth Geneva Convention 1949 all mention repatriation. For an analysis of the right of return in humanitarian law for individuals and in situations of mass expulsion, see BADIL Resource Center (2001), and Quigley (1997: 70–1).

60. For example the Dayton Peace Accord of 1995 provides explicitly for those expelled to be able to return to their homes of origin.

61. See for example UNCERD (1998: para. 18): 'The right of many Palestinians to return and possess their homes in Israel is currently denied. The State party should give high priority to remedying this situation.'

62. Amnesty International proposes that, where possible, Palestinians should be able to return to their original home or lands. If this is not possible, because they no longer exist or have been converted to other uses, or because of a competing claim, they should be allowed to return to the vicinity of their original home. Dr Salman Abu Sitta set out to demonstrate that the return of Palestinian refugees to their original lands is in most cases feasible, since the original sites of Palestinian communities can be located, 85 per cent of Israel is sparsely populated, and those Jews who do live on Palestinian land do not hold title to it (Abu Sitta 1999).

63. Article 1(1) of Annex 7, Dayton Peace Agreement of 14 December 1995, endorsed by UN Security Council Resolution 1031 of 15 December 1995.

64. Cyprus v. Turkey, application no. 25781/94, judgment of 10 May 2001.

65. Paras 175 and 187 of the Court's judgment.

66. Para. 174 of the Court's judgment.

67. Paras 186–7, relying on Loizidou v. Turkey, application no. 00015318/89, judgment of 18 December 1996, in which the Court had found a violation of Article 1 of Protocol 1 and ordered Turkey to pay compensation to the applicant, an individual Greek Cypriot landowner.

68. Application no. 28342/95, judgment (just satisfaction) of 23 January 2001.

69. UN Document E/CN.4/1998/53/Add.2 of 11 February 1998. Among others, the UN General Assembly, Commission on Human Rights and the Economic and Social Council have encouraged the application and wide dissemination of the principles.

70. The right of IDPs to return is based on the right to freedom of movement and the right to choose one's residence contained in Article 12 of the ICCPR, and the duty to transfer civilians evacuated during an occupation back to their homes as soon as hostilities have ceased under Article 49 of the IV Geneva Convention; Kalin (2000: 69–71).

71. UNGA Resolution 194(V) of 14 December 1950.

72. Sami Hadawi, who worked as an official land valuer during the British Mandate and later with the Palestinian Conciliation Commission, heavily criticized the way in which this assessment was carried out; Hadawi (1988: 94–7).

73. See for instance Ian Brownlie and James Crawford in Crawford (1992: 1–16 and 166). The right to self-determination is one of the foundation stones of the international human rights regime (it is found in Article 1 of both of the Covenants of 1966) and an important legitimization of collective identity and a collective right to determine their own destiny for groups such as the Palestinians. The precise implications of the right to self-determination in the context of the Palestinian citizens of Israel has not been a subject of detailed examination and certainly merits such attention.

74. Mrs Erica-Irene Daes discusses states' interpretation of the Resolution on Permanent Sovereignty over natural resources in her *Special Rapporteur's Report on Indigenous People and Their Relation to Land* (Daes 1999: para. 64). James Crawford presents the view that the principle can also serve as a limitation on states' powers; Crawford (1992: 64).

75. Convention no. 107 Concerning the Protection and Integration of Indigenous and Other Tribal and Semi-Tribal Populations in Independent Countries of 1957, and Convention no. 169 on Indigenous and Tribal People of 1989.

76. The Draft Declaration was elaborated by a Working Group under the UN Sub-Commission on Prevention of Discrimination and Protection of Minorities which completed its work in 1993. The Draft was adopted by the Sub-Commission in 1994, UN Doc E/CN.4/Sub.2/1994/56, and submitted to the UN Commission on Human Rights in 1995. The Commission has set up an open-ended intersessional Working Group on the Draft Declaration.

77. Decision 1997/114.

78. UN Doc E/CN.4/Sub.2/1999/18 of 3 June 1999.

79. ILO Convention 169, Article 14; Draft Declaration, para. 23.

80. ILO Convention 169, Article 14.

81. ILO Convention 169, Article 16, Draft Declaration, para. 9.

82. ILO Convention 169, Article 16, Draft Declaration, para. 25.

83. Draft Declaration, para. 19.

84. Bolivia, Brazil, Colombia and Paraguay have adopted new constitutions or legislation providing special protection for indigenous lands and requiring the demarcation of lands traditionally occupied by them. In Eastern Europe, following the fall of communism, countries such as Latvia, Bulgaria, the Czech Republic, Hungary and Romania have introduced policies based on the principle of restitution for landowners whose lands were expropriated without compensation by forced collectivization. In Australia and Canada courts have recognized native land title of indigenous groups, sometimes based on historical title and treaty rights, other times based on the concept of immemorial possession. For an analysis of developments in all regions up to 1994 see Plant (1994: 13–32).

85. *Independent on Sunday* (UK newspaper), 2 July 1995, p. 1.

86. ICJ Reports, 1975, p. 39; and McNeil (1989: 40–1). Courts in Canada, New Zealand and Australia have accepted that conquest did not extinguish pre-existing native land rights.

87. Mabo and Others v. State of Queensland, Commonwealth Law Reports, Vol. 175, 1992, p. 1, High Court of Australia.

88. Ibid., per Brennan, J., p. 58. In fact, some of the Canadian cases even seem to imply that in order to establish pre-existing rights it is necessary to establish that there was an existing system of laws regulating land. See McNeil (1997: 136–7), citing the 1994 Canadian Supreme Court judgment in R. v. Guerin, [1985] 1 Canadian National Law Reports (CNLR), 120. In other cases the courts are happy to rely simply on historic occupation and possession. See for example the 1973 Canadian Supreme Court judgment of Calder v. Attorney-General of British Columbia, 7 CNLC, 91.

89. Delgamuukw v. British Columbia [1998], 1 CNLR 14, in which the indigenous peoples of north-western British Columbia sought a declaration affirming their ownership and rights over lands in the area.

90. Article 27 of the International Covenant on Civil and Political Rights, below.

91. General Assembly Resolution 47/135 of 18 December 1992.

92. Report of the CSCE Meeting of Experts on National Minorities, Geneva, 1991, mentioned in Thornberry (1993: 22).

93. Hashim Sawa'id and Others v. Local Planning and Building Commission of Misgav and Others, HC 7960/99, and Ismai'il Sawa'id and Another v. Local Planning and Building Commission of Misgav and Others, HC 6032/99, judgments handed down on 5 September 2001.

94. Miriam Aukerman asks whether differences between indigenous peoples and minorities justify the differences in the rights attributed to them. She argues that rights standards should avoid treating similarly situated people differently, while recognizing where there are real differences that justify why particular groups need special protection, and should avoid being fixated on labelling as

an indigenous or minority group as the sole basis for differentiation (Aukerman 2000: 1011).

95. Representatives of Palestinian NGOs have attended sessions of the UN Working Group on Indigenous Peoples that meets every year in Geneva, and some Palestinian human rights organizations argue that indigenous peoples' rights do apply to the Palestinians.

96. See Chapter 8 for a description of the struggle of the Palestinian un-recognized villages in Israel, and Chapter 1 regarding the significance of land to the Palestinians.

97. Aukerman (2000) refers *inter alia* to the work of Eide on the protection of minorities, regarding the principle that one should treat similar people equally, while differential treatment can be justified only on the basis of differences in situation and problems; UN Doc. E/CN.4/Sub.2/1993, 34 of 1993.

98. General Comment 23, 50th session, 1994, para. 7 reads: 'With regard to the exercise of the cultural rights protected under article 27, the Committee observes that culture manifests itself in many forms, including a particular way of life associated with the use of land resources, *especially* in the case of indigenous peoples. That right may include such traditional activities as fishing or hunting and the right to live in reserves protected by law. The enjoyment of those rights may require positive legal measures of protection and measures to ensure the effective participation of *members of minority communities* in decisions which affect them' (emphasis added).

99. The principle that human rights and fundamental freedoms must be respected without distinction as to race, sex, language or religion is included no fewer than four times in the Charter of the United Nations of 1945. There is considerable support for the view that the principle of non-discrimination, particularly on the grounds of race, forms part of Customary International Law; Brownlie (1998: 602).

100. See also Broeks v. Netherlands, Views of the Human Rights Committee, 9 April 1987, communication no. 172: 1984.

101. Bourkhan v. Minister of Finance, HC 114/78, PD 32(2), 800.

102. Klein (1987: 18) does not believe that this case gives a clear answer on the ethnic question, since the court based its decision mainly on procedural grounds. However, one of the judges, Shamgar, did stress the right of the Israeli authorities to restore the Jewish Quarter.

103. PCIJ 34th Session, 6 April 1935, Advisory Opinion.

104. Particularly influential has been the Habitat International Coalition which since the late 1980s has run a global campaign on housing rights, complemented by dynamic national and regional campaigns. In his report to the Commission on Human Rights in 2001, the UN Special Rapporteur on Housing paid tribute to the role of civil society in giving definition and practical meaning to the right to housing; UN doc. E/CN.4/2001/51 of 25 January 2001, para. 53.

105. Article 25.1 proclaims: 'Everyone has the right to a standard of living adequate for the health and well-being of himself and of his family, including ... housing.'

106. Article 5(e) includes the obligation of States Parties to 'prohibit and

eliminate racial discrimination in all its forms and to guarantee the right of everyone, without distinction as to race, colour, or national or ethnic origin, to equality before the law, notably in the enjoyment of economic, social and cultural rights in particular ... the right to housing'.

107. Housing rights are also included, *inter alia*, in CEDAW, the CRC and the UN Draft Declaration on the Rights of Indigenous Peoples.

108. Additionally, the UN Sub-Commission on the Promotion and Protection of Minorities, the Committee on the Rights of the Child, the Committee on the Elimination of Discrimination Against Women and the Committee on the Elimination of Racial Discrimination have all focused on aspects of the right to housing.

109. See for example Leckie (1992: 28–30), and also the 'Limburg Principles', a set of interpretive principles developed by human rights scholars and representatives of UN bodies.

110. The Habitat Agenda, Istanbul Declaration on Human Settlements, 1996, Ch. II, Goals and Principles, para. 27.

111. Ibid., Ch. IV, Global Plan of Action, B., Adequate Shelter for All, para. 61.

112. Ch. IV C, Sustainable Human Settlements Development in an Urbanizing world, para. 113.

113. Resolution 1993/77 adopted on 10 March 1993 during the 49th Session of the UN Commission on Human Rights.

114. UN Commission on Human Rights, Resolution 1993/77, para. 3.

115. This has been done, for instance, in the case of the UN Genocide Convention, of 1948, which was incorporated by the Crime of Genocide (Prevention and Punishment) Law 1950, but not in relation to treaties mentioned in this para.

116. For instance the Human Rights Committee, after considering Israel's initial report on its compliance with the ICCPR in August 1998, found: 'The Committee notes with regret that, although some rights provided for in the Covenant are legally protected and promoted through the Basic Laws, municipal laws, and the jurisprudence of the courts, the Covenant has not been incorporated in Israeli law and cannot be directly invoked in the courts' (para. 9). The Committee on Economic Social and Cultural Rights, after considering Israel's initial report on compliance with the ICESCR in December 1998, said: 'The Committee calls upon the State Party to undertake the necessary steps to ensure the full legal application of the Covenant within the domestic legal order' (para. 33).

117. Articles 2–7, Basic Law: Human Dignity and Liberty, passed by the Knesset on 17 March 1992, amended on 9 March 1994.

118. Article 3, Basic Law: Freedom of Occupation, passed by the Knesset on 9 March 1994, replacing the former law enacted in 1992.

119. See Water Commissioner v. Simcha Perlmutter and Others, High Court appeal case 535/89, *Jerusalem Post*, 15 February 1993.

CHAPTER 3

Dispossession by Expropriation

§ DURING the twentieth century, Palestinians from the area that is now Israel were dispossessed of the vast majority of land they had previously owned and possessed individually and collectively. During the 1948 war the land of up to 840,000 Palestinians was seized.[1] But the process began in the period before the establishment of Israel in 1948, continued afterwards and is still ongoing, with the result that there is hardly a Palestinian family that has not been profoundly affected. The victims are not only the Palestinians driven out of the area in 1948, who are now refugees, but also those who remained and became citizens of Israel. Some one-quarter of this group were displaced from their land and became internal refugees. But even those who remained in their original homes have lost much land. For the refugees and citizens alike, the return of their expropriated land and bringing a halt to further expropriations are major priorities that rank above all other considerations.

This process of dispossession has taken place in clear violation of UN resolutions based on international law, and of international human rights and other international law standards that protect property rights. More recently, Israeli law itself has entrenched the right to property in a Basic Law enacted in 1992. These and other protections that should operate to protect Palestinian land rights are set out in the previous chapter.

This chapter traces Israel's expropriation of Palestinian land under various legislation enacted with the objective of seizing and taking over permanently the land of the Palestinian refugees and internally displaced, and its use of other legislation even after this objective was achieved, in a process that is still ongoing, to take the land of the Palestinians who remained in the state and make it available for Jewish settlement. A second method by which Israel sought to dispossess Palestinian citizens of the state of their remaining land was through the system of settlement of title, by which rights in land are determined and registered, and this is the subject of the next chapter. We start with a brief overview of Zionist land purchases before the establishment of the state, because it was during this period of Jewish colonization of Palestine that the main pillars of the Israeli land regime were set in place, namely the concept that land would be held in trust for the Jewish people and would not be transferred to individuals. The nature of this regime will be examined more closely in Chapter 5.

Zionist land acquisitions before the establishment of Israel in 1948[2]

Gaining control of the land was a central component of Zionist thinking from the time organized political Jewish migration from Europe began in 1882 (Lehn and Davis 1988: 5–6). Prior to 1882, the Jewish community in Palestine had been small but of long standing, consisting of some 24,000 people concentrated in the four cities of religious significance: Jerusalem, Safad, Tiberias and Hebron. The official Zionist programme was to create a national home for the Jewish people in Palestine, then a province of the Ottoman Empire. Jewish colonization of the area was a key component of the strategy. In 1901 a Jewish National Fund (JNF) was established, devoted exclusively to the acquisition of land in Palestine for Jewish settlement.[3] According to Lehn and Davis in their major work on the Jewish National Fund, the JNF made its first purchase from an Arab landowner in 1910 and by the 1930s had become the principal Jewish land purchasing agency, aggressively acquiring land by any means possible.[4] The JNF also persuaded other agencies that had sprung up to adopt its practice of retaining the legal title to land it acquired in the name of the institution and granting leases to Jewish settlers (Lehn and Davis 1988: 24, 86–7).

Following the First World War, Britain was given a Mandate over Palestine that lasted until the establishment of Israel in 1948.[5] Crucially, the British government had undertaken to use its best endeavours to facilitate 'the establishment in Palestine of a national home for the Jewish people',[6] although terms of the Mandate granted by the League of Nations imposed a dual obligation towards Arabs and Jews in the area. Article 6 of the Mandate included a specific undertaking as regards land: 'The Administration of Palestine, while ensuring that the rights and position of other sections of the population are not prejudiced, shall encourage, in co-operation with the Jewish Agency ... close settlement by Jews on the land, including state lands and waste lands not required for public purposes.'

The British administration did indeed promote the settlement of Jews on land in Palestine, for instance permitting the Zionists to acquire 'concessions' over state land in certain areas.[7] Although the several commissions of inquiry ordered by the British government prompted by Palestinian unrest invariably cited land loss as one of the most important causes of the unrest, it was not until the Arab Revolt of 1936–39 that the Administration placed restrictions on Jewish immigration and land acquisitions. However, the restrictions were too little too late to effectively brake Jewish land purchases, which continued. At the same time the Zionist groups adopted a more strategic approach; they began to try to create distinct Jewish settlement blocks and to purchase land in areas of military importance, frontier regions and areas contemplated for a Jewish state.[8] Thousands of Arab farmers were rendered landless and up to seventy entire Palestinian villages disappeared (Kanaana 1992: 96).[9] The Zionist land purchasing agencies insisted on the removal of tenants prior to transfer of property, and British regulations aimed at protecting tenant farmers from eviction were frequently circumvented (Anglo-American Committee of Inquiry 1946: 289–96).

In the sixty-five years between 1882 and 1947, the Jewish land settlement movement succeeded in acquiring ownership of between 5.6 and 6.6 per cent of the area of Palestine.[10] The movement's land holdings tended to be concentrated in areas where the best farmland lay: by 1947, it held some 15 per cent of the cultivable land.[11] Much was purchased from non-Palestinian absentee landlords who owned large tracts of land farmed by Palestinians as tenants. After acquiring the land, the Zionist Movement proceeded to colonize it, and Jews around the world were asked to contribute funds that would be divided between land purchases, settlement activities, national institutions and economic undertakings (Lehn 1974: 84).

Almost from the very beginning of the Zionist colonization project, purchase of land by the JNF or one of the other Jewish land purchasing agencies involved a fundamental change in the status of that land. Once land had been purchased, non-Jews were excluded from it and prevented from deriving any benefit from it. Land acquired by the JNF was automatically considered to be 'redeemed', and the property of the Jewish people as a whole. The JNF constitution prohibited its sale, and it was to be leased only to Jews. Herzl, one of the early Zionist leaders, wrote in his diary for 12 June 1895: 'we are not going to sell them anything back ... we shall sell only to Jews, and all real estate will be traded only among Jews' (cited in Lehn and Davis 1988: 13). British official Hope Simpson noted in 1930:

> Actually the result of the purchase of land in Palestine by the Jewish National Fund has been that land has been extra-territorialised. It ceases

to be land from which the Arab can gain any advantage either now or at any time in the future. Not only can he never hope to lease or to cultivate it, but, by the stringent provisions of the lease of the Jewish National Fund, he is deprived for ever from employment on that land. Nor can anyone help him by purchasing the land and restoring it to common use. The land is in mort-main and inalienable. It is for this reason that Arabs discount the professions of friendship and good will on the part of the Zionists in view of the policy which the Zionist Organisation deliberately adopted. (Hope Simpson 1930: 54)

This period therefore saw the beginning of the dual land regime which was later to characterize the Israeli land system: on the one hand, there was land that was still available to both Jews and Palestinians, and on the other, land that was for the exclusive ownership and use of Jews.

The war of 1948 and the Absentees' Property Law

In the course of the Arab–Israeli War of 1948–49 and subsequent Israeli military operations, Israel seized and subsequently expropriated enormous areas of land possessed or owned by Palestinians. The war of 1948 is known by Palestinians simply as '*Al Naqba*', the catastrophe. As many as 800,000 of the 1 million Arab inhabitants of Palestine were displaced and forced to flee outside the borders of the new state. The government of the newly declared State of Israel prevented the refugees from returning, declared them to be 'absentees' and expropriated all of their property. While some 150,000 Palestinians managed to remain within the area or infiltrate back and become citizens of Israel,[12] as many as a quarter of this group were displaced from their land and were also dispossessed.

The expropriation of the land left behind by the Palestinian refugees and internally displaced was a two-stage process. The first stage involved the establishment of de facto control over land. At this stage, the legal ownership of the land was unaffected. But Israel rapidly took steps to take control,[13] and ensure that its conquests would be irreversible, preventing the return of refugees, destroying abandoned villages and resettling Jews on the land (Peretz 1958: 143), and providing legal backing for its requisitions by enacting the Absentees' Property Law 1950. The second stage came in the 1950s and involved the purported transfer of legal title to the state or the Jewish National Fund, a step aimed at ensuring that the land would remain permanently in Jewish hands and out of reach of its Palestinians owners – and, indeed, the reach of all Palestinians.

Such actions to seize and expropriate Palestinian land and prevent the return of its owners flouted numerous resolutions of the UN General Assembly, among them Resolutions 181 and 194. Resolution 181 specified that there should be no expropriation of land owned by an Arab in the Jewish state, except for public purposes.[14] Resolution 194 instructed the UN Conciliation Commission to facilitate the repatriation, resettlement and economic and social rehabilitation of the Palestinian refugees, and determined that 'the refugees wishing to return to their homes and live at peace with their neighbours should be permitted to do so at the earliest practicable date'.[15] They also violated international agreements entered into by Israel itself. Article VI.6 of the Armistice Agreement signed between Israel and Jordan on 3 April 1949 provided that 'Wherever villages may be affected by the establishment of the Armistice Demarcation Line ... the inhabitants of such villages shall be entitled to maintain, and shall be protected in, their full rights of residence, property and freedom.'

The main legal instrument that Israel used in order to take possession and control of the land belonging to the Palestinian refugees and internally displaced was the Absentees' Property Law 1950.[16] Under the law, all rights in any property belonging to those defined as 'absentees' passed automatically to the Custodian of Absentee Property.[17] Anyone in possession of absentees' property was bound to hand it over to the Custodian, and failure to do so was made a criminal offence.

The definition of an 'absentee' in the legislation was extraordinarily wide. An absentee was any person who from 29 November 1947 was:

> a legal owner of any property situated in the area of Israel or enjoyed or held it, whether by himself or through another, and who, at any time during the said period:
>
> i) was a national or citizen of the Lebanon, Egypt, Syria, Saudi Arabia, Trans-Jordan, Iraq or the Yemen, or
> ii) was in one of those countries or in any part of Palestine outside the area of Israel, or
> iii) was a Palestinian citizen and left his ordinary place of residence in Palestine
> a) for a place outside Palestine before the 1st September, 1948; or
> b) for a place in Palestine held at the time by forces which sought to prevent the establishment of the State of Israel or which fought against it after its establishment.

This wording incorporated not only Palestinians driven out of the area during the war or who happened to be outside the area when war broke out, but also those who were forced off their land but remained within Israeli territory or returned to it and became Israeli citizens. The Initiative Committee for the Defence of Refugee Rights in Israel believes that as many as one-quarter of the Palestinians who became citizens of Israel may have been turned into internal refugees, or 'present absentees'.[18]

The definition of 'absentee' was ruthlessly enforced. Once a person became an absentee this categorization could not generally be shaken off.[19] So for instance when the residents of the Little Triangle, who became Israeli citizens after the cease-fire agreement with Jordan in April 1949, attempted to reclaim their farmland from the Custodian, citing the clause in the Armistice Agreement between Israel and Jordan that obliged Israel to protect the property rights of the residents of the Triangle, they failed to have the designation of their land as absentee property reversed.[20] The High Court rejected several appeals, refusing to uphold the clause on the grounds that as an international agreement it was not justiciable in the Israeli courts.[21] There are also no time limitations as to when a person may be officially declared an absentee, and people are still receiving notifications to hand over land.[22] The Custodian need only issue a certificate that someone is an 'absentee' for that person or property to be regarded as absentee unless and until the contrary is proved (section 30). The courts have held that it is the simple fulfilment of the criteria contained in the Absentees' Property Law, not any official certification that one is an absentee, that determines one's status.[23] Nor would the fact that an owner is unknown save the land: section 5 provides that the fact that the identity of an absentee is unknown will not prevent his property from being considered absentee property.

Following the peace treaty between Israel and Jordan in October 1994, Israel amended the Absentees' Property Law 1950, to the effect that *as from* 10 November 1994 no property would be defined as absentees' property on the basis that it was owned by a resident or citizen of Jordan.[24] However, since the legislation specified that the status of property already defined as absentees' property would be unaffected, it only operates to prevent further property becoming categorized as absentee property. Since most property belonging to those falling under the definition of 'absentee' in the 1950 law had already been declared absentee property, the amendment has little practical effect. There is also evidence that even these limited concessions are not being implemented.[25]

On the face of it, the term 'Custodian' might seem rather benign, suggesting some sort of trustee, assigned to look after property on behalf of the owners during their absence. This was not at all the case. The Absentees' Property Law itself merely provided that the Custodian 'shall take care of held property, either himself or through others having his consent' (section 7[a]). He was authorized, but not obliged, to incur expenses in order to care for, maintain, repair or develop property (section 7[b]). Similarly he was authorized, but not mandated, to grant small allowances to dependants of an absentee (section 9). On the other hand, the Custodian was given sweeping powers to expel people from land, not only unlawful occupiers but also protected tenants where the Custodian decides that the vacation of the land is required 'for the purposes of the development of the place or area in which it is situated' (sections 10 and 12).

The Absentees' Property Law says nothing about the rights or status of the absentee owners. The High Court ruled early on, in 1954, that the Custodian was not a trustee for the Palestinian 'absentees', and owed them no duty of care regarding the management of their assets.[26] On the contrary, he was given wide powers to deal with the property and its income, and even to sell it, without regard for the rights of the owners. He was empowered to hand over land to others for cultivation or other purposes, and did in fact turn over large areas of Palestinian land to Jewish settlers. But he was permitted to grant only short leases of up to six years (section 19[a][2]). Pressure mounted for the property to be assigned for Jewish development on a more permanent basis, and moves were made to activate a clause in the law (section 19[a][1]) that allowed the Custodian to sell absentees' property to a Development Authority. Such a body was established in 1950 and under an agreement made in 1953, the Custodian transferred all immovable property under his control to the Development Authority. The Development Authority was in turn authorized by its constitutive legislation to transfer property in its control to the state, to agencies settling Arab internal refugees, or to a local authority, with a stipulation that the JNF be given first option to purchase land.[27] The JNF subsequently acquired 2,373,677 dunams of land as a result of agreements with the government, most of which was property belonging to the Palestinian refugees (Granott 1956: 111).

By this series of legal manoeuvres, the Israeli government sought to sever the link between the 'absentees' – and indeed the entire Palestinian community – and their land, and to place the land at the exclusive disposal of Jewish settlers. The bodies to which title was transferred were immunized from legal claims, and the intention was to ensure that the only remedy or interest in the land remaining for the original owners, even those unlawfully deprived of their property, was compensation. In 1973 legislation was enacted in order to encourage those who had been displaced internally to accept compensation for land expropriated under the Absentees' Property Law.[28] However, relatively few Palestinians have applied for compensation, unwilling to surrender their historical claims to their land, and the Knesset was forced to extend the original time limit for claims, set at three years.[29] And the compensation envisaged is intended to cover loss of the value of the asset itself, not other losses such as income and profits from the land during the years the owner was denied the fruits of the land. It is particularly egregious that while the Absentees' Property Law of 1950 provides specifically that where property is returned to its owner (because it is established that he is not an absentee or in exchange for other property, as provided in sections 27 and 28 of the law) the Custodian will be paid remuneration and expenses incurred in maintaining the property (section 32), there is no provision for compensation to be paid to the owners for their loss of income during the time the land was in the possession of the Custodian.

The Absentees' Property Law was implemented with enormous zeal. During the 1950s and 1960s, Israeli government inspectors were sent out to the Palestinian villages and towns to claim the land of those who could be defined as absentees on behalf of the Custodian. Not only villages emptied during the war were affected; the Custodian also asserted his rights over considerable amounts of land within the Arab communities that survived the war, stepping into the shoes of refugees and asserting their rights over property whether as sole or joint owners of a given piece of land. Since it was extremely common for families to have been broken up and scattered during the war, the Custodian would often find himself deeply enmeshed in complex family webs. He acquired title to large and small pieces of land in and around villages, and joint interests in many others. Thus, for example, if four brothers jointly owned a piece of land and one of them was classified as an absentee, the Custodian would become owner of a one-quarter share in the plot of land. Sometimes historical accident produced patterns of ownership that were a goldmine to the Custodian. In the Galilee village of Kaukab, around half the cultivable land was lost to the Custodian even though only a handful of the inhabitants had left in 1948. Under the Ottoman regime, a large landowner had persuaded most families to allow him to register the land in his name in return for his paying the taxes. When the landlord fled to Lebanon in 1948, all his assets were declared to be absentee property and vested in the Custodian.[30] The Custodian continues actively to stake his claims to this day. Where a Palestinian landowner dies and one of his or her heirs is a refugee, that share is claimed by the Custodian.

The consequences of this phenomenon are exploited to the full by the state, particularly the Israel Lands Administration, which is responsible for land under the control of the Development Authority and the JNF as well as the state. Where the Custodian takes over a share of jointly held property, the Absentees' Property Law entitles him to 'participate in the management of the whole of the property, together with the owners who are not absentees, with the same rights as the absentees had' (section 25). According to Palestinian community leaders, the state often uses these powers to block development plans or use of land, or bides its time and seeks to exchange its interest in land within Palestinian villages for other land, often taking advantage of the high price of land within the village to obtain larger areas of land outside it.[31]

Once land has been considered absentees' property it is extremely difficult to reverse this status. The Absentees' Property Law provides only two ways for retrieving property from the Custodian of Absentees' Property: confirmation by the Custodian that the person did not fulfil the definition of an absentee, or certification by the Custodian releasing the property by way of exchange for other property. Achieving either is a lengthy and difficult process and finds little support in the courts. Yvonne Cokrin petitioned the Israeli High Court in 1979, claiming that she did not fall within the definition of an absentee under the law because she should not be considered a Lebanese citizen since she also held British and Irish passports.[32] The High Court rejected her challenge, holding that there was no doubt that she was an absentee according to the technical legal definition, and further, that the decision as to whether to release property should be based not on humanitarian but on political considerations. The law had legitimately defined absentee in a broad way due to the political circumstances at the time, the Court said, even though it might encompass those who were not hostile to Israel.

The Cokrin decision is typical of the approach taken by the Israeli courts, which have been consistently unwilling to intervene in decisions of the Custodian and the committees established under the Absentees' Property legislation. In the case of Nicola, the High Court expressed reluctance at being a forum for challenging decisions of the Custodian, who it said should be assumed to have acted in a bona fide manner unless the contrary is proved.[33] The Court was not willing to look at the merits in such cases, but only to satisfy itself that decisions had been reached in a proper manner following the correct procedures. Nowadays, the courts appear even more reluctant to entertain applications by those challenging their classification as absentees in the 1950s and 1960s, citing delay as the reason.[34]

Retrieval of property from the Custodian is made even more difficult by section 17 of the Absentees' Property Law, which states that if the Custodian disposed of the property 'in good faith', such a transfer would not be invalidated even if it were proved that the property was not absentee property. Frequently, the transfer of title to land from an 'absentee' to the Custodian, and from the Custodian to the Development Authority, is transacted at the Land Registry on the same day. In a welcome judgment in 1993, a District Court accepted for the first time the argument that this arrangement made it impossible that the transfer on to the Development Authority was 'in good faith' since the circumstances of the simultaneous transfer effectively prevented the claimant from having any legal remedy, a situation that the Custodian must have been aware of.[35]

Generally, however, the Israeli courts have failed to provide any significant degree of protection for the property rights of Palestinian citizens of the state over the years in responding to challenges to the implementation of the Absentees' Property Law. In the early years the High Court simply deferred to 'political circumstances', as in the Cockrin case, and the Court has consistently drawn back from intervening in decisions of the executive relating to 'absentees'' land.

Today, the Custodian's role in matters relating to land is much reduced, since he transfers on land that vests in him under the Absentees' Property Law. Nevertheless, the Custodian came under sharp criticism in the State Comptroller's Report 1990. Citing the lack of coordination between relevant ministries, lack of resources and an overbearing attitude on the part of the Israel Lands Administration, the State Comptroller found the Custodian to be unable to provide basic information about the property under his control, to be in effect little more than a minor clerical official in the ILA and, in sum, incapable of performing the functions given to him under the law.[36] Despite this public criticism, the role remains shrouded in secrecy that has proved difficult to penetrate. In January 2001, the Attorney General refused a request issued by Adalah, the Palestinian legal centre, that he order the Custodian to release information abut the movable property of Palestinian refugees.[37]

Israel's enactment and implementation of the Absentees' Property legislation, as has been mentioned, violated UN resolutions such as General Assembly Resolution 194 that called on Israel to allow the Palestinian refugees and displaced persons to return to their homes and land, in accordance with international law, and other resolutions such as Resolution 181 that specifically warned against expropriation of Arab land in a Jewish state. Israel's actions also violated general international

law and practice that give the Palestinians a right to return and to restitution of their property. Other internationally recognized rights such
as the right to peaceful enjoyment of property and the right not to be
arbitrarily deprived of one's property, outlined in the previous chapter,
together with Palestinian collective rights over the land of historic
Palestine and internationally recognized concepts such as historic title
are also ignored.

Israel's treatment of *Waqf* property

International law protects freedom to manifest one's religion, and
this protection extends to religious sites and practices. Article 18 of the
International Covenant on Civil and Political Rights of 1966 (ICCPR),
to which Israel is a party, provides:

1. Everyone shall have the right to freedom of thought, conscience
   and religion. This right shall include freedom to have or to adopt a
   religion or belief of his choice, and freedom, either individually or
   in community with others and in public or private, to manifest his
   religion or belief in worship, observance, practice and teaching.
2. No one shall be subject to coercion which would impair his freedom
   to have or to adopt a religion or belief of his choice.
3. Freedom to manifest one's religion or beliefs may be subject only
   to such limitations as are prescribed by law and are necessary to
   protect public safety, order, health, or morals or the fundamental
   rights and freedoms of others.

In its interpretation of this Article, the UN Human Rights Committee (1993: para. 4) has said that the concept of worship extends,
among other things, to the building of places of worship, and to
freedom of religious groups to conduct their basic affairs, such as
the freedom to choose their religious leaders, priests and teachers,
and the freedom to establish seminaries or religious schools. The UN
Declaration on the Elimination of All Forms of Intolerance and of
Discrimination Based on Religion or Belief of 1981 specifically provides
that the right to freedom of religion includes the freedom 'to establish
and maintain appropriate charitable or humanitarian institutions' and
'to solicit and receive voluntary financial and other contributions from
individuals and institutions'.[38] Importantly, this Declaration also recognizes the right of religious groups to choose their own leadership,
declaring the right 'to train, appoint, elect or designate by succession
appropriate leaders called for by the requirements and standards of
any religion or belief'.

The majority of Palestinian citizens of Israel are Muslim, while there are also Christian and Druze communities. Israel has shown little respect for Muslim holy places or for the right of the Islamic community in Israel to conduct its own affairs. Since 1948 mosques, graveyards and other sites have been damaged and destroyed with scant regard for their significance for the Palestinian collective memory and identity, or for their religious significance.[39]

Nor did Islamic religious property escape the Israeli land seizures. The Islamic *Waqf* was among the greatest losers from the land expropriations. *Waqfs* are Islamic trusts endowed with assets and established for religious or charitable purposes, and have existed all over the Islamic world for centuries.[40] Income from assets endowed is traditionally devoted to the social needs of the community as well as for religious purposes. Schools and institutions for the needy are established as well as mosques and holy sites. Ottoman law had recognized the legal validity of *Waqfs*. Subject to supervision by the Islamic religious courts, a *Waqf* could be created for the benefit of a particular family or institution, or for the community at large, and the trustees were under a duty to administer the assets in the interests of the beneficiary or the specified purpose. Under the British Mandate few changes were made: the British Mandate authorities had continued to recognize the *Waqfs* as distinct legal entities and had established a Supreme Muslim Council to oversee the shari'a court and *Waqf* systems.

By 1948 the *Waqfs* in Mandate Palestine were extremely well endowed.[41] Their assets not only included mosques, graveyards and other holy sites, but rich farmland, residential buildings, stores and other commercial property in the towns and villages which had been dedicated during the Ottoman and Mandatory period.[42] The *Waqfs* may have owned up to 20 per cent of the cultivated area of Palestine (Dumper 1994: 29). Israel refused to distinguish between *Waqf* property and any other land, and the Custodian of Absentee Property asserted his claim over *Waqf* property on the basis that the Supreme Muslim Council that had managed much *Waqf* property since 1921 had become an 'absentee' under the terms of the Absentees' Property Law 1950 because most of its members were refugees. This was notwithstanding the fact that many of the beneficiaries of the *Waqfs* were not absentees. As much as 85 per cent of all *Waqf* property within the state was transferred to the Custodian (ibid., p. 35). The move was widely opposed by the Palestinian community. As Sabri Jiryis wrote:

Not only was the decision considered illegal and unjust but also inexcusable, since waqf property is regarded as belonging to God and income from such property is devoted to charitable ends. In any case, God can hardly be classified as an absentee according to the Absentees' Property Law. Nor had the needy members of the Islamic community – for whose sake the waqf was endowed – disappeared from Israel; on the contrary there are thousands of them. (Jiryis 1976: 118)

Challenges reached the courts, in which the applicants claimed that the Islamic shari'a courts had jurisdiction to appoint new managers (*mutawalli*) in place of the absentees, and those managers were entitled to take back administration of the *Waqf* property from the Custodian.[43] Despite some success in the courts, the outcome was that only certain '*dhurri*' (family) and '*mulhaq*' (private) trusts whose '*mutawalli*' were not absentees succeeded in avoiding the Custodian (Dumper 1994: 32, 41). In order to remove any doubt, the Knesset in 1965 retroactively authorized the transfer of legal ownership of *Waqf* property to the Custodian free from all conditions that were attached when the property was endowed.[44]

The bulk of the *Waqf* property, including its rich farmland, commercial and other properties, was claimed by the Custodian and subsequently transferred by him to the Development Authority in 1953 in the same way as other 'absentee' property.[45] Any compensation paid on *Waqf* property under the terms of the Land Acquisition (Validation of Acts and Compensation) Law 1953[46] went not to the Muslim community in Israel, but to the Ministry of Religious Affairs (Dumper 1994: 34). Like other 'absentees'' property, much cultivable land belonging to the *Waqf*s eventually found its way into the hands of the JNF.

Only the mosques, graveyards and other holy sites avoided being passed to the state, but even these were passed not to the Islamic community, but initially to the Ministry of Religious Affairs in 1951. In 1965, after persistent demands from the Palestinian community that they be permitted to administer their holy sites and other properties, the government enacted an amendment to the Absentees' Property Law allowing the appointment of boards of trustees in seven cities to which the *Waqf* properties in those cities would be transferred.[47] However, these boards are government appointed, and have been heavily controlled and manipulated by Israeli governments. They have outraged the Muslim community by engaging in property speculation and selling land falling under their administration for development. In a number of cases, construction work has been carried out on mosques and cemeteries without first allowing the Islamic community to relocate the graves, causing an outcry in the Palestinian community.[48]

The 1965 Amendment Law was designed to ensure that the land

expropriated from the *Waqf* would not be returned. It specified that the Custodian took the *Waqf* property free from any restrictions if either the managers or the beneficiaries of the *Waqf* were absentees, and authorized the Custodian to pass the property to the Development Authority or to the boards of trustees. The law of 1965 also brought about a fundamental change in the status of most *Waqf* property. The law gave the Custodian the power to release property belonging to a *Waqf* to its beneficiaries, and gave the boards of trustees the power to deal freely in the property that came under their administration. These powers ran directly contrary to the distinctive legal and holy character of *Waqf* land, one of the fundamental aspects of which was that its assets could not be sold or transferred in any way (Dumper 1994: 34). Now freely transferable and no longer subject to the conditions on which it had originally been endowed, little remained of the *Waqf* character. Although *Waqf* continued to exist formally as a category of land tenure, in effect, the 1965 law abolished the category of *Waqf* land in Israel, other than in relation to mosques.[49]

For some reason, the Custodian's assertion of rights over *Waqf* property situated within the Palestinian villages that survived the 1948 war was not in all cases registered at the time. As recently as 2000, a number of Arab local councils were approached by the Israel Lands Administration (ILA) and asked to approve the registration of *Waqf* lands within their borders in the name of the state, rekindling resentment.[50]

Israel's plundering of the *Waqf* property, ending its status as endowed property, and preventing the Islamic community in Israel from appointing its own leadership and managing its own affairs, clearly violates internationally accepted principles, specifically freedom to manifest one's religion and the right of religious groups to conduct their own affairs, including the right to establish charitable institutions and to choose their own leadership. Article 18 of the ICCPR does permit restrictions on the freedoms set out in that Article, but only if limitations are prescribed by law *and* are necessary to protect public safety, order, health, or morals or the fundamental rights and freedoms of others. None of these conditions could reasonably be said to apply in the context of the Muslim community in Israel, so the restrictions imposed by Israel violate the ICCPR.

Furthermore, the international standards relating to freedom to practise one's religion all stress that discrimination based on religion or belief is absolutely prohibited.[51] However, the treatment afforded to Muslim *Waqf* endowments in Israel has been totally different to the favoured treatment offered to the Jewish religious communities, which have largely had their freedom to conduct their own affairs respected.

Even other established religious communities in Palestine, the Christian, Druze and Bahai, were not subjected to the same treatment as the *Waqf*. Although much of the Church leadership and administration could technically have fallen under the definition of 'absentee' in the legislation, for instance, the Absentees' Property Law was not applied in relation to many of their religious sites. However, the Israeli High Court has chosen not to step in to prevent and punish dubious dealings and corruption in relation to both Church and *Waqf* property.[52]

Expropriation of land under Emergency Regulations

The Absentees' Property Law provided the basis for seizing land belonging to the Palestinian refugees and internally displaced, but this still left Palestinian populations not affected by the law in possession of significant areas of land including valuable farmland. A series of Emergency Regulations were introduced or invoked by the Israeli government between 1948 and the early 1950s in order to seize further land belonging to Palestinians who remained within the state and became citizens of Israel. The whole of the Palestinian population was initially placed under military rule that was lifted only in 1966, and Emergency Regulations formed the main legal basis of that military government. These regulations offered only minimal opportunity for legal challenge, and imposed severe restrictions on freedom of movement and other civil liberties of the Palestinian population, while at the same time providing instruments for seizing further land.[53]

As with the 'absentees" land, the dispossession was carried out in two stages. First, the land was seized under Emergency Regulations. Later, in a second stage, laws were passed in an attempt to ensure that the transfer of the land was irreversible.

The Defence (Emergency) Regulations 1945, introduced by the British during the Mandate period, were used by the incoming Israeli government to control the movement of Palestinians.[54] Under Regulation 125, the Military Governor was empowered to declare 'closed areas' which nobody could enter or leave without a written permit. The areas in which Palestinians lived were divided into small pockets and each was declared a closed area, with movement in and out heavily restricted. But Israel also used these powers to prevent refugees from returning to their villages after the fighting.[55] The government did not try to hide its intention to use these powers to secure more land for Jewish development. Ben Gurion informed the Knesset that the military government 'came into existence to protect the right of Jewish settlement in all parts of the state'.[56]

Israel enacted three additional emergency laws that were also used for the purpose of seizing Palestinian land. The Emergency Regulations (Security Zones) 1949 empowered the Minister of Defence to declare areas bordering the frontiers of Israel a security zone and to order any persons to leave such areas.[57] This power was used to expel Palestinians from the villages of Iqrit and Bir'im near the Lebanese border. Initially the inhabitants were informed that they were being evacuated as a temporary measure while hostilities continued, and assured that they would be permitted to return two weeks later. Instead, despite High Court orders in their favour, they were prevented from returning and the villages were destroyed by the army. This case, and the families' struggle to return to the villages which is still ongoing, are discussed below.

A second law, the Emergency Regulations (Cultivation of Waste Lands and Use of Unexploited Water Resources) 1948, empowered the Minister of Agriculture to take over agricultural lands not being cultivated due to the war.[58] In practice, these powers were used in conjunction with other emergency enactments in order to requisition land, including land belonging to the internally displaced Palestinians who remained within the State of Israel as well as the refugees. Palestinians wanting to cultivate their land would be prevented from entering the area where their land was situated, which would be declared a closed area. The land would then be declared uncultivated, the Minister would take possession and hand it to neighbouring Jewish agricultural settlements to farm. A third emergency law enacted was the Emergency Land Requisition (Regulation) Law 1949, which permitted the requisition of land or buildings 'for the defence of the state, public security, the maintenance of essential supplies or essential public services, the absorption of immigrants or the rehabilitation of ex-soldiers or war invalids'.[59] By 1953, 1,126 orders had been issued under these regulations, around half of them for the purposes of settling new immigrants.[60]

A further British ordinance used by Israel was the Roads and Railroads Ordinance (Defence and Development) No. 29, 1943.[61] This ordinance permitted the expropriation of land for building roads and laying railway tracks in the interests of defence or development. Its implementation interfered with cultivation and reduced the value of land. Israel also introduced the Cultivators (Protection) Ordinance (Amendment) Law 1953.[62] An amendment to an ordinance designed to protect tenant farmers from eviction when land was sold, this law excluded from protection those who took up tenancies after 17 December 1942 and tenants of farms owned by the state. The effect was to remove protection from many tenant farmers of land whose owners were classified as absentees, and make them vulnerable to eviction.

By 1953, large amounts of land had been seized under these laws and regulations and put at the disposal of the Jewish community, though the land was still legally owned by Palestinians. In 1953, in a move purporting to terminate Palestinian proprietary rights in this land, the Israeli government enacted the Land Acquisition (Validation of Acts and Compensation) Law.[63] Section 2(a) of this law authorized the transfer to the Development Authority of any property:

1. that on 1st April 1952 was not in the possession of its owners; and
2. that within the period between 14th May, 1948 and 1st April, 1952 it was used or assigned for purposes of essential development, settlement or security; and
3. that it is still required for any of these purposes.

Upon the Minister of Finance certifying that these conditions applied to a certain piece of property, the property would be turned over to the Development Authority. According to the law, the state was given immunity from claims relating to the legality of the seizure of the land. Compensation was to be paid, but at an extremely low rate.[64] In very limited circumstances, other land could be offered in full or partial compensation.[65] The Israel Lands Administration (ILA) is responsible for payment of compensation to owners of property under the Absentees' Property (Compensation) Law 1973 and the Land Acquisition (Validation of Acts and Compensation) Law 1953. By the end of 2000, the ILA had dealt with 15,975 claims relating to 205,669 dunams of land that were acquired by the state under the two laws (ILA 2001).[66]

Challenging the application of either the Emergency Regulations and laws or the Land Acquisition Law was extremely difficult. The courts have been reluctant to interfere in military or ministerial discretion exercised on the grounds of security, and, in the case of Younis, effectively closed the door to judicial review of decisions under the Land Acquisition Act.[67]

Use of emergency legislation did not end with the end of hostilities or even the lifting of military rule over the Palestinian population in 1966. Emergency legislation has continued to be used to impose restrictions on Palestinian-owned land, particularly the designation of areas as closed military areas. These measures have caused considerable resentment among the local Palestinian populations, who have viewed such encroachments as another step in the continuing Israeli policy to dispossess them of their land. Their implementation also causes considerable hardship and deprives Palestinian communities of land they badly need for development.

One example is the experience of the Ar-Roha area in the part of the Little Triangle heavily populated by Palestinians. In the 1950s large areas of Palestinian farmland in the Triangle were designated for military training. Local farmers whose land was affected petitioned the High Court to be able to enter and cultivate their land.[68] The Court ordered the army to permit the farmers to enter and cultivate their land under appropriate restrictions. Subsequently, arrangements were made with the landowners such as permitting them to graze their animals on certain days only.[69] During the 1990s reports emerged that planning was in progress for the construction of a new Jewish city, Irron, as part of Ariel Sharon's 'Seven Stars plan', and that the land in the military area would be expropriated for this purpose. These rumours grew when restrictions on entering this land were enforced more strictly and in 1998 the borders of the military area were altered. A protest movement grew among the Palestinians in the area, demanding that the owners be allowed to use their land and for the people of the area to benefit from it. In September 1998 matters came to a head when police and security forces stormed a protest tent and Intifada-style clashes took place.[70] Perhaps surprised at the scale of the protest, the authorities agreed to review the status of the land and an agreement was signed on 30 December 2000 whereby the majority of the land would remain a military area, but the local community would be able to cultivate parts of it.[71] The government also agreed to establish a committee to look into the possibility of annexing areas no longer to be part of the military area to the local Arab municipalities. The terms of the agreement leave the vast majority of the area as a military area. This land is particularly badly needed by the local Palestinian population, given that these communities are not able to expand to the east because of the proximity of the Green Line. And because most of the land remains in the hands of the state, the Palestinian communities remain concerned that the plans to establish the major new Jewish city of Irron can still potentially go ahead. What happened in Ar-Roha shows how unprepared Israel is to compromise even in the face of large-scale protest. Minimal concessions were made but no change to the overall policy, which was to retain most of the land in state control for military use and future Jewish development.

In other areas, also, Israel has designated Palestinian-owned land as a 'military area'. In 1976, the Minister of Defence announced the closing off of 11,000 dunams of land planted with olive trees and other farmland owned by residents of the villages of Sakhnin, Arabe and Deir Hanna, as a military firing range: Area Nine. This order, which was strongly opposed by these villages, was eventually cancelled in 1986.

Such use of emergency legislation may not result immediately in dispossession but has a creeping effect. A person who owns land within a military area is unable to use and profit from the land and faces uncertainty as to its future, and will be under severe pressure to sell it.

Perhaps the harshest uses of emergency legislation have been in the Naqab, where large areas of land formerly possessed and historically used by Palestinian Bedouin have been designated military areas, and emergency powers are still being used. In May 2001 the authorities began to implement two orders issued under Emergency Regulations that purported to confiscate a total of 72,000 dunams for military purposes, and started demolishing Bedouin homes in five communities.[72]

That such measures are viewed by the Israel Defence Forces in national political terms as part of a struggle for land was demonstrated in a paper of the Israeli Land Use Research Institute of 1986 which states: 'The security authorities participate in preserving national land but much national land is given into foreign hands because of failed dealings such as Area 9 in the north or the Laqya training area and the Carmel area and the Bedouin settlements' (Land Use Research Institute 1986a: 26).

The fifty-year legal battle fought by the villagers of Iqrit and Bir'im, who were expelled under the Emergency Regulations (Security Zones) 1949 demonstrates the extent of Israel's determination not to allow Palestinians to return to their land. In 1948 the Israeli army ordered the inhabitants of Iqrit and Bir'im, Palestinian villages close to the border with Lebanon, to leave their villages due to security concerns along the border. They left on the basis of assurances that they would be permitted to return within fifteen days. When this did not happen the residents turned to the courts. The High Court ruled in July 1951 that the residents of Iqrit were entitled to return to their village since the reason for the temporary evacuation no longer existed, and there were no legal grounds for depriving them of their right to return.[73] However, the military defied the order, issued the inhabitants with expulsion orders, destroyed both villages and later declared them closed areas under Regulation 125 of the Defence (Emergency) Regulations 1945. Furthermore, title to the land of both villages was expropriated under the Land Acquisition Law of 1953 and the farmland turned over to Jewish farming settlements. In 1981 the High Court rejected an attempt to challenge these steps, expressing sympathy but holding that too much time had elapsed for it to examine the matter.[74]

Nevertheless, the former residents continued their campaign to return to the villages. In 1993 a Ministerial Committee was appointed, headed by the Minister of Justice, to advise the Rabin government how to resolve the problem of Iqrit and Bir'im.[75] The Committee took the view that in this particular case there was no reason of state security to continue to prevent those evacuated from returning to their villages.[76] It would be possible, they determined, to restore a limited area of land without harming the rights of those who had subsequently settled in the area. The Committee recommended that a total of 600 dunams be given to each village, and that the ILA be responsible for defining which particular land this would comprise. This was less than 10 per cent of the land originally owned by inhabitants of the two villages.[77] Each head of a family that had resided in the village in 1948 would be entitled to 500 metres on which to build a house, which he could assign to a family member of his choice. If the head of family was dead, a Committee would decide which family member would receive this privilege. At the same time, the person acquiring the rights would be required to sign a document giving up any further rights to land in the area.

Stalemate followed the Committee's recommendations. On the one hand branches of government refused to implement them, while on the other, the people of Iqrit and Bir'im rejected them as inadequate, arguing that their effect would be to limit the numbers who could return and expropriate the majority of the land, and left no scope for the future development of the villages and no option for agriculture or other employment opportunities to be established. The High Court was petitioned once again to resolve the issue, and again pressed the state to come up with a solution. On 10 October 2001, the Israeli cabinet finally issued its decision. There was no reason, the government said, to change the decision of Golda Meir in 1972, which had been to refuse to allow a return to the two villages on the grounds of security concerns and because it would set a precedent for other displaced Palestinians. In December 2001 the High Court ordered compensation to be paid, but this solution has been rejected by the displaced residents of both villages.

The role played by the Israeli High Court in the cases of Iqrit and Bir'im is interesting in that, unusually, it was willing to rule in favour of the Palestinian owners, at least in the initial stages. Subsequently, however, the Court has deferred to the government rather than applying a solution based on law.

The use of the emergency legislation, in combination with subsequent legislation, particularly the Land Acquisition (Validation of Acts and Compensation) Law 1953, to seize for the state large areas of Palestinian land, must be viewed as an unjustified interference with the fundamental rights of the Palestinian community to peaceful enjoyment of their property. International law does not allow states unlimited power to violate rights in times of emergency, and has developed standards governing such situations. Restriction of rights by the use of emergency powers must be exceptional, temporary, proportional, and only to the extent strictly necessary; and some rights, such as the prohibition on discrimination, can never be derogated from even in time of emergency.[78] If these standards had not been fully developed at the time the Iqrit and Bir'im case began and the legislation was introduced, they have certainly developed and become binding on Israel since, and should be applied in relation not only to Iqrit and Bir'im, but also all the other Palestinian land in relation to which the right to enjoy peaceful possession remains adversely affected by emergency legislation.

Israeli land expropriation policies under the Land (Acquisition for Public Purposes) Ordinance

After the pretexts of taking over abandoned property and security were no longer credible bases for seizing Palestinian land, Israeli policies nevertheless continued to demand that means be found to expropriate further land from the Palestinians. In particular, there was concern that Palestinians still formed a majority of the population in the Galilee. It was decided that steps must be taken to create a sizeable Jewish presence in that area and to break up the concentration of Palestinians there. This was known as the 'Project for the Judaization of the Galilee', and the security and political goals were openly discussed.[79] From the late 1950s, the major tool used for acquiring Palestinian land and turning it over for Jewish settlement and development was the Land (Acquisition for Public Purposes) Ordinance 1943 (the Public Purposes Ordinance). This legislation, introduced by the British Mandate administration, permits the expropriation of privately owned land in the public interest.[80] While most states have such powers, Israel has implemented this legislation in a highly discriminatory and arbitrary manner. From the mid-1950s, land that remained in Palestinian hands was under threat from this process.

The Public Purposes Ordinance gives the government extremely wide powers. The Minister of Finance is permitted to take permanent ownership or temporary use of land that she or he declares is required for public purposes, upon payment of compensation. 'Public purpose' is simply any purpose defined as such by the Minister. The Minister is not even required to provide details of the nature of the public purpose for which the expropriation is required. In practice, the Expropriations Committee of the Israel Lands Administration usually initiates the process and advises the Minister. Powers to expropriate land are given not only to local authorities and the Development Authority, but also the Jewish National Fund – a body dedicated to acquiring land to which Jews only will have access.

The powers given under the Public Purposes Ordinance have been used by successive Israeli governments since the mid-1950s in order to pursue state goals to 'Judaize' (populate with Jews) areas predominantly populated by Palestinians, particularly the Galilee. Fertile land farmed by Palestinians has been targeted for expropriation even where alternative state-owned land is available. Cities, towns and villages are then built on the land and settled with Jews. Some of the major examples are: 1,200 dunams expropriated in 1957 from Arab landowners of Nazareth and its surrounding villages, used to establish the Jewish town of Upper Nazareth; land expropriated from the Arab villages of Tarshiha and Mi'lia in 1957 for the establishment of the Jewish town of Ma'alot; 5,100 dunams expropriated from the Arab villages of Nahaf, Deir-El-Asad, Bia'neh and Majd-Alkrum in 1964 for the establishment of the Jewish city of Karmiel; and the expropriation of 20,103 dunams, including several large parcels of agricultural land bordering Arab villages in the Galilee, announced in 1975 to make way for the establishment of twenty new Jewish settlements and the expansion of existing Jewish cities (Shmueli 1983: 708; Rekhes 1977). In reaction to this last announcement, the Palestinian community established a Committee for the Defence of Arab Land. The Committee called a general strike and organized demonstrations on 30 March 1976. In response, the state used excessive force, in the course of which six Palestinians were shot dead and hundreds of others were wounded by the Israeli security forces. Its anniversary is still commemorated each year by Palestinians as 'Land Day'.

The expropriations significantly depleted the Palestinian land holdings already devastated by the Absentees' Property legislation and Emergency Regulations used during the 1948 war and afterwards. The impact of the expropriations announced in 1975 on one village illustrates the ways in which the Palestinian communities were affected. Ein Mahil is a Palestinian village near the city of Nazareth. The land expropriated from the village constituted the major portion of its potential building land, directly bordering the edge of its current built-up area, leaving the village almost no further land for expansion.[81] The expropriated land was to be used not to benefit the community of Ein Mahil, but to provide industry for the nearby Jewish city of Upper Nazareth. Further, there were substantial land reserves already under the administration of the state in the area that could have been used for the purpose.[82]

After Land Day in March 1976, the authorities took no steps to implement the expropriation order for several years, and an inquiry carried out by the Ministry of the Interior recommended the restoration of the expropriated land to the village, recognizing its need for the land. Despite this finding, in 1988 the Israel Lands Administration initiated proceedings against some 120 landowners of Ein Mahil to evict them from a total of 1,100 dunams of land that had been subject to the declaration of expropriation in 1975.

The Public Purposes Ordinance continues to be used to expropriate Palestinian land in pursuance of national political goals. The Israel Lands Administration's report of 1992 shows that in the years 1991 and 1992 the legislation was invoked on 1,850,000 dunams of land of which some 92 per cent was privately owned land (ILA 1993: Table IV/7: 125).[83] This period coincided with stepped up efforts to 'Judaize' areas of the state that have predominantly Palestinian populations and to create a wall of Jewish settlements along the Green Line to separate the Palestinians within Israel from those in the occupied West Bank, the so-called Seven Stars plan initiated by then Housing Minister Ariel Sharon.[84] The announcement of plans to establish sixty-eight new villages, towns and residential areas in October 2001, some of them on land already expropriated from Palestinians, came as a sign that this plan is still alive and of the intentions behind it: as the Hebrew daily newspaper *Ha'aretz* commented (14 October 2001), these aspects of the plan are based on the Israeli saying that 'if the Jews are not quick enough in grabbing the land, an Arab will come along and grab it'.

While the Public Purposes Ordinance has frequently been used to take land away from Palestinian communities and used to benefit the Jewish population exclusively, the reverse has not occurred. Indeed, the Palestinian communities find it extremely difficult to obtain from the state the land they need for their growth and development.[85] The Public Purposes Ordinance is not used in connection with development plans for the Arab sector. On the contrary, its implementation has served only to deplete further the Palestinian community's land base for future urban development and for agriculture. There is no requirement in the law for the impact that a proposed expropriation will have on affected populations to be investigated or taken into account. There is no requirement, for instance, to justify why it is necessary to take a prime piece of agricultural land from a Palestinian village rather than a piece of unused state land, in order to build a new Jewish town (a practice Palestinians have often accused the government of). But the impact and purpose of this discriminatory implementation of the Public Purposes Ordinance is far more than merely economic; the 'public' served by the

Ordinance has been the Jewish public alone, and the policies served are national-political strategic objectives such as 'Judaization'.

While the Public Purposes Ordinance has been the major instrument used to effect large-scale expropriations of Palestinian land since the mid-1950s, there have also been examples of pieces of legislation applying to specific areas of land. When Israel withdrew from the Sinai under the terms of the peace agreement with Egypt in 1979, the government decided to relocate an airfield from the Sinai to an area of the Naqab Desert inhabited by Palestinian Bedouin, Tel Malhata. A law was enacted to effect the expropriation to the state of 82,000 dunams of land claimed by the Palestinian Bedouin.[86] The terms of this law cannot be considered reasonable. Possession had to be surrendered within three months (section 4), after which the state was entitled to seize the land without the need for a court order (section 6). The affected land was in the middle of an area inhabited exclusively by Bedouin, on which tribes had been settled for generations, and was among the most intensively cultivated land still in the hands of the Bedouin. Some 750 families were forced to leave their lands, 80 per cent of which were being used for agriculture (Falah 1989a: 80). One might wonder why the government passed a separate law rather than relying on its powers to expropriate land for public purposes under the Land (Acquisition for Public Purposes) Ordinance 1943. A possible motive is that since laws of the Knesset cannot be challenged in the courts in Israel, neither the expropriation itself nor the framework for compensation could be challenged at that time (under the Basic Laws of 1992, the High Court has the power to review and even to revoke legislation, but that power did not exist previously). Compensation levels provided for in the law of 1980 were considerably lower than sums paid to Israeli settlers to relocate from the Sinai as part of the same peace process, possibly as little as 2–15 per cent of those sums (Madrell 1990: 11).[87]

A further example of specific legislation was the law enacted in 1994 to facilitate the acquisition of land for the construction of Route Number Six, a major new road slated to run through the country north to south.[88] Palestinians allege that this 'Trans-Israel highway' will cut off Palestinian farmers from their land and is deliberately planned so as to take in their land rather than other available land.[89] Passing through areas heavily populated by Palestinians, its construction will involve the expropriation of 1,833 dunams of private land from Palestinians, and 1,364 dunams from Jewish citizens.[90] But while plans are well under way to prepare for the commercial development of the areas around the Jewish communities that will enable those owners to benefit from the construction of the highway, no such initiatives have been taken as regards the Palestinian-owned land. It is hardly surprising that such pieces of legislation have been viewed by the Palestinian community with suspicion, as constituting yet more moves aimed at seizing further Palestinian land.

Judicial challenges to expropriation under the Public Purposes Ordinance It has proved extremely difficult for Palestinian landowners successfully to challenge decisions made under the Ordinance before the courts.[91] In an early challenge brought in 1955, Arab residents of Nazareth affected by the announced expropriation of land for the public purpose of building government offices petitioned the High Court. They argued that the expropriation discriminated against them as Arab citizens, and that the Minister's intention had not constituted a public purpose and therefore did not comply with the Ordinance, since the actual purpose was the prevention of the future development of Nazareth. The High Court held that it was not the role of the court to determine whether the purpose for which the land was expropriated was indeed a public purpose, since even if there was no such purpose, according to section 5(2) of the Ordinance, the mere publication of the Minister's declaration constituted conclusive evidence that the purpose had been confirmed as a public purpose and was sufficient to make it so.[92]

Nor was the Court willing to uphold the claim of discrimination, stating:

> It was not enough that the Plaintiffs claimed that they were Arabs and that only Arab land was taken when it was possible to take the land of non-Arabs or to use government lands. It would have to have been established that the fact that they were Arabs – that and not some other fact – was what motivated the Respondents to take their land and not someone else's. This has not been proven. We have no basis for the assumption that the Respondents chose the Plaintiffs' lands, not for the declared public purpose or because these lands were the most suitable for their purposes, but in order to harm the Arab residents of the town.

The Court's assertion that in order to constitute discrimination that would justify intervention the administrative action must be *intentionally* discriminatory certainly flies in the face of contemporary international standards, which require only that the result is discriminatory, but while the High Court would be unlikely to use such language explicitly today, it cannot be said with certainty that it would be willing to accept a claim of discrimination in a similar case.[93] In its decision in the Nazareth case, the High Court added that the opposition of the Arab population of Nazareth was not material; residents of a particular area should not be able to thwart a plan that had been considered by the appropriate authority to be for the good of the region and the country: 'This is a matter of the central government taking precedence over the wishes of the local people.'

Two years later, the same petitioners approached the High Court a second time, claiming that the expropriation should be cancelled because the land in question had been used not for the declared purpose of erecting government buildings, but rather for the settling of Jewish immigrants and the building of a new Jewish town, Upper Nazareth.[94] Once again the High Court rejected the petition, saying the fact that the authorities were using part of the land for the construction of housing and industry for those who were not the government employees envisaged in the original expropriation order did not affect the plaintiffs' case.

Similar issues have been raised before the courts after the enactment of the Basic Law: Human Dignity and Liberty in 1992, in which private property rights were elevated to the status of fundamental rights, and the impact of the Basic Law is evident. In three major cases decided since 1992, Makhul, Nusseibeh and Kersek, each of which will be considered below, the Israeli High Court has been called upon to hear claims that land declared expropriated had not then been taken by the state for a long period and/or had been eventually used for a purpose different to that originally declared. This phenomenon whereby the state announces expropriation under the Ordinance but fails actually to take possession of the land for many years is common in Israel and causes great hardship. A landowner is unable to continue to exercise his rights as possessor: he may not plan for or improve his land, and is uncertain as to when the state will claim possession. Its value will go down, but meanwhile he is still obliged to pay high land taxes. The High Court has ruled (in a case not involving Palestinian land) that where the state expropriates land for public purposes, it should start to prepare the land for the development purpose for which it was required, within a 'reasonable period', which may be up to six to eight years.[95]

The High Court's response to these three cases differed widely and illustrates on the one hand the national and political pressures on the Court and its refusal so far to offer protection for Palestinian landowners from abuse of the Public Purposes Ordinance, and on the other, the potential offered by the entrenchment of the right to property as a fundamental constitutional right. In the two cases involving Palestinians – one landowner in the Galilee and the other in East Jerusalem – the High Court rejected the petitions. In a third petition, brought by a Jewish citizen on very similar facts, the Court upheld the claim and signalled a new approach, giving due recognition to the constitutionally protected right to private property, and holding that if the reason for the expropriation no longer exists, the public authority must return the land to its original owners.

The first case involved a Palestinian from near Acre in the Galilee, Saliba Makhul. Makhul objected to notice of expropriation of his land under the Public Purposes Ordinance that formed part of the large-scale expropriations of 1976 which led to the events of Land Day. In 1987, after the authorities had taken no steps to use the land for more than ten years, Makhul petitioned the High Court, at which point the state suddenly came forward with plans for developing housing for the residents of the region including those who had been evacuated from the old city of Acre, and the High Court refused to intervene. By 1995, not only had Saliba Makhul's land still not been used for the declared public purpose, but this purpose had been changed, and the land was now slated to be used not for housing the relocated (Palestinian) residents of Acre, but for building housing for new Jewish immigrants. He therefore petitioned the High Court again, on the basis of the long delay and the change of purpose.[96] Again, the High Court rejected the petition, holding that the state was entitled to change the initial purpose of the expropriation if that later purpose itself justifies the expropriation of the land, that 'its hands are not necessarily tied to the original purpose on which the expropriation was based' and that the public interest required that the planning authorities 'not close their eyes to the changing needs of society and changes in the order of social priorities' (Dakwar 2000: 18). Regarding the long period of delay, the Court divided the twenty-year period into four periods, and held that none of them constituted substantive delay such as to make it unreasonable (ibid., p. 19). While acknowledging the harm done to property rights, now given constitutional protection in the Basic Law: Human Dignity and Liberty, and the strong emotional link between the petitioner and his land, the Court merely stated that compensation minimized the economic harm, and the petitioner had refused to accept it.

The second case involving Palestinian land since the Basic Law was enacted in 1992 was that of Nusseibeh, a Palestinian family in East Jerusalem. In this case twenty-five years had elapsed since the Minister of Finance announced the expropriation of their plot of land on the grounds it was needed for development to fulfil public need. The relevant authorities had still submitted no detailed plans for its use, though in 1986 the land had been included in an approved outline plan for the commercial development of the area. The family petitioned the court to cancel the expropriation, claiming there had been no public aim for which the land was needed at the time the expropriation was announced. There was also no similarity between the original purpose, and the aims of the 1986 outline plan. Nevertheless, they were prepared to accept the terms of the plan and to develop the land themselves for commercial purposes within the scope of the plan. Further, they argued, there had been unreasonable delay in implementation of the expropriation order and due weight should be given to their rights as owners. In 1994, the High Court accepted the petitioners' arguments, holding that there was no need for the state to impinge on the fundamental right of ownership where it was clear that the land was not really needed.[97]

However, the case was considered important enough to be referred to a larger bench of the High Court, consisting of seven judges. On 11 November 1995 this bench overturned the previous decision by a margin of four to three. The majority held that while the burden of proof to demonstrate that an expropriation was legal did fall on the state, if a petitioner was seeking not to challenge the legality of the expropriation itself, but to cancel a legally performed expropriation retrospectively, the burden fell on the petitioner to demonstrate that there were new circumstances that warranted the cancellation of the expropriation order. This petition had been brought three years after an outline plan had been approved, and three years was not an unreasonable period for the implementation of a plan. The long period of time between the original expropriation and the approval of the plan did not demonstrate that there had been a departure from the purpose of the expropriation. It was right that the Court should take into account the harm done to the right to property, and there was a need to balance this right with the needs of the public. In this case, where the area of the plan included many parcels of land, and the aim was to concentrate ownership and market the area as one unit in order to plan effectively and construct new development within a reasonable time, the plan was in the best interests of the area.

Nevertheless, the decision had the narrowest of margins and, in a significant minority opinion, Judge Dorner stressed the harm done to the fundamental right to property enshrined in the Basic Law: Human Dignity and Liberty, and said that the burden was on the state to persuade the Court that expropriation did not contradict this principle, which as a basic right should be interpreted narrowly. Compensation, he said, was not the same: 'The basic element of the right to property is ownership itself, as distinct from the right to compensation. It is the expropriation itself which harms the ownership. Compensation does not redress the harm itself.'

Judge Dorner went on to say that the practice of expropriating property for one purpose and later using it for another went against the law and contradicted the principle that the exercise of governmental power should not be interpreted so as to harm basic rights. The state, therefore, should be forced to prove that the right to property under the Basic Law had not been infringed. The fact that the purpose of the expropriation order had not been fulfilled in thirty years was enough to place a burden on the state to demonstrate that the original purpose for which the expropriation was announced still existed.

In the third of the three major cases under the Public Purposes Ordinance since 1992, the High Court departed from the majority in Nusseibeh. In its judgment of 13 February 2001 in the case of Kersek, the Court held that if the public purpose on which an order for expropriation was based ceases to exist, the land must be returned to its original owner.[99] In the early 1950s, the Minister of Finance had declared his intention to expropriate land belonging to the petitioner in the Hadera area, for the purposes of an army training area. In 1966 the land was transferred into state ownership. In 1993, the government decided to evacuate the army and turn the land over to the Ministry of Housing to build high-rise public housing and other projects on the land. The applicants appealed to the Court, asking for the land to be returned since the original purpose for which it had been expropriated was no longer applicable. The Court agreed, in principle, that where the original reason for an expropriation no longer existed, the land should be returned to its owner. Giving the leading judgment, Judge Heishin gave two main bases for the new ruling. First, he said that although previous decisions of the High Court on this issue had assumed that the expropriation severs the link between the original owner and the land, the Ordinance itself does not make such a provision, and the Court now reversed its ruling on this point. This 'link doctrine' rested on the need for there to be a connection between the law governing the expropriation itself, and the law applicable after the expropriation has taken place, which governs the legal status of the land at that point. The process of expropriation itself, according to the Court, should be proportional. In order to pass this test, the planned expropriation must meet three conditions: there must be a specific and defined public purpose; a link between the said purpose and the land in question; and the expropriation must be needed in order to achieve the said purpose.

The crucial point was that these conditions should not have to be met only at the point the expropriation takes place, but they must also continue to be met for the entire life of the period of expropriation, however long that may be. This is because the expropriation does not sever the link between the owner of the land and the land itself. An individual whose land is expropriated continues to have a link with his property even after its expropriation. Consequently, a public authority may not simply expropriate land on a whim and later alter the basis for doing so; it remains subject to the specific public purpose for which the land was acquired in the first place. It is on the basis of the exercise of the powers under the Ordinance alone that the land has passed into public ownership. If the reason for the expropriation no longer exists, the public authority must either return the land to its original owners, or pay compensation as appropriate. The second basis for the decision was fundamental principles of law, particularly the duty to protect individual property rights, which had been strengthened in the Basic Law: Human Dignity. The Basic Law, according to Heishin, imposes on the Court a duty to examine in a new way any laws that might harm the right to property. Finally, the Court considered the implications of the change in the law implicitly in the ruling. Would it be prospective only, or should it apply also to land expropriated in the past but where the public purpose ceases to exist at some point in the future? Or, should it be retroactive such that the new arrangements would apply even to expropriations of the past where the original public purpose ceased to exist in the past? This question, Heishin said, raised a number of important issues on which the Court had heard no argument. The Court therefore invited representations on this point.[99]

The ruling in Kersek, in which the applicant was Jewish, could theoretically have enormous implications for the Palestinians who have lost land due to expropriation in Israel, and the High Court judges, in inviting further argument on the temporal application of the ruling, were clearly aware of this. There are enormous areas of land that have been expropriated from the Palestinians since the 1950s, not only under the Public Purposes Ordinance but also under emergency legislation such as the Emergency Land Requisition (Regulation) Law 1949 or the Emergency Regulations (Security Zones) Law 1949. In many instances the land was expropriated purportedly for one purpose, sometimes by its very nature a temporary purpose such as the conduct of hostilities (as in the case of Iqrit and Bir'im) and later used for a quite different purpose such as the building of new settlements. Or will Saliba Makhul, whose land was expropriated purportedly for the relocation of Palestinian residents of Acre and subsequently used for settling new Jewish immigrants, now be able to return to the Court and ask for the return of his land? The Court, as well as asking for argument from the parties on the question of the temporal application of its ruling, also appealed to the legislature to address the issue.

Legislation permitting expropriation of land in the public interest exists in most states and has been used, sometimes on a large scale. However, international standards have developed arising out of this experience that aim to protect individuals and groups from the arbitrary use of such powers by the state.[100] One such protection is the prohibition on discrimination, which should operate to ensure that powers to expropriate property in the public interest are not used to the detriment of one group in society, including a national group. There is clearly cause for concern that this prohibition has been violated by Israel in its application of the Public Purposes Ordinance in the Palestinian sector. Another is the prohibition on arbitrary interference with a person's enjoyment of their property, and tests that have developed such as the European Court of Human Rights' 'fair balance' test, which aims to balance the fundamental right of the individual to peaceful enjoyment of property against the power of the state to deprive and control property in the public interest. The test, which also includes a proportionality element, might involve consideration of factors such as the objectives of any interference with property rights, whether there is any alternative, and whether adequate compensation has been paid.[101] If such a test were to be applied to Israel's use of the Public Purposes Ordinance in relation to Palestinian landowners, there is serious reason to believe Israel would fail the test in all respects.

The expropriation of land from one community to benefit another cannot be viewed as expropriation in the public interest. In reality, the application of the Public Purposes Ordinance in Israel has been used as a further convenient method of transferring land from Palestinian to Jewish hands.

Notes

1. This figure is based on the upper estimate of 800,000 representing the number of Palestinians who became refugees as a result of the 1948 war (see Chapter 1, note 9), plus around a quarter of the 150,000 Palestinians who remained and became Israeli citizens, who became internal refugees.

2. More detailed accounts of Zionist land purchases before 1948 can be found in works such as Lehn and Davis on the JNF (1988), Stein (1984), various works by Abraham Granott (who also used the name Granovsky), who held senior office in the JNF from 1919 until his death in 1962, and the Palestinian expert Sami Hadawi, and official documents from the time such as the reports of the British official Hope Simpson.

3. The decision to establish the Fund was taken at the Fifth Zionist Congress held in Basle in 1901, and it became active immediately. In 1907 it attained formal legal status by registering in the UK; Lehn (1974: 75–82).

4. The Zionist organizations were able to exploit the weakness of the

Palestinian rural economy in the early part of the twentieth century, and social and political factors such as the accumulation of land in the hands of large landowners who lived abroad. But researchers disagree on the degree of significance of such factors.

5. Article 22 of the Covenant of the League of Nations of 28 June 1919 provided the legal basis for the Mandate system. Britain was awarded a Mandate over Palestine at the meeting for the purpose of ratifying decisions made at the Versailles Peace Treaty, held in San Remo, Italy, on 24 April 1920. The Mandate was confirmed by the Council of the League of Nations on 24 July 1922, and came into operation in September 1923.

6. Balfour Declaration, 2 November 1917.

7. The Zionists worked hard to persuade the Mandate administration to make state lands available to them, though they were not as successful as they would have liked. One of the Zionist agencies, the Palestine Land Development Company, was granted a concession over land in the Huleh Valley in 1934, later transferred to the JNF. In Beisan, the Zionists failed to obtain direct concessions over state land but succeeded in acquiring land from Palestinian farmers who had been allocated state land under an Agreement of 1921 but had no means to pay for it. See Givati (1981: 76); and Stein (1984: 59–64 and 199–202). By 1947, state land leased to Jews constituted only 11 per cent of all land in Jewish possession at the time and the remainder was purchased; Tyler (2001: 207). Granott maintains that by 1947, the Jews had obtained 181,000 dunams in concessions from the Palestine government; Granott (1952: 278).

8. The British Mandate authorities were sometimes complicit in this trend towards the division of the area into Arab and Jewish sectors, for instance allowing Palestinian peasants who had lost their land to be resettled in areas dominated by Palestinians rather than in those areas where Jewish land holdings were concentrated; see Stein (1984).

9. On the lack of reliable statistics on the number of landless Palestinians, see Kamen (1991: 28 and 96).

10. Sami Hadawi puts Jewish ownership at 5.67 per cent of the land in May 1948 (Hadawi 1963: 18). Abraham Granott claimed Jews owned 6.6 per cent of land in 1948 (Granott 1956: 28).

11. Hadawi (1963: 18), citing the Palestine government.

12. This includes the inhabitants of the Little Triangle, which was annexed to Israel under the Rhodes Agreement.

13. Jewish agricultural colonies neighbouring Palestinian villages eagerly seized the land of the refugees and the hasty measures taken by the government, first temporary then permanent, to regulate what happened to this land were apparently aimed at imposing some order on the situation and making central government retain control; see Jiryis (1976: 80–1).

14. United Nations General Assembly Resolution 181(II) of 29 November 1947, para. 8, Ch. 2.

15. United Nations General Assembly Resolution 194 of 11 December 1948, Article 11.

16. LSI, Vol. 4, p. 68. Prior to this, ad hoc arrangements had been made to

supervise Palestinian property falling into Israeli hands, such as a Committee for Arab Property in the Villages established by the Haganah in March 1948, and Custodians for Arab Property in Haifa and Jaffa appointed in July 1948. In June 1948 the Abandoned Areas Ordinance was enacted by the Provisional Council of State; LSI, Vol. 1, p. 25.

17. According to section 4(a)(2), 'every right an absentee had in any property shall pass automatically to the Custodian at the time of the vesting of the property; and the status of the Custodian shall be the same as was that of the owner of the property'.

18. This estimate is based largely on research citing the numbers given help by UNRWA, the United Nations agency for Palestinian refugees, in the 1950s.

19. One exception was the Palestinian residents of East Jerusalem; when Israel annexed East Jerusalem in 1967 it decided that property of its inhabitants would not be considered absentee property unless its owners left Jerusalem; ILA (1967–68: 232) (in Hebrew). Also see below regarding the circumstances in which property could be retrieved from the Custodian.

20. Article VI.6 of the Armistice Agreement signed between Israel and Jordan on 3 April 1949 provided that: 'Wherever villages may be affected by the establishment of the Armistice Demarcation Line provided for in paragraph 2 of this article, the inhabitants of such villages shall be entitled to maintain, and shall be protected in, their full rights of residence, property and freedom.'

21. The Custodian of Absentee Property v. Samarah and Others, HC 25/55, 145/55 and 148/55, PD 10, p. 1825. Also Eliyosef v. the Military Governor of 'Ara, HC 225/53, PD 8, p. 341.

22. For instance in the case of Awadallah, being handled by the Abu Hussein Law Office in Um El Fahem, a person who tried to sell his land in 1999 received official notification that since he had inherited the land in 1966 from his father, who was in Jordan and an absentee, the land was absentee property.

23. Mohammed Masri v. Masri and Others and the Custodian of Absentee Property, case 1295, Decision of the District Court of Haifa, 10 August 1999. Upholding the Custodian of Absentee Property's claim to part of a plot of land, the Court said it was the fact that the statutory criteria for being an absentee were fulfilled, and not whether a certificate under section 30 of the Absentee Property Law had been issued, that determined a person's status as an absentee.

24. Implementation Law of the Peace Agreement (Treaty) between Israel and the Hashemite Kingdom of Jordan, Section 6, Law no. 1503 of 10 February 1995, Book of Laws, 1995, p. 110.

25. The Abu Hussein Law Office in Um El Fahem is handling a case in which a Palestinian in Jordan was registered in the Land Registry as an absentee in November 2000, directly flouting the Peace Treaty with Jordan.

26. Habab v. the Custodian of Absentee Property, HC 58/54, PD 10(1), p. 912, cited in Adalah (2001: 41, note 92).

27. The Development Authority (Transfer of Property) Law of 1950; LSI, Vol. 4, p. 151.

28. The Absentees' Property (Compensation) Law 1973; LSI, Vol. 27, p. 176. The law allows Israeli residents to apply for compensation if they were an owner or lessee of absentee property.

29. In practice, if a person is ready to accept compensation, the case is usually dealt with not under the 1973 law but by ordinary contract for sale. A contract is arranged, often with the JNF or a front company established by it, and the vendors are not always aware of the real identity of the purchaser. These companies are known to seek out Palestinians in exile, such as in Latin America, and to offer to purchase their 'absentee' property. There is also evidence of efforts to persuade Palestinians who remained in the new State of Israel after 1948 to leave. The Abu Hussein Law Office is instructed by a Palestinian family who in 1956 were persuaded to leave and told that the compensation would be waiting at the border for them to collect on their way out. At the last moment, the family changed its mind and decided to remain. Thirty years later, they discovered that the land had been transferred into the name of the state and they are now taking steps to retrieve it.

30. Interviews with the Mayor of Kaukab, Ahmed Haj, and other village leaders, November 1994.

31. This phenomenon and its consequences are explored in more detail in Chapter 6.

32. Yvonne Cokrin v. Committee constituted under s.29 of the Absentees' Property Law 1950, HC 518/79, judgment of 13 September 1979, PD 32(2), p. 326.

33. Shukri Nicola and Others v. Custodian of Absentees' Property and Others, HC 721/79, judgment of 19 June 1980, PD 34(4), p. 201.

34. In the case of Nicola, the applicants came to the Court in 1979 to challenge decisions of the Custodian in 1955 and 1963. The High Court said they should have asserted their rights sooner and the Custodian was not obliged to reconsider the matter after a lapse of sixteen years.

35. Eid Hussein Tabari v. Custodian of Absentee Property, HC 261/90. The case related to land in the centre of Tiberias which the claimant, an internal refugee, had lost to the Custodian in 1956.

36. Israeli State Comptroller's Report, No. 41 (1990), covering the financial year 1989 (in Hebrew).

37. Adalah had requested this information from the Custodian in July 1998, who had refused in August 1998. In January 1999, Adalah began asking the Attorney General to order the Custodian to release the information, on the grounds that it was information that should be publicly available and the Custodian had a legal duty to release it. The Attorney General rejected the request on the grounds that it might damage Israel's foreign relations, and that it would require an exorbitant amount of time and resources to comply with the request; *Adalah News Update*, 28 January 2002.

38. UN Declaration on the Elimination of All Forms of Intolerance and of Discrimination Based on Religion or Belief, proclaimed by General Assembly Resolution 36/55 of 25 November 1981, Article 6.

39. Among mosques damaged or destroyed are those at Tiberias, Lod,

Caesaria and Seedna Ali, and damaged graveyards include Lajon, Haifa and Blad Al Sheikh, in which the Palestinian religious populist leader Sheikh Izzadeen Al Qasam is buried.

40. The Arabic word *waqf* means endowment or gift made to individuals or institutions. *Waqfs* have played an important role in the history of Muslim society and in the development of Middle Eastern states. Although they are not explicitly mentioned in the Qur'an, their creation was inspired by Qur'anic passages; Dumper (1994: 1 and 8).

41. Dumper (1994: 8–14) explains the reasons for so much property being endowed to *Waqfs* during the late Ottoman Empire, including the desire of the elites to avoid confiscation by the state or division on inheritance.

42. Knesset Reports, Fourth Session, Vol. 42, p. 1143 (in Hebrew).

43. Yacoub Hassuneh v. Custodian for Absentees' Property, 1952, HC 332/52, PD 6, p. 1198, and Boulos Boulos v. Minister of Development, 1955, HC 69/55, PD 10, p. 673.

44. Absentees' Property (Amendment No. 3) (Release and Use of Endowment Property) Law 1965; LSI, Vol. 19, p. 55, new section 1A.

45. Under the Development Authority (Transfer of Property) Law of 1950.

46. LSI, Vol. 7, p. 43.

47. Absentees' Property (Amendment No. 3) (Release and Use of Endowment Property) Law 1965, section 29B.

48. For instance *Kul El Arab* weekly newspaper (in Arabic) on 10 December 1993 reported that a housing corporation in Jaffa began construction work on a cemetery site ignoring a court order that work should only take place in the presence of an Islamic official; *Al-Ittihad* newspaper (in Arabic) reported on 3 January 1995 that a cemetery of the Bedouin Azazme tribe in the Naqab had been disrupted by construction of a road.

49. The Land Law 1969, which aimed to sweep away the Ottoman categories of land tenure, nevertheless did not formally abolish the category of *Waqf* property, probably because the annexation of East Jerusalem in 1967 had brought under Israeli control many important Muslim *Waqfs* and it was thought to be politically unacceptable to abolish the *Waqfs*. The traditional *Waqf* characteristics did continue to exist in East Jerusalem: *Waqf* property in East Jerusalem was specifically exempted from the Absentees' Property Law.

50. *Al-Ittihad*, 19 December 2000, reported that Majd Al-Krum local council had been approached with such a request and had refused to comply; an ILA spokesperson was quoted as saying this was merely a change in registration status of the land to reflect what had already occurred in 1950 and did not represent a new confiscation. Other local newspapers from the same period reported that other Arab local councils had also been approached.

51. For example the UN Declaration on the Elimination of All Forms of Intolerance and of Discrimination Based on Religion or Belief.

52. In 1991, a Trust Committee of the Islamic *Waqf* appealed to the High Court against implementation of a contract for the sale of a plot of land in a Jaffa cemetery, on the grounds that the requirement to obtain permission of the religious court had not been met (Trust Committee for the Islamic *Waqf*

Properties v. Usi Investment Company Ltd and Others, Civil Appeal 3997/91, PD49[3], p. 766). The Court refused to intervene. In 1995, a Catholic Church charity went to court seeking an order directing a bishop to disclose financial information regarding Church property. They based their application on the law of trusts, arguing that they were entitled to this information as beneficiaries. They suspected corruption in the administration of the Church properties and sales to the JNF, housing corporations and the ILA. The High Court confirmed the Haifa District Court's refusal to consider the case, holding that the religious courts had sole jurisdiction over such matters according to laws dating from the Mandate period, and that trust law did not apply (Galilee Sons Non-Profit Association and Others v. Bishop Maximus Salon and the Catholic Church, Civil Appeal 544/95, Takdin, 1997, 3,772). In both cases, the High Court chose not to apply principles of legal control and transparency as regards public bodies that it could have invoked to scrutinize the dealings.

53. The period of military rule and the ways in which it was exploited as a pretext for seizing Palestinian land is well documented in Jiryis (1976) and Nakkara (1985).

54. *Official Gazette*, No. 1442, Supp. 2, 1945, p. 1058

55. For instance, Sabri Jiryis says that this law was used to prevent the inhabitants of twelve villages in the Galilee from returning (Jiryis 1976: 89–90).

56. Prime Minister Ben Gurion to the Knesset on 20 February 1963, cited in Quigley (1990: 107).

57. Schedule to the Emergency Regulations (Security Zones) (Extension of Validity) Law 1949; LSI, Vol. 3, p. 56. These regulations were extended regularly until 1972.

58. Schedule to the Emergency Regulations (Cultivation of Waste Lands) (Extension of Validity) Ordinance No. 36 of 1949, LSI, Vol. 2, p. 70. These regulations were repealed in 1984.

59. LSI, Vol. 4, p. 3.

60. Knesset Debates, November 1953; Knesset Reports, Vol. 15, p. 336 (in Hebrew).

61. *Palestine Gazette*, no. 1305, 10 February 1943, Supp. 1, p. 55.

62. LSI, Vol. 7, p. 28.

63. LSI, Vol. 7, p. 43.

64. Compensation was to be based on the value of the land in 1950, which due to devaluation in the currency and other factors made the sums payable derisory. The same guidelines were used for calculating compensation under the Absentees' Property Law; see Jiryis (1976: 127).

65. Since 1 April 1993 compensation was calculated at 1.5 per cent interest plus inflation. By the end of 2000, a total of 55,474 dunams of land had been given in compensation.

66. In the year 2000, fifty-two claims relating to 248 dunams of land were dealt with. From 1967, official figures include Jerusalem, annexed by Israel in that year.

67. Younis v. Minister of Finance, HC 5/54, PD 8, 1954, p. 314, analysed in Nakkara (1985).

68. Yusef Abed Alfateh and Others v. Minister of Defence and Military Commander of Um El Fahem, HC 92/57, PD 11, p. 1524. The petitioners also asked for the cancelling of the order, but the Supreme Court denied this request since the declaration of the military areas was made legally.

69. For example, letter of 7 January 1990 from the Minister of Defence to the Mukhtar of the village of Mu-awya confirming arrangements for villagers to use land in Military Training Areas 105 and 109 for grazing at certain times (in Hebrew).

70. Although about 500 people were injured, many of whom were left with long-term disabilities, the Attorney General refused to investigate police behaviour on the grounds that the identity of the police units concerned was unknown.

71. According to the terms of the agreement, one area would no longer be within the military area and a second area would continue to be used as a military area for fifteen years, but its owners may cultivate it with the permission of the army.

72. The first order, issued in 1995, covered the villages of Qatamat Al-Mitaher and Mazra'a; the second, issued in May 2001, covered Kahelah, Al Bat and Sao'e. The total population of the five Bedouin villages is 4,600.

73. Judgment of the High Court of Justice of 31 July 1951, HC 64/51, translated in the *Palestine Yearbook of International Law*, Vol. II, 1985, p. 121.

74. HC 141/81, in ibid., p. 129.

75. Government Decision 2071 of 7 November 1993.

76. Report of the Committee, 24 December 1995 (in Hebrew).

77. The people of Iqrit had owned a total of 12,500 dunams, and of Bir'im, 16,000 dunams, before they were evacuated.

78. For example, Article 4 of the ICCPR of 1966 provides: 'In time of public emergency which threatens the life of the nation and the existence of which is officially proclaimed, the States Parties to the present Covenant may take measures derogating from their obligations under the present Covenant to the extent strictly required by the exigencies of the situation, provided that such measures are not inconsistent with their other obligations under international law and do not involve discrimination solely on the ground of race, colour, sex, language, religion or social origin.' A state of emergency was proclaimed in Israel in May 1948 and has remained in force ever since. So, for example, when becoming party to the ICCPR in 1991 Israel declared a derogation of Article 9 of the Covenant.

79. The perceived dangers of having a stretch of land from Nazareth to the northern border where Jews were in a minority included creating a potential security threat and increasing the likelihood that the area would be claimed by the Arab states; Jiryis (1976: 104–11).

80. This is the equivalent of the power of compulsory purchase in the UK or the right of eminent domain in the USA.

81. Interview with the Mayor of Ein Mahil, Ahmed Abu Leyl, at the local council, July 1990.

82. Interview with the Reverend Shehadi Shehadi, former chair of the National Committee for the Defence of Arab Land, 20 March 1990. The same point was made by many other Palestinian community leaders.

83. The report does not specify how much of the private land was owned by Arabs, but perhaps around half privately owned land in the state is Arab owned.

84. This plan will be discussed further in Chapter 7.

85. See Chapter 6, where obstacles to Palestinians obtaining access to state land are elaborated.

86. The Negev Land Acquisition (Peace Treaty with Egypt) Law 1980; LSI, Vol. 34, p. 190.

87. Nevertheless, the scheme set out in the 1980 law has also been used as the basis for calculating compensation due to Bedouin when they move to the urban townships as part of the government's relocation plan for the Bedouin.

88. State Road of Israel Law 1994, Book of Laws, no. 1493 of 20 December 1994, p. 38 (in Hebrew). The law provides for a committee to be established to determine levels of compensation.

89. In the Galilee, the road would cut off farmers of seven villages from their land, and would use thousands of dunams in the fertile Batof valley belonging to Palestinians from the towns of Arabah and Sakhnin. See for example Alternative Information Center (1997: 26).

90. Sikkuy, <www.sikkuy.org.il>.

91. For an excellent analysis of the cases see Dakwar (2000: 14).

92. The Nazareth Committee for the Protection of Expropriated Lands v. Ministry of Finance and Others, HC 30/55, PD 9(3), p. 1261.

93. See the discussion of Israel's approach to discrimination and a comparison with international standards in the previous chapter.

94. Ahmad Suliman Kassem and Others v. Minister of Finance and Others, HC 181/57, PD 12(4), p. 1986.

95. Klems v. Tel Aviv Local Planning and Building Commission, HC 75/57, cited in Gouldman (1966: 71).

96. Saliba Makhul v. Minister of Finance and the ILA, HC 2739/95, PD 50(1), p. 309.

97. HC 4466/94, PD 49(4), p. 68.

98. Kersek and Others v. State of Israel, the ILA and Others, HC 2390/96, PD 55(2), p. 625.

99. When the parties did not submit further pleadings on this point, the Court postponed consideration of the matter for one year.

100. These standards are developed in the previous chapter.

101. This test was first elaborated in the case of Sporrong and Lonnroth v. Sweden, European Court of Human Rights, 1982, 5EHRR 35, pp. 52–4.

CHAPTER 4

Dispossession through Denial of Palestinian Land Rights, and Forced Eviction of Bedouin in the Naqab[1]

§ THE seizure and expropriation of Palestinian land described in the previous chapter brought enormous areas of land under the control of the state, including the land of the refugees and internally displaced. But when the dust had settled after the war and the large-scale seizures of Palestinian land that took place between 1948 and the mid-1950s, the Israeli government believed that the surviving Palestinian communities still retained possession of too much land. The Public Purposes Ordinance was one instrument used to take over some of this land, and thousands of dunams were expropriated including large blocks in 1957 and 1964 for the building of new cities such as Upper Nazareth, Ma'alot and Karmiel, part of a policy to 'Judaize' the Galilee. At the same time, Israel began to exploit another legal process, namely that for determining rights over land, known as the settlement of title process.[2] When Israel was established in 1948 a process aimed at surveying all land and registering rights that had been initiated by the British Mandate administration had not yet been completed. Israel exploited this situation to the full, restarting settlement of title operations, amending legislation and applying laws and procedures with the single-minded purpose of registering as much land as possible in the name of the state. Palestinian landowners, disadvantaged by Israel's manipulation of the settlement of title process, lost many of these battles. This process took place mainly during the late 1950s and through the 1960s but continues in some areas to the present day.

Particularly egregious is the way in which the land rights of the Palestinian Bedouin in the Naqab have been dealt with. Israel is avoiding settling the thousands of land claims submitted by the Bedouin, instead settling Jews on the disputed land and putting enormous pressure on the Bedouin to give up their land claims and resettle in urban townships. The Bedouin community rejects this policy, and almost half of them have resisted by continuing to live in 'unrecognized' communities in harsh conditions, without basic amenities and services. This chapter deals with the way in which Israel has manipulated the settlement of title process and how in the Naqab this has gone hand-in-hand with policies aimed at forced eviction and relocation of the Palestinian Bedouin. Israel used a number of creative devices in order to achieve its goals in the settlement of title process, but was assisted in part by the nature of the land regime it inherited.

The pre-1948 land regime

Prior to 1948, the land regime in Palestine was governed by Ottoman law, as modified by the British Mandate administration. The principal rules of Ottoman land law were, following reforms in the mid-nineteenth century, contained in the Land Code of 1858 and the Civil Code (*Mejelle*) of 1869. The main objectives of these reforms were to award individual land rights, protect the peasant population and stabilize existing patterns of possession, while at the same time maintaining the role of the state and centralizing its power (Owen 2000: xiix–vii). According to these rules, all land was classified as one of five different categories, and legal interests in land were to be defined and recorded. In practice, it was not always clear under which category a plot of land fell and many rights in land, acquired by long possession and use, were not formally registered. But even where Palestinians did not have formal legal title, the state's title to much land was already considered merely nominal and the land actually belonged to Palestinians through long use and possession, or was communal land held in trust for the inhabitants of the Arab villages and used by them for generations (Hadawi 1963: 18–23; Shehadi 1993: 21). In the Naqab Desert, Palestinian Bedouin tribes laid claim to large areas of cultivable and other land. It was not considered necessary for Palestinians to prove title of specific pieces of land since they had collective historical rights over the vast majority of the land of Palestine. But such uncertainty opened the way for Israel to manipulate the system, denying the existence of some Palestinian rights over land, and sweeping aside others through legislation. A number of characteristics of the pre-1948 land regime made Palestinian landholders particularly vulnerable in such a context:

- the nature of the Ottoman land regime
- the fact that most legal interests in land were not formally registered
- the importance of possession and use, as opposed to formal registration, in acquiring rights over land

- changes to the land regime introduced by the British Mandate administration.

The nature of the Ottoman land regime Very few possessors of land in Ottoman Palestine held full formal ownership rights. Ottoman land law was originally based on the idea that upon conquering an area, all of the land came under the Sultan's fiefdom and he was free to grant rights in that land as he chose.[3] Following Ottoman land reforms, all land was divided into five categories, each governed by different rules. The five categories were *Mulk, Waqf, Miri, Mewat* and *Matruka*. Of these, the sovereign retained a legal interest in all but two types: *Mulk* and *Waqf*. *Mulk* was absolute ownership, with rights of possession, use and disposition assigned to the owner. In Palestine, relatively little land was *Mulk* other than in built-up areas within towns and villages. *Waqf* property was dedicated to Islamic trusts for the benefit of specific groups or the community as a whole.[4]

The other three categories of land – *Miri, Mewat* and *Matruka* – made up the majority of land in Palestine. In these categories the sovereign retained a legal interest, the *Raqabe*, or ultimate ownership. *Miri* was land over which a temporary right had been granted to use it for the purpose of cultivation, pasture, meadow or woodland, resembling leasehold rights. Most importantly, someone who used and cultivated a piece of land for ten years continuously (the prescription period) was then entitled to ask for that land to be registered in his name. Rights in *Miri* land could be inherited according to certain rules. Such rights could also be assigned to others, which allowed for the accumulation of large estates in the hands of wealthy landowners, worked by tenant farmers. Only where there was no heir would the land become *Mahlul*, or vacant, and would revert to the state which could then make a new grant. Under Ottoman rule, most agricultural land in Palestine fell in this category. Theoretically, a *Miri* holder could exercise only such rights as were accorded under the terms of the grant. However, in reality, the only interests comprised in the *Raqabe* were the ultimate reversion and the financial interest: fees and taxes. The grantee was largely free to use and transfer his land as he pleased. Thus the nature of the interest retained by the sovereign in *Miri* land was largely hypothetical and nominal, and diminished with time (Shehadi 1993: 21).

The second category of land in which the Sultan retained a legal interest, *Mewat*, literally meaning 'dead', was undeveloped or unused land not owned or possessed by anybody that was situated at least one and a half miles from inhabited areas, 'at such a distance from towns and villages from which a human voice cannot be heard at the nearest inhabited place'.[5] *Mewat* included mountainous or rocky areas considered not usable, but also land in the vicinity of a village that was potentially cultivable but had not yet been developed and brought under cultivation.

The third category was *Matruka*. This was land intended ('left') for public benefit, including land assigned for general public use, such as roads and markets, or for the use of inhabitants of a particular area, such as common pasture.[6] Such land formed an essential part of Palestinian rural life and economy, for grazing flocks, as a source of wood, and other purposes. It could not be bought or sold and individuals could not acquire rights over it. Although technically the *Raqabe* of such land remained with the sovereign, in practice such land was not regarded as being under the sovereign's actual control. This view is supported by the fact that *Matruka* land was not included in the Mandate authorities' definition of public land, which was defined as land subject to the control of the government.[7]

The ultimate ownership of the sovereign (*Raqabe*) had a different meaning in each category. As regards *Miri* and *Matruka* land, *Raqabe* had come to mean little more than sovereignty, a concept of supreme authority over a territory that does not, in itself, confer ownership in the sense of legal tenure over land within the territory.[8] The individual right, in the case of *Miri,* and the collective right, in the case of *Matruka*, to possession and occupation, went to the possessor. As regards *Mewat*, the state retained the right to assign the land.

Thus, while the reality was that possession and use were the most important factors in determining interests in land, the remnants of the formal legal interest of the sovereign still remained and this precarious situation was exploited by Israel as a pretext for claiming land for the state.

The fact that most legal interests in land were not formally regis-tered Systems for the formal registration of interests in *Mulk* and *Miri* land existed during the Ottoman period, and title deeds were issued. By the time Ottoman rule ended in Palestine, however, most land rights were still not registered. The British Mandate administration set out to reform the system for settlement of title and registration of legal interests in land. While maps had been prepared, no comprehensive cadastral survey of the area had ever been carried out. The Ottoman system of land registration had been confusing, inaccurate and incomplete, and, on leaving, the Ottoman authorities had removed many of the registers and records. The British Mandate administration decided to design a new system, announcing in 1920 that every transaction in land must be registered. In 1922 it established a Department of Lands to ascertain, register and record all state lands (Goadby and Doukhan 1935: 299).

The objectives of land settlement were: 'The examination of rights to land and the solution of disputes about the ownership, boundaries, category and other registrable rights in land, its cadastral survey for the purpose, and the eventual recording of the rights in Land Registers' (Anglo-American Committee of Inquiry 1946: 234).

Sir Ernest Dowson, a British expert in land surveying, was invited to advise on reform and decided to adopt the Australian Torrens system of settlement and registration of property rights. The Torrens system involved the topographical surveying and mapping of land, followed by its subdivision into blocks and parcels, and the recording of rights in these blocks and parcels in the Land Registry. This resulted in a more accurate and precise definition of parcels of land. Registration of rights in the Land Registry would now be regarded as conclusive evidence of their existence, cancelling all other rights and taking precedence over all contradictory claims, except where fraud or omission were proved.

A process for determination of rights over land, 'settlement of title', was established. First the High Commissioner would declare an area to be under settlement. A Settlement Officer would invite claims and then post a Schedule of Claims showing claims that had been submitted including ownership and all other rights and interests in the land. The Settlement Officer then investigated claims, heard evidence and settled them publicly. His function was therefore both an administrative and a judicial one. He had the option to refer legal questions to the Property Court. State interests in land could be considered even where the government had not submitted a claim, and land over which no claim was proved would be registered as state land. Government-owned land intended for public use, or *Matruka* land allocated for the use of a village, could be registered in the name of the local council. However, only three Arab localities had local councils before 1948, with the result that the others lost the opportunity of preserving land around the village for the use of the community.

It seems that Jewish communities were the principal beneficiaries of the implementation of the system in its early days (Gavish 1990: 185).[9] Dowson, himself a supporter of the Zionist colonization, encouraged the official adoption of the land-holding books kept by the Zionist colonies, and in 1926 persuaded the administration to order that all unofficial books should be turned over to the Land Registrar.[10] From the time the surveying process was begun in 1920 until 1946, some 35 per cent of Mandatory Palestine was measured and mapped, and in

1947 the British Mandate administration published a map summarizing the outcome. The map was prepared for the special inquiry committee of the UN, which recommended the division of Palestine into two independent states, one Arab and one Jewish, a recommendation that was accepted by the UN General Assembly (Gavish 1992: 202). Most of the land that had been surveyed fell into the part proposed for the Jewish state. This raises important questions about the relationship between the mapping process and the UN's partition plan.

Following on from the mapping process, by 1948 settlement of title operations had been completed in some 20 per cent of the area (ibid.; Oded 1964: 10, 13). The principle that rights and interests in land were to be proved and registered on an individual basis had been established.

The importance of possession and use, as opposed to formal registration, in acquiring rights over land Ownership can be viewed as a de jure relationship between a person and property, and is a question of law; the law gives certain rights to those able to prove ownership, such as the power to use and dispose of the land. Possession, on the other hand, is de facto and the law may recognize differing weight and rights attaching to it. A person may lose control and possession over land without losing ownership itself. Conversely, a person may have possession of land but that possession might not be recognized as conferring ownership. In the Ottoman land system, rights over land could be acquired in different ways, according to the rules governing the different categories of land. Article 78 of the Ottoman Land Code allowed a person to acquire *Miri* land by implied grant, where he or she possessed and cultivated it unchallenged for an uninterrupted period of at least ten years, the prescription period. After this period had elapsed that person would become entitled to be issued with a title deed. His right to continue to possess the land, however, did not depend on obtaining a title deed (Goadby and Doukhan 1935: 266). Despite Ottoman efforts, most *Miri* owners did not obtain title deeds.

As for *Mewat* land, the rule was that a person who 'revived' *Mewat* land by cultivating it could thereby transform the land into *Miri*. A person who cultivated land with prior consent would be entitled to a title deed automatically and without payment. A person who cultivated without permission was not entitled to a title deed but might, upon payment, be granted one. The prescription rules did not apply to *Mewat* land.

In the case of both *Miri* and *Mewat*, then, possession and use gave rise to rights. It was relatively easy to 'revive' *Mewat* land by cultivating it and thereby transform it into *Miri,* and to acquire rights over land that was already *Miri* by long use on the basis of the prescription rules. The fact that *Miri* conferred the strongest rights on the possessor was a reflection of a predominantly agricultural society: if land was cultivable, it was *Miri*; if barren land was made cultivable (revived or improved), it could become *Miri*. The principle of possessory title, which gives a possessor the right to be presumed owner until a better claim is asserted, applied in practice through the prescription laws. Although formally *Matruka* rights could only arise from grant by the state, in practice this too was often presumed from use (Anglo-American Committee of Inquiry 1946: 230–2). Most importantly, as already mentioned, there was a presumption that lands surrounding a village were in the patrimony of the local population.

The fact that the system was based largely on possession and use rather than formal registration, however, made it vulnerable to Israeli manipulation since it was dependent on proof of possession and use. When Israel took over the land system it acted to ensure that the rules were weighted heavily against those trying to prove possession.

Changes to the land regime introduced by the British Mandate administration The British Mandate administration had started a process designed to regulate and limit the acquisition of rights over state land, aimed at improving efficiency and certainty. The Mahlul Land Ordinance of 1920 and Mewat Land Ordinance of 1921 aimed to prevent farmers from encroaching on these two categories of land without obtaining permission, and to put a stop to the practice of bringing land under cultivation and acquiring title without permission. The Mewat Land Ordinance stated that any person who had revived *Mewat* land without permission must apply for a title deed within two months or lose his right to acquire the land. Nevertheless, in practice the Mandate authorities tended to recognize rights to *Mewat* land even where a person in possession had not applied for a title deed within the required period (Goadby and Doukhan 1935: 47). In fact, the Mandate authorities gave contradictory messages in terms of the nature of the rights they were willing to recognize, sometimes allowing custom to prevail and at other times insisting on strict adherence to the rules. But in general, the authorities were not interested in securing the rights of the state over land in order to attain the right to allocate it, as Israel later was; rather they were guided by concerns and policy objectives, that shifted over time, whether to give farmers security of tenure in order to promote land development or to avoid social and political problems caused by landlessness (Bunton 2000: 147–9).

The changes brought in under the British Mandate were not hugely significant at the time. They represented moves towards a more formal system of regulating possession of land, the main purpose of which was not to dispossess Palestinians but to introduce greater order and certainty. But they had certain implications for the future in that they assisted Israel to impose an even more rigid system.

Typical Palestinian land-use patterns prior to 1948

In a typical Palestinian village the built-up area would be *Mulk*, the farmland around it would be *Miri*, other land close to the town might be *Matruka*, while land further away from inhabited areas would be *Mewat*. The pattern of land tenure following the Ottoman Land Code has been aptly summed up by Raja Shehadi:

> Thus, if we conceive of concentric circles with the village as the nucleus, the first circle around the nucleus would consist of lands which are cultivated by the inhabitants, or *miri* lands. This circle may be criss-crossed with radii representing the connecting roads, and the land comprising these would be *matrouk* land. Within this same circle there may be lands dedicated and turned into *waqf*, and there may also be *mulk* lands. If another larger circle is drawn, representing the distance from the nucleus from which a human voice cannot be heard, then all the lands lying beyond the circumference of that circle would be lands falling into the category of *mawat*; those within it would be *miri* lands. (Shehadi 1993: 17)

Palestinians relied upon their ability to use extensive common lands around the village for grazing and gathering, and where more land was needed for cultivation, they were able to bring formerly unexploited land under cultivation and obtain a title deed either with permission or without prior consent upon payment. In the communities, some land was known to belong to individual families while other land was considered to be available for communal use (*Matruka*). These arrangements were well known and accepted among the population. Some of this land was held on the basis of *Musha'*, a system of common village ownership in which an identifiable group of people were each entitled to a certain share in an area of land. Although the *Musha'* system was criticized for holding back Palestinian agricultural development and was gradually being phased out, the system still existed in many Palestinian communities during the Mandate period.[11] The important point is that these common or collective forms of landownership and use are conceptually different to the category of state land. The rights of a community in common land are individual rights. So for instance as regards land held on the *Musha'* system, rights were distributed among a certain group and non-members could be excluded. *Matruka* land was land intended for the benefit of a certain community. State property, on the other hand, is land that is available to be allocated by the state.

Land that was not owned by individuals or the community was state domain, and this also was largely in the possession of Palestinians. A British Commission of Inquiry in 1929 found that 70 per cent of all state land north of Birsheba was leased to Arab cultivators (Stein 1984: 13).[12]

Distinct patterns of landownership and use existed in the Naqab among the Palestinian Bedouin.[13] The Naqab is the arid region that comprises the southern part of Israel, making up more than 60 per cent of Israel's total area. Prior to 1948, the area had been for centuries inhabited almost exclusively by semi-nomadic Bedouin tribes who were settled in the area and possessed and used specific lands. In the 1940s, between 65,000 and 90,000 Palestinian Bedouin inhabited the Naqab, constituting almost 90 per cent of its population (Maddrell 1990: 6).[14] 'Bedouin', literally meaning 'desert-dwellers', as distinct from village- or town-dwellers, were traditionally divided into three categories: true Bedouin (nobles), *Fellaheen* (peasants) and *A'beed* (blacks), of which the first was the landowning class (Abu Saad and Fredrick 1993: 1–3). Originally semi-nomadic, by 1948, the Palestinian Bedouin were in the process of settling down; they cultivated most of the land in the Naqab that was suitable for agriculture, concentrating on the more fertile northern Naqab, and part or all of the tribe would move seasonally with the herds in search of pasture areas. Although some moved seasonally, they would return each year to cultivate the same land. While most lived in tents, some had begun to build stone houses and several hundred had moved to the town of Birsheba, established in 1900 (Maddrell 1990: 5). The boundaries of land belonging to each tribe were delineated and known, and maps exist from the Mandate period that show areas cultivated and owned by the different tribes. Aref El-Aref, District Officer for Birsheba during the Mandate period, wrote that fighting took place over land boundaries and that: 'Every inch of land is owned by someone and everyone knows his own land in spite of the absence of boundary fences' (El-Aref 1974: 179–80). Not only did the Bedouin themselves recognize patterns of ownership, but the land rights of the Bedouin Palestinians in the Naqab had been recognized by both Ottoman and British Mandate authorities.[15] Ottoman land law recognized long possession and use of land as giving rise to legal rights. The Ottoman authorities had demonstrated their recognition of

Bedouin land rights, for instance when they purchased 2,000 dunams from the al-Azazmeh tribe in 1900 in order to establish the town of Birsheba (Maddrell 1990: 5). The Zionist land purchasing agencies had also purchased land from Bedouin. For instance, the Company for the Preparation of the Yishuv had purchased 25,351 dunams in the Birsheba area by 1931 (ibid.).

The land formed the basis of subsistence for the Bedouin Palestinians. It also played an important role in maintaining the social, cultural and economic integrity of the Bedouin communities, particularly their independence and dignity: organized in tribes based on kinship, each tribe had a definite territory (Abu Saad and Fredrick 1993). As one observer of Bedouin culture wrote:

> For the Beduin, who lived in the Negev for centuries, it represented their home, economic security, history and tradition – until Israel took it over. In its wadis, they grew winter grains, 80 percent of their diet; on its hillsides they pastured goats, which gave them wool for their tents, meat for their guests, milk for their children and when sold, money for what needed to be bought. This was a way of life that most Beduin wanted to go on living. Israel has dispossessed the Beduin and destroyed this way of life.[16]

Most Bedouin had not registered their interests in land either under Ottoman or British administrations, however, wishing to avoid taxation and because it did not appear to be necessary: nobody doubted their right to possession. Indeed, possession without title deeds was the norm in Palestine prior to the settlement of title process initiated by the British Mandate authorities. Nevertheless, at least some tribes kept written records of land boundaries and transactions in land.[17]

The British Mandate administration was aware of the difficulty of defining Bedouin land rights in the Naqab. In 1930, the British official Hope Simpson reported that the land rights of the Bedouin in the Naqab had never been determined, but recognized that any plans to develop the area must take account of their rights, which it would be necessary 'to consider, and scrupulously to record and deal with' (Hope Simpson 1930: 73). Again in 1946, the Palestine government admitted that, pending settlement of title operations, it was not possible to assume that land in the Naqab did not belong to anyone (Hadawi 1963: 22). Some attempts were made to calculate the amounts of land possessed and used by the Bedouin. The British Mandate authorities' Village Statistics of 1945 show that of a total of 12.5 million dunams in the Naqab: almost 2 million dunams, or 15 per cent, were used by Arabs; 0.5 per cent was owned by Jews; 0.2 per cent was public land;

and the remaining 84 per cent was 'uncultivable' and with no defined ownership.[18] Nevertheless there was recognition that even the latter was used by the Bedouin, including by tribes from outside the area, for grazing purposes at certain times of the year (Hadawi 1988: 108–9).[19]

The experience of the Palestinian Bedouin in the Naqab during the war of 1948 and the early years after the establishment of Israel was somewhat different to that of the rest of the Palestinian community. In 1948, the natural process of sedentarization being undergone by the Bedouin Palestinians was interrupted. During the war of 1948, all but 11,000 Bedouin left or were driven out by the Israeli army, including the entire Arab population of Birsheba, the only urban centre in the Naqab at that time. Of ninety-five sub-tribes, only nineteen remained. During the early 1950s, the Israeli army forcibly moved the entire Bedouin population that remained within the state into an area east and north-east of Birsheba known as the *siyag*.[20] Many were informed this was only a temporary measure. The area was declared a closed military area; nobody could enter or leave without the permission of the military government. Confined to a space less than 10 per cent of the area of the land they had formerly possessed, in moving to the *siyag*, many Bedouin were forced to give up better agricultural land for the less good land within the *siyag* (Falah 1985: 38). When military rule ended in 1966, the Palestinian Bedouin were still not permitted to move back to their own lands. By this time the government was claiming most of the Naqab as state land and Jewish immigrants were being settled there. Since that time the Bedouin have been allowed to use some 40 per cent of the area of the *siyag*, for habitation, cultivation and grazing (Ben David 1993: 9). Israel has sought to prevent the Bedouin from acquiring rights based on uninterrupted possession and cultivation.

Even within the *siyag* the Israeli authorities imposed strict controls, including over land use. Most of the land within the *siyag* belonged to one of the tribes, the Tayaha tribe, who were allowed to keep their land (Nakkara n.d.: 145). The other eleven tribes, who did not own land within the *siyag*, were granted leases of land within the *siyag* which belonged to Palestinian Bedouin classified as 'absentees' under the Absentees' Property Law 1950. The leases were renewed annually, thus preventing acquisition of rights by long possession and use.[21] Only those who owned land within the *siyag* were permitted to lease land outside it. Others were forbidden to cultivate their land outside the *siyag* or to lease other land outside it.

Israeli settlement of title operations after 1948

After the establishment of Israel in 1948 the goal of seizing as much land as possible and registering it in the name of the state (or the JNF) guided state policy. Manipulating the system for determining rights and interests in land – the settlement of title process – became part of that policy. New legislation and a proactive approach from governments and the courts created changes that robbed the Palestinians of much land that had formerly been owned, possessed or available to their communities.

There is general agreement that the amount of land already acquired by Jewish national institutions or individual Jews by 1948 was in the region of 6–7 per cent.[22] The amount of land actually owned by Palestinian landholders at that time is less clear. According to statistics published by the Mandate administration in 1945, just over half of the land not in Jewish ownership was owned by Palestinians, and the other half by the state.[23] The lack of clarity is due partly to the fact that Ottoman land records were inaccurate and incomplete, and the British Mandate administration had not completed settlement and registration of title throughout the country. By 1948, legal interests in land remained undetermined in vast areas, particularly the Naqab Desert that comprises over 60 per cent of the area of the state and was still untouched by settlement of title operations, and many areas in the Galilee and Triangle where sizeable Palestinian populations remained after the establishment of Israel.

Israel radically changed the law governing privately owned land. The objective of the Land Law, enacted in 1969,[24] was to sweep away the three layers of legal sources of land law, the Ottoman, Mandate and Israeli laws, and replace them with a single law to govern private rights in land (Weisman 1972). The pre-existing Ottoman categories of land were abolished and the one form of ownership in land was defined as 'the right to possess and use it, and to do anything and effect any transaction in respect thereof, subject to the restrictions imposed by law or by agreement' (section 2). Owners of the former categories of *Mulk* and *Miri,* and those who had established title to *Mewat* land, would be entitled to be registered as owners (sections 153 and 155). Some *Matruka* land, that situated within the area of jurisdiction of a local authority consisting of roads or open spaces used mainly by the residents of that local authority, would be registered in the name of the local authority (section 154[a]). The old Ottoman categories of land tenure still remain relevant for determining rights in land which has not undergone the process of settlement of title, which in 2000 still amounted to over 1 million dunams of land, most of it in the Naqab.[25] Once settlement of title operations have been completed throughout the state, the ILA confidently expects that at least 93.5 per cent of all land will be owned by the state, the Development Authority or the JNF (ILA 1993: 131). This is categorized as 'Israel Lands', ownership of which cannot be transferred. The status of Israel Lands is dealt with in other legislation and is discussed in the next chapter.[26] The Land Law is therefore relevant only to that part of the land in the state that is capable of being privately owned – only some 6 or 7 per cent of all land in Israel – and has already undergone settlement of title. The Land Law by itself was not hugely significant for Palestinian access to land since it did not undermine the rights of private landowners and even strengthened those rights since it brought rights in *Miri* and *Mewat* up to full ownership. The main difficulty for Palestinians in Israel has been the enormous obstacles placed before them in establishing those rights, which is not dealt with in the law of 1969.

From the mid-1950s, Israel took up the process of determining interests in land through settlement of title operations, and that process is still ongoing, though it has now been completed in most, though not all, Arab populated areas outside the Naqab.[27] The British Mandate system was largely retained unchanged; powers regarding settlement of title were simply transferred to the Israeli Minister of Justice and powers to hear and decide disputes vested in the District Courts.[28] However, the way in which the system was implemented changed, in what can only be described as an obsessive drive to register as much land as possible in the name of the state. The late Hanna Nakkara, a land lawyer practising at the time who documented the process, described how during settlement of title operations Israel registered land of Palestinian villages evacuated during the war in the name of the state, and how where Palestinian populations remained and submitted claims regarding their legal interests in land, rights were hotly contested.[29] Israeli officials responded with thousands of counterclaims, asserting that land should be registered in the name of the state. Every plot was inspected and anything that could be used to form the basis of a claim by the state was vigorously asserted. In the many cases where there were conflicting claims, the courts were called upon to adjudicate. The struggle was intense but the odds weighted heavily in favour of the state. By the end of the 1960s, 8,000 disputed claims in the Galilee had been decided by the courts, 85 per cent of which were decided in favour of the state (Kedar 2001a: 923). Sandy Kedar examined decisions of the District courts and High Court and demonstrates that there were possible alternative findings, but that where the lower courts found in favour of

Palestinian possessors, the High Court often overruled, while on the other hand, it rarely intervened in decisions favouring the state.[30]

A majority of Palestinians had not registered their interests in the land they farmed, and did not possess title deeds. For them, and for the villages and other Palestinian communities that used land without formal title, registering their rights in the context of the settlement of title operations was hugely problematic. A person attempting to establish a claim must first prove which category the land he is claiming falls under, i.e. whether it is *Miri* or *Mewat*, or another category (such as *Mulk* or *Matruka*).[31] This is a question of fact and depends initially on the nature of the land itself (although subsequently a claimant might be able to prove that *Mewat* had been transformed into *Miri*).

Having proved the category of the land, the claimant must then prove that he has acquired a legal interest in that land. The manner in which he must do this depends on the classification of the land. In order to prove rights over *Miri*, the claimant must prove he acquired rights by express grant or long use and cultivation. For *Mewat*, he must prove he acquired rights under Article 103 of the Land Code by reviving the land with consent or upon payment within the given time. Much land used by Palestinians had been regarded as *Miri*. Since after the Land Law of 1969 tenure of *Miri* land was recognized as full ownership, the ability of Palestinians to establish such interests was crucial. It was also important for Palestinian communities to establish rights over *Matruka* and *Mewat* land if they were to preserve their access to that land and protect its potential as land reserves for the future expansion of the communities. The problem was that the new Israeli regime made all these rights extremely difficult to prove.

The courts created an entire new set of restrictive basic ground rules. As a result of the Badran decision, where a person is not able to establish a right to more than 50 per cent of a particular plot for the entire relevant period, the whole plot will be registered in the name of the state.[32] Palestinians believe the state has tended to divide up plots in such a way that it takes the maximum amount of land, and the courts will not usually accept objections to the way in which the division is carried out. In another case, that of Mas'ad Kassis, the court held that where a claimant failed to prove the precise boundaries of a plot, he would lose the entire plot.[33] The surest way to claim ownership is to prove title on the basis of a title deed (*Kushan*). However, even possession of a *Kushan* is not conclusive. Typically the deed identifies a property by describing the borders and stating its area. Frequently, however, the two do not correspond, and the description reveals a much larger area than the number of dunams stated, which had been artificially minimized in order to avoid taxes. A further obstacle is that the nature of the surrounding land will not be considered a relevant factor, so for instance in attempting to prove that land fell under a particular category, a landholder was not assisted by being able to prove that neighbouring land was of that category.[34]

Registering rights in *Miri* land and manipulation of the Prescription Laws

A second major focus of disputes in the settlement of title process was over land located a little further distant from the Palestinian villages, where the dispute often centred on whether the land was *Mewat* or *Miri*, and whether Palestinians could successfully establish rights over it. One subject of intense disputes in the courts was the determination of title of *Miri* land. Most agricultural land close to Palestinian villages fell under this category. Under the Ottoman land regime, *Miri* was cultivable land, granted in a manner similar to a lease, and the grant could either be made expressly or presumed from continuous possession and cultivation. Under Ottoman and Mandate law, a person who had continuously possessed and cultivated *Miri* land unchallenged for a period of ten years – the prescription period – became entitled to have the land registered in his name. Most Palestinian farmers relied on these rules for gaining rights over land, rather than on express grants of ownership. While, according to the Ottoman Land Code, *Miri* grants should be registered and evidenced by a title deed, in practice most were not, and this was true throughout the Ottoman Empire. The prescription rules were therefore of enormous importance for Palestinians' prospects of establishing their rights over land when Israel took up the settlement of title process. In order to substantiate a claim to *Miri* land on the basis of implied grant for a period greater than the prescription period, a person must show that they possessed the land for the relevant period and cultivated it continuously. Section 78 of the Ottoman Land Code requires cultivation in addition to possession.

In 1958, Israel enacted the Prescription Law, introducing crucial changes that made it much more difficult for Palestinians to establish rights on the basis of long possession and cultivation.[35] The law extended the prescription period from ten to fifteen years for land that had not yet undergone settlement of title (sections 5[2] and 22). For land that had already undergone settlement of title, the law extended the prescription period to twenty-five years (section 5[2]), but the Land Law 1969 subsequently abolished all rights of prescription in registered land altogether (section 159[6]). Once title is established, acquisition of rights by prescription will no longer be possible. Those already entitled to interests in land by right of prescription at the time of the coming into force of the Land Law in 1970 could still pursue their claims.

The extension of the prescription period in unsettled land from ten to fifteen years had an insidious purpose. The law was to apply retro-actively, so rights that had already been acquired before the law came into effect were also affected. Thus a person was required to prove cultivation for fifteen years as soon as the new law came into force, even though the original prescription period of ten years had already passed and he was able to prove continuous cultivation for that period (section 29[6]). But this was not the only change. The Prescription Law also provided that where a claimant came into possession after 1 March 1943, the five years after the coming into force of the law in 1958 would not be counted towards the prescription period. The purpose behind the inclusion of this provision only makes sense in combination with the settlement of title activities that were going on at the time the Prescription Law was passed. Of the areas most densely populated with Palestinians, many were declared subject to settlement of title operations before March 1963 – in other words, within five years of the Prescription Law 1958. Since the announcement that settlement of title operations were under way halted the running of time for the purposes of acquisition of rights by prescription, the combination made it impossible for farmers who came into possession after March 1943 to fulfil the requirement, since time effectively stopped in 1958. The com-bination of these provisions provided the government with an effective tool for knocking out the claims of those only able to prove that they came into possession after March 1943 in the affected areas.

A further difficulty is presented by the requirement that a claimant must have cultivated the land continuously during the prescription period, since any evidence that the claimant has neglected to cultivate at any point during the requisite period would negate the claim. This was crucial, since in contesting claims, the state has frequently relied on aerial photographs taken in a comprehensive aerial survey of 1944–45 that the Israeli authorities inherited from the British Mandate adminis-tration. When a Palestinian attempts to prove cultivation of land for the requisite period, the state produces photographs that appear to show that the piece of land was not cultivated in 1944–45. The problem Pales-tinians raise is that because land was cultivated during certain seasons only, a photograph taken during another time of the year may not reveal any sign of cultivation, so the photographs do not necessarily indicate that land was not cultivated during the entire year. But the evidential value of the photographs cannot be effectively challenged because the state controls these records and uses only those that support its case, and the courts have accepted this situation.

Lawyers and local community leaders say that, compounding these problems, a range of obstacles are placed in front of Palestinians seeking to establish ownership based on prescription. Aside from the unequal position created by the state's use of aerial photographs, to which it had exclusive access, in court proceedings, other rules of evidence that were developed put Palestinian claimants at a disadvantage. Palestinians attempt to bring other evidence such as tax, records and witnesses, but many potential witnesses have died, records have been lost, and the courts give less weight to such evidence than to the aerial photographs. In the case of Hawashleh, the High Court said that a single payment of tax would not be sufficient to prove continuous possession and cultivation, and that tax receipts, evidence of expenditure on improvement and deeds of purchase from other Arab owners are considered sufficient only in cases of conflict between two rival owners (for instance in establishing where boundaries lie), but not as proof of ownership against the state.

Dealing a further heavy blow, in 1992 the High Court had to consider a conflict between the Prescription Laws and the law governing state lands. The plaintiffs were Palestinians who had possessed and cultivated land in the village of Arab Al Shibli near Mount Tabor in the Lower Galilee. In 1943 this land had been registered in the name of the High Commissioner as a result of settlement of title operations. Accordingly, it was inherited by Israel as state land after 1948. The plaintiffs issued their case in the Nazareth District Court, claiming that they had possessed and cultivated the land without interruption since before 1943, and were therefore entitled to be registered as owners under section 78 of the Ottoman Land Code, as amended by the Prescription Law 1958 (which extended the ten-year period to twenty-five years in the case of settled land) and the Land Law 1969 (which put a stop to acquisition of rights by prescription over settled land as of 1 January 1970). They claimed to be able to prove more than twenty-five years' use before 1970. The state claimed that it would be unlawful to register the land in the name of the petitioners, relying on the Basic Law: Israel Lands 1960, which provided in section 1 that land owned by the state could not be transferred 'either by sale, or in any other manner'. The District Court accepted their claim, on the basis that they had possessed and cultivated the land from 1944 until 1 January 1970 (the date on which the Land Law 1969, which revoked the Ottoman Land Code, came into force). However, making new submissions in the High Court, the state argued that the Basic Law: Israel Lands prevents the acquisition of rights over state land under section 78. The High Court agreed, holding that where there was a conflict between the prescription provisions in Ottoman law, and the prohibition of alienation of state lands contained in the Basic Law, the latter would prevail.[36]

The consequences of failure to meet the stiff requirements are critical. Those claiming rights over *Miri* land who are not able to substantiate their claim are not entitled to any right over the land in question, even though they might have used that land for generations. The land is registered in the name of the state and becomes classified as Israel Lands; access for any Palestinian, not only the claimant, is then severely limited.

Obstacles to establishing that land is *Miri*

Many Palestinian claims to land were based on the possibility of converting *Mewat* land into *Miri*. *Mewat*, literally meaning 'dead', was defined in the Ottoman Land Code as undeveloped or unused land which was not owned or possessed by anybody and was situated at least one and a half miles from inhabited areas, 'at such a distance from towns and villages from which a human voice cannot be heard at the nearest inhabited place' (Articles 6 and 103; see Goadby and Doukhan 1935: 263). In Ottoman times such land could be brought into use, or 'revived', and a person who did so with the administration's consent would be entitled to cultivate the land, the land would become *Miri*, and the possessor entitled to a title deed. If a person 'revived' *Mewat* land without consent, although there was no automatic entitlement to a title deed, there was a discretion to award a deed if consideration was paid.

However, a combination of British Mandate and Israeli measures and policies closed off the option of converting *Mewat* into *Miri*, following which it became crucial for Palestinians to establish that land was *Miri* and not *Mewat* for there to be any prospect of establishing rights over it. In 1921, the British Mandate administration legislated to put a stop to the acquisition of title to *Mewat* land by revival.[37] Those who had already acquired rights could still claim title by registering their interest at the Land Registry, but they were required to do so within two months of the publication of the Ordinance. The Ordinance of 1921 was to have a particularly harsh impact on the Bedouin in the Naqab after 1948. Few Bedouin were aware of the new rule and the British Mandate authorities, when deciding claims in settlement of title operations, did not in practice discount claims where land had been revived and cultivated without permission (Goadby and Doukhan 1935: 47).[38]

It was the practice to grant title deeds on payment of a fee to those able to show that they had revived land prior to the 1921 Ordinance without consent. Furthermore, the British and the pre-state Zionist institutions continued to recognize Bedouin land rights after the Mewat Land Ordinance came into effect, and where land was sold the Land Registry noted the Bedouin as vendors with title. This is strong evidence that the British themselves did not intend the 1921 Ordinance to sweep away at a stroke all the acquired rights of the Bedouin. Nevertheless, relying on the Ordinance of 1921, Israel argued that most Bedouin had lost their rights through failure to register. In the case of Hawashleh, the High Court confirmed that those who revived *Mewat* land prior to 1921 but failed to register their interest within the time prescribed in the Mewat Land Ordinance of that year did not acquire any right in the land.[39]

In 1971, the Naqab area was declared subject to settlement of title operations, and one study found that some 3,220 claims relating to a total of 776,856 dunams were submitted by Bedouin in order to establish their rights.[40] Since few had land deeds, the Bedouin had to base their claims, which they asserted over both cultivated and grazing land, on long possession and use. The claims included rights over both *Miri* and *Mewat* categories of land. Typically, the Palestinian applicants asserted rights over land they claimed was *Miri* and had been cultivated by their family for generations, while the state claimed that the land was *Mewat* but had not been registered following the 1921 Mewat Land Ordinance, and must therefore be registered in the name of the state. The state vigorously contested the claims, and in a series of decisions the Israeli High Court not only supported the state's claims, but developed rules that placed further restrictions on the Ottoman law. Many of these cases involved the Naqab.

In one early case, that of Hussein Sawaid, the High Court found that the burden of establishing the status of the land – whether *Mewat* or *Miri* – was on the person claiming the land.[41] The Court also held that for these purposes it would consider only the land that was the subject of the claim, and not the land surrounding it. In other words, it would not assist a claimant if neighbouring land had already been established as *Miri*, and if the plot were part of a larger area, some of which was cultivated but the plot itself was not suitable for cultivation, that plot would be lost.

The High Court introduced further restrictions focusing on the element of distance in the definition of *Mewat* (Article 103 of the Ottoman Land Law established that *Mewat* land is land far enough from the inhabited area that a human voice could not be heard). The case law effectively establishes a presumption that land that is not close to an inhabited settlement is *Mewat* unless otherwise proven. In the case of Saleh Badran, the High Court noted that the test in Article 103 is far from precise and it was better to rely on the measure of distance (one and a half miles).[42] Thus a presumption was established that land located more than one and a half miles from a village will be *Mewat*. In Hawashleh, the Court said that the element of distance should be measured at the time the Ottoman Land Law was passed, and not at some later date.[43] This raises particular difficulties in proving the location of inhabited areas in the Naqab, given the Bedouins' settlement patterns and semi-nomadic lifestyle. There were very few permanent settlements in the Naqab in 1858, and the difficulty in proving the location of permanent Bedouin settlements leads to difficulty in proving that land is not *Mewat*, i.e. not at a distance greater than one and a half miles from the nearest inhabited area.

Having established these rules as to how to distinguish between *Mewat* and *Miri*, which resulted in much land being considered as *Mewat* despite Palestinian protestations, the courts then made it almost impossible for Palestinians to establish rights over *Mewat* land. In Badran the High Court also confirmed that since according to this definition the land was *Mewat* and not *Miri*, rights could not be acquired by prescription. Applying the Mewat Land Ordinance of 1921, according to which those who revived *Mewat* land prior to 1921 but failed to register their interest within the two months prescribed lost their rights, the Court found that Badran had no basis on which to be registered as owner of the land. Unlike the Mandate authorities, who had tended to recognize unregistered rights over *Mewat* even after 1921, the Israeli High Court applied the terms of the 1921 Ordinance strictly. After this was established in Badran, subsequent cases followed this approach.[44]

The High Court has also insisted on a restrictive interpretation of what it means to 'revive' *Mewat*, holding in the Hawashleh case that it must involve an improvement in land such that its nature is totally changed, and that it must involve continuous cultivation of the land.[45] The Ottoman system was less severe as regards activities that could amount to revival; whereas sowing seed or preparing for irrigation would constitute revival, mere enclosure of land is not considered sufficient (Goadby and Doukhan 1935: 48).

In such circumstances, proving that land had become *Miri* in the Naqab became an almost impossible task. Lawyers acting for the Bedouin say they have been unable to convince the courts to recognize rights based on long possession and use even as regards Bedouin with land within the *siyag* (the area to which the Bedouin were relocated and confined in the 1950s) who are on their own land and never left it during the war and throughout the 1950s.[46] As the then-High Court judge Halima wrote in 1985, commenting specifically on the Naqab: 'Who is the hero who is able to prove these things?' (Halima 1985: 15).

To date, the settlement of title process in the Naqab remains dead-locked, with 95 per cent of claims unresolved. Claims are not being adjudicated. Government policy has been to suspend the process in order to try to reach arrangements with the Bedouin and persuade them to accept compensation and renounce their claims.[47] While some have done so, most have not. Only where there are no claims or Bedouin have renounced theirs has registration been completed. Thus, most of the land in the southern Naqab, the most arid part of the Naqab, has now been registered in the name of the state.

The state's ambition to ensure that the Bedouin are not registered as owners of the land they have possessed and used for centuries through the settlement process is undisguised. In July 2000 the Israel Lands Council, the decision-making body of the Israel Lands Admin-istration, said in Decision 884 regarding the compromise agreements being negotiated with the Bedouin aimed at persuading them to move to the planned townships: 'It is important to emphasise that in these compromise agreements, the Bedouin give up all their claims to land made in the settlement of title process, and that lands claimed by them are registered in the name of the state.'[48]

State officials boast of their success in retaining hundreds of parcels of land for the state. In 1985, the head of the Lands Department in the State Prosecutors' Office, Plia Albek, claimed: 'Those responsible for the defence of state land succeeded in preventing every attempt by land thieves to acquire land without legal justification' (Albeck 1985: 9).

Above and beyond the right to property, the right not to be forcefully evicted and other fundamental rights that have been violated, there is a further dimension to the land rights of the Bedouin. The Bedouin in the Naqab share with all Palestinians their historic and collective rights over the land they have been dispossessed of during the past century. They also share characteristics of indigenous peoples around the world, including a special relationship with lands traditionally occupied, this relationship being essential for their survival as distinct peoples and to preserve their way of life and culture. The international movement for indigenous peoples' rights has gained strength in recent years and certain legal rights in relation to land are already recognized. Among them the right of ownership and possession of lands traditionally oc-cupied.[49] This aspect has been ignored by Israel.

Registering rights in *Matruka* land

Matruka land, used by villages for generations for grazing, wood gathering and other purposes, was mostly lost to Palestinian communities during the settlement of title process. The Land Law 1969 specified that *Matruka* land situated within the area of jurisdiction of a local council which is used mainly by the residents of the area is to be registered in the name of the local council.[50] However, only three Arab localities had municipal status prior to 1948: Kafr Yasif, Nazareth and Shefa'Amr. Kafr Yasif, for example, succeeded during settlement of title operations in 1945–46 in having the village's communal land registered in the name of the local authority. As a result, this village today has land for general purposes such as schools, local council buildings, sports facilities and so on.

However, most Arab localities did not have local authorities until the 1960s or 1970s or are still too small to merit one. Where there is no local council at the time settlement of title takes place, whether before or after 1948, *Matruka* land is registered in the name of the state, and the villages have found it difficult to gain control of it, even where, as in some cases, it is registered with the proviso that it be used for the purposes of the community, such as in the city of Um El Fahem. In 1970 the High Court heard an appeal concerning *Matruka* land in Um El Fahem that was claimed both by the local authority which had by then been established, and the state. The land in question had originally been used for the grazing of animals by residents of the village but since 1948 had been built on, needed for the expansion of the community. The Court held that in order for the land to be recognized as *Matruka* and registered in the name of the local authority, its use as grazing land must continue right up to the time a claim was submitted in settlement of title proceedings, which in this case had not occurred, so the land had lost its character as *Matruka* and should be registered in the name of the state.[51]

The Israeli High Court considered the claims of a Palestinian village over *Matruka* land in a case concerning the village of Yaffa, near Nazareth. In 1947, thousands of dunams of uncultivated land had been registered in the name of the High Commissioner on behalf of the village, on the basis that there was at that time no local council as a legal body able to represent the village.[52] Unusually, the land in question had been described in the land register as *Miri* lands even though it was uncultivated, and was also expressly described as waste land. After a local council for the village was established, it applied to have the land registered in its name. This was contested by the state. The High Court denied the state's claim that it was impossible for *Miri* land to registered as *Matruka*, holding that the definition of *Matruka* under Ottoman law was sufficiently unclear to permit such a registration. It also rejected the state's claim that since it was waste land, it could not be used for the benefit of the village, saying that such land could still be useful and in fact evidence had been brought to the effect that the villagers had used it for grazing. However, the Court rejected the petitioners' argument that since the land would have been registered in the name of the local council had one existed at the time, it should be transferred to the local council now that it had been established. The Court said that this could not be known for certain, and the fact that the land had not been registered as *Matruka* in 1947, when it could have been, was conclusive. The outcome was that the application to register the land in the name of the local council was rejected, but the Court ordered that a note be made in the register to the effect that the state held the land on behalf of the village. The legal effect of this note remains unclear.

The case of the village of Mi'lia in the upper western Galilee is unusual. In the course of settlement of title operations the villagers claimed thousands of dunams of uncultivated land on the basis they had used it for grazing and gathering, and other land was also in dispute, the issue being whether or not it had been cultivated. In 1982 the village reached an agreement with the authorities. The local authority was to take a belt around the village and the small plots claimed by the state within the village, on condition that it be used only for public purposes including housing. As for the disputed agricultural land, 1,200 dunams were registered in the name of the local council for grazing and owners could elect to take 50 per cent of the amount they claimed. Even some *Mewat* land was included. Although the state gained thousands of dunams as a result, the village retained more land than other villages had succeeded in securing, and the local council was left in a better position to look after the future interests of the community than elsewhere. This experience is unique, as other Palestinian villages have not been able to achieve a similar deal. And even for Mi'lia, implementation of the deal has required persistence and determination. Eleven years after the agreement described was reached, all the land was still registered in the name of the state. The local community was forced to take legal steps in order to oblige the state to implement the agreement by registering some land under the name of the local council in accordance with the agreement.

Another practice, deeply resented by the Palestinian population, has been the designation of woodland surrounding a village, some of which would have been considered *Matruka,* as state forestland.[53]

Palestinian writer and lawyer Sabri Jiryis found that by 1970, at least ten Palestinian villages had lost over 40,000 dunams of land in this way (Jiryis 1976: 117). A number of nature protection laws introduced by Israel have also imposed restrictions on permitted uses of land within forests, parks and nature reserves.[54]

Once again we see the familiar pattern of loss of access for Palestinians. The application of the law relating to *Matruka* has been problematic not so much because of the fact that uncultivated land surrounding Palestinian villages was registered in the name of the state, but because the Israeli intention has been to prevent this land being used by the Palestinian communities and for their benefit, and to win the right to allocate it instead for Jewish settlement. In other words, the problem is with the status of state or public land in Israel in general, which is that state land is not land that can be made available for all sections of the public, but only to the section of the population that is Jewish.

Dispossession of the Bedouin: forced evictions and relocation

Registering their historic lands in the name of the state has been one central objective of Israeli policy towards the Bedouin in the Naqab, but at the same time Israel has developed other policies, pursued with equal vigour, aimed at uprooting the Naqab Bedouin from almost all of their traditional lands and resettling them in a limited number of urbanized communities. Even if they were to overcome all the obstacles placed in their way in the settlement of title process, prove their rights over land to the satisfaction of the Israeli legal system, and resist the application of the expropriation laws, the Bedouin would still have to overcome this further hurdle before they could live on or use their land. The relocation policy involves forcing the Bedouin to move to one of the planned urban townships – of which there are currently ten in existence or in their planning stages. According to this policy, the entire Bedouin community must be concentrated in these townships within a few years. The Bedouin community in the Naqab, numbering approximately 120,000 (about 19 per cent of the population of the Naqab),[55] actually occupies, according to one estimate, around 220,000 dunams of land (Ben David 1999: 65), compared to formal claims submitted to around three-quarters of a million dunams and a total estimated pre-1948 possession of some 2 million dunams. The Bedouin have resisted the relocation policy and approximately half of the Bedouin in the Naqab, some 70,000 people, are living in around forty-five so-called 'unrecognized' communities considered illegal by the authorities.[56]

The uprooting of the Bedouin began as early as the 1950s when the entire Bedouin population that remained after the war was forcibly moved into an area east and north-east of Birsheba known as the *siyag*, supposedly in a temporary measure. Like the rest of the Palestinian population, they were subjected to military rule until 1966 and the *siyag* was declared a closed military area. During this time they were confined to a space of less than 10 per cent of the area of the land they had formerly possessed. But when military rule was lifted in 1966, those Bedouin whose land was outside the *siyag* were not permitted to return to their land, which was claimed by the state, and those who did so were considered to be encroaching on state land and acting illegally.

The concentration of the Palestinian Bedouin population of the Naqab in a small area of land, which began with their relocation in the *siyag*, was continued and intensified in the 1970s with the urbanization programme. The policy envisages that the entire Bedouin population of the Naqab will be concentrated in a limited number of urban townships – the current policy is around ten – all situated within the *siyag*. Even many of those resettled within the *siyag* since the 1950s are being forced to move again. The area of land that the Bedouin are permitted to occupy is ever shrinking. Within the *siyag*, much of the land is now planned for purposes that exclude the Bedouin: an airport, military training areas, industrial areas such as Ramat Hovav. Every new regional master plan designates more land for other purposes, leaving less and less land available to the Bedouin. Sometimes, land is designated but not used. For instance, according to a plan of 1978, Ramat Beker was designated an industrial area and 56,000 dunams of land south of Birsheba was expropriated under the 1943 Public Purposes Ordinance, and the same year forty-seven Bedouin families were evicted. However, by 1995 the land had still not been developed.[57]

Meanwhile, over the years, entire cities (Dimona, Arad and Yeruham) as well as numerous agricultural villages, settlements and farms, all for Jews only, and military areas, have been established on land claimed by the Bedouin. National and regional plans disregard the reality of the existence of the Bedouin communities. In 1994, a new 'Master Plan for the Southern District' was deposited which envisaged further development projects and forests to be located on land claimed and in some cases settled by Bedouin.[58]

Resettlement is the only legal alternative open to the Bedouin Palestinians. They are offered no choice whatsoever – even as to which one of the townships to move to, which is dictated by extended family membership. Government reports and ILC decisions indicate that the government has continually set objectives in relation to the speed at which the relocation policy can be realized that are plainly unrealistic.[59]

The relocation policy forms an integral part of the process of taking away Palestinian Bedouin land rights. Concentrating the Bedouin in as small an area of land as possible goes in tandem with steps to gain possession of the land for other uses. Measures have been taken against the large numbers of Bedouin who have refused to reach agreement as regards their land (i.e. surrender their rights) and who refuse to move into the townships. In the eyes of the state, they remain 'trespassers'. While the government tries to enforce its policy, the Bedouin employ the most effective form of resistance in their power – their presence on the land. Around half are still outside the townships and the failure to resolve the ownership issue as well as the relocation policy are the major causes of this situation. Thus, the Bedouin who have not moved into the townships live in a permanently temporary situation, unable to develop or to build permanent homes, and facing severe difficulties in obtaining basic amenities and services.

Given that the Palestinian Bedouin were already largely sedentarized by 1948, with only part of the tribe moving seasonally and each tribe with defined lands and growing permanent centres, the concentration policy amounted to forced displacement and resettlement rather than state-enforced sedentarization. The government has employed a mixture of coercion and persuasion tactics to force the Bedouin to comply with its policy, including demolishing homes (many of which are not permanent buildings but corrugated iron shacks and huts). Such actions, which will be discussed in more detail in Chapter 8, cannot be justified under international law standards, and Israel has been severely criticized by international human rights bodies for violating human rights in relation to the Bedouin. The prohibition on forced eviction is considered by the UN Commission on Human Rights to be among the most fundamental of all human rights, and the Commission has declared that forced evictions constitute a gross violation of human rights, in particular the right to housing.[60] The international human rights bodies urge states to protect populations against forced eviction and have said that it can be justified only in the most exceptional of circumstances.[61]

In particular, it is clear that Israeli government policy to relocate the Bedouin Palestinian population of the Naqab and concentrate them in a small number of planned urban townships is not motivated by overriding legitimate considerations or by development policies aimed at benefiting the public as a whole. The policy is closely linked to the dispute over ownership of land and Israel's desire to register most of the Bedouin land in the name of the state, and to use it for Jewish development. The facts speak for themselves. Since 1948 a massive development drive has been underway in the Naqab, involving numerous development plans and investment, and the establishment of dozens of new towns and villages, including agricultural communities, which are exclusively for Jews. At the same time, the government would allow initially only three, then seven recognized communities for the Bedouin, and only of one type: urban townships. There have been indications that the government may be prepared to recognize three to five more, including possibly agricultural villages.

Several branches of government cooperate to regulate Bedouin life, including land allocation, through a Bedouin Office in Birsheba: the ILA, the Ministry of Agriculture, the Green Patrol, the JNF and the army. Dependency is encouraged and Bedouin are forced to form good relations with officials, sometimes involving collaboration such as informing on other Bedouin or other forms of cooperation with the authorities, if they wish to lease land (Abu-Rabia 1994: 25–40). The ILA serves as the main instrument of the government in uprooting the Bedouin from their encampments and concentrating them in the planned settlements. An ILA Directorate for (Furthering) the Situation of the Bedouin in the South, the so-called 'Compromise Committee', is charged with 'reaching compromises in land and population arrangements with the Bedouin in the Naqab'. Its role in practice involves the evacuation of the Bedouin from their land and their concentration in urban townships. In order to implement government policy, the ILA is authorized to allocate plots of land for building in the planned townships without going through the normal process of public bidding. Where the number of applicants exceeds the number of available plots, the Committee for Bedouin Affairs makes recommendations regarding allocation according to criteria defined by the Housing Ministry and 'relevant considerations'.[62]

While Israeli governments have always refused to accept the Bedouin land claims, in the 1970s the government decided to offer compensation to Bedouin when they comply with the government's relocation policy, whether or not they are surrendering recognized legal rights. The Israel Lands Council has issued a series of decisions setting out the levels of compensation payable to Bedouin who agree to move to the planned townships. Levels of compensation and terms of resettlement differ depending on whether the Bedouin are able to establish that they have been in possession of the land they are giving up. The levels of compensation are far below what would be needed to purchase and develop a building plot in one of the planned townships, but some subsidies are available.[63] The level of compensation also depends on the type of land and its development value to the state. For instance, those who claimed grazing rights would receive 20 per cent of the value of the land,[64] and those who had acquired rights over cultivable land but not registered their rights would be able to claim 50 per cent of the relevant rate. Compensation is also payable for the homes that are left behind, the rate depending on whether the construction is made of zinc, concrete block, stone or other material; the more substantial the building, the greater the level of compensation.[65] Bedouin are also entitled to minimal amounts of compensation for loss of assets such as fruit trees and water wells. The government has introduced a number of incentives aimed at persuading the Bedouin to move quickly, such as offering higher rates of compensation for a limited time only.[66]

It should be stressed again that successive Israeli governments have been prepared to recognize Bedouin land rights only in the context of their agreeing to comply with the relocation policy, and in the context of a specific agreed resettlement. The terms of ILC Decision 884 of July 2000 make it clear that the Bedouin are expected to give up all claims they submitted in the settlement of title process when they reach compromises with the state to relocate. While the Bedouin are not forced to surrender their land claims when they move into the townships, there are strong pressures on them to do so. Those who agree to relocate but refuse to surrender ownership of their original land will be granted a lease but not title over the plot allocated to them in the township. Only those who agree to surrender their land claims will be eligible to receive ownership of their plot in exchange (those offered land according to the terms of the Negev Land Acquisition [Peace Treaty with Egypt] Law of 1980 are an additional exception).[67] However, the circumstances in which compensation is given in the form of land rather than money are carefully limited. Transfer of state land is limited by the exceptions set out in the Basic Law: Israel Lands, and a number of ILC decisions seek to ensure that compensation in land is exceptional and restricted to small areas on which the Bedouin will actually live.[68]

From the Israeli government's point of view, proving ownership becomes irrelevant other than for the purposes of compensation. In effect, there is little difference between those who still live (in the government's eyes, illegally) on the lands they claim, and those who have been forced off their land but still claim ownership of it. In both cases, even if they could prove ownership, according to current government policy, they would not be permitted to live on the land. Nor does the government recognize Bedouin rights over land on which they were placed within the *siyag* in the 1950s. All of the Bedouin community are victims of the two-pronged government approach: (i) the government's policy of concentrating the Bedouin in planned urban townships, and (ii) the planning of the disputed land for other purposes, frequently for the development of Jewish communities or for industry, housing, military use or forest land.

In the townships, the Bedouin are given forty-nine-year leases over land registered in the name of the state and mortgages and housing subsidies are made available as incentives for complying with the policy. Very often, land that is allocated to one tribe is claimed by another tribe in the settlement of title process. The townships are planned without consulting the Bedouin, and the layout of the communities is inappropriate for Bedouin culture and society. For instance, the Bedouin complain that the plots are too small and close together, and do not allow for agricultural pursuits such as keeping animals.[69]

That the government's objective is to limit the land area taken up by the Bedouin is not a secret. It is clear from official language that control of land is the core of the issue: from the chair of the governmental Board for the Advancement of the Bedouin saying, 'There is no justification in a few dozen families in every Bedouin center controlling huge areas of land',[70] to accusations that they are 'encroaching' on state land required for Jewish settlement (Falah 1989a: 75). Israel is reportedly prepared to leave only 100,000 dunams in Bedouin hands, compared to some 220,000 that they now possess and 775,000 to which they lay claim (Ben David 1999: 65). If the Israeli government succeeds in implementing its policy in the Naqab in full, it will therefore have reduced the amount of land possessed and used by the Bedouin from some 2 million dunams before 1948 to an area amounting to only a mere 5 per cent of that.

Israeli policies have had a particular impact in the Naqab, where in 1948 the Bedouin were only just adapting to a sedentary as opposed to a semi-nomadic lifestyle and where fewer landowners had registered their legal interests in land. The work of contemporary Israeli sociologist Ronen Shamir demonstrates how Israeli public officials and also the courts have embraced a culturally superior attitude towards the Bedouin and used this as a basis for dismissing and delegitimizing their land claims (Shamir 1999: 525–46). Once the Bedouin have been portrayed as backward and simply opposed to a modern system of law, it has appeared more acceptable to deny their links with the land and dismiss their claims to ownership and possession. Certainly Israel's actions have been influenced by such attitudes. But Israel's policies are about more than wilfully ignoring customary or traditional forms of land tenure. Before 1948 the pre-existing rules were applied in the same way throughout Palestine, and Israel also applied the same policies in all areas of the new state. But Israeli governments simply took advantage of factors in the Naqab that made it easier to deny the claims of those in possession of the land.

The outcome of Israeli manipulation of the settlement of title process

Israel fully exploited the fact that so much of the Palestinian land that remained after 1948 was situated in areas where title was formally undetermined, and by the early 1970s it had completed settlement of title in most of these areas other than the Naqab. During this process, tens of thousands of dunams were transformed from being considered the private or communal property of Palestinians into the name of the state. The state fought over every last piece of land and, as with the Absentees' Property Law, found itself as registered owner of many pieces of land, small and large, scattered in and around the Palestinian communities.[71]

The Israeli use of the settlement of title process to strip Palestinians in all parts of the state of their property rights flies in the face of internationally recognized legal principles that oblige a new sovereign to respect private property rights held under a prior regime, and to continue to recognize and protect forms of land tenure previously recognized even if they are different to those established under the new sovereign.[72] The Ottoman system of land tenure, as adapted both by the Ottoman authorities and the British Mandate administration, was based on a well established set of norms and practices that was known to all and recognized by successive administrations in Palestine. In this system actual possession and use, by communities as well as individuals, were the main basis for acquiring rights over land. As 1948 approached, the British Mandate authorities had established a more formal system for defining and registering these various existing rights in land and were in the process of registering all rights in land. But Israel exploited this situation, altered the rules in crucial ways and manipulated the process so that Palestinian individuals and communities could only with great difficulty establish their right to have land registered in their names.

Where Palestinian possessors lost their claims, their land would be registered in the name of the state, drastically curtailing access to it by Palestinians in the future. Because what Israel essentially gained by its drive to accumulate most land in the hands of the state was the right of allocation over that land. Whereas before 1948 much state land was leased to Palestinian farmers (70 per cent of all state land north of Birsheba in 1929), after Israel was established and, as will be described in the following chapters, the Israel Lands Administration was given responsibility for land belonging to the state, the JNF and the Development Authority (amounting to more than 93.5 per cent of land in the state), this land has been devoted to settling Jews and providing them with a livelihood, and the circumstances in which Palestinians can obtain leases over state land are extremely limited.

Summary of Palestinian land losses due to expropriation and settlement of title operations

Palestinian loss of land due to the laws and policies described in this and the previous chapters has been catastrophic. On the eve of the 1948 war the JNF and other Jewish institutions owned in the region of 6 per cent of the land of Mandatory Palestine between them. The precise amount of land privately owned by the Palestinian communities whether individually or in common is not known, since many legal interests in land were not yet formally registered, but data from the period indicate that Palestinians either owned or used the majority of land in the area. The typical pattern was for land surrounding a Palestinian village to be owned by residents of the village either individually or in common, and Palestinians also leased a majority of state land.

After the State of Israel was declared in 1948, the State Property Law 1951 was enacted, transferring all property within Israel that had previously been vested in the Mandatory administration of Palestine to the State of Israel.[73] Israel claimed some 15 million dunams as state property on this basis.[74] In the years that followed, a massive transfer of land into the name of the state occurred. Israel added to the state domain the land it claimed under the Absentees' Property Law, the Land Acquisition (Validation of Acts and Compensation) Law 1953, the Public Purposes Ordinance 1943 and other legislation, and land it claimed in the course of settlement of title operations. Today more than 94.5 per cent of all land in Israel (over 20,400 dunams of land) is directly administered by the state, owned or claimed by the state or the JNF (some of that is land of which ownership is disputed, such as land claimed by Bedouin in the Naqab) (ILA 2000: 163).[75] The ILA has predicted that once title to all land in the state has been finally determined, it expects to control some 93.5 per cent of it. Of the land in private ownership, some is owned by Jews and the rest by Palestinians; the exact proportion owned by Palestinians is unknown but may be as little as 2 per cent of all land in the state.[76]

The largest group of victims were the 800,000 Palestinian refugees of 1948, whose land was seized under the Absentees' Property Law. Israel has never released official figures relating to the amount of property belonging to Palestinian refugees from 1948 that it expropriated. Table 4.1, taken from a study by Cano, shows Palestinian land losses in the early years of the state under the Absentees' Property Law, including the refugees outside the state who lost all of their land, and also the 16–17 per cent of the pre-war Palestinian population who remained or returned, and have been citizens of Israel.

TABLE 4.1 Land ownership immediately after the establishment of the State of Israel (in dunams)

Land privately owned by Jews	801,000
Land privately owned by Arabs	867,000
Land owned by the state	18,754,000
Total	20,422,000

Source: Cano (1992: 79), based on Tzur (1972: 42).

According to Cano, the 867,000 dunams left in Arab ownership was all that was left after some 4.6 million dunams had been claimed by the state as land 'abandoned' by external and internal refugees under the Absentees' Property Law 1950.

The Palestinians who remained and became citizens of Israel have had their land holdings further whittled away since 1948. Subsequent expropriations under the Land Acquisition Act 1953 and other legal measures reduced Arab land holdings even further. Cano found that following these expropriations, land held by Palestinians remaining in Israel had been further reduced from 867,000 dunams to 529,428 dunams by the 1950s (Cano 1992: 79, citing Baer 1957: 193).

TABLE 4.2 Arab land transferred to the state by 1954 (in dunams)

Transfer of absentees' land	4,589,013
Transfer under the Land Acquisition Law 1953	1,288,000
Confiscation of land in the north	118,000
Total	5,995,013

Source: Cano (1992: 102, Table 23).

If Palestinian Bedouin land in the Naqab transferred to the state is added, Cano estimates that the total area of Arab land transferred amounted to between 6.5 and 7 million dunams, which was more than 30 per cent of all land in the state. The figure of 7 million dunams for global Palestinian losses was also asserted by the UN Conciliation Commission for Palestine (see Peretz 1958: 143–4; Hadawi 1988: 94–7).

Others have attempted to estimate how much land was lost by the Palestinian communities that survived the war of 1948. According to studies, Arab residents of Israel initially lost 40 per cent of their land under the Absentees' Property Law, and by the time the major land expropriations had been completed, a total of some 70 per cent as a result of a combination of all the land expropriation measures (Peretz 1958: 142; Lustick 1980: 179).[77] While there has been no comprehensive survey to establish the precise extent of the loss across the whole community, it seems the figure of an average of at least 70 per cent of land lost to the Palestinian communities is plausible. Abu Kishk compared landownership in thirty-eight Arab villages in 1945, 1962 and 1972. He found that between 1945 and 1962, the villages lost 68 per cent of their land, and by 1972 had lost a total of 72 per cent of their original lands (Abu Kishk 1981: 128). His figures accord with a sample of data from a representative eighteen Arab villages carried out by Ian Lustick, who also concluded that an average of 70 per cent had been lost (Lustick 1980: 179). Sabri Jiryis looked at land lost by seventy-eight communities between 1945 and 1962, and found an overall reduction of 65 per cent, of which 21 per cent was due to the Land Acquisition Law 1953.[78] Another study carried out in 1963 found that the state owned about 55 per cent of the total land area within the boundaries of Palestinian villages, and that 11.1 per cent of the cultivable land in Arab villages was public land (Abu Kishk 1963). A later study by Professor Barukh Kipnis of Haifa University revealed that the process of expropriations continued through the 1980s: 60,000 dunams were added to state lands in the Galilee alone during the period 1978 to 1987, as a result of settlement of title operations, acquisitions and expropriations.[79]

Calculation of the amount of privately owned land that was taken away from the Palestinians, whether through expropriation or because the possessors were unable to prove ownership under the stringent rules devised by Israel in the settlement of title process, does not present the full picture of Palestinian land loss. Two further factors must be considered. The first is that Palestinians were dispossessed not only of land to which they claimed individual ownership rights, but also of other land to which the Palestinian communities had communal rights of access. The land area privately owned by the Palestinian community does not represent the full amount of land actually possessed, worked, lived on and used for a wide range of purposes by this community, rights that had been recognized by the Ottoman and British rulers as conferring right of possession and use if not right of absolute ownership. Nor does it take account of the fact that further land would have been available to the Palestinian communities had their natural growth and development not been arrested. This approach was accepted by the Palestinian Conciliation Commission set up by the UN to arrange for the implementation of UN Resolution 194, which in 1951 estimated that the land lost to Palestinians amounted to 16,324 square km of a total area of 26,320 square km of Mandatory Palestine (Hadawi 1988: 94–7).

A second and vital factor is the far-reaching consequences for Palestinians of the fact that at least 93.5 per cent of land in Israel has been brought under the formal ownership of the state. The JNF, which cannot be considered a private body, owns more than 2.5 million dunams of this land, including large amounts of cultivable land belonging to the Palestinian refugees, and allocates this land only to Jews (ILA 2000: 163). The rest is registered in the name of the state (including some registered in a state body, the Development Authority) and Palestinian access to this land is also in reality severely limited. As the following two chapters seek to demonstrate, because of the regime that has been established in relation to state land, Palestinians have not only lost access to land that they claim is rightfully and legally owned by them, but they have also been largely stripped of access to land over which they do not claim ownership, but which had been, and should be, accessible to them.

Notes

1. Naqab is the Arabic name for the region in the South of Israel that is known in Hebrew as the Negev. Large parts of the Naqab are desert.

2. Sabri Jiryis says Israel had already taken much of the good farmland belonging to Palestinians and wanted to prevent Palestinians from 'seizing' it back or from using the less good but still cultivable or usable land such as hilly or rocky land. Since much of the country was still unsurveyed and rights were not defined, and according to existing law Arab farmers would have the right to ask that land they were actually farming be registered in their name, the government decided to take urgent action (Jiryis 1976: 111–12). Sandy Kedar explains how around 1955, after the state had completed a massive set of land transfers under the 1953 Land Acquisition (Validation of Acts and Compensation) Law, it grew concerned at the amount of land in the central Galilee that remained in Palestinian hands, an area still largely untouched by settlement of title operations. The state therefore began settlement of title in the area in 1955 but progress was slow and numerous legal disputes arose regarding interpretation of the Ottoman Land Law. As a result, the government

decided more drastic steps were required, and took the measures described in this chapter such as amending the law in order to make it more difficult for Palestinians to prove their rights (Kedar 2001a: 923).

3. The Ottoman land system is described in detail in Goadby and Doukhan (1935).

4. Prior to 1948 the Islamic community had been left to administer its own affairs and property as part of the Millet system, but, as already described in the previous chapter, Israel broke up the *Waqfs* and their administrations, and expropriated most of their property. The religious shari'a courts, which had previously had supervisory jurisdiction over the *Waqf* system, lost this role.

5. Ottoman Land Code, Articles 6 and 103.

6. Ottoman Land Code, Article 5.

7. Palestine Order in Council 1922 regarding Public Lands, cited in Goadby and Doukhan (1935: 60). Hadawi (1988: 42) also stresses that the government did not regard these lands as being within its control.

8. See McNeil (1989: 80), generally and, with regard to Palestine, Shehadi (1993).

9. Gavish asserts that the intention to fulfil the British commitments made regarding the establishment of a Jewish home in Palestine was a major driving force behind the creation and early implementation of a land registration system. The Zionist movement had been promised possession of lands that were registered in the name of the Mandate administration. Thus for example two parcels of land that were considered crucial for the Zionist enterprise were surveyed: the Ghur Mudawrah (Beit She'an) and Huleh valleys.

10. Ordinance for the Amendment of Land-Holding Books, *Official Gazette* 175, Supplement 1, pp. 75–8.

11. British High Commissioner Arthur Wauchope estimated in 1933 that there were 4–5 million dunams of land held under the *musha'* system. As surveying and registration of land progressed, *musha'* land was often divided and villagers were given individual title; see Stein (1984: 14–15).

12. Just under 1 million dunams, out of a total of 26.3 million dunams of land in Mandatory Palestine as a whole, was leased to Arabs. This excludes the Naqab south of Birsheba.

13. There are also smaller Bedouin communities in the north of Israel, and Israel has pursued similar resettlement policies there, establishing new communities for some while others continue to live in 'unrecognized' settlements.

14. The widely varying estimates are due to lack of reliable data from the period.

15. The authors are indebted to lawyer Meir Lamm, who has represented Bedouin in land cases for many years, for clarifying the legal context of the Bedouin land claims in the Naqab, in an interview in February 1991.

16. C. Bailey, 'Dispossessed of the Desert', *Jerusalem Report* magazine, 26 January 1995.

17. According to a tribe leader interviewed by Moshe Arens in *Ha'aretz* (Hebrew daily newspaper), 20 April 1979, each tribe kept a book recording the

boundaries of its land and any transactions which took place, and each year any changes would be recorded in an identical copy of the book kept by the district governor. After 1948, it seems, Israeli officials collected these and never returned them. Unpublished manuscript of Palestinian land lawyer H. Nakkara (n.d.: 201).

18. The Survey of Palestine prepared in 1945–46 for the Anglo-American Committee of Inquiry also asserted that there may be private claims to over 2 million dunams (of a total 12.5 million dunams) of cultivated area; Anglo-American Committee of Inquiry (1946: 257).

19. According to Shimoni, writing in 1947, of 4.3 million dunams of cultivable land in the Naqab, the Bedouin used 3.4 million; Association for Support and Defence of Bedouin Rights in Israel (1990).

20. The Arabic word for fence or enclosure is *siyaj*, but this is pronounced *siyag* by the Bedouin in the Naqab, so we have adopted this spelling.

21. They would not be able to acquire rights by prescription both because the lease was granted by consent and because it was for a short time.

22. The Jewish communities kept their own land-holding books and succeeded in persuading the Mandate administration to recognize them; see note 10 above.

23. Palestine Government, *Village Statistics*, 1945.

24. LSI, Vol. 23, p. 283.

25. By 2000, the ILA administered over 20,400 dunams of land, amounting to 94.5 per cent of the total land area of Israel; ILA (2000: 163, 'Ownership of settled land administered by the ILA'). But at least 1.1 million dunams is land that has not yet undergone settlement of title.

26. Nevertheless, the Land Law does contain a few provisions designed to protect state land: for instance, section 113 limits the acquisition of rights in state land by prescription.

27. According to ILA (2001) more than 1.1 million dunams of land remained unsettled.

28. The Land (Settlement of Title) Ordinance (Amendment) Law 1960; LSI, Vol. 14, p. 12.

29. Unpublished manuscript by the late H. Nakkara. The authors would like to acknowledge Nakkara's work and his meticulous documentation of the settlement of title process in the Galilee in particular.

30. Kedar shows how this pattern helped to establish restrictive rules such as relating to *Mewat* land and the 50 per cent rule – see note 32.

31. State of Israel v. Hussein Sawaid and Others, HC 342/61, PD 15, p. 2469.

32. State of Israel v. Saleh Badran and Others, HC 518/61, PD 16, p. 1717.

33. Mas'ad Kassis v. State of Israel, HC Civil Appeal 298/66, PD 21(1), p. 272.

34. Cases of Hawashleh and Sawaid.

35. LSI, Vol. 12, p. 129.

36. State of Israel v. Abdulla Shibli and Others, HCA 520/89, PD 46(2) 81, judgment given on 16 March 1992, also reported in English in the *Jerusalem Post Law Report*, 4 May 1992.

37. The new Article 103 of the Land Code, introduced by the Mewat Land Ordinance, *Official Gazette*, no. 38, 1 March 1921, or *Legislation of Palestine 1918–1925*, Vol. 1, p. 135.

38. Furthermore, Nakkara argues that in the revised version of the Mewat Land Ordinance of 1934, the paragraph requiring registration of acquired rights within two months was omitted, following which the legal position was that anyone who had revived *Mewat* land without leave prior to 1921 was entitled to a title deed upon payment of a fee; Nakkara (n.d.: 155).

39. This was confirmed in the leading case of Hawashleh in 1974, see note 43, below.

40. Association for Support and Defence of Bedouin Rights in Israel (1990: 19–20). This does not represent the full amount of land used by Bedouin before 1948, which is close to 2 million dunams; see Anglo-American Committee of Inquiry (1946).

41. State of Israel v. Hussein Sawaid and Others, HC 342/61, PD 15 p. 2469.

42. State of Israel v. Saleh Badran and Others, HC 518/61, PD 16, p. 1717.

43. Salim Hawashleh and Others v. State of Israel and Others, HC 218/74, PD 38(3), p. 141.

44. For instance State of Israel v. Hussein Sawaid and Others and Salim Hawashleh and Others v. State of Israel and Others.

45. Hawashleh, see note 43, above.

46. Interview with lawyer Meir Lamm, 12 February 1991, Tel Aviv.

47. Plia Albek admitted this in the discussion group on 'The Negev Lands from a Legal Point of View' (1985). According to statistics from the ILA Birsheba office, in 1979, 3,220 claims had been submitted concerning 776,856 dunams of land; Association for Support and Defence of Bedouin Rights in Israel (1990: 20).

48. ILC Decision 884 of 18 July 2000.

49. ILO Convention No. 169 of 1989, Article 14, and Draft Declaration on the Rights of Indigenous Peoples, para. 23.

50. Section 154(a) Land Law 1969. This was confirmed in the case of the village of Julis v. State of Israel, HC Civil Appeal 501/83, PD 40(2), p. 131

51. Um El Fahem Local Council v. State of Israel, HC Civil Appeal 438/70, PD 26(1), p. 813.

52. Yaffa Local Council v. State of Israel, HC 13/76 and 10/76, PD 31(2), p. 605.

53. The government has power to convert *Matruka* land to another category where it is in the public interest, so long as existing rights and interests are compensated by reasonable substitute: The Land Law Amendment (Conversion of Matruka) Law 1960, LSI, Vol. 14, p. 92.

54. For instance the Forests Ordinance 1926 and the Parks, Nature Reserves and National Sites Law 1963, which prohibit grazing, the building of residences and other activities on designated lands.

55. According to the Statistical Abstract (2000), the 'arab' population of the Naqab is 106,400, but a general note is included to the effect that the statistics regarding the Bedouin are incomplete. The figure of 120,000 is based on field surveys by Palestinian community-based organizations in the Naqab such as the Regional Council for the Unrecognized Villages of the Palestinian Bedouin in the Naqab, and the Association of Forty.

56. These figures are estimates of the Regional Council for the Unrecognized Villages of the Palestinian Bedouin in the Naqab. The phenomenon of the unrecognized Palestinian villages in Israel is examined in Chapter 8.

57. Interview with town planner Esther Levinson, March 1995.

58. See Chapter 8 for a discussion of this plan and of legal challenges by the Bedouin community.

59. For instance, the government-commissioned *Markovitz Report* of 1986 recommended that the relocation policy be completed by the year 1990 and targets set by the Israel Lands Council also overestimate the speed at which plots of land in the urbanized centres will be taken up; see Chapter 8.

60. Resolution 1993/77 adopted on 10 March 1993 during the 49th Session of the UN Commission on Human Rights.

61. See for example UNCESCR (1991, para. 18).

62. ILC Decision 340, session 285 of 28 October 1986.

63. According to ILC Decision 813 of 9 October 1997, a building plot in the township of Rahat, of around half a dunam, would cost NIS 60,000, whereas according to the same decision, a Bedouin would be entitled to NIS 2,000 per dunam for good (flat) land if he was not in possession and NIS 3,000 if he was in possession, and only NIS 1,100 per dunam for mountainous land in possession. ILC Decision 813 also provides for subsidies of up to half the cost of purchasing and developing a plot (an average of 20,000 with a maximum of NIS 35,000).

64. ILC Decision 626 of 12 January 1994.

65. ILC Decision 885 of 18 July 2000 specified the amount of compensation payable per square metre depending on whether the house was built of stone, wood or other material. Decisions 585, 595 and 601 of 1993, and Decision 626 of 1994 also dealt with this.

66. ILC Decision 859 of 3 May 1999 offered compensation of NIS 100,000 to those who signed evacuation agreements before the end of 1999.

67. ILC Decision 550, session 270 of 28 October 1991.

68. ILC Decision 813 of 9 October 1997 and Decision 884 of 18 July 2000. For instance ILC Decision 813 authorized the ILA to compensate Bedouin in the form of land to the extent of up to 20 per cent of the area claimed, where the area claimed is over 400 dunams.

69. The relocation policy and conditions in the urbanized townships are discussed more fully in Chapter 8.

70. Yosef Algazi in *Ha'aretz*, 10 January 1994, translated in 'The Other Front', Alternative Information Center, Jerusalem, Issue 255, 12 January 1994.

71. See Chapter 3 for a discussion of some of the implications of such land-holding patterns, including the fact that the state uses such plots to exchange for consolidated plots outside the village which it then uses for Jewish settlement.

72. The first principle is known as the doctrine of continuity and is well established under international law, and the second is finding increasing support in international practice; both are described in Chapter 2.

73. Section 2, State Property Law 1951; LSI Vol. 5, p. 45.

74. Israel Government Yearbook 1962–63, p. 107, cited in Jiryis (1985: 21).

75. The ILA administers some 1,129,631 dunams of land that has not yet undergone settlement of title procedures and whose ownership has not yet been established.

76. Salman Abu Sitta (2001: 13) says that estimates of land in the state privately owned by Palestinians vary from 2–3 per cent.

77. Lustick bases his estimate on data from a representative eighteen Arab villages.

78. Jiryis's benchmarks are the Village Statistics of 1945, an estimated index of landownership undertaken by the British Mandate authorities but not conclusive since surveying and settlement of title had not been carried out in many areas, and the Israeli Government Yearbook for the year 1963/64. He found a total overall reduction from just over a million dunams to around 375,000 dunams, an overall loss of approximately 65 per cent; Jiryis (1976: 292–6).

79. Conference concerning the Galilee held at Haifa University, reported in *Ha'aretz*, 13 June 1989.

CHAPTER 5

The Concept of 'Israel Lands'

§ WITHIN the first decade or so of its establishment, Israel had taken the vast majority of land into the ownership and control of either the state or the Jewish National Fund (JNF) in the manner described in the two previous chapters. This included some 7 million dunams of privately owned Palestinian land expropriated under the Absentees' Property Law and other legislation. It also included all land that had been regarded by the Mandatory administration of Palestine as public land, which was transferred to the State of Israel.[1] Third, it included land purchased by the Zionist land purchasing agencies, chiefly the JNF, before 1948. By 1960, these three categories already accounted for over 90 per cent of all land in the state, and today amount to a total of around 94.5 per cent.[2]

Debates about what to do with this land – whether to keep it in public ownership, how to manage it and what role, if any, to give to the JNF – began almost immediately after 1948. But it was not until 1960 that two major pieces of legislation were enacted to define the status of this 'national' land: the Basic Law: Israel Lands and the Israel Lands Law. Under this legislation, all land owned by the state and the JNF was to be known as 'Israel Lands'. This land was to be administered by a new public body, the Israel Lands Administration (ILA). It would be misleading to view the new system as merely a centralization of landownership in the sense known in other countries. The terms 'public land', 'national land' or 'state land', used elsewhere to denote central ownership in the interests of all citizens of a state, are given a very specific application in Israel. Here the term 'Israel Lands' is broadly intended to mean the land of the Jewish people, meaning not only those living in Israel but Jews anywhere in the world. The legislation of 1960 and the new regime for non-private land has had an enormous impact on Palestinian access to land in Israel.

The concept of public land under Ottoman and British rule

In 1948 the State of Israel inherited some form of legal interest in the majority of land in the state, though the precise nature of this interest varied from one category of land to another. Under the Ottoman land system, ultimate ownership of all land was vested in the Sultan by right of conquest, other than *Waqf* land, which was vested in God, and *Mulk*, which the Sultan had granted in full ownership to a private person.[3] Most agricultural land used and possessed by Palestinians fell under the category of *Miri*, in which the Sultan retained the *Raqabe*, meaning the ultimate ownership.[4] Over time, however, the *Raqabe* became a mere theoretical interest, as those who possessed and used this land were given more and more rights, so that, by the end of the Ottoman era, the government had no effective control over it. Other land around the towns and villages was *Matruka* and *Mewat*, and was recognized as being at the disposal of the local population for a variety of purposes.[5]

The British Mandate administration, when it took over responsibility for Palestine after the First World War, essentially recognized the de facto situation, which was that most usable land was in the possession of the local population and such possession conferred rights. The Mandate authorities did, however, set out to clarify legal interests in land by initiating land surveying and a process for determining rights in land (this was the settlement of title process, discussed in Chapter 4). The administration defined land falling under its control 'by virtue of Treaty, convention, agreement or succession' as 'Public Land',[6] and one of the objectives of the settlement of title exercise was to identify which land fell into this category. The main factor used to determine if land was public land was whether or not the administration exercised control over it.[7] By the time the Mandate came to an end in 1948, this process of identifying public land was far from completed.

Meanwhile, as Jewish immigration and settlement in Palestine grew, and the Zionist organizations consolidated their control over certain areas of land, a division started to appear between 'Jewish' land, which was land taken over and made subject to the Zionist restrictions on sale and insistence on Hebrew labour, and 'Arab' land, which was land still available for Palestinian use.[8] After 1948, Palestinians who became citizens of Israel found that whereas previously they had had access to all land other than that owned by individual Jews or the Zionist organizations, or the relatively small areas of state land leased to Jews, under Israel the situation was reversed. Palestinians now faced enormous obstacles in obtaining access to all land other than land that was recognized as privately owned by members of the community.

The Zionist concept of national land

The idea that land acquired by Jews in Palestine was to be the property of the Jewish nation as a whole and that it could never be sold but only granted to Jews under temporary grants of use, dates from the earliest Zionist thinking. The idea was first presented by several rabbis active in the Zionist movement, notably Herman Schapira, at the First Zionist Congress held in Basel in August 1897 (Lehn and Davis 1988: 1). His rationale was based on the Old Testament; since God is ultimately the owner of the land, humans may only have use of it and not ownership: 'The land must not be sold in perpetuity; for the land is mine' (Leviticus 25: 23). According to the Tora, every fiftieth year the land must be redeemed, or restored to its original owner (ibid.: pp. 1–3). The idea was adopted by secular Zionist leaders who realized that they could retain the support of religious Jews while redefining the concept in national and political terms so that the place of God as ultimate owner of the land was taken by the Jewish state (ibid.: p. 5). Its appeal was based on the assumption that measures were required to ensure that land, once acquired by Jews, would remain in Jewish hands.

Jewish land acquisition before the establishment of Israel was led by Zionist agencies, principally the Jewish National Fund (JNF). The JNF was established following a decision of the Fifth Zionist Congress, registered in England in 1907, which began raising funds (Lehn and Davis 1988: 24). Its role was to provide the foundations for a Jewish state by acquiring and settling land based on the principles recommended by Schapira, and 'guaranteeing the land basis of the enterprise' (Granott 1956: 38). Initially, a debate took place within the Zionist movement as to whether ownership of land that had been purchased in Palestine should be transferred to individual Jews or held by the Zionist institutions that would allocate it to members of the Jewish community. This dilemma of choosing between private or national ownership was resolved in 1920 when the Zionist Conference in London decided that 'the guiding principle of Zionist land policy is to transfer into the common possession of the Jewish people those areas in which Jewish settlement is to take place'. The JNF was to be the sole instrument of Jewish land policy, and all the resources of the Zionist movement that were allocated for land acquisition were to be channelled to the organization. At the same time, detailed guidelines for leasing JNF land were approved (Lehn and Davis 1988: 49–50). Although private ownership of land by individual Jews was permitted, the main thrust of Zionist policy was to be pursued through national ownership of the land. Without this, it was thought, there could be no effective guarantee that the ownership of the land would remain in Jewish hands. Retaining land in national hands was also considered important in order to protect the notion of Jewish labour (Granott 1956: 51).

The advantages of 'national' ownership of the land were presented by one of its main architects, Granott, who argued on the grounds of both political expediency and of efficiency:

1. It precludes the danger that the land may cease to be Jewish.
2. It will be possible to avoid concentration of land in the hands of a few; the size of units leased will not be greater than the capacity of the farmer and his family to work it.
3. It promotes an efficient agricultural sector by allowing planning, which cannot be done if land is controlled by many owners.
4. It facilitates the role of land in the state economy since the exploitation of land for public benefit is feasible under a single owner. (Granott 1956: 52)

By the time of the establishment of Israel in 1948, the principle that land acquired by the Zionist colonizers would be considered the inalienable property of the Jewish people as a whole was well established. After debating the issue, the Israeli Knesset decided to retain this principle of inalienability of the land as the foundation stone of the new land regime, and to formalize it in legislation of the most entrenched kind possible in the Israeli constitutional system: a Basic Law. During the debates in the Knesset that preceded the adoption of the legislation of 1960, a range of ideological, religious, national and sociological arguments were raised. These arguments fell into three main categories: national/religious justifications and the need to absorb Jewish immigrants; the need to guarantee control of land use; and the need to prevent speculation in land.

When proposing the Israel Lands Law in the Knesset, the chair of the Constitution, Law and Justice Committee, Zerah Verhaftig, said:

> The reasons for recommending this law, as far as I understand it, are to provide a legal cover for a principle that at its core is religious, and that is 'the land shall never be sold, for the land is mine' (Leviticus 25: 23). And if this is repeated in the law as has been recommended, or even if it is not, here now is a legal cover for it, the same rule that is to be found in the Torah. In this is a law that can be interpreted as expressing our original view on the holiness of the Land of Israel ...

> The second argument is an active principle. The land was acquired and conquered by the whole nation. It was promised from the beginning by the Lord our God, to Abraham, Isaac and Jacob, and it was first

conquered by the entire nation by Joshua and the whole nation that left Egypt and then by David and the entire nation ...

The lands of the JNF were also purchased with the small change collected by the entire nation in every part of the Diaspora, and the land was developed by the blood of our youth, our soldiers, and so we do not have any right to turn this property, these assets, that were acquired and conquered by the entire nation, to individual inheritances, to private inheritances.[9]

For some, then, it was the national-religious concept of 'redemption' or Judaization of the land that justified its central ownership. Harking back to the objectives of the early Zionist colonization movement, they saw the drive to 'redeem' the land and to take in Jewish immigrants as a duty to the Jewish people. They believed that measures still needed to be taken in order to ensure that the land remained Jewish.

The Knesset debated the question of whether or not the role of the Jewish national institutions was now redundant or whether these institutions still had an important part to play now that the state was established.[10] Some criticized the land regime proposed by the government on the grounds it gave too much state power to non-governmental bodies. Member of Knesset Yohanan Bader of the Herut Party criticized the fact that the government had approved the transfer of land from the state Development Authority to the JNF, charging that the government's purpose in so doing was to remove that land from the supervision of the Knesset and from the democratic processes.[11] In the end, however, it was decided that the JNF would be given a central role in the new land regime. One of the main reasons why it was decided to assign such a huge role to a formally non-governmental organization rather than to the state was to ensure that land use policies in Israel would continue to be guided by Zionist principles, at the expense of Arab interests, including Arab Palestinian citizens of the state. As one JNF official admitted: 'The economic impact of our land purchases and our activities on Arabs is not considered ... The government would have to look after all citizens if they owned the land; since the JNF owns the land, let's be frank, we can serve just the Jewish people' (Lustick 1980: 106). In other words, by giving central roles to the JNF and the other Jewish national institutions, the Israeli government thought that it would be able to ensure that resources were channelled to Jewish citizens alone while denying accusations of discrimination.[12] Another factor was financial: the JNF was an important institution for Jews abroad, and continued to be able to attract large-scale funding to Israel.[13]

The Knesset also discussed whether the term 'Israel Lands' was the most appropriate to adopt. Its proponents had made it clear that this was not to mean 'land belonging to all citizens of the state of Israel'; rather, it was intended that the land would be at the disposal of Jews from anywhere in the world. So for instance a proposal to adopt instead the name 'the people's lands' was rejected on the basis that this would necessarily include all the residents of the state, including non-Jews.[14]

Other arguments were also raised in support of a land policy based on public ownership. Many of those who supported retaining central ownership of land believed that such a system guaranteed greater public control over land use, facilitated planning and development, and made those using the land more easily held accountable to planning needs. The premise was that centralized supply of land, the country's most precious resource, can ensure that sufficient land is available when and where it is required for agricultural, residential, industrial and commercial uses. It was also argued that public landownership would ensure that land prices remained low and would discourage speculation in land. By fixing prices, the ILA could control fluctuations and prevent steep rises in land values, and control who would benefit from rises in land value.

The debates that led to the adoption of the legislation of 1960 establishing the new land regime are illuminating. They indicate a majority favouring a system that would allow the exclusion of non-Jews from some centrally owned land (that owned by the JNF) and an understanding that all centrally owned land, even that owned by the state, was primarily intended to be used for building Israel as the Jewish state. Indeed, this was hardly a contentious issue. The major concerns expressed were how best to ensure efficiency, control and the state's national and religious objectives.

The Israeli reorganization of the land regime

In the years immediately following the establishment of Israel in 1948, the land falling under the control of the new state had been administered by various authorities. The Custodian of Absentee Property and the Development Authority took charge of the property of 'absentees', the Department for State Lands in the Finance Ministry managed state lands, the Lands Division of the Ministry of Agriculture allocated agricultural land for cultivation, and the JNF managed the land under its ownership. Pressure mounted for a more coordinated policy. The Basic Law: Israel Lands, and the Israel Lands Law, both enacted in 1960, established the new land regime governing non-private land in the state. The major characteristics of the new regime were:

- Ownership was to remain unchanged.
- The principle of inalienability was retained.
- Management of land owned by the state and the JNF was centralized in the hands of a public body.
- The roles of the JNF and the Jewish Agency were continued and institutionalized.

Ownership was to remain unchanged A first key decision taken was that there was to be no comprehensive nationalization of land: the minority of land in the state still in private ownership could remain so. A second important decision was that land owned by the JNF was not absorbed into state ownership; the JNF was to be allowed to keep its land, and indeed to continue its function of acquiring land for the purpose of settling Jews.

Section 1 of the Basic Law: Israel Lands provided that lands belonging to the state, the Development Authority and the JNF were now to be known as 'Israel Lands'.[15] The existing distribution of land between these three bodies has remained fairly constant, though some additional land has been passed by the state to the JNF. The state acquired ownership of land from various sources and by various legal procedures. The State Property Law 1951 transferred all property within Israel that had previously been vested in the Mandatory Government of Palestine, to the State of Israel.[16] The law also granted the state the right of reversion on all land, stating that all ownerless property would be the property of the state. Under the Succession Law 1965, the property of a deceased person who has no heir reverts to the state.[17] The Development Authority was a state body established by the Development Authority (Transfer of Property) Law 1950,[18] specifically to receive from the Custodian of Absentees' Property the property belonging to Palestinian refugees and that expropriated from Palestinian owners under the emergency and defence regulations.[19] In 1953 the Custodian formally sold to the Development Authority all the lands vested in him at the time. In 1961, after having sold some of its land to the JNF, the Authority held 2,596,000 dunams, or 13 per cent of all Israel Lands.[20] This remained almost unchanged in 2000, at 2,499,000 dunams (see Table 5.1). The Authority's power to sell land was already restricted prior to 1960.[21] The JNF owns a little over 12 per cent of all 'Israel Lands', a total of 2,542,000 dunams. This includes around half of all non-privately owned land outside the Naqab and most non-private cultivable land, and the Fund is still actively involved in purchasing land. The distinction between state- and JNF-owned land is often blurred. JNF land is administered by the ILA which is a state body, and the Fund enters many joint ventures;

for instance acting as trustee and administering properties on behalf of the Ministry of Housing or other government ministries.[22]

TABLE 5.1 Ownership of settled land administered by the Israel Lands Administration in 2000 (in thousands of dunams)[23]

District	Total	JNF	Devel. Auth.	State
Total	19,281	2,542	2,499	14,240
[...]	[...]	[...]	[...]	[...]
Haifa	635	209	192	234
South	12,008	378	166	11,464

Source: (ILA 2000: 163).

The ILA administers an additional 1.1 million dunams of land that has not yet undergone settlement of title procedures. The ILA estimates that of this, some 130,000 will eventually be registered in the names of private owners and the remainder in the name of the state (ILA 1993: 131).[24] The ILA believes that once settlement of title operations have been completed throughout the state, 20,235,000 dunams, or almost 93.5 per cent of the 21,650,000 dunams which is the total area of land in the state, will fall under its administration. The amount remaining in private ownership will be 1,415,000 dunams (ibid.). In 2000, the amount of settled land in private ownership was 1,406,325 dunams.

The principle of inalienability was retained The basic principle established in section 1 of the Basic Law: Israel Lands 1960 was as follows: 'The ownership of Israel lands ... shall not be transferred either by sale or in any other manner.' In other words, the principle that land, once acquired, would not be sold but would be held centrally and leased, which had been the practice of the JNF since before the establishment of the state, was to be not only maintained but extended to all 'Israel Lands', including state-owned land. This decision had already been made and recorded in the Covenant between the JNF and the government of Israel concluded in 1954. This document describes how the JNF had been engaged in acquiring land in Palestine and transferring it to the ownership of 'the people': 'The fundamental principle of Keren Kayemeth Leisrael [the Hebrew name of the JNF] is that its lands shall not be sold, but shall remain the property of the people and shall be given on lease only.'

Article 4 of the Covenant had affirmed that not only JNF-owned lands but all Israel Lands would be administered on the principle that land is not sold, but only leased. Israel Lands were to be centrally held and transferred only by lease. Agricultural land, for example, would be leased solely for cultivation and related purposes; use of the land for another purpose would result in the termination of the lease and the return of the land to the ILA.[25]

Management of land owned by the state and the JNF was centralized in the hands of a public body The legislation of 1960 provided for the centralized administration of all Israel Lands, including land owned by the JNF, by the Israel Lands Administration (ILA).[26] As a consequence of the principle of inalienability of 'Israel Lands', which means that land will be leased but not sold, the ILA, as the chief organization responsible for the management and supply of land in the state, has enormous influence on who has access to land. The way in which this public body operates and, in particular, its discriminatory policies as regards Palestinians in the state, are discussed in the following chapter. Its governing body, the Israel Lands Council, had no Arab representative until one was appointed following a successful legal challenge in 2001,[27] and it is dominated by the JNF.

The roles of the Jewish National Fund and the Jewish Agency were continued and institutionalized For Palestinians, perhaps the most significant aspect of the reforms of 1960 was the decision to give the JNF, the major agent of Zionist land acquisition before the establishment of the state, a central role. After 1948 the JNF had in fact continued to operate in the same way it had previously, and the legislation of 1960 reinforced and formalized this role. The JNF was registered as a corporation in Israel and permitted to continue its activities.[28] It had been agreed in a Covenant between the JNF and the state, in 1954, that the administration of JNF lands would be carried out by the state, which would also administer state and Development Authority lands.[29] The Memorandum and Articles of Association of the JNF, accepted in May 1954, specified that the objects of the organization were: 'to purchase, acquire or lease or in exchange, or receive on lease or otherwise, lands, forests, rights of possession, easements and any similar rights as well as immovable properties of any class ... for the purpose of settling Jews on such lands and properties'.[30]

The JNF emerged as one of the most powerful institutions in the state, gaining a role in three key areas. First, it was permitted to remain a large landholder, keeping the land it had owned before 1948 and acquiring vast new areas from the Israeli government, much of it agricultural land belonging to Palestinian refugees and the internally displaced. As a result of two agreements with the government, the JNF received 2,373,677 dunams of land including both urban and rural property, for which payment was agreed in annual instalments with interest at 2.5 per cent (Granott 1956: 11). By 1959, however, the JNF had paid little more than a third of the amount it owed at that time, less even than the accrued interest.[31] As late as 1989, the state transferred over 40,000 dunams of green land in Hula to the JNF.[32] The JNF's land holdings consist mainly of agricultural land, but the vast majority of residential units in cities such as Jerusalem and Haifa are built on JNF-owned land (Land Use Research Institute 1986b: 9). It owns approximately two-thirds of the forest land in the state (Givati 1981: 116, 184). It has a considerable budget; income for 1992 amounted to almost 350 million shekels (approximately US$117 million).[33] In 1996, the JNF received 850 million shekels (approximately US$240 million) in income from its lands from the ILA, more than the Development Authority or the state.[34]

The JNF is still actively involved in purchasing land, and still considers its main goal to be 'redeeming' land.[35] According to its report of 1994: 'The JNF purchases and "redeems" land (primarily from non-Jews) at fair market prices in all parts of the country.'[36] It now acts via companies such as Hemanuta Ltd, through which the Israeli government habitually makes land transfer deals with Arabs, exchanging either money or land in compensation for property that is then transferred into the ownership of the JNF. In practice, Hemanuta Ltd acts as the state's land purchasing agent. Its head defined the company as 'actually a dummy company of the State of Israel'.[37] Hemanuta is reported to be actively engaged in taking steps to prevent land or apartments from falling into Arab hands, financed by government funds, and even to have secretly subsidized apartments in one city, Upper Nazareth, in order to prevent Arab citizens from competing for them.[38]

A second key role given to the JNF was to be assigned specific tasks in the state that were by their nature governmental functions. Under its Covenant with the JNF of 1954, the government gave the Fund exclusive responsibility for rural land development in Israel, including land reclamation and afforestation. The Fund's Land Development Administration was to be governed by a board on which JNF appointees form a majority, and government representatives a minority. The JNF has been granted other quasi-governmental powers, such as the power to expropriate land for public purposes.[39] It also cooperates with government ministries in large-scale public projects such as water reservoirs and tourism.[40]

Third, the JNF was given shared responsibility with the state for managing Israel Lands, now over 93 per cent of all land in Israel. On the Israel Lands Council, the policy-making body of the ILA, 45 per cent are JNF representatives. In this way the Fund continues to play a major role in shaping government land policy.

It seems extraordinary that despite the JNF's extensive land holdings and powers, and despite its central role in Israeli land policy, the Israeli state has allowed the Fund to continue to work for the benefit of Jews alone, and to exclude Palestinians from land registered in its name. The intention to exclude non-Jews is implicitly rather than explicitly stated in the Memorandum and Articles of Association adopted in 1954 and accepted by the government, in which the 'primary object' of the JNF is stated to be to carry out its functions 'for the purpose of settling Jews on such lands and properties' (Article 3[a]). The Covenant between the state and the JNF, also concluded in 1954, declares that land owned by the JNF will remain the property of 'the people', which has been taken to mean not the citizens of Israel, but the Jewish people. The Memorandum and Articles of Association do not explicitly prohibit the leasing of its land to non-Jews, as the Memorandum and Articles of the company registered in England in 1907 had done. Indeed, the Fund is authorized to let its property 'on such terms and in such manner as it may deem fit' (Article 3[e]). However, the Fund has regarded the condition that its land must not be leased to non-Jews as unchanged. The established practice, based on the 1907 document, of leasing to Jews only, is still considered to be in force, and, in practice, non-Jews have been prohibited from leasing JNF land. Standard JNF lease agreements reflect this understanding, prohibiting transfer of the lease to 'a person or a company to whom the Fund according to its Memorandum of Association is prohibited from leasing its land' and explicitly state that cultivation of the land is to be 'only and exclusively by Jews'.[41]

In carrying out its role as manager of JNF land, the ILA is mandated to observe the restrictions contained in the Memorandum of Association regarding the use of land owned by the Fund. The Covenant between the JNF and the government concluded in 1954 specifies that 'the lands of [the JNF] shall be administered subject to [its] Memorandum and Articles of Association'. Thus, for example, where the ILA is offering a contract relating to JNF land by public bidding, it may discount an Arab tender on the basis that the purpose of the contract is to settle Jews.[42] The exclusion policy was emphasized still further by the enactment in 1967 of the Agricultural Settlement (Restrictions on Use of Agricultural Land and of Water) Law, which was enacted specifically with the intention of preventing lessees of JNF land from subleasing to Palestinians.[43]

Quite apart from these formal arrangements relating to the status and functions of the JNF, the attitude of the JNF itself and its senior officials has been of crucial importance to the Palestinian community in Israel and has continued to ensure that Palestinians will be denied access to JNF land. Instead of adapting to its new status as effectively a governmental arm in a state that includes not only Jews but also Arabs among its citizens, the JNF has kept the same basic attitudes that it developed when it was a part of the Zionist movement before the establishment of the state. So, for instance, the Fund still views its main objective as redeeming the land for the Jewish people and strongly resists any suggestion that it might end its practice of discriminating between Jews and Arabs.[44]

The JNF is not the only relic of the pre-state era to be given a special status and governmental functions in relation to land in Israel. The Jewish Agency (JA) also has a special status in Israel conferred by statute: the World Zionist Organization – Jewish Agency (Status) Law 1952. Its relationship with the government is established by the terms of a Covenant between the Jewish Agency and the government of 1958. The role of the JA is to take care of immigrant absorption and rural settlement in the state, as well as major public functions with a significant impact on land policy and access to land. Like the JNF, its special status extends to representation in key public decision-making authorities. And, like the JNF, it has a policy of excluding Palestinians from its projects.

The JNF and JA: private, quasi-governmental or public bodies?

The legality of the exclusionary policies of the JNF and the JA in relation to Palestinians has not been addressed directly by the Israeli High Court. A key question in any challenge would be whether the JNF and the JA are independent, non-governmental organizations, as they claim to be, or whether they must be considered to be public bodies, at least in relation to some of their functions. If the latter, they would be subject to the normal principles of Israeli administrative law, which includes the principle of equality and the duty not to discriminate. If they are considered to be private organizations, they would be subject only to general law which, at present, does not prohibit discrimination by private bodies (a claim of discrimination can still be brought against a purely private body by ordinary civil proceedings, but only where the law imposes a duty not to discriminate in the private sphere, such as in the field of employment).

Both the JNF and the JA are registered in Israel as independent private organizations; for instance the JNF was registered as a company in Israel in 1954. And when the Israeli government permitted this registration and concluded Covenants with the two organizations in 1954 and in 1958, its intention was clearly to allow the organizations to act independently of the state abroad as well as at home. One of the reasons why the two organizations were allowed to retain their roles after 1948 was in order for them to continue as international organizations catering to Jews all over the world, and not to limit their activities to Israel and its citizens, who include Jews and non-Jews. In its Covenant with the Israeli government of 1954, for instance, it is stated in Article 16 that the JNF 'shall continue to operate, as an independent agency of the World Zionist Organization, among the Jewish people in Israel and the Diaspora'.

However, in all essential respects, the JNF and JA have all the characteristics of public bodies and should be considered as such. Two elements can be identified as particularly crucial in the definition of a public body: that the source of its powers is a statute, so that the body is acting under law; and that its functions are 'powers of a public law character' (Wade and Forsyth 1994). Both are true of the JNF and JA: both organizations have been given their functions and powers under a law of the Knesset, and both carry out functions of a public law character.

Even where a body is established with a private status, it is possible for it to be considered a public body for certain purposes. The primary purpose of administrative law is to protect the citizen from the abuse of powers of public authorities, and, particularly since powers necessarily confer discretion, to ensure that the citizen has an effective legal remedy to challenge the exercise of that discretion (Wade and Forsyth 1994: 4, 245). So, in Israel, it has been recognized that certain bodies which do not form part of the central or local government structure but which do carry out public functions – such as public utility corporations and universities – should be subject to some of the rules of administrative law, including the prohibition against discrimination (Kretzmer 1990: 14).[45] In the Kistenbaum case, where the issue was whether a private company with a monopoly over burials in Israel could be considered a public body subject to public law rules, the High Court found that because the company carried out functions that were of a public nature, it had a public status and any contracts made by the company must therefore conform to rules governing contracts entered into by public authorities.[46] Even when it was carrying out private activities, Chief Justice Shamgar said, this company had duties based on its public status, and where there was a conflict between the two legal spheres, the rules of public law prevailed over those of private law as *lex speciale*.[47]

This is in line with the law elsewhere. In the UK, for example, it is possible for a body to be subject to judicial review with respect to some of its powers but not others.[48] In the USA, as in Israel, constitutional provisions such as the prohibition on discrimination apply to state action only, and not to the private sector unless legislation specifically imposes them in certain spheres, such as housing. However, a long line of cases have established that where government delegates to private actors functions that the government itself could perform, that private actor is bound by constitutional and administrative standards. In determining whether or not a function is a public function of this nature, the US courts will look at whether the delegated function is so predominantly governmental in nature that the private actor's action may be fairly attributable to government (Buchanan 1997). So, for instance, as long ago as 1883, the US Supreme Court held that a private railroad company had acted unlawfully in prohibiting a black woman from riding on a train, because 'when the owner of property devotes it to a use in which the public has an interest, he in effect grants to the public an interest in such use, and must, to the extent of that interest, submit to be controlled by the public, for the common good, as long as he maintains the use'.[49] In 1995 the Supreme Court held that Amtrak, the national railroad company, was an agency of the state for the purpose of individual rights guaranteed by the constitution, even though the legislation that created it declared that Amtrak would not be a state agency.[50] The decision rested on the fact that the government had established the corporation by special law for the furtherance of governmental objectives, and had retained the authority to appoint a majority of its directors.

Despite the overwhelming case for considering the JNF and JA to be public bodies, the Israeli courts have so far refused to subject the Jewish national institutions to any significant degree of judicial scrutiny. In a case relating to the Jewish Agency, the Bet Rivka case, the Israeli High Court in 1993 denied that the JA was fulfilling public functions according to law, and held that consequently its actions were not subject to judicial review. The JA, the Court held, is an independent voluntary organization fulfilling self-imposed tasks, not functions it is obliged to fulfil by law, and neither the law establishing the JA's status nor the Covenant with the government involved the delegation to it of governmental functions.[51] The Court did, however, acknowledge that there were circumstances in which a claim for discrimination could be brought on the basis that a private body had taken on a dual nature (i.e.

a private and public nature), in which case an action could be brought under administrative law, just as a branch of the administration may act in its private capacity. The Court did not clarify in which circumstances and on what basis such challenges could be brought.

The Bet Rivka decision seems extraordinary in light of the Kistenbaum judgment. It is difficult to understand also given the fact that the JA is clearly allocated functions under law (the World Zionist Organization – Jewish Agency [Status] Law 1952), and the fact that those functions – taking care of immigrant absorption and rural settlement in the state – cannot be viewed as voluntary and independent tasks. The JA is not simply a rather large-scale non-governmental organization working in community development. Nor is the JNF simply a large private organization that governs its own land in accordance with its own regulations. If this were the case the situation might be rather akin to that of a charity that focuses on assisting a particular community. The situation of the JNF and the JA is entirely different. First, the JNF's land is managed by the ILA, which is a public body. The clause in the Covenant of 1954 obliging the ILA to administer JNF land in accordance with the JNF's Memorandum and Articles of Association effectively calls upon the ILA to discriminate between different classes of citizens.[52] Second, the state has given the JNF many functions that are of a governmental nature, such as giving it an equal share of power on the governing body of the ILA, which manages all state land. The JA, also, has been given functions that are clearly of a governmental nature: absorption of immigrants and establishment of rural settlements throughout the state. But it is not only that they carry out what are essentially public functions; in some spheres, the JNF and JA are actually the *sole* bodies in the state given certain functions in relation to Jews, but with no parallel body for non-Jews. There are no other bodies in the state that acquire land for settlement, or that develop rural communities, for all citizens or for Palestinians in particular. Professor David Kretzmer (1990: 98) rightly says, 'one may question whether allowing a body which is restrictive in nature sole authority over these activities is consistent with the duty of the state to ensure equal rights to all citizens, irrespective of race, religion and sex'.

In other words, even if it were to be conceded that the JNF and the JA themselves are not public bodies, then the state has violated fundamental legal principles by giving them such functions and allowing them to act only for Jews. The government should not be able to avoid its own obligation to abide by the principle of equality simply by transferring land to another body (the JNF) and giving that body full licence to give only Jews access to it, or simply by delegating important development functions to another body (the JA) and giving it the power to cater only to Jews. In the case of the JNF, the situation is particularly egregious since most of the land in the ownership of the JNF was sold to the JNF by the state after it had been expropriated from Palestinians. The state, which authorizes these agencies to carry out functions in the public sphere, is responsible for the discriminatory way in which they are carried out. The roles of the JNF and JA are defined in Covenants with the Israeli government, and their functions are defined in enactments of the Knesset. There is therefore a duty on the state to ensure that these powers and functions are not exercised in a discriminatory manner. It is immaterial whether the terms of these Covenants and laws actually direct or permit discrimination and unequal treatment; this in practice results and the state is responsible. Additionally, the JNF and the JA should themselves be subject to public law norms, at least in so far as the functions they exercise are of a public character.

To date, however, the Israeli High Court has not only been unwilling to scrutinize the Jewish national institutions, but where it has commented has made it clear that it views their role as untouchable. In the case of Qa'dan, the High Court was asked to find that the exclusion of a Palestinian family from building a house in Katzir, a community established by the Jewish Agency, violated the principle of equality.[53] 'Adil Qa'dan had been informed by the Katzir Cooperative Association, upon applying to join the community, that he would not be accepted due to the fact he was an Arab and the land was for Jews only. The Association for Civil Rights in Israel, which represented Mr Qa'dan, claimed that the ILA, in allocating state land to a third party that established unlawful discriminatory criteria, was breaching its duty as a public body not to discriminate. While the JA's policy of building for Jews only was clearly a central issue in the case, not only did the Court decline to deal with this question, but it went to great lengths to assert that the issue was outside the scope of the petition, and to affirm the role of the Jewish Agency in the development of the Jewish state, a role given expression in legislation. The petitioners, the Court said, are not focusing their claims on the policy of the settlement bodies to settle Jews only, or on the historical role of such institutions.

A situation where Palestinians, only by virtue of the fact that they are Palestinians, are effectively excluded from leasing, or even being employed to work most agricultural land in the state other than that in private ownership, cannot be considered to be in accordance with principles of administrative and constitutional law as understood in Israel and elsewhere, and certainly does not comply with the prohibition on discrimination that is a fundamental principle of international human rights law.[54] And this situation is particularly egregious given that much of the land in the hands of the JNF had been expropriated from the Palestinian community.

The ongoing debate in Israel on nationalization of land

While the ownership and management of 'national' land was resolved in the legislation of 1960, this did not end the debate in Israel on this question. The lobby for denationalizing land has become increasingly strong. Two questions in particular have been debated in recent years. The first is how the benefits resulting from any denationalization would be distributed. The second is what to do about the reality that much land classified as 'agricultural' is no longer being used for agriculture. Only 20 per cent of the 450,000 people living on moshavs, kibbutzes and other Jewish agricultural settlements are actually working in agriculture (Leaber 2000: 21). This has resulted in pressure to develop land for other purposes, bringing lucrative profits, and the question is who should be entitled to those profits.

In 1982 the government appointed a committee, headed by Dr Amnon Goldenberg, to reveiw the state's landownership policy. In its final report submitted in 1986, the Committee recommended that state ownership should be preserved, but that leases of Israel Lands should become more akin to absolute ownership (Goldenberg 1987: 12). According to the proposal, leases of forty-nine years could be extended (renewed in perpetuity) in exchange for a payment of 99 per cent of the value of the land, with the state preserving the right to transfer ownership. In support, Dr Goldenberg cited several court rulings that recognized long-term leases as approaching near ownership. In his opinion, whether a lease was for forty-nine years or 1,000 years, it would not contradict the intent of the Basic Law: Israel Lands on a strict interpretation, which merely prohibited the *transfer* of Israel Lands. He believed that the Committee's recommendations coincided with the view already prevalent among the Israeli public, which was that leases resembling ownership were legal, desirable and fair. Another leading authority on land law in Israel, Professor Joshua Weisman, has opposed this view, arguing that such an interpretation would empty the Basic Law: Israel Lands of any meaning, and that long-term leasing would be thought of as ownership (Weisman 1987). Pliah Albek, former head of the Lands Division of the Attorney General's office, believes that the law as currently framed is already wide enough to allow greater rights to be given to leaseholders without sacrificing the principle of inalienability.[55]

For instance, a form of leasehold could be created in which the lessee makes an initial payment of 99 per cent of the value of the land, but the grantor of the lease preserves the full right to object to the transfer of the lease to anyone who does not meet certain criteria.[56] So, for example, if the land was owned by the JNF, the lease agreement would include a condition that the lease could not be transferred to persons who, according to the JNF regulations, would not normally be entitled to lease property from the JNF – in other words, non-Jews.

The government of the time rejected the Goldenberg Committee's recommendations, and decided to continue the existing system.[57] However, the question was reopened in response to the increased pressures on land resources created by the large-scale immigration from the Soviet Union from the early 1990s. Perceived problems included high housing prices, overcrowding in the central areas but under-usage of land in outlying areas. In April 1997 a report emerged from another inquiry, the Ronen Committee. The Committee had been appointed by the government to carry out a comprehensive review of Israeli land policy including the merits of selling state land into private ownership, the status of urban and agricultural leases, the extent to which land-use policies were achieving government settlement policies, and the role of the ILA. No change in attitude towards Palestinians is evident in the *Ronen Report* compared to earlier reviews. For instance, among the dangers warned of by the Committee if steps are not taken are 'illegal possession of land by Bedouin and Arabs'.

The Ronen Committee recommendations do nothing to address Palestinian concerns about the present land system. As regards Israel Lands classified as agricultural land, the Ronen Committee recommended the immediate denationalization only of land that was to have its status changed and was no longer designated for agricultural use. Otherwise, Ronen proposed that agricultural land should remain in national ownership for at least a further ten years. Any land that was denationalized would be registered in the name of the lessee only after it had been registered in the name of a particular settlement (such as a kibbutz) or the Jewish Agency. Since only Jews can be given leases by these organizations, this recommendation would effectively exclude Palestinians from acquiring any of this land. Among the Committee's other recommendations, relating to ILA policy and the distribution of the population, are proposals to prevent illegal possession of land and to give greater incentives for Jewish construction in the Naqab, Galilee and border areas.

It is hardly surprising that the *Ronen Report* was criticized by the Palestinian community as ignoring their needs, branding them as trespassers, and leaving intact the roles of the organizations which exclude

Palestinians from land, namely the ILA, the JNF and JA and Jewish settlement organizations. Although part of a trend towards a more market-led economy in Israel, the recommendations carefully ensure that the new situation would not create a truly open market where Palestinians would enjoy equal access to land. Instead, Palestinians would largely remain excluded from the land presently owned by the state or Jewish national institutions. Alarm in the Palestinian community was fuelled by reports in 1998 that the government had agreed to transfer millions of dunams of land expropriated from Palestinians in the Galilee and the Naqab to the JA.[58] If the Ronen Committee recommendations were to be implemented, the effect would be to entrench still further the dispossession and exclusion of Palestinians from land; if land no longer designated as agricultural land were to be transferred to kibbutzes and other private Jewish owners, this would mean that the land taken from Palestinians in 1948 would be placed even further beyond the reach of its former owners.

The recommendations of the Ronen Committee were not formally adopted by the government. However, some steps were taken to privatize property in the urban sector. In line with the Committee's recommendation to convert residential and industrial leases into full ownership, in 1998 the Public Housing (Rights of Acquisition) Law was enacted, allowing tenants of public housing to purchase full ownership rights in their apartments.[59] Palestinians will not benefit from this law, since there is virtually no public housing in the Arab sector, and in any event its implementation was subsequently frozen by the Knesset on the basis that too heavy a burden was imposed on the state budget, and amendments were made in order to reduce the cost.[60]

As a result of the widespread criticism provoked by the *Ronen Report*, in February 2000 the government appointed yet another committee, the Milgrom Committee, to look specifically into the question of agricultural land. In its report, issued in December 2000, the Milgrom Committee accepted that most agricultural land would remain in state hands, and focused mainly on the highly politically sensitive question of what should happen to land once its status has been changed from agricultural to another designation and it can be developed for other purposes. Milgrom suggested lower levels of payment to possessors of land on a change of use than had previously been proposed.

This sensitive question of who benefits from the huge profits to be made from the development potential of land is intrinsically linked to the question of the future of Israel Lands, particularly agricultural land. The kibbutzes, moshavs and other collective farms have held the best farm land in Israel on renewable long leases since the establishment of the state. Recent years have seen an increasing trend for the designation of agricultural land to be changed so as to allow development of housing and other projects. The *Gazit Report*, issued in 2000, found that of more than 22,000 cases of illegal construction in the country (excluding the south), one-third was in the Jewish agricultural sector, mainly in the moshavs, where people turned to building outside the legal process in order to make profits 'due to the difficult situation of the agricultural sector'.[61]

Once the status of agricultural land is changed and it becomes land that can be developed, its value increases enormously. According to the original philosophy behind the Israel Lands regime established in 1960, if, under exceptional circumstances, agricultural land was changed to another use, the lease would automatically expire and the land would return to the ILA. The lessee would be entitled to compensation for any investments and improvements he made to the land, and for the ending of the lease.[62] However, by the 1990s, changes in land policy reflected the rather more ambiguous status of land that had now been in the hands of the kibbutzes and other farming communities for forty years or more. From 1992, those who had been in possession of agricultural land for more than twenty-one years were given an entitlement to compensation for the change in use, calculated as a percentage of the new value of the land.[63] Further, as an alternative to receiving compensation they were given the right to acquire the land upon payment of only 51 per cent of its new value. Other decisions followed, giving holders of agricultural land in kibbutzes and moshavs greater rights to change the status of land and to take the profits.[64] These new policies not only departed from the principle that state-owned agricultural land was leased for cultivation only or returned to the state, but also gave land directly to one sector, the kibbutzes and moshavs, bypassing the usual requirements for putting out to tender that were intended to create an open process for allocating land.[65]

This situation has proved to be too much of a temptation for many kibbutzes, and they have pressed both for a change in status of the land they occupy and for the benefits of that change to go to them. The Knesset agricultural lobby presented a draft bill that aimed to transfer 4.2 million dunams of prime agricultural land into the permanent ownership of the some 130,000 people in the kibbutzes and other communities that currently possess it (Kedar 2001b). The lobbyists claimed that such a measure would benefit the agricultural economy, and that in any event the recipients deserved to benefit after decades of hard work. Further, the draft bill would give those currently in possession of the land considerable financial benefits if the status of the land is changed. Professor Gabriella Shalev, who advises the agriculture lobby, argues that the ILC has in effect acknowledged the rights of the agriculturalists by routinely renewing their leases and by acting to all intents and purposes as if they are the actual owners of the land, giving them the feeling that their status on the land was permanent (Benyan 2001). Relying on the principle of legitimate expectation, she argues that the behaviour of the ILA and other state bodies gave rise to a reasonable expectation on the part of the agriculturalists that their rights over the land go beyond the actual language of the renewable contracts, and that they would be full partners in any change in status of state land. She also asserts that the agriculturalists have come to rely on the consistent renewal of the leases, and on the fact that the long leases were virtually equivalent to ownership.

In response to these developments, members of the *Mizrahi* (Eastern Jewish) community in Israel calling themselves the Eastern Democratic Rainbow petitioned the Supreme Court. In their petition, they claimed that the series of decisions issued by the ILC in the 1990s easing the restrictions on change in status of agricultural land and granting the considerable financial benefits that flowed from it to the kibbutzes and other collective farms that held the land, enriched one sector of society at the expense of other citizens and had no legal or moral basis. Such developments, the Eastern Democratic Rainbow claimed, compounded the already existing discrimination that gave the basic resources of the state, which should be available to meet the needs of all citizens, to one small sector.[66]

The situation reached an impasse at the end of 2001, with neither the government nor the Supreme Court apparently wishing to decide between the different competing groups that were vying and hustling for their own interests. The agricultural lobby, upon hearing of the appointment of the Milgrom Committee, began to draft a law that would grant full ownership to possessors of agricultural Israel Lands and high payments in case of change of use. The aim was both to influence the Committee and to bypass it by securing the enactment of legislation that favoured their interests (Lekhtman 2001: 118). The draft law proposed by the agricultural lobby was opposed by the nature defence groups who say it will encroach on green areas, by the Eastern Democratic Rainbow who say it offends the principle of social equality, by the ILA which fears losing its power and ability to carry out land planning in the state, and by Attorney General Rubenstein who took the view that it goes against the basic laws relating to Israel Lands and fundamental rights, and the JNF which fears losing its land. Some voices within the JNF even called for a separation of JNF land from the ILA so that the JNF could administer its own land. The JNF's fears were fuelled by the High Court's decision in the Qa'dan case, which appeared to some to raise the prospect that land could fall into non-Jewish hands, contravening the JNF's mantra that national land belongs to the Jewish nation (Neive 2000: 5; Vitkon 2001: 131). In August 2002, the situation was partly resolved when the High Court ordered the ILC to cancel its decisions granting compensation to the Jewish farms when the status of agricultural land was changed, agreeing with the Attorney General that the lessees of the agricultural land should not be entitled to take the benefit.[67] But the longer-term question of whether agricultural land should be transferable into private hands remains open.

Palestinians, lacking a powerful political voice in the state, seem unlikely to gain significantly whichever interest group wins. If there is no change and the land is not denationalized, their exclusion from Israel Lands will continue unless and until the policies of the state and the JNF in relation to their access to that land change. If the land is transferred to the kibbutzes and others, there is little prospect of access for Palestinians.

The impact of the concept of 'Israel Lands' on Palestinians

What standards should be used for evaluating a country's system for regulating access to public land? Equality, certainly, is one measure that applies both as a fundamental principle of Israeli law and as a matter of international law.[68] Other measures might include efficiency, the extent to which the system delivers an ability to control land use in the public interest and the extent to which it helps to achieve national goals.[69]

Public ownership of land exists to varying degrees in many states in the world with varying degrees of success in terms of guaranteeing equality of access to land. The example of Israel demonstrates that public ownership is not, in itself, sufficient to guarantee fairness and equality, and that the extent to which such principles are upheld depends on other factors. In Israel, no measures have been taken to ensure fairness and equality of access to land, certainly not in relation to the state's Palestinian Arab citizens. Where state ownership of land has come about against the background of one ethnic group striving to dominate and displace another, as in Israel, greater diligence will be required to ensure a culture of equality in the land system. And if one rationale for public ownership is that it ensures the supply of land when it is required, a system that expropriates the majority of the land belonging to a proportion of the population and then excludes that population from access to land is clearly far from satisfactory. In fact, arguments relating to equality and fairness have been almost wholly lacking from debates within the Knesset and among senior state officials and academics. Palestinians have not been included in or consulted by any of the review committees appointed to look into the status of national land. Aside from questions of efficiency, the debates have focused on public perceptions, vested interests and the need to control land in order that it could be used in the interests of state policies that include national goals.

The Eastern Democratic Rainbow case highlights the ways in which the inherent inequalities in the Israeli land system discriminate not only against the Palestinians, but also against other sectors of Israeli society that have less power than the kibbutzes, moshavs and the rest of the agricultural lobby. Mizrahi Jews tend to be consigned to sub-standard public housing in the cities. Nevertheless, the situation of the Palestinians differs from that of the Mizrahi Jews not only because of their historic claims to the land, but also because unlike the Mizrahi they are excluded in law as well as in practice from access to some Israel Lands, and in practice from others.

The continued role of the pre-state Jewish national institutions is a particular cause for concern to Palestinians. It is extremely difficult to see how a fair and equal land system can prevail when Palestinians are automatically denied access to a proportion of land in the state, owned by the JNF, which excludes non-Jews from land owned by it, and when the same organization wields a heavy influence on the entire land policy. The problem does not lie only with the legal framework. The Jewish national institutions, together with sections of the Israeli media and some of the political parties, have continued regularly to adopt the language used by the Zionist movement in the pre-state era, warning of the need to prevent 'encroachment on national land by the Arabs'.[70] The JNF still considers one of its most important roles to be 'protecting' Israel Lands and 'preserving the principle of national land', which means ensuring that 'this land remains the property of the entire Jewish people'.[71] The terms 'national' and 'redeemed' are used to describe Israel Lands, even by Israeli ministers, even though such lands include not only JNF-owned land but also state-owned land (Lustick 1980: 107, 296 note 68). Such attitudes are not merely a question of terminology; they demonstrate an underlying shared belief system that is translated into substantive policy relating to land. For instance, 'lookout' settlements are placed around the Galilee to watch over Arab villages; tree-planting campaigns are initiated to guard against Arab encroachment on land;[72] and legislation has been enacted specifically to prevent land leased to Jews falling into non-Jewish hands.[73]

If the Israeli land system fails to score well on the scale of equality, it fares little better in terms of efficiency. Israeli and international experience has shown that public acquisition of land alone does not necessarily ensure sufficient and appropriate supply of land. Without proper coordination with other public authorities, such as those responsible for planning, finance and municipal authorities, this goal cannot be achieved. In a study comparing land policies in different countries, Israel was used as an example of where a lack of such coordination has led to disastrous results (Lichfield and Darin-Drabkin 1980: 216). The study particularly identified the problems caused where the land authority has its own vested interests.

The assertion that public ownership of land guarantees greater control of land use in the public interest has also been disproved in Israel. Land use is determined by the planning authorities more than by those responsible for landownership, and Israel already has a highly interventionist planning system at the national, regional and local levels. Public ownership can even act against the interests of effective planning: Israeli land law expert Professor Weisman believes that although the Israeli public assumes that a lease will automatically be renewed for a further forty-nine years, the possibility that one might have to surrender the land at the expiry of the lease period acts as a disincentive for land-use planning (Weisman 1987: 96).

Similarly, the claim that central landownership facilitates the implementation of national goals such as the dispersal of the population has also not always been borne out. One example is the ILA's inability to enforce its decision to freeze the allocation of land in the coastal areas of Nahariya and Ashkalon (Weisman 1987: 96, citing Zorea and Poznisky 1976: 3). The argument that central ownership prevents speculation is also flawed: the ILA sells and leases land at the price dictated by the market. Although it does itself influence the market, for example by setting prices for leases of residential property and taxing profits derived from an increase in land values whether due to the rise in market prices or to planning decisions, it has proved unable to prevent fluctuations in land values.

In the following chapters, we will examine how the Israeli land system is implemented in practice, focusing on the extent to which it delivers equal access to land for Jewish and Arab citizens of the state.

Notes

1. Section 2, State Property Law 1951; LSI, Vol. 5, p. 45.
2. The ILA currently administers 94.5 per cent of land in the state, but

more than a million dunams of it is land to which title has not yet been formally determined. Once settlement of title operations have been completed throughout the state, the ILA expects that at least 93.5 per cent of all land will be owned by the state, the Development Authority or the JNF; ILA (1993: 131).

3. See Chapter 4 for more details of the Ottoman land system. *Mulk* was full ownership. *Waqf* was property dedicated to Islamic trusts for the benefit of specific groups or the community as a whole.

4. *Miri* was the grant of a temporary right to use a piece of land for the purpose of cultivation, pasture, meadow or woodland, and resembled a lease.

5. *Matruka* was land intended ('left') for public benefit, including land assigned for general public use, such as roads and markets, or for the use of inhabitants of a particular area, such as common pasture. *Mewat*, literally meaning 'dead', was undeveloped or unused land which was not owned or possessed by anybody and was situated at least one and a half miles from inhabited areas, but if a person developed it and started to use it, it could be converted into *Miri* and he could claim rights as the *Miri* holder.

6. Palestine Order in Council of 1922, Article 2.

7. Sami Hadawi (1988: 42) asserts that the government did not regard *Matruka* as being within its control. Goadly and Doukhan (1935: 60–1) believe that *Matruka* did fall within the category, although not *Miri*.

8. See for instance the comment of British official Hope Simpson in 1930 that land purchased by the JNF 'ceases to be land from which the Arab can gain any advantage either now or at any time in the future. Not only can he never hope to lease or to cultivate it, but, by the stringent provisions of the lease of the Jewish National Fund, he is deprived for ever from employment on that land' (Hope Simpson 1930: 54).

9. Knesset Record 29, 19 July 1960, p. 1917 (in Hebrew).

10. Major Knesset Debates, Vol. 2, pp. 600–9, regarding debates which took place in May 1950.

11. Ibid., p. 681.

12. See the JNF's report to the 23rd Zionist Congress in 1951, in which it stated that it would 'redeem the lands and … turn them over to the Jewish people – to the people and not the state, which in the current composition of the population cannot be an adequate guarantor of Jewish ownership' (Lehn and Davis 1988: 108).

13. Speech of Finance Minister Eshkol when introducing the 1960 legislation in the Knesset (Lehn and Davis 1988: 104).

14. Z. Wahrhaftig, Minister of Religious Affairs, to the Knesset (Lehn and Davis 1988: 107).

15. Section 2 of the Israel Lands Law 1960 lists seven permitted exceptions to the prohibition on alienation of 'Israel Lands', but the total amounts of land transferred under these exceptions has been small. The transfer of land belonging to the JNF also requires its agreement.

16. State Property Law 1951; LSI, Vol. 5, p. 45. In the case of Yaffa Local Council v. State of Israel, HC 13/76 and 10/76, PD 31(2), p. 605, the High Court rejected the claim that the legislative intent of the State Property Law 1951 was to withdraw existing rights over land and found that it was simply intended to confirm the normal situation whereby one sovereign succeeds to the property of its predecessor.

17. Section 17, Succession Law 1965, LSI, Vol. 19, p. 58.

18. LSI, Vol. 4, p. 151.

19. Under the Absentees' Property Law 1953 and the Land Acquisition (Validation of Acts and Compensation) Law 1953. Property in Israel owned by Germans was also transferred to the Development Authority; LSI, Vol. 4, p. 142.

20. Knesset Record 29, 1961.

21. It could not transfer any land other than by specific decision of the Israeli government, was permitted to transfer ownership in most of its land only to the state, the JNF, an institution for settling landless Arabs (never established) or a local authority, must give the JNF the first option to purchase urban land, and must not sell more than 100,000 dunams of urban land.

22. For example, a tourist complex mentioned in the JNF Proposed Budget for the Fiscal Year 1994, p. A3. See the discussion below regarding whether the JNF should properly be considered a private or a public body.

23. Settled land means land regarding which settlement of title has been completed and title determined. Some one million dunams of land in the state are still unsettled.

24. The implementation of the settlement of title process is highly contentious and many Palestinian claims, mainly in the Naqab, are outstanding; see Chapter 4.

25. ILC Decision 1, 17 May 1965, set out the ILA's policy as regards leasing agricultural land; and the Agricultural Settlement (Restrictions on the Use of Agricultural Land and Water) Law 1967 introduced strict powers of enforcement against those making non-conforming use of land leased to them by the ILA.

26. In Professor Weisman's opinion, the State Property Law 1951 gives the government a parallel authority to carry out transactions in state land, though also subject to the Israel Lands Law. He argues that this constitutes an additional exception to the general prohibition on alienating Israel Lands contained in the Basic Law: Israel Lands; Weisman (1981: 79, 89).

27. Association for Civil Rights in Israel v. Government of Israel and Others, HC 6924/98, judgment of 9 July 2001, CD Rom Takdeen High Court 2001 (9).

28. Keren Kayemeth Leisrael Law 1953; LSI, Vol. 8, p. 35.

29. Unofficial translation of the Covenant in the *Palestine Yearbook of International Law*, Vol. II (1985), pp. 206–17.

30. Article 3(a) of the Memorandum and Articles of Association, in ibid.

31. Givati (1981: 681), reporting the words of Knesset Member Yohanan Bader.

32. ILC Decision 822, 10 February 1989; it seems the decision to make the transfer had been taken in 1952 and, in 1962, the JNF had paid the state for the land.

33. According to the ILA report for 1992 (ILA 1993: 222–3), the ILA transferred 27 per cent of its total net income for the year to the JNF.

34. Land income transferred by the ILA to the JNF for 1996 was 851.0 million shekels, while the Development Authority received 605.9 million and the state 576.1 million (ILA 1997: 107).

35. 'One hundred years of the JNF', interview with Shlomo Gravitz, head of the JNF Council, *Globes* (financial newspaper), 5 October 2001, p. 29 (in Hebrew).

36. JNF Proposed Budget for the Fiscal Year 1994, p. 8.

37. In the Hebrew daily newspaper *Yediot Aharanot*, cited in I. Shahak, 'The Israeli citizens are not equal', *Middle East International*, 12 July 1991.

38. Ibid.

39. Keren Kayemeth Leisrael Law 1953, Section 6.

40. According to the JNF's budget proposal for 1994, in 1993 the Fund constructed twenty reservoirs.

41. Articles 17 and 25 of the standard lease translated and reproduced in the *Palestine Yearbook of International Law*, Vol. II (1985) p. 221.

42. Regulation No. 25 of 1993 of the Minister of Finance under the Obligation to Put Out to Tender Law 1993, Section 27; *Laws of Israel* (1992), p. 114 (in Hebrew).

43. LSI, Vol. 21, p. 105, and see Chapter 6.

44. 'One hundred years of the JNF', interview with Shlomo Gravitz (see note 35). See Chapter 2 for a thorough review of this article.

45. See also Religious Educational Body of Bet Rivka and Others v. Jewish Agency and Others, note 51 below.

46. Kadisha Company v. Lionel Kistenbaum, civil appeal 294/91, PD 46(2), p. 464. The applicants were relatives of a deceased who wanted to write on her tombstone in Latin and using dates based on the Western calendar. The company's regulations permitted use of the Jewish calendar only.

47. Ibid., judgment, p. 485b.

48. R v. Independent Broadcasting Authority ex parte Rank Org. plc 1986, *The Times*, 14 March 1986, cited in Wade and Forsyth (1994: 637).

49. Robinson and Wife v. Memphis and Charleston Railroad Company, Supreme Court of the United States, 109 US3; Supreme Court 18, judgment of 15 October 1883.

50. Michael A. Lebron v. National Railroad Passenger Corporation, 513 US374, 115 Supreme Court 961, judgment of 21 February 1995.

51. Religious Educational Body of Bet Rivka and Others v. Jewish Agency and Others, High Court of Justice case 4212/91, 27 May 1993, PD 47(2), p. 661.

52. Professor Kretzmer, while declining to give a view on the legality of the

restrictions placed on non-Jews by the JNF, suggests that on this ground the Memorandum and Articles should be declared invalid (Kretzmer 1990: 65–6).

53. 'Adil Qa'dan v. ILA and Others, HC 6698/95, judgment of 8 March 2000, PD 54(1), p. 258.

54. See the discussion of applicable human rights principles, including the prohibition on discrimination, in Chapter 2.

55. Pliah Albek has also been behind much of the confiscation of Palestinian land in the Occupied Territories.

56. Albek adds that the lessor must stipulate this condition expressly in the original leasehold agreement and it must be implemented reasonably. Report of the State of Israel for the fiscal year 1992, pp. 167, 169.

57. Report of the State of Israel, 1986, p. 5.

58. This was reported by the Hebrew daily newspaper *Yediot Aharanot*, 2 March 1998.

59. According to the law, those who have had legal possession of an apartment constantly for at least five years are entitled to acquire ownership and will only have to pay 15 per cent of the actual value.

60. According to section 23 of the State Economy Law 2001, implementation of the Public Housing (Rights of Acquisition) Law would be frozen until the end of 2001.

61. Report of the Inter-Ministerial Committee to Examine Illegal Construction in the State of Israel, March 2000 (in Hebrew).

62. ILC Decision 1 of 17 May 1965.

63. ILC Decision 533 of 11 May 1992, cancelled in 1995.

64. For instance, ILC Decisions 717 of 20 June 1995 and 737 of 17 December 1995.

65. These points were raised in a petition to the High Court issued by the Eastern Democratic Rainbow and others, Petition no. 244/00, January 2000.

66. Petition 244/00, issued in January 2000. The High Court agreed to consider the petition and a temporary injunction was in force from 15 November 2001 freezing all changes in status of the land in question. The Court requested the government to discuss the issue and publish its recommendations for a solution.

67. <www.court.gov.il>.

68. Although not constitutionally entrenched in a Basic Law, the principle of equality has long had a fundamental status in Israel law; see Chapter 2.

69. See Lichfield and Darin-Drabkin (1980), who assess a number of national land systems on the basis of efficiency, and see the writings of Israeli land law expert Professor Joshua Weisman, who criticizes Israeli official assertions as to the latter two measures.

70. This language was used by the Jewish Agency when justifying the establishment of fifty new settlements in the Galilee, cited by H. Law-Yone in the *Jerusalem Post* English daily newspaper, 17 March 1994.

71. JNF Proposed Budget for the Fiscal Year 1994, p. 6. It is not clear whether the JNF is here referring only to JNF land or to all Israel Lands.

72. JNF head Shlomo Gravitz, in his interview in *Globes* newspaper (see note 35 above), states that 'afforestation, besides its important environmental purpose, puts facts on the ground and signals ownership in theory and in reality'.

73. The Agricultural Settlement (Restrictions on Use of Agricultural Land and Water) Law 1967, see note 25 above, and Chapter 6.

Administration of 'Israel Lands': Policy towards the Palestinian Sector

'State ownership in itself guarantees no human rights' (Chomsky 1975: 384)

§ ONCE the decision had been taken to keep most land in the state under the ownership of the state and the JNF, and to rename it as 'Israel Lands', it was then decided that management of this land would be centralized in the hands of a new state body, the Israel Lands Administration (ILA). In addition to managing all Israel Lands, the ILA also plays a key role in land policy, development, planning, land acquisition for public purposes and a myriad other functions that are crucial to Palestinian access to land in the state. The ILA was established in 1960 as part of the major reform of the land system implemented in that year.

In examining the role of the ILA and other bodies in the management of Israel Lands, two themes in particular dominate this chapter. One is that the legislation of 1960 established a system for the administration of public land that inherently discriminates against non-Jews in the state. So, for example, the ILA's governing body, the Israel Lands Council (ILC) is dominated by the Jewish National Fund (JNF), which excludes Arabs from land owned by it. In other words, the state created a situation where a body that acts in the interests of one category of citizens only is given an enormous amount of influence over the management and control of all public land in the state. In addition, another of the Zionist organizations that survived the establishment of the state, the Jewish Agency (JA), which like the JNF operates only for Jews, was given a central role in state development. A second theme is the discriminatory manner in which the ILA carries out its functions as the public body responsible for managing centrally held land in the state. Pursuing familiar state goals such as containment of the Palestinian communities, Judaization of areas with a Palestinian majority and forced relocation of the Bedouin, the ILA effectively limits access for the Palestinian communities to state land under its control.

Taking land into public ownership is not in itself sufficient to guarantee that it will be administered on the basis of fundamental rights and principles, such as that of equality. Nevertheless, the state as landowner has legal duties different from those of a private owner. In Israel, general principles of administrative law, particularly case law, require public bodies to treat citizens equally, and international law applicable to Israel also creates this obligation. The problem is that these principles are not adhered to, while attempts are made to disguise their breach with a thin legal cover.

The public body responsible for 'Israel Lands': the Israel Lands Administration

Until 1960, land was administered by different bodies: the state administered land it acquired from the Mandate authorities, the Development Authority administered land taken over by the Custodian of Absentees' Property, and the JNF administered land under its ownership. One of the key elements of the reforms of 1960, which brought in the new Israeli land system regulating state and JNF land, was to centralize the management and administration of this land in the hands of a single public body, the Israel Lands Administration (ILA).[1] In 1960, the Knesset passed the Basic Law: Israel Lands, confirming the existing distribution of ownership of non-private land in the state between the state, the Development Authority and the JNF, and categorizing all of this land as Israel Lands.[2] In the same year, the Israel Lands Administration Law was enacted, establishing the ILA as a public body and charging it with administration of Israel Lands.[3] The ILA now controls over 94 per cent of land in the state.[4] Although the ILA is the major body responsible for management of Israel Lands, the Jewish national institutions were also given powers in certain spheres by statute: the JNF has responsibility for 'the cultivation, development and afforestation' of Israel Lands, while the JA is assigned responsibility for rural settlement.

The ILA is directly accountable to the government. Its director is appointed by the government, and is directly subordinate to the Minister of Infrastructure who also serves as chair of the Israel Lands Council (ILC), the ILA's governing body.[5] The High Court has offered the following guidelines for interpreting the ILA's role:

When we consider the written statements in the Basic Law: Israel Lands, the Israel Lands Law of 1960 and the Israel Lands Administration Law of 1960, enacted and implemented at the same time, it is very clear that the goal of the legislature is to ensure that land policy, on which all future actions and transactions of the Development Authority and the JNF concerning Israeli state land in Israel will be based, will be official, Zionist and coordinated, based on the principles set out in these laws ... and to ensure that the implementation of such actions and transactions ... will henceforth be centralised in the hands of a single administration, which is appointed by the government and acts under the supervision of the Council, and to ensure that its actions are also subject, due to the government's duty to report concerning them, to the scrutiny of the Knesset.[6]

One point to note at the outset is that the ILA, as a public body, is bound by principles of Israeli public law, including the principle of equality. This means that it must not exercise its discretion in a discriminatory fashion. Nor must it ignore or ascribe insufficient weight to basic rights including not only the principle of equality but also, particularly since the enactment of Basic Laws in 1992, other fundamental rights such as human dignity and the right to property.[7] A public body must observe other administrative law rules, for instance it is prohibited from exercising its discretion for purposes other than those for which the power was granted, taking into account irrelevant considerations, taking a decision which is patently unreasonable or ignoring procedural rules of natural justice (Kretzmer 1990: 14).[8] The Israeli High Court has explicitly stated that authorities responsible for public land are subject to the same administrative law standards as all state authorities, particularly when dealing with state land, a standard that involves 'dealing with the public fairly and with equality according to the rules of property administration'.[9] The Qa'dan case, in which the High Court in March 2000 found that the ILA had breached its duty to treat all citizens equally when it transferred land to a settlement body that discriminated against Arabs, represents a recent affirmation of this principle.[10]

The ILA's governing body, the ILC, is responsible for laying down land policy, supervising the ILA's activities and approving its budget. The ILA's activities are financed through the state budget but income earned on land goes to the property's registered owners.[11] In the mid-1970s, the JNF and ILA reached an understanding whereby the JNF would shoulder 38 per cent of the ILA's administration costs, despite the fact that the JNF owns only 18 per cent of the land administered by the ILA (Vitkon 1999: 35). This understanding, which has been the practice ever since, has no basis in any formal decision or law.

The legislation of 1960 gives the ILA extensive powers, but subsequent interpretations of those powers have expanded them even further. The High Court has held that the ILA's administrative authority includes the right to sue and settle legal actions on behalf of the land's owners. The ILA also undertakes land acquisition on behalf of the state. High-ranking ILA officials are authorized to represent the government in transactions relating to Israel Lands and to sign documents on behalf of the state. Since the late 1960s the ILA has taken an increasingly proactive role in implementing state land policy, in addition to granting leases and generally managing public land. One area in which the ILA has been extremely active is in land-use planning and development and generally overseeing the utilization of land in urban and rural areas (Phorolis et al. 1979: 506). As the main body responsible for the supply of land for both private and public use in the country, the ILA engages in long-term planning and is a major actor in planning activities at all levels. The ILA has its own planning body responsible for furthering the development of lands coming under its administration, locating new land reserves, and following every planning process carried out on state land from the national to local levels. At the national level, the ILA's planning body participates in the preparation of national plans including plans for immigrant absorption and tourism and national road plans. At the regional level, the ILA's planning arm defines medium- and long-term policies and prepares outline plans which determine the planning goals. At the local level, the ILA prepares local outline plans in coordination with national plans. In response to waves of new Jewish immigration in the early 1990s, for instance, the ILA prepared plans for their absorption across the country, including providing for the establishment of new communities.[12]

The ILA also has responsibility for ensuring a supply of land to meet the needs of government ministries, public institutions and agricultural or urban settlements. Transactions are carried out between the different bodies owning Israel Lands and between the ILA and private owners. Where it proves impossible to acquire land through negotiations, the ILA expropriates land from private owners using the power of compulsory purchase under the Land (Acquisition for Public Purposes) Ordinance 1943. Although formally the authority to exercise this power rests with the Minister of Finance, in practice it is the ILA that recommends where it should be exercised and that deals with the acquisitions, including conducting negotiations as to compensation.

Another example of an area in which the ILA has a wide discretion is the power to evict those it views as trespassing on land under its control, without recourse to the courts. Acting only on a belief that a person has illegally encroached upon land, the ILA may give a maximum of fourteen days' notice of eviction, following which this notice has the force of a court order and may be enforced by the bailiff. The burden is on the alleged trespasser to obtain a court order to prevent the eviction.[13] This has led to criticism that the ILA is bypassing normal legal processes and taking on a quasi-judicial function.

Cooperating with the government, the ILC and ILA work to implement Zionist and national goals such as guaranteeing the supply of suitable land for settlement and population dispersal. For instance, policies to settle Jews in border areas and development towns resulted in the establishment of over thirty development towns between 1948 and 1964 and of several development regions in the Galilee. Other national goals such as security and national–religious considerations often take priority over economic or other considerations (Peret 1988: 2), and political motivations have also guided settlement policies in the Occupied Territories.

Other national goals the ILA seeks to implement include the protection of agricultural land and control of the size of plots of land leased. Despite pressure from local authorities and developers, a central aspect of government land policy has always been to protect agricultural land as far as possible and prevent it from being used for urban expansion. So, for example, the Minister of Agriculture initially chaired the ILC, and a Committee for the Preservation of Agricultural Land was established. The ILA has worked to resist the encroachment of urban development on agricultural land. Another feature of Israeli land policy is the commitment to avoid both the accumulation of plots of public land in the hands of individuals, and the fragmentation of plots through inheritance or sale. The principle that each should have sufficient for his own needs and no more is upheld. The ILA imposes strict controls to maintain this situation.

The ILA has come under sharp criticism from several quarters for the way in which it behaves. Despite the ILA's formal role as an administrative body subordinate to the government,[14] it is criticized for acting too independently, pursuing its own vested interests and behaving as a domineering monopolist. It is also accused of accumulating wealth for the state budget rather than making land available at lower cost to the benefit of a greater number.[15] In its defence, former ILA head Wexler asserts that the ILA fulfils its function of administering state lands and supplies land according to market needs.[16]

Lack of effective accountability is certainly a major problem. The ILC and ILA as public bodies are answerable to the courts and the State Comptroller as well as the government and the Knesset, but they have been criticized for lacking a proper legal framework to make them truly accountable for the way in which they exercise their far-reaching powers over public and JNF-owned land. Zamir, a leading Israeli expert on administrative law, finds it extraordinary that the law of 1960 that establishes the ILA and provides the source of its authority to administer more than 90 per cent of land in the state, fails to set out objectives, methods and criteria for its operation and leaves the Administration itself to develop its own directions. He believes that this state of affairs sits uncomfortably with the principle of rule of law (Zamir 1996: 233–8).

Similar criticisms have been raised by the Israeli State Comptroller. In her report for the year 1993, the State Comptroller strongly criticizes the ILA's unchecked and inefficient administration, and recommends reform (State Comptroller's Report 1993: 221). Among her findings were that the participation of government representatives in meetings of the Council was minimal compared to that of JNF representatives; during the period 1990–91, there was never once a majority of government representatives at any meeting. Further, the JNF had a majority on all five sub-committees, and government representatives were frequently absent from meetings, thus reducing significantly the government's ability to influence its decisions (ibid., p. 230). Protocols of the Council's meetings are frequently not signed, and in some instances the Council failed to receive from the ILA all the information it needed in order to discuss matters on its agenda and take decisions (ibid., p. 228). Of 155 decisions taken by the Council in the period 1990 to April 1993, only a third were published in the *Official Gazette*, despite the fact that some had far-reaching legal consequences. In a previous report, in 1990, in which she investigated the Custodian of Absentees' Property, the State Comptroller had concluded that the Custodian was little more than a 'clerical officer' for the ILA, and that the ILA directed the work of the Custodian without any authority for doing so, and without coordination with or consent from the responsible ministry (State Comptroller's Report 1990).

Aside from the general lack of public accountability evidenced by this catalogue of criticisms, the allegation that the ILA is dominated by the JNF, with its mandate to act exclusively in the interests of the Jewish population and as a tool of the Zionist bodies, the JA and the World Zionist Organization, is of particular concern to the Palestinian community. Indeed, the extent to which the ILA deals with the public fairly and equally may have been brought into public question, but mainly in relation to the Jewish sector. So, for instance, public pressure resulted in a duty being imposed on all state bodies and governmental corporations to go through a process of offering contracts by public bidding when granting contracts (for leases, development, services and other purposes), in order to ensure equal opportunities.[17] However, the ILA, which as controller of some 94.5 per cent of all land should, arguably more than any other body, be bound by such requirements, is entitled to be exempted from putting contracts out to public tender in certain circumstances, and these exemptions often apply particularly to the Arab sector.[18] For example, the Authority is not restricted by such requirements in leasing agricultural land owned by the JNF, and in relation to residential building in Arab villages and Bedouin townships.

An international comparative study of land policies in different countries singles out Israel for criticism on the basis that the degree of autonomy and financial independence accorded the ILA in Israel undermines its legitimacy as a public body representing the public interest (Lichfield and Darin-Drabkin 1980: 216–17). The lack of co-ordination between the ILA, as the public authority in charge of supply of land, and other public authorities, is highlighted in the study. Pointing out that the ILA has a tendency to act in its own interests which may sometimes contradict planning interests, the study cites by way of example the decision to allow high-rise building on the hills of Jerusalem, in which one of the deciding factors was the higher immediate income for the ILA, but the result was a bad planning decision which contradicted the policies of the planning authorities. In chasing short-term profit and acting in its own vested interests, the study concludes, the ILA differs little from private developers.

Despite such severe criticisms both at home and abroad, the ILA's functions and powers have not been amended over the years. However, the government has not ignored them altogether. In 1997, the government appointed a committee to carry out a comprehensive review of Israeli land policy, and its terms of reference included looking at the role of the ILA. The *Ronen Report* included a recommendation that the ILA should continue to administer state-owned land, but that its role should be limited to that of a professional body administering land, and it should lose many of its policy-making functions.[19] So far, however, no Israeli government has seen fit to change the status quo.

Land administration policy and the Arab population

The ILC, which has responsibility for the ILA's land policy, has adopted no formal land policy as regards the Arab sector, only sporadic decisions affecting the Arab sector or parts of it. Of some 900 decisions taken by the ILC from its establishment in 1961 until 2001, very few relate to Palestinian citizens. However, its actual policies, as evidenced by its activities, in relation to Arab citizens are entirely different to those implemented in relation to the Jewish population. From 1986, the ILC belatedly started to devote attention to the Arab citizens of Israel, but not by initiating a process aimed at positive development projects. Examination of the long lists in the ILA's Annual Reports of planned development projects to be initiated and carried out by the ILA throughout the country reveals that scarcely any were intended for the benefit of the Arab sector. Those that relate to Palestinians are overwhelmingly negative, such as measures to cooperate with a committee to submit recommendations as to how to combat illegal building in the Arab sector, or are aimed at implementing policies such as the relocation in planned townships of Palestinians in the Naqab or the north living in unrecognized communities.[20] Other ILC decisions relate to the Palestinians indirectly, in that they are aimed at 'Judaization': reducing a Palestinian majority in a certain area. For example, a decision of 22 January 2001 reduced the cost of land for housing in the Galilee and the north 'in order to encourage settlement and prevent negative abandoning of these areas'.[21] It is clear that the intention when the ILA was established was to make sure that the Administration would remain closely wedded to such state policy. The passage from the High Court cited earlier in this chapter on the ILA's role provides insight into this intention: 'When we consider the written statements in the Basic Law: Israel Lands, the Israel Lands Law of 1960 and the Israel Lands Administration Law of 1960, enacted and implemented at the same time, *it is very clear that the goal of the legislature is to ensure that land policy*, on which all future actions and transactions of the Development Authority and the JNF concerning Israeli state land in Israel will be based, *will be official, Zionist and coordinated*, based on the principles set out in these laws' (emphasis added).[22]

One aspect of Israeli land policy that has caused particular disaffection among the Palestinian communities in Israel has been land taxes. Until 2001, Israel imposed steep taxes on privately owned land that was unused, the objective being to encourage development of vacant land and discourage accumulation and speculation in land. While Israel Lands were always exempt from land taxes, privately owned land attracts a range of taxes, including: property tax, betterment tax, land improvement tax, inheritance tax and municipal betterment tax. The system, however, disproportionately penalized Palestinians who tend to retain land not in order to speculate and profit from it, but to keep it for family members to build on in the future. Such a phenomenon largely does not exist in the Jewish sector. The taxes imposed a heavy burden on Palestinian landowners and by 1995 this had become one of the major issues raised in the political arena by the Palestinian community's leadership.[23] In 1999, the land taxes were abolished, with effect from 1 January 2000.[24]

Despite the importance of this powerful body in controlling land policy, Palestinians have never been represented on the Israel Lands Council (ILC). According to the Covenant signed in 1961 between Israel and the JNF, the ILC was to consist of thirteen members, six to be proposed by the JNF, and seven by the government.[25] Subsequent amendments allowed the Council to be enlarged, and by 2000 the Council comprised twenty-seven members, half of whom were JNF nominees. In practice, both the government representatives and the high-ranking JNF officials who represent the Fund on the Council are usually from the Jewish agricultural sector, giving this sector the greatest weight on the Council, a state of affairs that had been criticized by the State Comptroller in 1994 (State Comptroller's Report 1994: 221). When the Council membership was to be renewed in 1997, the Association for Civil Rights in Israel (ACRI) called for Arab members to be nominated to the Council. No Arabs were in fact nominated, and when the ACRI persisted, the organization was informed by the Ministry of Infrastructure in April 1998 that the government intended to amend the law so as to enlarge the ILC to thirty members, of whom at least six would be representatives of the public. Of these six, the Minister planned to nominate one representative of the Arab community. Although a draft law was published and received a first reading in the Knesset, it did not progress further.

ACRI petitioned the High Court, demanding the appointment of Arab members to the Council in order to give proportional and adequate representation to the Arab community.[26] In the petition, ACRI cited a decision of the High Court in which it had affirmed that the principle of adequate representation of women on public bodies flowed from the principle of equality.[27] The case had decided that the Minister had a legal duty to ensure adequate representation of women in the nominations for the position of deputy to the Director General of the National Insurance Institute. In view of the very important role played by the ILC in distribution of land resources in the state, ACRI argued that it was vital to the interests of equality that the Arab community have the opportunity to participate in this decision-making body. This was particularly crucial since half the Council members were representatives of the JNF, a body whose fundamental goals discriminate directly against Arab citizens by excluding them from its land. In support, the ACRI cited the serious underrepresentation of Arabs on all public bodies and the fact that, as a result, they were unlikely to be among the senior public officials appointed by the government.

In its response, asserting that it would be impossible to give representation to all of the many ethnic groups in Israel, the government stated that while it did not concede the principle that it was bound to nominate Arab members, in practice the Arab community would have a maximum of one out of the six places to be allocated to representatives of the public.[28] An Arab had in fact been nominated but, following checks on his political links, his appointment had been withdrawn after six months.

The High Court, in its judgment of 9 July 2001, declined to give a remedy to the petitioners. The Court said that the question it was asked to address was whether the principle of equality required, as the petitioner claimed, that the government must give due representation to the Arab community on the ILC, not only by appointing one Arab from among the representatives of the public, but also by nominating further Arabs from among the state officials who would be appointed, so as to ensure due representation for this community on the ILC as a whole.[29] The Court noted that the principle of equality required the government to *take into account* the need for due representation and to give it due weight, but did not require it actually to achieve a *result* of greater Arab representation. Since at present the lack of high-ranking state officials in the Arab sector made it difficult to find suitable nominees, then the only way forward was to wait until there were sufficient numbers. The Court noted that legislation had recently been enacted specifically aimed at increasing the number of Arab state officials. In the meantime, the Court suggested that the government consider whether or not to nominate further Arab members to the ILC from among the academic and public representatives, but stressed that it was not obliged to do so. The Court was not willing to order that even one Arab should be nominated to the ILC. The most it would say was that ministers should review the list of nominees in light of the Court's decision. While the decision represented a partial victory for the applicant, in that the applicability of the principle of equality was recognized, the result was disappointing. Regardless of the outcome of any move to appoint an Arab member to the ILC, it seems doubtful whether one or two Arab representatives on the ILC would be able to have a significant influence on Israeli land policy, particularly as long as the JNF continues to dominate the Council. Their ability to represent the Palestinian community might in any event be questioned if they were appointed by the government rather than nominated by their community.

Leasing agricultural land to Palestinians Prior to 1948 Palestine was a largely rural community and farming was the main source of livelihood for a majority of the population. The massive expropriation of Palestinian land from 1948 involved the seizure of all of the agricultural land of the refugees and internally displaced, and even the Palestinian communities that remained after the 1948 war lost some 70 per cent of their land.[30] The result is that little privately owned cultivable land remains in the hands of the community, and most agricultural land in the state is now classified as Israel Lands, owned either by the state or the JNF and managed by the ILA. Perhaps 85 per cent of all agricultural land is Israel Lands. Palestinians wanting to lease agricultural land from the ILA are forced to compete with Jewish agriculturalists. However, Palestinians wishing to lease land for farming face severe difficulties. A large proportion of agricultural Israel Lands is owned not by the state but by the JNF, which excludes Palestinians from leasing or even working on its land even though it is clearly a body exercising public functions.[31] But even when it comes to agricultural land owned by the state, it has proved extremely difficult for Palestinian farmers to obtain leases, particularly long leases. Very little state-owned agricultural land outside the Naqab is leased to Palestinians. The facts speak for themselves. Some 90 per cent of all agricultural Israel Lands are leased to Jewish collectives (kibbutzes, moshavs and other cooperative settlements) (Tzur 1989: 38). Almost 99 per cent of land farmed by Jewish cooperative villages and institutions is Israel Lands, and 70 per cent of land farmed by other Jewish agriculturalists. Meanwhile, land farmed by Arabs is 50 per cent Israel Lands and 50 per cent privately owned land (Haidar 1990: 17). According to the agricultural census of 1981, a little over 2 per cent of all cultivated land in the state was in the hands of 'non-Jewish localities' (Tzur 1989: 37). Of this, some 9 per cent was grazing land. Another phenomenon that has developed in the Arab sector is that most of the land actually cultivated by the community is formally classified not as rural or agricultural land, but as urban land. A large part of this is land used by Bedouin in the Naqab, while some of it represents olive groves and market garden areas within the boundaries of the Arab villages. Palestinians tend to cultivate most of the cultivable land in their possession (Haidar 1990: 17).

The ILC defined its policy regarding the leasing of agricultural land in its very first decision.[32] Agricultural land administered by the ILA would be leased only for agricultural production and related purposes, and a lessee must use it constantly for these purposes or must return the land to the ILA. There are two main types of lease of agricultural Israel Lands: long leases (*nahala*) for renewable periods of forty-nine years, and short leases for predetermined purposes of one to three years. According to the ILA *Report for the Year 2000* (ILA 2001), the long *nahala* leases existed in 740 agricultural settlements. Of the 2.8 million dunams leased in this way, none at all is leased to Palestinian citizens of the state. Long leases are normally granted only to agricultural settlements, rarely to individual farmers (Phorolis et al. 1979: 586). The lease is granted to a kibbutz or moshav, or to the Jewish Agency or the Histadrut (labour union). The ILA has also leased land to lookout posts and settlements in the Occupied Territories. This practice of leasing land to collectives, rather than directly to individual farmers, is one factor that puts Palestinian farmers, who are not organized in collectives, at a disadvantage.

As for short leases, Palestinians receive only a tiny proportion of all agricultural Israel Lands that are leased. In 1986, only 1 per cent of all recipients of short leases were non-Jewish, the remainder going to moshavs, kibbutzes and other Jewish agricultural settlements (Tzur 1989: 38).[33] Short leases are granted for a specified agricultural purpose, such as for pasture, irrigated or unirrigated crops or orchards, and are strictly supervised by the ILA. (Land granted on a long-term *nahala* lease, on the other hand, may be used for whatever agricultural purpose the leaseholder wishes, in many ways resembling private ownership, conferring wide choice to use and pass on land to heirs, subject to restrictions such as on division and subleasing [Phorolis et al. 1979: 56–60].) Rights in non-*nahala* leases terminate if the lessee does not live on the land or use it for the purpose for which it was leased. A lessee may not transfer the property to another without the consent of the ILA, and this principle is strictly enforced. If the designation of the land is altered, for instance by planning changes, and is no longer classified as agricultural land, the lessee must surrender his lease, but will receive compensation.

Having their options limited to only short-term leases presents a number of problems for Palestinian farmers. One is that rents on short leases are several times higher than the rent on long-term leases, which are extremely low. Leasing fees are determined on the first of every year by the ILC. Another is that they are frequently allotted less land, and for less time, than they need. The Bedouin in the Naqab, who cultivate almost half the total amount of agricultural Israel Lands leased to Palestinians, habitually receive leases of only one or two years and, for pasture land, only ten months (a season). This severely limits their ability to undertake long-term planning and development. Palestinians are also likely to be given smaller tracts. The size of a plot to be leased is determined (by the Ministry of Agriculture and the ILA), supposedly on the basis of what is sufficient to sustain a family. In the Naqab, the conditions on which Palestinian Bedouin may obtain short-term leases from year to year are published annually in the newspapers. The conditions tend to be restrictive and linked to government policy relating to the unresolved land disputes. Examples of conditions that have been imposed are that the age of the applicant is fifty years or above, or that the applicant does not hold any land for which he has filed a claim of ownership.[34]

The policy and criteria concerning the circumstances in which agricultural land will be leased, and how it will be determined whether long or short leases will be granted and on what conditions, are not generally made known. Neither the law establishing the ILA, nor subsequent legislation or statutory guidelines, define these matters. A wide discretion is left to the ILA. The preference that is in practice given to farming collectives and communities rather than to individual farmers is not, on the face of it, a criterion that discriminates on the basis of national origin. However since it is only Jewish farming communities that organize themselves in this way as collectives, and there are barriers preventing Palestinians from establishing rural settlements, the criterion is indirectly discriminatory.[35]

At times there have been even more blatant and sinister steps taken, aimed at actually preventing Palestinians from leasing agricultural land from the state. In 1967 the Agricultural Settlement (Restrictions on the Use of Agricultural Land and Water) Law was passed, bringing in strict powers of enforcement against those making 'non-conforming use' of land leased to them by the ILA.[36] The law was presented to the Knesset as being in the interests of agricultural planning, designed to prevent lessees of agricultural Israel Lands from subleasing land and water quotas to others rather than working it themselves or from selling the right to harvest their crops. The real intention behind the law was widely believed to be to prevent Jews from subletting their land to Arabs. Measures were taken to enforce this law in the years that followed; the vast majority of cases involved subleasing of land to Arabs.[37] Following the passage of the law Palestinian farmers found that kibbutzes and moshavs were no longer willing to sublease land to them. Periodically, there are still calls to enforce the law against farmers leasing state-owned land to Arabs.[38]

Leasing urban land to Palestinians No proactive policy for leasing state-owned urban land to the Palestinian sector has emerged from the ILC. Rather, the ILC tends simply to take decisions in response to government policy directions. A lower proportion of urban land than of agricultural land is Israel Lands, and therefore managed by the ILA. Since there is a high level of public intervention in planning and development, urban land will be leased only within the framework of city planning processes, and usually the ILA will ensure that the stages of planning, development and infrastructure are completed before agreeing to allocate a residential or commercial unit of land.

Allocation of urban land is usually required to be done by public competitive bidding, but the ILC frequently exempts the ILA from this duty, giving it a freer hand to pursue government policies in relation to the Palestinian communities. So, for example, according to an ILC Decision of 1989, the ILA is authorized to release building plots in certain listed Arab villages without public bidding for residents of the village who are seeking to build a home.[39] The effect of such measures is to increase governmental control over Palestinians and limit their freedom to choose where to live. If Palestinians wish to move to another location outside their indigenous village or town, they must first approach the Ministry of the Interior. Other measures designed to control and direct where Palestinians live are described in Chapters 7 and 8.

Palestinian areas regularly receive fewer financial benefits than Jewish areas in the granting of leases over urban land. Payment for a lease usually consists of a First Payment when the lease agreement is concluded, a fee which may be as much as 91 per cent of the value of the land and as little as a complete exemption, and annual payments of the remainder. An ILC Decision of 1986, for instance, specified that on the granting of leases for building in Arab villages, the First Payment should constitute between 40 and 80 per cent of the value of the land.[40] Jewish areas are granted substantially greater benefits. In its Annual Report 1992, the ILA listed localities where there were to be substantial reductions on the First Payment; no Arab localities were included in the list other than some Druze communities (ILA 1993: 50–4). Again, in areas designated as National Priority Areas needing special assistance, residents pay only 31 or 51 per cent of the value of housing land, and further reductions are granted for allocation of land for industry, tourism and other commercial purposes.[41] But only a handful of Arab towns have ever received this designation, despite the fact that the socio-economic status of the Palestinian communities is consistently among the lowest in the country.[42] Reductions are also granted in areas in which the government wishes to encourage Jewish settlement ('Judaize'), such as the Galilee and the north.[43] Even in localities where there are both Jewish and Arab inhabitants, such as Bokia'a and Kufr Same', reductions in lease payments were stated to apply only to those who had completed military service, thereby excluding most Palestinian citizens (other than Druze, who do serve in the army) automatically.

As with agricultural leases, urban leases are subject to strict control by the ILA and may not be transferred by one lessee to another without ILA approval. Urban public land is usually leased for periods of forty-nine or ninety-nine years, with an option to renew for an additional forty-nine years. However, shorter-term leases are granted for buildings administered by government housing corporations operating in the cities. These corporations control almost 70 per cent of Arab housing in the 'mixed' cities of Acre, Haifa, Jaffa, Lod and Ramle because this land was claimed by the state under the Absentees' Property Law (Arab Association for Human Rights 1996: 56). Israeli land law places few restrictions on arrangements between lessors and lessees, and while general statutory safeguards for tenants exist,[44] the rights of a possessor of Israel Lands are not specifically defined by law and are dependent on the terms in the leases granted by the ILA. As a result, the nature of such agreements is determined by the relative bargaining power of the parties (Weisman 1972: 18). Since one party is the state, the individual lessee is in a very unequal position, particularly since there is machinery in place for establishing terms and conditions for leases of Israel Lands, and a large measure of standardization. Rents can be increased during the term without limit and without consent, entirely at the discretion of the ILC.[45] There are no representatives of lessees as such, or by Arabs in general, on the ILC. The lessor may require the lessee to surrender part or all of the leased property if convinced it is not required or used by the lessee for the purposes for which the lease was granted (Weisman 1970). The ILC insists that all leases granted by the ILA must contain clauses prohibiting work on the leased property during the Jewish Sabbath or Israeli holidays.[46]

Relations between the ILA and Palestinian towns and villages Due to the large-scale land expropriations in and around the Palestinian towns and villages, most Palestinian urban and rural communities are to some extent dependent on the ILA for the land they need for a variety of purposes whether for residential or commercial use, public purposes, agriculture, industry or any other purpose. According to a study carried out in 1963, the state owned about 55 per cent of the total land area within the existing boundaries of Arab villages.[47] The ability of Arab local authorities to obtain access to this land is therefore crucial to local development.

The ILA's reluctance to release land under its control within Arab villages to the local authorities was stressed by a number of heads and other officials of Palestinian local councils and lawyers interviewed by the authors. Among other complaints, these community representatives drew particular attention to a number of points. First, they say that it is difficult for local authorities to obtain sufficient land for public projects such as schools. Second, they say that it is even more exceptional for state-owned land situated within Arab built-up areas to be released for housing projects, which the ILA does not appear to regard as a legitimate community purpose (although it does not take this view in the Jewish sector). Only in a few places has the ILA agreed to lease land as building plots on forty-nine-year leases at high prices. For instance, in Eilabun, there was a new neighbourhood under construction on 300 dunams of ILA land. However, contrary to the usual practice in the Jewish sector, the ILA leases out land without the necessary infrastructure (roads, water, sewerage etc.) in place. The inhabitants then look to the local authority to provide the infrastructure even though it is not receiving income from the lease, all of which is going to the ILA. In the Jewish sector, it is the Jewish national institutions that take on these functions. Third, the Palestinian community leaders say that the ILA allocates state land to Arab local authorities only reluctantly and after extremely hard bargaining. When negotiating the release of land, wherever possible the ILA will prevaricate, delay and threaten non-cooperation in future if forced into making concessions. Expressing frustration, the local council representatives felt that the ILA, exploiting the unequal bargaining position, when approached by an Arab local authority and asked for land, acts like a private individual protecting its land, trying to gain something in return, or asking why the local authority has not approached private owners instead. Instead of allocating land for the public benefit, such as a project of a local authority, the ILA prefers to lease it out and receive an income from it. Fourth, the ILA is careful never to lease land that has been expropriated from Palestinians to its former owners, concerned about appearing to recognize their rights.

If it does not allocate it for the development of the local Palestinian communities, one might ask what does the ILA do with the land it controls in the Arab villages? As a result of the Absentees' Property Law, under which land of Palestinian external and internal refugees came into the hands of the state Development Authority, the state frequently owns tiny plots or shares in plots of land in the Arab villages. The mosaic patterns of landownership in Arab villages significantly restrict the potential use of the land. Villages where the Custodian of Absentee Property took over substantial amounts of land, such as where there were a large number of absentees or extensive areas of land registered in the name of absentees, have been permanently rendered more vulnerable to losing their land base. According to many local officials, the Development Authority usually retains land within the villages as a bargaining chip, in order to exchange it for other land outside the village. In such circumstances, because land within the villages fetches a high price and is in huge demand since there is a severe shortage of land within the building zones, the Authority is able to obtain much larger pieces of land in exchange for its tiny plots within the village.[48]

Where, as a result of the Absentees' Property Law, the state Development Authority is a joint owner of a piece of land (say, because it steps into the shoes of one brother in a family who is classified as an 'absentee' whereas the other brothers who are joint owners are not 'absentees'), and the Authority's share is less than the minimum area permitted for a building plot, it may offer its portion for sale to the other co-owners, but at a very high price. Another option is to undergo a 'parcellation' process whereby co-owned land is divided and each joint owner takes his share, terms being reached by agreement or by court order.[49] However, this is a long and expensive process. In order to avoid it, the ILA sometimes makes 'use agreements' with co-owners whereby the parties agree to divide the land between them, without the ownership being affected. Where no parcellation or use agreement takes place, either party is able to block plans to develop the property. Co-ownership with the Development Authority can result in paralysis, preventing the use of the land and causing its economic freezing (for instance, although the price of land within Arab villages is high, owners cannot sell because the Custodian is a co-owner) with implications for private owners and for local authorities.

As a result of this experience, it is hardly surprising that the Palestinian communities view the ILA with suspicion and believe that the ILA's attitude and policies are intended to prevent their development and growth.

Rural settlement, the role of the Jewish Agency and the Qa'dan case

The JNF is not the only Jewish national institution that has played a key role in excluding Palestinians from state land. The Jewish Agency (JA), like the JNF, is a Zionist institution that played a key role in the pre-state era. Established originally in order to represent Zionist interests to the British Mandate authorities in Palestine, it focused on immigrant absorption and settlement while the JNF concentrated on land acquisition. Like the JNF, the JA is an organ of the international Zionist movement, and together with the World Zionist Organization constituted the 'state in waiting' before 1948. Following the establishment of the state, the Knesset debated the JA's future status. Some felt it was no longer appropriate for an independent body to fulfil such a role, now that elected and accountable institutions were in place. One Member of Knesset commented: 'Anyone who decides on matters of settlement, absorption and development automatically decides what the extent of all the government's other activities will be.'[50] Others, including Prime Minister Ben Gurion, took the view that the institutions of the Zionist movement were still required.

The latter view prevailed and in 1952 the World Zionist Organization – Jewish Agency (Status) Law was passed, providing that the Jewish Agency's role was 'to take care as before of immigration and directing absorption and settlement projects in the state' (section 3).[51] Its continued role was necessary because, it was stated, 'the mission of gathering in the exiles, which is the central task of the State of Israel and the Zionist Movement in our days, requires constant efforts by the Jewish people in the Diaspora' (section 5). The details of the JA's relationship with the government were spelt out in a subsequent Covenant between the Jewish Agency and the government.[52]

The JA was to have primary responsibility for rural settlement, which was defined as a national and Zionist goal of the Jewish people. Its mandate covers initiating the planning of rural settlements (on the basis of decisions of a Joint Committee for Settlement comprising the government, WZO and JA), financing the creation of the necessary infrastructure and continuing to support rural settlements until they are self-sufficient including helping in matters of agricultural production (Kretzmer 1990: 94–5). Such assistance extends to acquiring animals, equipment, water rights and required permits, and granting low-interest loans repayable only when the settlement becomes self-sufficient.[53] Acting in close collaboration with government ministries, by 1981 the JA had established 861 agricultural settlements.[54]

The JA's role also extends to other spheres that both in nature and in scale have an enormous impact on Israeli land policy in general, and on Palestinian land use in particular. The JA is jointly responsible with the Ministry of Agriculture for the Rural Planning and Development Authority, the supreme body responsible for agricultural and settlement policy including allocating agricultural land and making agricultural development plans. In this capacity, its role includes recommending who should be awarded short-term agricultural leases, and sitting on a Short Term Leases Appeals Committee together with the ILA

(Phorolis et al. 1979: 75). Such a role gives the JA an influence over allocation of agricultural land to Palestinian farmers. The JA's role is not limited to rural settlement; it has also built public housing and established industrial projects in urban areas, working closely with the government, the JNF and the ILA. It owns shares in the Israel Land Development Company, the water company Mekorot, and the housing corporation Amidar (Lustick 1980: 104). These corporations are major public corporations affecting the lives of all citizens of the state. As in the case of the JNF, the fundamental contradiction between a body performing public and governmental functions while at the same time remaining committed to promoting exclusively Jewish interests, has far-reaching consequences for the Palestinian minority in the state. As in the pre-state era, the JA continues to work for the benefit of Jews alone, and restrictions on non-Jews benefiting from its activities are openly adopted in the process of establishing new settlements and in selection of inhabitants. It is not only the fact that it plans and implements projects for Jews alone that has an impact on the Arab sector. Like the JNF, the JA pursues political goals such as 'Judaization', aimed at achieving a Jewish majority in areas with sparse Jewish populations and significant Palestinian populations, and preventing the spreading of Palestinian communities on 'national' land (Falah 1989b).

In recent years, the JA's role in establishing new rural communities for Jews has been challenged by Palestinians also wanting an opportunity to make a new home in a rural community. The establishment of new rural communities in Israel is the result of partnership between the government, the ILA (which allocates the land) and the JA. The JA, together with the government, the WZO and any other body 'engaged in settling persons on the land and recognized by the Minister of Agriculture', is defined by law as a 'Settlement Institution'.[55] In addition, 'National Settlement Bodies', which must also be recognized by the Minister of Agriculture, are defined as bodies organizing persons for agricultural settlement. A number of settlement institutions and bodies exist in the country corresponding to the different types of rural settlements that exist in the Jewish sector such as kibbutzes and moshavs. When a new rural settlement is to be established, the JA signs an agreement with one of these organizations, and the ILA leases land to the settlement body itself or to the individual members.

An example of how the ILA and the JA work together is ILC Decision 433 of 2 November 1989. Decision 433 sets out the conditions on which the ILA will allocate land to the JA for the development of rural settlements in the Galilee, Wadi 'Ara, the area south of Hebron, the Naqab and the Jordan valley. The Decision specifies that steps will be taken to ensure that the settlement is established according to the terms of the World Zionist Organization – Jewish Agency (Status) Law of 1952 and the Covenant Between the Jewish Agency and the Government, which define the role and objectives of the JA. For this purpose, the Decision says, the JA will establish community associations in each settlement, and will have to give its approval to each allocation of a plot of land within the settlement. In this way the state, through the ILA that is one of its organs, hands over land for the development of settlements that will be exclusively for Jews.

If the JA is the body responsible for the establishment of rural settlements in Israel that are only for Jews, a vital question for Palestinians is, how do non-Jews establish rural settlements. No Palestinian organizations are currently recognized as settlement institutions or national settlement bodies. It is difficult to envisage circumstances in which any of the Zionist settlement bodies would become involved in establishing a rural community for Palestinians. The government, which is also defined as a settlement institution, also has the power to establish rural settlements. Palestinians living in 'unrecognized' villages, a phenomenon that will be discussed in Chapter 8, have repeatedly requested the establishment of rural villages. However, Israeli governments have rejected this option, and the reality is that no new rural settlements have been established in the Arab sector since the establishment of the state.

Where new rural settlements are established in the state, controls are in place designed to ensure that only Jews will be able to live in them. JA internal guidelines state that in order for applicants to be accepted to live in the settlements established by the Agency, they must have completed military service (thus excluding most Palestinian citizens other than Druze), and must be accepted by a committee set up for the settlement comprising representatives of the JA, the settlement institution and the inhabitants.[56] Furthermore, standard lease agreements between the JA and settlers include a declaration that the lessee agrees to be bound by the JNF's restrictions of the use of land by non-Jews.[57]

Recently, a number of Palestinians have applied to live in settlements established by the JA and attempted to challenge its policy of not leasing property to non-Jews. Khaled Nimer Sawaid applied in 1988 for a housing unit in the *mitzpe* (lookout settlement) of Makhmanim in the Galilee. He was already settled nearby on land on which his family had lived for generations, but which the government does not recognize as a legal community.[58] In correspondence the Ministry of the Interior, the planning authorities and the ILA each insisted that he seek housing in one of the concentration points allocated for Bedouin

Arabs. The ILA informed him it was impossible for him to obtain a plot in Makhmanim since plots were allocated only upon referral from the JA, in order to guarantee the 'aims of the settlement'. After protracted correspondence, the ILA proposed to change their plans for the area, rather than agreeing to Sawaid's application.[59] In 1994, Tewfiq Jabarin applied for a house in a new settlement in the Triangle, Katzir. When his application was rejected – on the basis the project had been initiated by the JA and therefore only Jews could benefit – he threatened legal proceedings. In 1995 he was permitted to purchase a home in Katzir, though his agreement was not with the JA or the settlement institution, but directly with the company contracted to build the settlement.

In 1995, a High Court petition was filed by the Association for Civil Rights in Israel on behalf of 'Adil Qa'dan and his wife, who had also applied for a new house in Katzir.[60] On their initial application, they were informed the new housing was not targeted for Arabs. The entire settlement was built on state land that had been confiscated from the residents of the Wadi 'Ara in the early 1950s. Part of it consisted of public housing constructed by the Ministry of Housing and marketed through a government corporation. The other part was controlled by a settlement body, a cooperative that had received the land from the ILA and had organized a 'build your own home' scheme with the Jewish Agency. Allocation of a parcel in the latter part of Katzir was conditional on being accepted as a member by an admissions committee, and was administered by the settlement body according to an agreement with the JA. The conditions included having completed military service or been exempt from it – a condition that automatically excludes most Palestinians who do not serve in the army – and being recommended for acceptance by the JA. Qa'dan had in fact approached the settlement body and been told his application would not be accepted due to the fact he was an Arab.

Before the Court, Qa'dan argued that since the ILA and Ministry of Housing were public bodies and bound to respect the principle of equality, they could not lawfully transfer public land to the Jewish Agency and a private settlement body that were not committed to the principle of equality in distributing public land. On the contrary, the JA was committed to settling Jews only, and its involvement in building a settlement ensured that obstacles were placed before any non-Jewish citizen wishing to live there. The state and ILA had given away their control over the land and given complete discretion to the JA and the settlement body to determine who could live in the new settlement. This process of permitting the JA to carry out such a policy, the petitioner argued, amounted to discrimination on the basis of nationality and was unlawful.

In response, the state asserted that it was bound to respect the agreements between the state and the JA, which were enshrined in law, and the lawful role of the JA was to concern itself with settling Jews only. To accept the petition, the JA argued, would mean the end of the JA's settlement project that had continued since the beginning of the twentieth century and included legitimate aims such as settling Jews in parts of the country where their numbers were small. In its judgment of 8 March 2000, the Israeli High Court said it was only called upon to consider whether the ILA, as a state body, was permitted to allocate land to a communal settlement that was exclusively for Jews.[61] It would deal only with the narrow question of whether the ILA had offended the principle of equality in allocating land to a communal settlement that discriminated between applicants on the basis of religion or national origin and admitted Jews only. The Court found that it had.[62] In a curious follow up, a Jewish Israeli, Uri Davis, applied under the same home development scheme in Katzir and his application was accepted. After signing agreements with the settlement body and the JA, and constructing a house, he promptly handed it over to a Palestinian from Um El Fahem, Fathi Mahameed, claiming that he had acted as an agent for Mahameed all along. The JA and the Katzir cooperative, Haresh Limited, immediately went to Court claiming that their agreement with Davis had been obtained by fraud and should be cancelled.[63] The Magistrates' Court rejected the application, finding that Mahameed had been a victim of discrimination and that Davis was entitled to transfer his rights. On appeal, the Haifa District Court overturned this decision, on the grounds that the applicant refused to cooperate with the admission committee of the community council and the ILA, although this may itself be appealed.

The High Court's judgment in the Qa'dan case has been heralded by some as a victory for the principle of equality in Israel, while others have given it a more cautious welcome.[64] On the surface, the decision might appear to mark a step forwards in recognition of the right of Palestinians in the state to equality. It did confirm that the state cannot avoid its obligation to respect the principle of equality by allocating land to another body that discriminates against non-Jews. And it provoked an attempt to introduce a bill in the Knesset that would have reversed the effect of the decision.[65] But a closer look reveals just how small is the advance made in Qa'dan. One problem is that it simply does not address the main issues at stake. Palestinian commentators have rightly criticized the decision for its failure to address the context of the collective national struggle of the Palestinians in Israel, and point out that the case must be considered as an individual case and was not brought to the court by the Palestinian community but by a Jewish institution, the Association for Civil Rights in Israel.[66]

Another issue the decision fails to address is the role of the Jewish national institutions in Israeli life. The state, by granting a special status to the Jewish Agency and allowing it at one and the same time to carry out one of the most important development functions of the state and to behave as a private body and exclude non-Jews from its programmes, effectively sanctions an unequal position between Jews and Arabs in the state, but this state of affairs was not questioned by the Court. In fact, the Court was at pains to point out the issues that it was *not* addressing, including the 'difficult and complicated questions' of the functioning of the JA and its role in developing Jewish settlements and the lawfulness of the establishment of exclusively Jewish settlements. Instead the Court specifically emphasized the importance of the historical mission of the Jewish Agency, and did not question for a moment the legitimacy of the overall national programme that lay behind the Qa'dan situation. Other issues the Court said it would not address included whether a party other than the state is allowed to discriminate (presumably referring to the JA), and questions of security. And in the end the High Court was not even prepared to give Qa'dan a satisfactory remedy: it did not actually order that he should be permitted to live in Katzir, merely that the state must consider whether it could find a way to enable him to build a house there, within the framework of the law.

So long as the State of Israel remains committed to giving the JA and the JNF what are central roles in governmental functions, while allowing them to continue as nominally private bodies acting in the private interests of one category of citizens, and to escape the reach of judicial review on the basis of discrimination and other public law principles, Israel's claim to be a democratic state committed to principles such as equality must be seriously questioned. In the previous chapter, we argued that the JNF and the JA, as nominally private bodies performing what are in nature public functions, should be subject to public law principles such as the principle of equality, and that the state could not avoid its obligation not to discriminate, and to respect the principle of equality, by handing over control of public land to nominally private bodies. It is not sufficient for the state to hide behind the World Zionist Organization – Jewish Agency (Status) Law and the Covenant Between the Jewish Agency and the Government. The legislation defining the role and functions of the JA should now be amended so as to ensure that, if the institution continues to exist and to perform public functions, it is not permitted to perform its functions in a discriminatory fashion.

Notes

1. The question of whether the ILA has sole authority to administer Israel Lands is unresolved. Israeli land law expert Professor Weisman (1981: 79 and 89) believes that the government is given a parallel authority under the State Property Law of 1951.

2. See Chapter 5.

3. LSI, Vol. 14, p. 50.

4. The ownership of over 1 million dunams of land has still not been determined, but the ILA predicts that once settlement of title operations have been completed everywhere, it will be left with 93.5 per cent of all land in the state under its control; ILA (1993: 131).

5. According to the Israel Lands Administration Law 1960 the Ministers of Finance and Agriculture were responsible for the ILA. They were replaced in 1990 by the Minister of Housing, and in 1996 by the Minister of Infrastructure.

6. Civil Appeal 55/67, N. Kaplan v. State of Israel, PD 21, p. 726.

7. Basic Law: Human Dignity and Liberty, passed by the Knesset on 17 March 1992, *Official Gazette*, 25 March 1992.

8. See also Ben Haim v. ILA, HC 292/75, PD 30 (1), p. 412, and Israeli Center for Contractors and Builders v. the Israeli Government, HC 840/79, PD 34(3), p. 729.

9. Chief Justice Shamgar in a High Court judgment given on 31 March 1992 in the case of Avraham Poraz MK and Others v. Minister of Construction and Housing and Others, HC 5023, 5438 and 5409/91. It was held that the ILA had unlawfully failed to allocate building land without putting it out to public tender; *Jerusalem Post Law Report*, 13 April 1992.

10. 'Adil Qa'dan v. ILA and Others, HC 6698/95, judgment of 8 March 2000 at PD 54(1), p. 258.

11. This arrangement had been agreed in the Covenant between the state and the JNF concluded in 1954, Article 6.

12. In 1992, for example, the ILA prepared dozens of plans in the Zichron Ya'akov, Fanimina, Pardes Hanna, Harhour, Or Akiva, Givat Ada settlement cluster and the Nativot, Sederot and Ofakim cluster, providing for housing, trade, tourism and infrastructure.

13. Public Land, Eviction of Trespassers Law, 1981; *Laws of Israel*, 1981, pp. 105, 142 (in Hebrew).

14. For instance Beneliezer, when Minister of Housing, insisted that the ILA yields to him; *Ha'aretz* (Hebrew daily newspaper), 12 March 1995.

15. It was reported that at a meeting in which top-level government and other officials discussed the ILA, the latter remark was made by the deputy Housing Minister; *Ha'aretz* (Hebrew daily newspaper), 12 March 1995.

16. Ibid.

17. Even where it is obliged to allocate land on the basis of public tender, the ILA does not always do so. In the 1991 case of Poraz, the ILA allocated building land to non-profit associations (on the basis of a decision of the ILC)

despite the insistence of the State Legal Advisor that this should not be done until regulations had been drawn up regarding how allocation should be opened to the public. The High Court criticized the ILA, saying that non-competitive allocation should occur only in extraordinary circumstances which did not exist in this case: everyone must have an equal opportunity to acquire land in public ownership, and this could only be achieved through bidding (in the case of contractors) or drawing lots (in the case of competition for housing aimed at young couples, new immigrants and disadvantaged socio-economic groups); Avraham Poraz MK and Others v. Minister of Construction and Housing and Others, HC 5023/91, PD 46(2), p. 793.

18. Regulations 25, 26 and 28 of 1993 of the Minister of Finance, under the Obligation to Put Out to Tender Law 1993; *Laws of Israel*, 1992, pp. 114 and 250 (Hebrew version), as amended in 1993 and 1994. Regulation 27 authorizes the ILA to handle tenders relating to JNF land in a manner compatible with the Covenant between the JNF and the state.

19. *Ronen Report*, 7 April 1997, see Chapter 5. The Ronen Committee had been appointed by the government to carry out a comprehensive review of Israeli land policy including the merits of selling state land into private ownership, the status of urban and agricultural leases, the extent to which land-use policies were achieving government settlement policies, and the role of the ILA.

20. Examples include ILC Decision 859 of 3 May 1999 raising the compensation levels due to Bedouin in the south who sign evacuation agreements before the end of 1999, and ILC Decision 864 of 3 May 1999 regarding compensation for evacuation of land and properties of Bedouin in the north.

21. ILC Decision 897 of 22 January 2001.

22. Civil Appeal 55/67, N. Kaplan v. State of Israel, PD 21, p. 726.

23. In March 1993, the Nazareth tax office had 11,000 outstanding tax demands, and people were protesting that they could not afford to pay. Interview with Jaber Asakli of the Israeli non-governmental organization Shatil (which gives technical support to community organizations), Haifa, 30 March 1995.

24. Amendment to section 3 of the Tax on Property and Compensation Fund Law 1961.

25. Article 9, Covenant Between the State of Israel and Keren Kayemeth Leisrael, 1954.

26. ACRI v. Government of Israel, Minister of Infrastructure and Minister of Finance, HC 6924/98.

27. Women's Group of Israel v. Minister of Work and Welfare, HC 2671/98, judgment of 11 August 1998.

28. The state's response was given in an affidavit of Ya'cov Katz, General Director, Ministry of Infrastructure, on 3 May 1999.

29. Reported on CD Rom Takdin High Court 2001 (9).

30. See Chapter 4.

31. See Chapter 5.

32. ILC Decision 1 of 17 May 1965.

33. Source: Land Use Research Institute, *Final Report, Long Lease Rents in*

Agricultural Lands (Jerusalem 1986), section A, p. 12 (in Hebrew). Figures were not available for more recent years.

34. Announcement of the ILA in the Hebrew daily newspaper *Yediot Aharanot*, 12 June 1989.

35. Some Jewish communities also claim that they are disadvantaged and discriminated against in this process; petition of the Eastern Democratic Rainbow v. Minister for National Infrastructure, the ILA and Others, Petition no. 244/00 of January 2000.

36. LSI, Vol. 21, p. 105. ILC Decision 243 of 14 September 1980 defined as breaches of this law any use contradicting conditions in the lease, and any transfer of rights granted under a lease.

37. See, for example, *Yediot Aharanot*, 3 May 1971, reporting the first time the law was enforced against a Jewish farmer who sold his crop to an Arab, and *Ha'aretz*, 5 November 1971, reporting ten legal actions against Jewish farmers who had rented their land to Arabs. The latter also reported that an investigating commission had found 267 cases of 'national' land being rented to others, 80 per cent of whom were Arabs. Both reports are translated in Davis and Mezvinsky (eds) (1975: 71–2).

38. For example, in the *Jerusalem Post*, 27 June 1990, it was reported that Likud Agriculture Minister Rafael Eitan threatened legal action against offenders.

39. ILC Decision 425, session 256 of 3 August 1989.

40. ILC Decision 65, session 82 of 28 October 1986.

41. ILC Decision 817 of 10 February 1989.

42. A petition was filed in the High Court in May 1998 by Adalah: the Legal Center for Arab Minority Rights in Israel, on behalf of the High Follow-Up Committee on Arab Affairs and others to challenge the selection of towns to the 'A' or 'B' lists of towns that are given national priority status, HC 2773/98.

43. Under ILC Decision 897 of 22 January 2001, the prices of housing land in certain areas of the Galilee and the north are reduced by almost a half. The purpose of the Decision is stated to be to encourage settlement in those areas and prevent them from being abandoned.

44. For instance, Tenant Protection Laws, the Standard Contracts Law of 1964 (which empowers a court to declare void provisions that are prejudicial to lessees), the Land Law of 1969 (which provides for judicial examination of reasons for a lessor objecting to the assignment of a lease or sublease), the Lease and Licence Law of 1971.

45. Israel Lands Administration Law 1960, section 37.

46. ILC Decision 102, session 113 of 26 July 1971.

47. 472,798 dunams is state land, while 385,993 dunams is private, while 11.1 per cent of the cultivable land in Arab villages is public land; Abu Kishk (1963).

48. For instance, the Abu Hussein Law Office represents a Palestinian family from Faradis who owned land nearby in what had become the Jewish town of

Zichron. Two-thirds of this land had been registered in the name of the Development Authority after being sold by the Custodian of Absentees' Property. The ILA offered to exchange this land for a plot of land in Faradis. On drawing up the terms of the agreement, the ILA inflated the value of the land in Faradis to almost twice its market value, and undervalued the land in Zichron.

49. One co-owner may not take his share unless the entire piece of land is divided and all take their share; Liddawi v. the Israel Lands Administration, Nazareth District Court case 78/79, 1979.

50. Major Knesset Debates, Vol. 2, pp. 600–9. The debate took place on 15 May 1950, the speaker was MK Z. Aharonowitz of Mapai.

51. LSI, Vol. 7, p. 3.

52. *Official Gazette*, 595, 17 April 1958, p. 831.

53. Lustick (1980: 111), referring to JA documentation, Budget Proposal 1973–74, p. 3.

54. Map of Settlement in Israel, Jewish Agency Settlement Department, 1981.

55. Candidates for Agricultural Settlement Law 1953; LSI, Vol. 7, p. 103.

56. *Preconditions, Criteria and Procedures for Acceptance of Applicants to Settlements*, Jewish Agency, 1987.

57. The preamble of standard lease agreements reviewed by the authors for settlements established by the JA states that the lessee agrees to be bound by the provisions of the Covenant between the state and the JNF and of the Memorandum and Articles of the JNF and acknowledges that he takes the lease on this basis.

58. The issue of the 'unrecognized' Palestinian communities will be dealt with in Chapter 8.

59. The Association for Civil Rights in Israel filed a petition to the High Court on his behalf in 1993, Khaled Nimer Sawaid v. Minister of Finance, ILA, JA, Local and District Planning and Building Commissions and Mitzpe Makhmanim, HC 1686/93.

60. 'Adil Qa'dan v. ILA and Others, HC 6698/95.

61. PD 54(1) 258.

62. Paragraph 34 of the Judgment.

63. Katzir, Haresh Ltd v. Uri Davis, Fathi and Nawal Mahameed, case 154/99, Hadera Magistrates' Court.

64. For instance Alexandre (Sandy) Kedar gives the decision a cautious welcome; Kedar (2000: 3).

65. Rabbi Haim Druckman of the National Religious Party introduced a bill that would enable state land to be allocated to build communities in Israel for Jewish settlement only. 'Plan to keep Israeli Arabs off some land is backed', *New York Times*, 9 July 2002, p. A4. Although the government initially decided to back the bill, it was withdrawn a week later.

66. Jamil Dakwar, 'Qa'dan: to what extent an achievement?', *Ha'aretz*, 15 March 2000. And see a series of critical articles in the *Adalah Review*, Vol. 2, Fall 2000.

CHAPTER 7

Control of Land Use: Planning and Housing

> The apparatus of town planning can be a powerful force for the good of a community. On the other hand, it could be an even more powerful means of oppression. Much will depend on whether the aspirations of the community are shared by the central authority, or the extent to which the central authority is prepared to tolerate representative institutions which promote the aspirations of their local communities in the use and development of their land. (Coon 1992: 9)

§ PLANNING should be a dynamic mechanism that enables societies to develop and flourish. In Israel, two very different pictures exist side by side. For the Jewish sector, government ministries and the Zionist Jewish national institutions (principally the JNF and the JA) work together in a proactive drive to establish and develop hundreds of human settlements from large cities to small rural communities.[1] Since 1948, Israel has established around 700 communities specifically aimed at settling Jews.[2] Public money is poured into urban renewal projects, large-scale housing schemes and other projects. A totally different situation exists for Palestinians. In 1948, Palestinians were forced to leave some 418 towns and villages, many of which were destroyed. The 150,000 Palestinians who remained inhabited 108 towns and villages. More than fifty years later these communities have remained almost entirely static. Not a single new community has been established other than townships intended to concentrate the Palestinian Bedouin. There are still only 123 Palestinian communities. In a recent report to the United Nations, the Israeli government stated: 'new Arab settlements are not planned, because of a policy of developing the current settlements' (State of Israel 2001: 100). But the existing Palestinian communities are not being permitted to develop either. While the Palestinian population has increased to a million, the built-up areas of the existing communities have not been allowed to expand sufficiently. As a result of planning decisions, the Palestinian communities, some of them now classified as cities, are hemmed in on all sides, prevented from expanding and developing. They experience severe overcrowding and, left with little choice, a proliferation of unlicensed building that is harshly penalized.

How did this situation come about, and why does it persist in spite of rhetoric and apparent legal protection of the principle of equality in the state? One reason is that Israeli planning policy is dominated by the same ideological and political objectives that have already been described in relation to land policy. These include creating a Jewish majority in all areas of the state ('Judaization'), breaking up Palestinian population concentrations, strategic placing of Jewish settlements such as in border areas and minimizing the land area possessed by Palestinians whether for housing, agriculture, industry or any other purpose. Major land-use projects put into practice since the establishment of the state have been based on these policy objectives: the establishment in the 1950s and 1960s of Jewish towns and cities in areas where the Jewish population was sparse (Upper Nazareth, Ma'alot, Karmiel) and of Jewish 'development towns' in all regions of the state (Khamaysi 1990: 57–8), and the 1970s plan to establish tiny *mitzpim*, or lookout settlements, intended to fill the gaps in Jewish settlement in the north in order to protect state land from 'unauthorised Arab agricultural, residential and grazing activity', and to monitor illegal land use by Arabs (Yiftachel 1992: 143). In other words, it is not merely as a result of neglect and default that Palestinians are discriminated against in planning matters. In planning and housing policy as in land policy, Palestinians in Israel are treated as hostile competition for land rather than as part of the population with an equal entitlement to use the land. Discrimination is the result of deliberate policy decisions at the highest level and permeating the entire system.

The same goals have continued to underlie planning policy. A core objective of a new master plan developed during the 1990s for the Northern District, the area in the state with the largest proportion of Palestinian residents,[3] was to increase the number of Jewish residents in the region. Guidelines sent to planners working on the plan in 1990 stated that the plan should aim to achieve a significant Jewish presence in all different areas of the Galilee region and to address the 'problems' of territorial continuity of the Arab villages and of illegal possession of land and illegal construction.[4] Political and security factors also continue to dominate planning policy. So for instance the plan reflects concerns to prevent the Palestinian community in the area from establishing links with the Palestinian Authority in the West Bank. In the 1990s Ariel Sharon, in his capacity as Minister for Housing Infrastructure, developed his so-called Seven Stars Plan, which aimed to construct a line of settlements straddling the border between Israel and the Israeli-occupied West Bank, effectively moving the Green Line westwards, and to establish Jewish populations in parts of Israel where they were sparse. Construction on both sides of the Green Line was stepped up, both the enlargement of existing settlements and the establishment of new ones.

In October 2001, the government announced plans to establish sixty-eight new villages, towns and residential areas, none of them intended for Palestinians other than the Druze community. The objectives are highly political. As the Hebrew daily newspaper *Ha'aretz* commented, the main reason behind the plan was based on the Israeli saying that 'if the Jews are not quick enough in grabbing the land, an Arab will come along and grab it'.[5] Seventeen of the new settlements will be in the Galilee and the northern Triangle, the areas of the state most heavily populated by Palestinians, and will be located close to the Palestinian communities, further cutting them off from each other and strangling them so as to prevent their further development.[6] A second motivation appears to be related to security and political reasons: a number of the new settlements will be surrounding Jerusalem, along the Green Line, or in areas of the Naqab that have been the subject of negotiations with Israel's neighbours for withdrawal or exchange.[7]

Clearly, then, securing equal opportunity of access to land for all is not one of the goals of the Israeli planning system. The demands of maintaining Israel as 'the Jewish state' are clamouring far more loudly than the rhetoric of Israel's identity as a democratic state committed to fostering 'the development of the country for the benefit of all its inhabitants'.[8] But in Israel, as in any country, society consists of a multiplicity of differing interests and while it is the role of central government to develop policy in the public interest, it should not be allowed to become the sole judge of the public interest (Reade 1987: 216).

A true test of a democratic system is one in which the interests of all groups are taken into account. Accountability and transparency are increasingly viewed in today's world as essential for good governance. One way to ensure these principles, and to cope with differing and conflicting interests, is to allow effective participation in policy-making by all interested groups, a degree of local self-government and consultation of affected communities. This chapter sets out to examine how far these principles are applied in relation to the Palestinian communities in Israel.

Another theme is the extent to which the Israeli system guarantees that the planning needs of the Palestinian sector are met. The purpose of planning should be to facilitate and encourage development as well as to control it. While positive planning involves encouraging development (through planning schemes), planning regulation involves restriction and control of specific development (through licensing building and enforcement of violations of planning laws). A proper legal framework is needed to ensure that this dual function – of positive and regulatory planning – is exercised in accordance with the principles of equality and non-discrimination. In Israel, such a framework does not exist and the result is that the Israeli system has failed to ensure that planning for the Arab sector either respects principles of equality or is appropriate to meet the development needs of the sector. Legislation fails to provide a framework for guaranteeing that the interests of all sectors will be taken into account in planning; for instance, requirements for consultation and participation of all sectors, and assessment of the impact of plans of affected communities, do not exist. Instead, government ministers are given wide powers, such as to determine what sort of local planning body will be appointed in a particular area, the boundaries of local planning bodies and their areas of jurisdiction and other matters that are crucial to the control and development of land. The Israeli High Court, competent to review decisions of public bodies, is charged with ensuring that the statutory planning bodies exercise their powers reasonably and fairly, which includes upholding the principles of non-discrimination and equality. But the courts have not played an active enough role intervening to protect these principles. At each of the different stages in the planning process – policy-making, plan preparation and the process of approval – the system as implemented operates to restrict the Palestinian community's access to land. Housing, also, is a sector in which both direct and indirect discrimination are experienced by Palestinians. Israeli governments have played a highly interventionist role in housing and pump enormous sums of public funds into housing, but have neglected the Palestinian communities that not only comprise more than 17 per cent of the population but are also in socio-economic terms the most needy, and are suffering from a severe crisis in housing.

The Israeli land-use planning system

The Planning and Building Law of 1965 (to be referred to as 'the 1965 law'),[9] provides the formal legal framework for both positive and regulatory planning in Israel. The 1965 law regulates the functions and powers of planning authorities, the preparation of plans and enforcement procedures. In a highly centralized, top-down system, almost any activity relating to land is regulated and a high degree of intervention is assumed in both state and privately owned land. The law provides for a pyramid of planning bodies with three levels: national, district and local. Underneath the National Planning and Building Board are six district commissions and around 130 local planning and building commissions. The major functions of each are set out below. The parameters of plans developed at each level are dictated by the level above; district schemes prevail over local schemes and national schemes over any other scheme.[10] So, for example, the objects of district schemes are stated to be 'the determination of the details necessary for the implementation of the National Outline Scheme in the district and any matter of general importance to the district and likely to form the object of a Local Outline Scheme' (section 55). Only at the local level is there any provision for input by local communities; the national and district commissions are appointed by the government.

PLANNING BODIES AND THEIR FUNCTIONS[11]

National Planning and Building Board
- Advises the government on planning and building policy.
- Directs the preparation of national plans and submits them to the government for approval.
- Approves district plans and, in some cases, local plans.
- Decides objections to district plans and, in some cases, local or detailed plans.

Six district planning and building commissions[12]
Administrative functions:
- Prepare district outline schemes and submit to National Board.
- Approve local outline schemes and detailed schemes, and sometimes initiate them.
- Fulfil the role of a local commission in areas not included within the area of a local commission.
- Ensure local planning and building commissions carry out functions.
- Prescribe conditions for issuing building permits pending approval of schemes.

Quasi-judicial functions:
- Take certain decisions regarding building permits.
- Hear appeals against the rejection of plans by local commissions.
- Decide objections to local plans.

Local planning and building commissions (one for each local planning area)
- Prepare local outline schemes and detailed schemes.
- Initially approve detailed schemes submitted by private persons.
- Grant permits for building and other specified uses of land which conform to a scheme.

- Permit deviations from plans, subject to the approval of the district commission and after considering objections.
- Take primary responsibility for enforcement.
- Expropriate land for public purposes.
- Levy betterment taxes.

Special planning and building commissions (one for each special planning area; mostly areas designated for new settlement and where most of the construction is public)
- Prepare outline or detailed scheme for all or part of a special planning area and submit to Minister of Interior for approval.
- Decide objections to detailed schemes.

Committee for the Protection of Agricultural Land
- Declares land as 'agricultural land'.
- Regulates use of agricultural land, including consenting to the use of such land for non-agricultural purposes.

The 1965 law envisages that national, district and local *outline* plans will be produced via the system set out in the law, while *detailed* plans can be prepared by bodies outside the statutory system. However, one central feature of the Israeli planning system is that external to the formal planning process, a number of other actors in practice have a major input in planning. The same actors as have been discussed in previous chapters in relation to land policy are also active in planning. In addition to government ministries (primarily the Housing Ministry), the ILA and the Jewish national institutions, the Jewish Agency (JA) and the Jewish National Fund (JNF), play a central role. While these bodies frequently work in contradiction to each other rather than pursuing a uniform strategy, they all draw up and implement plans which have a major impact on Arab communities. These bodies are active both within and outside the statutory planning system: they either feed their plans into the statutory system or bypass it altogether. For instance, the concept of *mitzpim* was introduced by a Jewish Agency plan of 1978 and was implemented in breach of the statutory planning procedures, exploiting an apparent loophole in the law (Yiftachel 1992: 142–246).

The impact of this combination of forces leaves the Arab sector at a severe disadvantage. On analysing the objectives of plans initiated by a range of bodies including the statutory system, government ministries, the ILA and the JNF and JA, Oren Yiftachel found that only the statutory system involved any element of promoting the interests of both Arabs and Jews, while the JNF and JA plans involved an explicit aim to contain Arabs, and the plans of the ILA and ministries as well as most elements of the statutory system involved an open promotion of Jewish interests tied with an implicit aim to contain Arabs (Yiftachel 1992: 150).

In recent years, there has been a growing awareness in the Palestinian community of the advantages of attempting the same strategy of putting forward plans from outside the statutory planning process. Since the late 1980s, non-governmental organizations representing the unrecognized Palestinian communities have pursued a strategy of commissioning planners to draw up plans reflecting their own aspirations for their communities, which contrasted sharply with government plans.[13] A recent amendment to the 1965 law enacted in 1995 made it easier for bodies outside the planning system to propose plans.[14]

While independent preparation of alternative plans is a relatively new phenomenon in the Palestinian sector, a long-standing tendency is for key aspects of planning in this sector to be dealt with through informal means rather than using the legal framework provided by the planning system. Both the authorities and the Palestinian community tend to rely heavily on negotiation and other non-formal processes for achieving their objectives.[15] So, for example, the authorities in the Naqab approach Bedouin extended families and seek to negotiate relocation deals. The Palestinian community, and particularly the traditional leadership, frequently perceive their best chances of influencing things in their favour to be through negotiation rather than through the legal and planning system, which they view as loaded against them. Some have proved more successful than others at this, but in general it has led to a divided approach with less ability to influence the system as a whole effectively. Many matters are dealt with at the level of each community or family, with local officials or leaders cultivating relations with the relevant government departments. A major problem with such informal approaches from the point of view of the Palestinian minority is their unequal bargaining power in this relationship, and the fact that so many elements of policy are predetermined in a sphere outside the formal planning process and from which they are excluded. Behind the scenes, government ministries cooperate with the ILA and the Jewish national institutions to decide on policy, including in areas that have a greater or lesser impact on the Arab sector. They then use the planning system to implement it. A key impediment for the Arab sector is the lack of effective lobby groups to represent the community's interests. The National Committee of Arab Mayors for years struggled to be recognized by the government as a spokesperson for the Palestinian community. Although the Committee briefly achieved recognition by the Labour government in the mid-1990s, the subsequent Likud government reverted to the previous situation whereby governments have refused to recognize and deal directly with this body.

The extent of Palestinian participation and consultation in the planning process

Identifying the needs of the affected population, and involving them in the planning process, is essential for a planning process that responds to the needs of the communities and respects the principle of equality. In the Israeli system, Palestinians are given little opportunity to have input in the planning process at its different stages, with the result that their needs and views are not taken into account. Little attempt is made to identify the needs of the Palestinian communities or to assess the impact of plans on these communities, there is negligible Palestinian representation on planning bodies and minimal Palestinian participation in either the process of preparation or approval of plans.

Lack of needs or impact assessments Until recently, Israeli law had no requirements for impact assessments to be carried out or for consultation with affected communities during the planning process. The 1965 law was silent on this issue, providing only for notice to be posted when preparation of a plan begins, and for objections to be lodged once a plan has been deposited.[16] Recently there have been some indications of a change in attitude and greater acknowledgement of the importance of participation. In 1994 some progress was made when a requirement was introduced for an environmental impact survey to be carried out when roads are being planned, and for steps to be taken to mitigate any negative impacts.[17] In the same year, the law was amended to give planning and building committees the discretion, though not the duty, to ask for an environmental impact assessment.[18]

Despite this advance, planners at all levels continue to make little or no effort to identify needs in order to provide positive planning for development. The process of developing National Outline Scheme 'Tama 31', approved in February 1993, illustrates this tendency. The plan's major objective was to encourage construction, development and immigrant absorption over several years. One of its stated goals was the creation of conditions for equal development in the Arab sector. However, little attempt was made to identify the needs of the Arab sector or consult with or involve the Arab community in its preparation. Moreover, the plan revealed no overall goals for the Arab sector, merely ad hoc provisions, and no practical measures to close existing gaps between the Jewish and Arab sectors (Abu El Haija 1994). The Arabs are directly mentioned only in the context of negligible allocations for tourism (0.7 per cent of the countrywide budget) and housing, and the relocation policy relating to the Palestinian Bedouin in the south and the completion of settlement of title. Indicative of the government's approach is the fact that on the official website of the Centre for Local Authorities in Israel, the planned population levels of all cities, towns and villages in Israel are listed – except in the case of the Arab communities, for which the column showing planned future inhabitants remains empty (Sikkuya 2001).

At the district and regional level similar practices prevail. The consequences have been felt particularly keenly in the environmental sphere. While it is common international practice to require the preparation of environmental impact assessments in relation to any development likely to have a significant effect on the environment,[19] the Israeli planning system has no such requirement, and the Palestinian community has suffered as a result. A number of environmental problems confront the Palestinian communities, including the building of quarries close to them. In 1992, plans were approved for the construction of the Phoenicia glasswork factory close to several Palestinian villages, in the Tzipori industrial zone. The factory as planned would have emitted large quantities of poisonous sulphur dioxide that, according to environmental experts, would pose a threat to health, to flora and fauna, and to buildings and vehicles in several nearby Palestinian villages.[20] However, the inhabitants of these villages knew nothing about the plans for the factory until bulldozers arrived to prepare the land for construction. It was only after the affected Arab local authorities, together with a non-governmental organization, petitioned the High Court that the factory agreed to take steps to limit the hazard to the environment. The factory was only the first of several heavy industrial factories proposed for the site which, placed so close to an area heavily populated by Palestinians, would constitute an environmental hazard. The Phoenicia experience highlights the dangers of a system that does not require environmental impact assessments to be prepared for development projects as part of the planning process.

Arab representation on planning bodies There are few Arab representatives at any level of the planning system, resulting in a low level of participation by the Arab population in policy and decision-making. The National Planning and Building Board, the pinnacle of the highly centralized Israeli system and a crucial body in setting national planning policy, comprises members and appointees of the government, including professional experts. Six representatives of local government are included: mayors of the major cities and others designated by the Minister of the Interior. No Arab had ever been nominated to the National Planning Board until the appointment in May 1995 of the mayor of one Palestinian community, Eilabun, who was appointed not as a representative of the Arab sector but as one of the local authority delegates. Meanwhile the Zionist Jewish national institutions have always been well represented; for instance, there is always a representative of the settlement institutions recommended by the Jewish Agency.[21]

At the district level, Palestinians are also underrepresented. Members of the six district commissions are all either representatives of government ministries or appointed by the Minister of the Interior.[22] In the Northern District, for instance, where the proportion of Arab inhabitants is the highest of all the districts (just over 50 per cent), two out of fifteen members are Arab. There is one Arab representative on each of the Haifa and Central districts, and none on the other three district commissions. A legal challenge directed at the low Arab representation on the Northern District Commission was rejected by the High Court.[23]

At the level of local planning, the statutory planning system does display some commitment to community representation.[24] Where a local planning area includes the area of only one local authority, the elected municipal council will itself be appointed as the local planning and building commission (1965 law, sections 18–19). The advantage for the community is that its members are elected by the local residents as opposed to being appointed and dismissed by the government.[25] The law does not set out criteria for appointment of a municipal authority as a local planning and building commission, and the matter is at the discretion of the Minister of the Interior. Of the 130 local and regional planning areas in Israel, more than half are single municipal authorities.[26] However, whereas all the Jewish localities with city status and the majority of Jewish towns have their own local planning and building commissions, in the Arab sector even some cities do not. Of the all-Arab communities only Nazareth, Taibeh and Tira have their own local planning and building commissions. As a result, the Palestinian community has significantly fewer elected bodies with a direct role in planning than does the Jewish sector.

Where a municipal council is not appointed as a local commission, or where there is no municipal council, local planning is in the hands of a local commission that is given responsibility for several communities. The majority of Palestinian towns and villages fall within the latter type of local commission. The thirteen-member commission will comprise government representatives, who serve in an advisory capacity, and seven members recommended by the municipal authorities in the area. The 1965 law provides that, as far as possible, 'all the area authorities are represented and that the number of residents of each of them is taken into account' (section 19[2]). Despite this stipulation, Arab representation on local commissions tends to be minimal even where there are significant Arab populations. For example, all seven of the Bedouin planned townships in the Naqab – including the city of Rahat – fall under the Shimonim Local Planning and Building Commission, together with a number of small Jewish settlements, which over the years has had little or no Palestinian participation, even though Palestinians form an overwhelming majority in the area.[27] The unrecognized villages are particularly disadvantaged by having no voice on local planning bodies. For instance, the 70,000 Palestinians in the Naqab living in forty-five unrecognized villages come under a regional planning committee that they are unable to influence even though it exercises crucial powers not only in relation to the development of plans, but also regarding questions such as issuing and implementation of demolition orders.

Two other influential bodies on which Palestinians lack representation are the Committee for the Protection of Agricultural Land and the Council for National Parks, Nature Reserves and National Sites. The former was established under the 1965 law with the aim of protecting green areas and preserving land for agricultural use. The Committee's function is to declare which land is 'agricultural land' and to regulate use of such land, including consenting to the use of such land for non-agricultural purposes.[28] In so far as they relate to agricultural land, all planning schemes must be approved by this Committee. Since most land that is not within the built-up areas is designated as agricultural land, an expansion of the Palestinian towns and villages often requires the consent of this body. It is therefore an important body for the Palestinian community. The Committee's eleven members comprise six government representatives and others appointed by the Minister of the Interior, including one representative recommended by the Jewish Agency. The Arab sector is not represented. The Committee's decisions are based on expert advice and it is not obliged to hear landowners who stand to be affected by a declaration of land as agricultural land. The High Court has held that it will intervene in its decisions only where there is a fundamental flaw in the exercise of its discretion.[29] The operation of the Committee has often had negative consequences for the Arab sector.[30]

The Council for National Parks, Nature Reserves and National Sites is also an important decision-making body for the Palestinian community, since it has powers relating to land situated near Palestinian-inhabited areas that are designated as parkland or nature reserve. Nevertheless, the government-appointed Council of nineteen members comprises representatives of a number of ministries, of the ILA, JNF, local councils and nature institutions, and four representatives of the general public. Once again, there is no Palestinian representative on this body.

Palestinian participation in the preparation of plans A range of different bodies is involved in planning for the Arab communities, including not only the planning authorities but also government departments and the ILA. Only a small number of these bodies include any Arab representation at all. Arab local authorities are permitted to initiate local plans,[31] but plans are only rarely prepared by locally elected authorities.[32] Because of the limited role of Palestinians in the statutory planning bodies, the community has little opportunity to participate in the process of preparation of plans.

Power disparities exist in the relationship between the Arab local authorities and the planning bodies during this process. A key factor identified by Oren Yiftachel is the alienation between planner and community that leaves the local authority feeling dissatisfied (Yiftachel 1992: 242–3). One problem is that the appointed planners and architects are almost always Jewish (ibid., p. 238).[33] Only in recent years have trained planners, architects and engineers emerged within the Palestinian community. Although this ought not to be an influential factor, since it is internationally recognized that planners, like other professionals, have a duty to promote equality of opportunity and seek to eliminate discrimination (Coon 1992: 209),[34] it has been a factor in the alienation of the Palestinian communities from the planning process in Israel.

When plans are not initiated by the Arab communities themselves, the 1965 law contains no formal requirement for consultation with the local community or for a study to be made of what impact plans would have on the affected community (Alexander et al. 1983: 138). The only requirement of district and local commissions is to publish notice of their intention to prepare a plan in the *Official Gazette* and in a daily newspaper. There is no statutory duty on the planning authorities to allow the public to share in the formulation of planning proposals.[35] This is contrary to well established practice in other countries, which give considerable weight to the principle of consultation and participation in planning.[36] Often the Palestinian community affected knows nothing of a plan until it is formally deposited, even though this is in breach of the notice requirements. Where more than 10 per cent of the local planning area is Arabic-speaking, there is a requirement that the notice must also appear in an Arabic-language newspaper. In practice, these notices are often not published (ibid.), even though failure to do so could lead to the cancellation of the plan.[37]

The courts have recently taken some small but important steps to promote the principle of consultation in planning for the Palestinian sector. In September 2001 the High Court considered a petition regarding the Palestinian unrecognized village of Kamaneh, challenging the exclusion of parts of the village from the plans prepared by the planning authorities as part of the implementation of a government decision to recognize the village. The consequences for the two areas of being excluded from the plan were that they would have remained unrecognized. In its decision, the High Court stressed the importance of participation by the affected community in plan development.[38] Ordering that the excluded parts of the village should be included in the plan, the Court directed that the residents of those parts be given the opportunity to submit their own proposals, and that the residents of the areas affected should be heard during the process.[39] In another case relating to an unrecognized village in process of recognition, this time the village of Husseiniya, the Acre Magistrates' Court ruled that since there was no local municipal authority, a local planning and building commission should have consulted with the local committee of inhabitants before ordering the demolition of buildings within the community.[40]

Despite these small advances, it remains the norm that Palestinians do not have a significant input in much of the planning that is carried out in relation to their communities. It is hardly surprising that the plans that result primarily reflect government policies relating to the Palestinians, including the policies of containment and 'Judaization', rather than being in keeping with the aspirations and needs of the communities.

Palestinian participation in the process of approval of plans Once plans are drawn up, they must go through a formal process of approval. In most cases, the Palestinian community is in the position of having to respond to plans drawn up without their input. Their ability to respond effectively to plans once they have been drawn up and deposited is limited. This is partly due to their lack of representation on the key decision-making bodies, but also to the fact that the statutory system presents little opportunity for objection to national and district schemes. National plans are approved by the government and there is no procedure for objections or appeals.[41] District plans are approved by the National

Board, and opposition may be lodged by local commissions and municipal authorities – of which there are few under Palestinian control – and by certain representative bodies on a list approved by the Minister of the Interior, on which no Palestinian body is included.[42] The National Committee of Arab Mayors, for instance, is not on the list. So far as local plans are concerned, the 1965 law provides that objections may be lodged by anyone with an interest in land who believes he or she is prejudiced by the plan. An analysis of appeals brought against decisions of local commissions in the Yahiam region during the period 1975 to 1987 found that the success rate for Jews was much higher than that of Arabs. During 1986–87, Jews had a 100 per cent success rate while the rate for Arabs was 48.3 per cent (Yiftachel 1992: 235).

The role of the courts in planning decisions is limited to procedural review and does not extend to hearing appeals. Despite the detailed listing in the 1965 law of matters that plans are to cover, the statutory system leaves a wide discretion, particularly in the upper levels of the system, leaving little scope for individuals and groups to bring legal challenges to decisions that affect them. The difficulties faced by the Arab sector in successfully opposing plans were highlighted by the case of a stone quarry in the vicinity of the Palestinian village of Tamra. An application for planning permission to develop a quarry was approved by the local and district planning and building commissions, despite objections by the Tamra local council and others on the grounds that it would create a nuisance to nearby villages. When Tamra local council attempted to appeal to the National Board, the question of whether or not it had the standing to do so went to the High Court, which decided that only members of the district commission could appeal to the National Board.[43] In other words, an elected body representing the interests of a particular locality is prevented from making representations before the National Planning and Building Board. The prospects of persuading the district commission to back such an appeal were slim. Similar obstacles face Palestinians wanting to appeal even at the local commission level. Smaller or unrecognized Palestinian communities that do not even have municipal status will not be represented on the local commission either at all or in sufficient numbers to carry a decision to back an appeal, and are at a particular disadvantage.

Drawing the boundaries of local municipal and planning authorities

Two layers of local government authorities exist in Israel that are highly important in regulating access to land: municipal and planning authorities. Both have a considerable ability to exercise control over land falling under their respective jurisdictions, despite the centralized nature of both systems. The municipal authorities consist of local, city and regional councils that are assigned an area of jurisdiction over which they exercise municipal powers. Second, there is the layer of local planning authorities that also have an area of jurisdiction over which they exercise powers under the 1965 law. There is considerable overlap between the two functions. In larger communities a city or local council will itself be the local planning and building commission. Sometimes a local commission will be coextensive with a regional council. But it is not always the case that a community will look to the same authority for both municipal and planning functions. Some communities do not have any municipal status at all, but all will come under the jurisdiction of one or other of the planning authorities.

The designation of a community as a certain type of municipal authority, and the assignment of areas of jurisdiction to the different bodies responsible for local government and planning, have important consequences in terms of control over land. The power to determine the type of municipal or planning authority a community will have, and the areas of jurisdiction of these bodies, lies with the Minister of the Interior. Palestinian areas are consistently given smaller areas of control than Jewish authorities of equivalent size. Land surrounding the Palestinian communities that has for centuries been considered part of the community, even if it has become state land due to the operation of the Absentees' Property Law, is placed under the jurisdiction of Jewish-controlled municipal and planning authorities. This opens the way for that land to be used for residential and other projects that are developed for Jews only, military areas, national parks and other uses that have the effect of putting the land out of use for the Palestinian communities. The issue of inequities in the allocation of areas of jurisdiction was raised by many of the local council representatives that the authors interviewed, and this is perceived to be one of the major obstacles to local municipal authorities being able to carry out their responsibilities to maintain and develop their communities. Almost all the Palestinian communities are engaged in some form of border dispute with neighbouring authorities.[44] Some have attempted to challenge the drawing of the borders, even in the courts, but with few results.

Municipal government and control of land use in the Arab sector Local government administration is so centralized in Israel that municipal authorities have very little independence and few decisions can be taken at the local level without the permission or confirmation of the Minister of the Interior.[45] Municipal budgets are also controlled by the Minister, an effective tool to pressure councils to bend to his/her will. Nevertheless, Palestinian access to land is heavily influenced by the Israeli local government system, and under which municipal authority's jurisdiction a piece of land falls is significant in a number of ways. Municipal authorities have the power to expropriate up to 40 per cent of a plot for public purposes without paying compensation,[46] and the option to develop planning schemes for the community. Where the municipal authority is also a local planning and building commission, its ability to influence land-use planning in the community is even greater as it will have the power to grant initial approval to a detailed scheme, grant building permits and carry out other planning functions.[47] There are also other benefits to municipal jurisdiction, including the important power to levy taxes on land. Municipal status draws government funding, and cities are able to attract the highest budgets for development as regional centres. Whether a locality has any municipal status at all (many small communities do not), and which status they are granted (city, local council, locality within a regional council) is therefore a matter of considerable significance.

One of the grievances of the Palestinian communities is that land immediately surrounding their communities, including agricultural land owned by the residents as well as state land, is often included not in their jurisdiction but in the jurisdiction of another – Jewish dominated – local authority. In this situation the Arab city or local council is no longer able to exercise a measure of control over the future use of that land, including its use in any future expansion of the community. Instead it may find that plans have been put forward for some other use of the land, such as for the development of a community intended for Jews only.

Another grievance is that Palestinian communities are not given the status they deserve. The highest level of municipal authority is the individual community that is designated with an elected municipal authority, either as a city or as a local council. City status is desirable because it draws more resources. There are only eight Arab cities even though some of the other Palestinian communities have larger populations than some Jewish cities.[48] There are also sixty-nine Arab local councils, some 60 per cent of the 123 Palestinian recognized communities, reflecting the forced urbanization that the sector has undergone since 1948. A further complaint is that even after councils are established in the Palestinian communities they are frequently not permitted to hold elections for several years, thereby remaining effectively under national governmental control.[49]

Smaller communities that do not have their own local council will come under the jurisdiction of a regional council, which provides municipal services. Communities within a regional council are administered by local committees, which are represented on the regional council. In the Jewish sector there are over 900 rural localities that are organized in this way.

It is the smallest Palestinian communities, those lacking their own local municipal councils and allocated to a regional council, that face the greatest problems, having little voice in policy- and decision-making. Because of the way the boundaries are drawn, Arab localities tend to form a minority in Jewish dominated councils, as shown in Table 7.2. Research has shown that the vast majority of Palestinians living within these regional councils are dissatisfied, claim discrimination, and express the desire to leave their jurisdiction (Abu Raya 1995: 31). Those Palestinian localities that lack municipal status at all, or are unrecognized, have particular problems in getting their concerns heard. Regional councils cover 85 per cent of the area of the state and incorporate 10 per cent of the population. Until the establishment of the Mashosh Regional Council in 1988, there were no all-Arab regional councils (ibid., p. 5). Only very recently have exclusively Arab regional councils been established in the form of the 'Villages Council', a new category introduced in 1992. Four regional or villages councils comprising only Arab localities have since been established (ibid., p. 11). They incorporate several villages, but are smaller than a regional council and have fewer powers.[50] For instance, Mashosh has jurisdiction over only three Palestinian localities and a fraction of the area of Jewish-dominated regional councils, as Table 7.2 indicates.

Given the benefits, both financial and in terms of independence and control, that accompany a promotion in municipal status, the process by which municipal status is determined is important. However, there

TABLE 7.1 Localities In Israel

	Cities	Local councils
Jewish	61	87
Arab	8	69
Total:	69	141

Source: Statistical Abstract of Israel 2001: Table 2.3; Sikkuy <www.sikkuy. org. il> and Arab Association for Human Rights, Nazareth.

TABLE 7.2 Jurisdictions of selected regional councils

Regional councils	Jurisd. (in dunams)	Inhabitants	Of whom Arab	No. of localities	Of which Arab
Gilboa	250,000	20,000	7,000	29	5
Matai Yehuda	600,000	24,000	1,550	60	3
Mashosh	35,000	13,010	13,010	3	3
Emeq Israel	500,000	28,500	10,000	39	5

Source: Abu Rayah (1995: 7).

are no published criteria for the designation of municipal status and for determining whether a community is to be declared a city, or a local council. These matters are at the discretion of the Minister of the Interior, who also specifies the area of jurisdiction of a new city or council. Before granting city status, the Minister is obliged to appoint an investigation committee and consider its findings.[51] The committee's function is not a judicial one, but to deal with public policy considerations.[52] Implementation of these powers *vis-à-vis* the Arab sector has been discriminatory in a number of ways. Israeli governments since 1948 have been slow to accord municipal status to the Palestinian communities (Jiryis 1976: 227). They have also been slow to promote Arab localities to the appropriate status for their size of population. Sizeable Palestinian towns are less likely to achieve city status than Jewish towns of comparative size.

Areas of jurisdiction of the Palestinian municipal authorities When the government establishes a city or a local council it has to define an area of land that comes under the control of that council. Because of the important elements of independence and control that come with municipal authority, the areas of jurisdiction allocated to Palestinian cities, local councils and localities have been a key aspect of the struggle for access to land. Successive Ministers of the Interior have limited the areas of jurisdiction of Arab local councils, which tend to have a far smaller jurisdiction than their Jewish counterparts. The tendency is to place little more than the actual built-up area of the village or town under the jurisdiction of the council, and not the surrounding area. Most of the Arab local councils were established during the 1960s and 1970s, and the areas of jurisdiction they were given excluded large areas of land owned by the residents and previously recognized as part of the community.

Meanwhile the agricultural land around the village remains with no municipal status or is annexed to a Jewish dominated regional council and becomes available for future planning by that council. This is true even of the new Arab Villages Councils of Nof Hagalil and Irron. Nof Hagalil, established in October 1992 and comprising six Arab villages, was allocated jurisdiction over only the built-up areas of the villages, and Irron consisted only of the built-up areas of eight Arab villages.[53] Agricultural land owned by the inhabitants of the villages included in Irron were annexed to other regional and local councils on which Palestinians have little or no representation. Anomalous situations arise such as that of the area known as Shbrentzak, an area of land within the city limits of the Arab city of Nazareth that was confiscated in the 1960s and put under the control of the municipality of Jewish Upper Nazareth, even though there is no geographic or other link with Upper Nazareth.[54]

Table 7.3 shows the extent to which the areas of jurisdiction of a number of Palestinian villages have been reduced since 1948. 'Arab village area before 1948' includes the lands surrounding a village that were acknowledged as being used for agriculture and grazing by the inhabitants of the village. In most cases the area under the jurisdiction of the present-day local councils is drastically reduced.

The average area of jurisdiction of the Palestinian cities and local councils has decreased by 46 per cent compared to the area recognized as lands belonging to that community during the British Mandate. Meanwhile, the built-up areas of the Palestinian communities has increased sixteen-fold since 1948, and the population density within these areas has increased eleven-fold.[55]

TABLE 7.3 Areas of jurisdiction of Jewish and Arab local councils (in dunams)

Place	Population	Arab village area before 1948	Current area of jurisdiction of local council
Kabul	8,600	8,000	7,000
Sha'ib	5,300	18,000	2,300
Deir Hanna	7,300	16,000	8,900
Sakhnin	23,000	68,000	9,700
Nahf	8,800	15,600	4,900
Deir Al Asad	8,900	15,000	4,300
Majd Al Krum	11,000	20,000	9,300
Arrabe	17,300	5,000	8,350

Source: Sikkuy 2001b: Table 13, p. 26.

Again, it is the Palestinian communities that are included within regional councils that face the greatest problems. The establishment of the Misgav Regional Council in 1982 was particularly damaging for the Palestinian communities involved. Misgav was created in an area of the Galilee where there are a number of large Arab villages that still retain extensive agricultural lands. The new council was given jurisdiction not only over twenty-seven small Jewish communities but, in addition, over large areas of agricultural land belonging to neighbouring Arab villages. Half of its jurisdiction of 180,000 dunams constitutes agricultural land owned by Palestinians from twenty-three villages (Falah 1989b), plus the Batof valley, an area of considerable economic significance to several Arab communities in the region.[56] The decision to place this land under the jurisdiction of a Jewish dominated regional council instead of under the control of the Arab local councils in the area must be viewed in the context of the state policy of domination and control of land in the country generally, and in the Galilee in particular. Misgav now has power to decide the future of large areas of land lying around the Arab villages in the area.

Industrial areas are treated in the same way; Arab neighbourhoods are forced to suffer the environmental consequences of having industry nearby while losing the benefit of the taxes paid by these industries, which go to other councils. A quarry near the Arab town of Tura'an, for instance, was annexed to the Lower Galilee Regional Council instead of to the local council of Tura'an. Similarly, the industrial area of Rosh Ha'ain, which is situated on land that was expropriated from the Arab village of Kufr Qasem, was annexed to the Jewish town of Rosh Ha'ain.[57] As we have seen above, the Phoenicia glasswork factory, planned in the Tzipori industrial zone in 1992, is another example. Although this zone is situated in the midst of an Arab populated area, particularly close to the villages of Mashad and Kufr Kana – on land originally owed by residents of Mashad but expropriated from them progressively since 1948 – it was placed under the jurisdiction of Upper Nazareth Local Authority and Local Planning and Building Commission in February 1991. The inhabitants of the area knew nothing about the plans for the factory until the bulldozers arrived. The first question that should be asked is why this land was annexed to the jurisdiction of Upper Nazareth when it was situated in the middle of an area encompassing several Arab villages and not geographically contiguous to Upper Nazareth. And why was the area given top development status (A), attracting high levels of tax incentives and government subsidies, when none of the neighbouring Arab villages, including their tiny industrial zones, was given such a status. Placing it under the jurisdiction of Upper Nazareth made sure that the nearby

Palestinian villages gained no share in benefits such as municipal taxes and economic investment. It was only after intense negotiations and the discovery that the villagers were in a strong legal position due to the harmful environmental effects the factory would have that Upper Nazareth began to talk of the Arab villages sharing the industrial zone.

Palestinian communities have been hit not only by the initial drawing of boundaries but also by subsequent boundary changes. Ministers of the Interior have on a number of occasions exercised their discretion to alter the areas of jurisdiction of municipal councils so as to reduce the areas controlled by Palestinian authorities. A wide discretion is given to the Minister by law and the courts are unwilling to intervene. Decisions to alter boundaries of jurisdiction must, according to the law, be preceded by an investigation committee; however, this is nominated by the Minister and its membership is left to his or her discretion.[58] The Minister is not tied by its recommendations, but the committee should look into the merits, commission a survey of the impact of the change of boundary and consider all the circumstances. Local councils must be informed and the committee must give an opportunity for a fair hearing to any interested person or body.

Palestinian areas have not so far met with much success in attempting to challenge decisions to reduce their areas of jurisdiction. In 1990 the Minister of the Interior approved the merger of two Palestinian villages in the Triangle: Arara and Ara. The populations of both villages strongly opposed the merger, but were prepared to agree if *all* the land owned by the inhabitants of the two villages was included in the jurisdiction of the local council (according to the proposal, only the built-up area of Ara was to be included). A new committee was appointed to reconsider the issue but little change resulted. In February 1991 the Minister of the Interior announced that the area of jurisdiction of the Arab city of Um El Fahem would be reduced; the area taken out of its sphere of influence included some of the land surrounding the city and 80 metres each side of a road leading to a small Jewish locality.[59] Furthermore, complete blocks belonging to the inhabitants of Um El Fahem that had been without municipal status were given to regional councils on which there was little Palestinian representation. In the same month, the area of jurisdiction of the predominantly Jewish city of Upper Nazareth was expanded by 7,330 dunams at the expense of the villages around Nazareth: Reineh, Ein Mahil, Mashad and Kufr Kanna. This was despite the fact that Upper Nazareth already had a jurisdiction of 19,200 dunams for a population of 25,000, compared with Arab Nazareth, which has an area of jurisdiction of 12,500 dunams for a population of 65,000.[60] Being brought under the jurisdiction of a predominantly Jewish area does not bring the benefits that accrue to those areas, however. The Palestinian village of Ein Mahil, which as a result of the changes became an island within the area of Upper Nazareth, did not gain the status that this mainly Jewish city has. Whereas Upper Nazareth is designated an area of national priority A, Ein Mahil has no development status at all, which means its residents will not be granted reductions in the price of land for housing, industry, tourism and other commercial purposes.

One Arab village, Kufr Yasif, has attempted to challenge the reduction in its area of jurisdiction in the courts. Of 6,880 dunams within its jurisdiction on the establishment of the local council in 1925, the village now only has 2,655 dunams. The local council of Kufr Yasif issued its first petition to the High Court in 1982, in response to which the Court invited the Minister of the Interior to review the application for an enlargement of jurisdiction. Seven years later, no determination had been made, so the local authority petitioned the High Court again.[61] While the petition was pending, a review committee recommended that the village's jurisdiction be slightly enlarged, but not so as to encompass the land that fell within the traditional area around the village, rather to add land belonging to inhabitants of two nearby Druze villages, Yarka and Abu Sinan. Not satisfied with this result, the local authority petitioned the High Court for a third time.[62] The High Court dismissed the petition in July 1993, saying it was not willing to intervene in the exercise of discretion by the Minister. The Minister of the Interior, the Court said, had appointed a committee that had heard all interested parties, and had confirmed its recommendations. The Court found no procedural irregularity and was unwilling to look into the merits of the case.

In the Naqab, residents of two Palestinian Bedouin unrecognized villages in 2000 also turned to the courts to challenge the government's decision to expand the area of jurisdiction of the Jewish town of Omer so as to annex the land on which the 6,000 inhabitants of the two villages resided.[63] Since the decision ignores their presence entirely, the villages are arguing that it means an end to any prospects for recognition and development and people assume that they will be forcibly evicted. The review committee had neither heard representations from the Bedouin community nor even referred to their existence.

Areas of jurisdiction of the planning bodies It is not only the areas of jurisdiction of the municipal authority that have crucial implications for control over land. The drawing of the boundaries of the local planning areas is also important. Planning authorities have the power to expropriate up to 40 per cent of the land for public purposes without paying compensation, may initiate local plans, grant permits and take enforcement measures. The power to create and draw the boundaries of local planning areas again lies with the Minister of the Interior. The 1965 law gives little guidance as to how the Minister should exercise this discretion, beyond stating that he or she should consult with the National Board, the district commission and the local authority concerned (section 13[a]). In practice, successive ministers have exercised their discretion in such a way as to minimize direct Palestinian input into planning. Oren Yiftahel analysed the jurisdiction of local commissions in the Galilee as a whole and found that commissions dominated by Ashkenazi Jewish majorities controlled 62 per cent of the area, although that group comprised only 6 per cent of the inhabitants, while Arab dominated commissions covered only 16 per cent of the area despite comprising 72 per cent of the population (Yiftachel 1999b: 330).[64] A similar pattern was repeated in the Naqab.

For instance, areas inhabited by Palestinians are commonly not placed under the jurisdiction of local planning commissions on which there is Palestinian representation, even where such commissions exist in the area. In the Triangle, for example, the local commission of Menasheh Alona includes in its jurisdiction most of the lands of the Palestinian town of Baqa Al-Gharbiya, and lands of the villages of Barta'a, Jat, Arara, Ara, Al-Arian and Kafr Qara, and the commission of Yizraelim includes extensive areas of the city of Um El Fahem and the villages of Muawiya, Musmus, Musherfa and Biada. Neither has a single Arab representative. These villages could have been placed under the jurisdiction of the Irron local commission, situated in the same area, on which Palestinian communities do have representatives, but they were not. The same is true of extensive areas of land surrounding Arab villages and owned by village residents, which are placed under Jewish dominated commissions even though there is no territorial link between this land and those commissions. In general, Ministers of the Interior have rarely exercised their discretion so as to establish local planning commissions comprising only Arab local authorities, despite requests from heads of local authorities to do so. Those few local commissions that contain mainly Palestinian localities and that do have Palestinian representatives, such as Irron, cover an extremely narrow area incorporating the immediate vicinities of the localities only.

A further practice is to leave many sensitive areas of Palestinian-owned land (meaning areas where the authorities wish to keep the land available for central planning initiatives or to pursue certain policies in relation to the Arab sector) unaffiliated to any local planning commission, in which case they come directly under the jurisdiction of the relevant district commission, which is controlled by government representatives. Such areas include unrecognized communities, communities that are recognized but have no municipal status, and communities that the Minister of the Interior does not declare to be part of a local or regional planning area. In the Jewish sector, on the other hand, small localities are invariably included within regional councils.

The way in which the drawing of boundaries of the planning bodies is done in order to maintain central government control and to carve out as much land as possible for Jewish development, is well illustrated by the example of the Misgav Regional Council in the Galilee, established in 1982, which has already been mentioned in relation to its municipal powers. Misgav is also a planning commission, and exercises planning control over large areas of land bordering several Arab villages including agricultural land owned by Palestinians from twenty-three villages and the fertile Batof valley (though, as noted in the section above, not the villages themselves; Palestinian villages in the area are subject to the jurisdiction of the Central Galilee Planning and Building Commission). In other words, the decision was taken to give to Misgav the power to decide the future of large areas of land lying around the Arab villages in the area, rather than to give that power to a planning authority on which those communities would be able to exercise influence. In a context in which the main problem for the Palestinian communities is to find land for building in order to keep up with natural growth and development, this situation gives Misgav the power to prevent such development. An Arab landowner who wishes to build on his land that falls within the jurisdiction of Misgav, or initiates any use of land that requires permission, has the difficult task of seeking permission for the status of the land to be altered from agricultural to building land, and then beginning the planning process. The Palestinian communities bordering on Misgav also have difficulties in having state land within the Misgav region allocated for their needs. Sakhnin's request for land on which to build a football stadium was refused; it was said the land in question was needed instead for the expansion of a nearby Jewish community.[65] The Palestinian communities bordering Misgav also find themselves powerless to prevent unwelcome developments on land. In 1999 a military base was constructed on land within the Misgav Regional Council but directly bordering on Sakhnin and right next to a high school in the town.[66]

As a result of the allocation of jurisdictions to both municipal and planning authorities, a considerable proportion of land owned, used or potentially used by the Palestinian community has been placed under the control of authorities on which Palestinians have little or no representation or influence. This process contributes towards the steady erosion of Arab land reserves and the restriction of Palestinian access to land in the state. It seems difficult to avoid the conclusion that decisions regarding the allocation of jurisdiction are motivated by the objectives of limiting the expansion of Palestinian communities and putting land surrounding them under the control of Jewish-dominated authorities in order to further policy objectives of ensuring geographical containment of Palestinian communities, and making land available for development exclusively for Jews. It is hardly surprising that the Arab communities view the removal of municipal and planning jurisdiction over land as attacks on the integrity and independence of their communities.

The failure of 'positive' planning in the Arab sector

One of the key purposes of land-use planning is to facilitate and encourage development. Development plans should 'provide *opportunities* for the expected range and scale of future development, they should provide *guidance* for potential developers, and they should be *relevant* to current conditions' (italics in original; Coon 1992: 206). The 1965 law provides a framework for positive planning. For the Jewish sector, a combination of the operation of this law and the dynamic role played by other actors (government ministries, the ILA and the Jewish national institutions) has resulted in development on a large scale, even if not always according to sound planning principles.[67] For Palestinian citizens of Israel, the experience has been very different, with neither appropriate planning nor adequate development taking place. Positive planning for the Arab sector over the years has been extremely limited, and almost the only example of a centrally planned large-scale project to develop the community was a five-year plan for developing infrastructure and services in Palestinian villages initiated in 1962 (Jiryis 1976: 229). In October 2000, a 4 billion shekel plan for development of the Arab sector communities was announced by the Barak government, including boosting preparation of plans, developing older neighbourhoods, developing new neighbourhoods using high-density construction, and cultural, sports and social institutions for the Arab sector (State of Israel 2001: 7–15), but it was frozen by the subsequent Sharon government. Consequently, gaps have continued to grow between the two sectors in relation to infrastructure and housing. As already noted, national and regional planning tends either to ignore the Palestinian communities or seek to contain them and to pursue national political goals; the policy of developing urban townships for the Bedouin can be viewed as falling under these categories rather than as positive development planning.[68]

The development of outline plans at national, district and local levels is governed by the 1965 law, is mandatory and is supposed to occur within set time frames. The 1965 law sets out the objects of outline plans and provides guidance regarding the matters they might cover.

THE OBJECTS AND SUBJECT-MATTER OF OUTLINE PLANS

National outline scheme
- Assigns land for various purposes and uses (industry, roads, recreation areas, forests, holy places etc.).
- Determines the major communications and supply systems.
- Forecasts and plans population distribution in the state.
- Estimates the future size of existing settlements and determines the location, type and size of new settlements.
- Directs the subject of district schemes.

District outline schemes
- Implement national outline schemes.
- Determine matters of general importance to the district, likely to be the object of local schemes, including security and employment.
- Provide for development, areas for agriculture and industry, forest, roads, cemeteries, frozen areas.
- Set conditions for non-conforming use.

Local outline schemes
- Control development.
- Ensure conditions for public health, security and transport.
- Protect places of special historical, natural etc. importance.
- Enact provisions on many matters including designating areas for specific purposes and setting building regulations.

After outline plans are in place, the last stage in the planning process is the preparation of detailed plans. These may be prepared by a local planning and building commission, either on its own initiative or when directed by the district commission, or by others, including anyone with an interest in the land, the state or the local authority. Once a detailed plan has been submitted, the local commission should accept or reject it within four months, failing which the applicant may submit the plan directly to the district commission. Detailed plans cover the same subject matter as local outline schemes, and can cover other matters such as the division of land into plots; designation of roads, open spaces and public facilities; the number of buildings that may be erected on a plot and other regulations relating to buildings.

This statutory framework for positive planning has not been applied in the Arab sector. In practice, severe delays in approval of plans have resulted in a prevalence of out-of-date plans, and inadequate short-term interim arrangements are put in place to deal with the problems caused by this situation. Further problems are created by the fact that planning policies are designed to contain Palestinian opportunities for development rather than to create them, and by the existence of pressures tending to result in planning that is inappropriate for the desires and needs of the community.

Out-of-date plans The effectiveness of the statutory planning system is heavily dependent on plans being kept up to date. However, delay in approving plans is endemic. While the 1965 law lays down that district outline schemes be submitted within five years of the law's coming into force and local outline schemes within three years of the law's coming into force or of the declaration of the local planning area, in practice these time limits are not adhered to (sections 56 and 62). One researcher examined the time taken to develop plans in one region in the Galilee and found that, by the end of 1988, the average time for the Arab sector was 20.6 years as compared with seven years in the Jewish sector (Yiftachel 1992: 240). Astonishingly, only as few as 15 per cent of Arab municipalities have current approved outline plans in place.[69] According to Ministry of the Interior figures from January 2000, only forty-nine out of 107 Palestinian locations had plans that dated from 1990 or later, while nineteen had no plan at all and the remainder had older plans – the oldest being Nazareth with its plan dating from the 1940s.[70] In sixty-one cases, new plans are stated to be at various stages of preparation or approval. The Israeli High Court has criticized delays: 'A planning authority must be alive to the fact that powers and authority are bestowed upon it in order to serve the public interest, and this interest includes handling applications from the citizen within a reasonable time.'[71]

The lack of an approved plan has severe consequences and seriously hampers the possibility of communities to develop. Plans are often out of date almost as soon as approved: plans are usually based on a fifteen- to twenty-year projection but for Arab localities can take that long to be approved. Another problem is that building permits will generally only be issued in line with an approved plan (the district commission must approve conditions for granting permits once a plan has been submitted for approval), and building outside the approved building zone is a criminal offence. The lack of approved plans thus creates a major obstacle to development since building cannot take place legally.

Having an approved plan is also a prerequisite for obtaining government resources such as budgets for infrastructure and services, such as sewerage systems and local roads. Local councils are unable to carry out public projects and implement their power to expropriate land for public purposes other than in the framework of an approved plan. Based on several studies that showed that very few Arab localities possess approved outline plans, one researcher concluded that the Minister of the Interior delays approval of plans in the Arab sector as a matter of deliberate policy, as a means to restrict spatial growth (Falah 1989b).

Where plans are not kept up to date, interim arrangements for regulating development in the absence of an approved plan become of crucial importance. Over the years a practice has developed of adopting detailed plans for parts only of a planning area, using powers under section 68 of the 1965 law.[72] Such a practice was accepted by the High Court in the case in which the Palestinian village of Beit Safafa challenged the approval of a plan to construct a road from Gilo to Jerusalem, arguing that in the absence of a local outline scheme for Beit Safafa, a detailed plan for a road that would cross the village's land should not be approved. However, the High Court held that the 1965 law allowed a local commission to prepare a detailed plan 'at any time', whether or not an outline plan was in existence, and commented: 'From the practical standpoint it cannot be otherwise ... How could it be possible to prevent the preparation of detailed plans throughout the entire local planning area of a Local Commission just because of the fact that it has not yet managed to prepare a Local Outline Scheme for its entire area?'[73]

A second measure to avoid the freezing of development for long periods of time during the consideration of plans, particularly where the existing plan is completely out of date, was introduced in 1981. A district commission may grant a building licence in accordance with a plan that has been submitted but not yet approved, where the existing plan was approved before 1950 and no objections to the submitted plan have been received or, if objections have been received, they are unlikely to influence the commission's decision (Revital 1993: 93).

Use of these powers to obtain the approval of local detailed plans and building permits in the absence of an overall approved plan can help relieve chronic housing shortages in the short term. But where such measures become not rare and interim but the normal method of planning, they result in an ad hoc pattern of development and are bad planning practice. They also create confusion, since it leads to uncertainty in people's minds as to where construction will be tolerated or permitted.[74] Preparation of detailed plans before the completion of an outline scheme, and by way of amendments to an outline scheme, has become routine in the Arab sector, as in the Jewish sector, since it allows development to take place even if by a clumsy patchwork method.[75] Thus, for example, the city of Nazareth is still operating on the basis of an outline scheme from 1941, which has been amended over the years by countless detailed plans. More than 60 per cent of the planning area of the Arab city of Um El Fahem that is designated for development is subject to a series of detailed plans at varying stages of preparation and approval. The currently valid local outline scheme for Um El Fahem dates from 1963, and is unable to provide planning solutions for a population that has increased enormously since that year. Such measures can actually serve to prolong the time taken to consider proposed plans, by taking away the urgency of the need for a decision.

Israeli governments have displayed a willingness to overcome some of these problems in the Jewish sector but not as regards the Palestinian community. In 1990 the government made special arrangements to cope with the housing crisis in the Jewish sector caused by the pressure of absorbing hundreds of thousands of Jewish immigrants from the Soviet Union. A speedy procedure was announced that bypassed or shortened the normal requirements as regards notices, approval and objections, and gave wide powers to a special committee to approve any plan that involved construction of more than 200 housing units.[76] In 1992, the Israeli High Court confirmed that this summary process could even be used for the construction of an entire new town, holding that the only requirement was that a plan should not contradict a national outline scheme.[77] Israeli planners warned of the dangers of this law, under which construction of some 400,000 housing units had been approved by September 1992.[78] However, almost no Palestinian housing projects were able to take advantage of this procedure, despite the urgent need for housing in the community.

Containment of Palestinian development Palestinians continue to inhabit almost the same number of localities as they did after the war of 1948, even though their population has risen during that time from 150,000 to almost one million. The number of recognized communities stands at 123 compared to 108 that survived 1948. The only new Palestinian localities that have been established are the small number of concentration points for Bedouin, which is part of a policy to shrink the amount of land inhabited by these communities rather than to provide for their development. Many established communities that existed before 1948 have never been recognized by Israel.

Israel's explanation for not establishing new towns and villages, reported to the UN in July 2001, was: 'New Arab settlements are not planned, because of a policy of developing the current settlements' (State of Israel 2001: 100). But even in relation to existing communities, Israeli planning is aimed primarily at containment of those communities rather than their development. Plans often do little more than define existing areas of development. Particularly when it comes to smaller Arab localities that come under the jurisdiction of a district commission by default (not being assigned to any local commission), the plan may consist of no more than a circle depicting the area within which building is permitted (the 'blue line'). The smallest Jewish localities, by contrast, have detailed building plans and regulations regarding land use. Meanwhile the Palestinian communities are already densely built up. A study of eight Palestinian villages showed that there was an average of 160 square metres per person in the built-up area permitted under the zoning maps. This compared to 524 square metres per person in the Jewish city of Karmiel (Sikkuy 2001b: 26, Table 13). There is a constant tension between the desire on the part of the Palestinian communities to expand the built-up area in order to cope with the needs of growing populations, and pressure from the authorities to limit the expansion of the built-up areas. This is a major source of conflict between the Arab communities and the planning authorities (Khamaysi 1990: 90). From the cities to the smallest communities, the authorities are concerned to restrict the so-called 'blue lines' of Palestinian communities.

Central planning authorities operate on an assumption that privately owned land reserves in the Palestinian communities are sufficient to meet the needs of these communities. So, for example, the plan for the Northern District initiated in 1990 and deposited in 1999, which was based on this assumption, failed to acknowledge a shortage of available land for Arab development, even though Palestinians – 50 per cent of the district's population – have only 6 per cent of the district's land reserves.[79] On the other hand, the plan includes extensive discussion of the shortage of land immediately available for building faced by the Jewish population of the district, when the land reserves available to this group are substantially larger. For instance, the plan notes that the Jewish rural population, comprising 32 per cent of the population of the district, has 16 per cent of the land reserve available to it.

The content of the Northern District plan deposited in 1999 serves as a good example of the aim to contain Palestinian development displayed in Israeli planning. The officially stated aims included increasing the Jewish population so as to create a Jewish majority, preventing the territorial continuity of Arab towns and villages and putting a stop to Arab illegal building and possession.[80] The Committee for Planning in the Arab Sector, a community-based group, analysed the plan from the perspective of the Arab community of the Northern District. Its criticisms of the plan include the following:

- There is no reference to plans relating to the Palestinian communities, either plans already approved or those being prepared or considered, although there is reference to other plans.
- There is no attempt to deal with the underdevelopment of the Palestinian towns such as shortages of housing and land, job opportunities and illegal building. Although the development of Arab towns is listed as an aim of the plan, there are no steps to put this into effect other than the intention that the Arab communities benefit indirectly from the development of the Jewish towns.
- Different questions were asked of Palestinian communities than of Jewish communities. For instance, the former were not asked about the demographic balance of the area while latter were asked this question.
- The main aims of the plan ignore the aspirations and preferences of the Palestinian communities, and indeed go contrary to their desires and national aspirations.
- There is no attempt to address the serious problems of infrastructure, such as lack of sewerage systems, suffered by Palestinian communities.
- District plans determine which towns are to be developed as regional centres, but options outlined in the plan failed to designate a single Arab town to be developed as a regional centre, despite the fact that half the district's population is Palestinian.

In December 2001, twenty-six Palestinian local councils submitted a formal objection to the Northern District plan on the basis that it discriminates against Palestinians. They demanded the cancellation of the plan and the development of a new one based on the principles of equality, public participation, transparency and adequate representation of Arabs in the planning process.[81]

Instead of enjoying opportunities for development, Palestinians often find themselves pushed aside to make way for housing projects built exclusively for Jews. The Arab village of Reineh near Nazareth has seen its land base eroded over the years through expropriations (for the construction of Upper Nazareth) and substantial reduction in its area of jurisdiction (also to Upper Nazareth). The village is badly in need of housing and other development projects but attempts by its local council to expand the building zone have constantly been rejected. In

1990 the government announced plans to construct a new residential neighbourhood on land that had belonged to Reineh residents and was still used by them, although its expropriation had been announced in 1976 and its annexation to the jurisdiction of Upper Nazareth was later announced in February 1991. In a press conference in Jerusalem in June 1991, Hassan Khutaba, the Mayor of Reineh, asked why housing projects were being planned for Jews on land that was owned by Arabs and badly needed for housing for the village.

There is also little planning for economic development within Palestinian communities. Insufficient land is allocated for industrial zones in Arab towns and villages. Where functioning industrial zones do exist (in 30 per cent of communities), they are too small and lacking in infrastructure, and, in 1990, only 20 per cent of Arab industry was located in industrial zones, the remainder was in the residential areas (Attrash 1994). In the Northern District, where half the population is Arab, according to the planning authorities some 3,500 dunams of industrial area exists in the Jewish sector, only 175 dunams in the Arab sector.[82]

Ensuring a sufficient supply of land for housing and other needs is a basic function of a planning system. In the UK, for instance, local planning authorities are obliged by law to ensure that a five-year supply of land is earmarked for housing.[83] A landowner, Fourth Investments Ltd, objected to a local plan on the basis that its land had not been included in the area zoned for building but was in a green belt. The High Court in London upheld their objection, on the grounds that the planning inspector had unreasonably failed to consider allocating the land in question as building land given that there was insufficient land earmarked for housing to satisfy the legal requirement.[84]

Inappropriate planning The Israeli planning authorities too often pay insufficient attention to the particular characteristics and needs of the Palestinian communities, such as the patterns of landownership and social and cultural factors. One aspect of this is the authorities' insistence that all Arab communities take on urban characteristics, including denser building patterns and multi-storey construction. Like all societies, Palestinians have varied preferences regarding the type of communities in which they wish to live. While there is a demand for decent city housing, there is also a sector wanting to live in a more rural environment. At present Jews but not Arabs are permitted to establish rural communities. The objectives of protecting the countryside and limiting the spread of urban areas, while legitimate, should be applied equally. Planning should take account of social, cultural and economic factors such as traditional rural lifestyles. For instance, farmers could be permitted to live on their agricultural land if regulations permitted very low density building, as was the case before 1948. It was only in the 1950s that the National Planning Board decided to ban all construction of dwellings on land zoned for agriculture, in direct response to Arab building activity in Lower Galilee.

A further problem is that planning authorities in Israel frequently fail to take sufficiently into account the economic and social dislocation caused by plans. For instance, Israeli plans for Palestinian Bedouin communities in the Naqab aim to uproot them from a rural to an urban lifestyle in one step and as yet no rural communities have been established.[85] In other countries, concepts such as 'existing use' serve to ensure gradual and controlled adaptation of present uses of land to uses envisaged in plans, with minimum economic waste and individual hardship. In the UK, for instance, there is a presumption that a lawful use may be continued and it will be harder to take enforcement action against a use the longer established it is.[86]

While it is true that some obstacles to planning and development come from within the Palestinian communities themselves, because the family-based pattern of landownership and the fragmentation of land have made effective planning difficult, and there is little land for sale and only at high prices, a flexible and innovative planning approach could address these problems.

Enforcement: the implementation of regulatory planning in the Arab sector

A planning system requires enforcement mechanisms to ensure orderly planning. However, in Israel, although illegal building is common in both Jewish and Arab sectors, enforcement mechanisms are not implemented equally in relation to the two communities. Whereas the harshest penalties are used to prevent and punish breaches of the planning laws in the Palestinian community, the authorities are ready to adopt a much more tolerant approach towards the Jewish sector.

The planning authorities in Israel possess far-reaching enforcement powers, set out in Chapter 10 of the 1965 law. All development must conform to approved schemes and permits. Construction is forbidden on land designated as agricultural land, which is all land outside the building zones.[87] 'Blue lines' ring the existing communities and demarcate the limit of permitted building. Enforcement of the regulatory system is rigid, cumbersome and slow. Activities requiring permission that are carried out without or in breach of a permit are criminal offences, and the courts have power to administer fines and an additional sum double the value of the structure, or to order that the illegal construction be demolished. The courts sometimes imprison those convicted of offences against the planning rules, a practice approved by the High Court in the interests of upholding the law.[88]

The demolition of a building is the most extreme sanction available for unlicensed construction. The power of the courts to issue a demolition order is discretionary and not mandatory.[89] Demolition is considered an exceptional procedure and one court has said that it needs to be persuaded there is a good reason to implement it beyond the fact that the building was constructed illegally.[90] A major factor considered is a desire not to legitimize illegal building and open up what amounts to an alternative licensing procedure. A person ordered to demolish his house who fails to do so may be subject to further criminal charges for failure to obey a court order, with the possibility of fines and imprisonment. The likelihood that the owner will subsequently obtain a building licence may at best delay the implementation of the order, and will not constitute a sufficient reason to prevent the issuing of the order.[91] The planning authorities have administrative powers to order work to stop or even the demolition of work in progress but must then apply to the court for confirmation of such an order.[92] In 1981, the Knesset amended the 1965 law, prohibiting the connection of electricity, water or telephone networks to buildings prior to a building licence being obtained.[93]

In both the Jewish and the Arab sectors there is a high instance of building without permits; in the Jewish sector primarily on state land and in the Arab sector mainly on privately owned land. There are an estimated 30,000 'illegal' buildings in Palestinian communities.[94] Common practices include building in breach of building regulations within the built-up areas of the Palestinian communities, as well as construction outside the 'blue lines' on land designated as agricultural land. It is the latter that has been the subject of strict control by the planning authorities. Since most land in Israel not specifically designated for another purpose is declared to be agricultural land, much illegal building in Arab towns and villages has been on land outside the built-up area that is classified as 'agricultural land' even though it is not actually used for agricultural purposes. In a context where expansion of Arab land use is perceived as a threat to the Jewish nature of the state, construction outside the approved building lines of the Arab communities is perceived in a political context. On the other hand, the major cause of the extensive breach of planning schemes is the fact that the authorities are unwilling to approve schemes that allow for sufficient and appropriate development. In other words, Palestinians build illegally out of necessity.

The government has acknowledged that there is a housing problem in the Arab sector, but tends to imply that this is partly the fault of the communities themselves (for resisting living in higher density multi-storey buildings)[95] and continues to do almost nothing to alleviate the underlying causes, while treating the symptom (the building in breach of the law) with strict law-enforcement measures. In November 1985 the Markovitz Commission was appointed to investigate unlicensed construction in the Arab sector and to make recommendations as to how to deal with the problem. The Commission recommended granting retroactive legalization to some 'illegal' buildings by incorporating them into expanded development plans, while the remainder would be either demolished or have their status frozen. At the same time, the Commission recommended that the planning system should become more efficient and clamp down on all future illegal building. In the words of the *Report*, 'a dividing line should be drawn between the handling of the illegal building thus far and illegal building begun from here on' (Markovitz Commission 1986: 4). The *Markovitz Report* failed to deal with the underlying causes of the problem of unlicensed building in the Arab sector, most of its chapters focusing on ways to ensure a stricter enforcement of the planning laws. While the *Report* recognized the need for speedier planning, it failed to look more deeply into the reasons for the illegal building or to make recommendations as to how the underlying problems could be addressed. Essentially, it treated the problem as a law and order issue and the failings identified are mostly to do with failure to *enforce* the law rather than with inadequate implementation. The recommendations of the *Markovitz Report* were confirmed in principle by the government in February 1987, and subsequently followed up by the cabinet and an inter-ministerial committee established for the purpose and headed by Markovitz.[96]

When the implementation of the Markovitz recommendations had failed to address the problem and the number of unlicensed buildings continued to increase, another investigation commissioned into illegal construction resulted in a report issued in 2000 known as the *Gazit Report*.[97] Like its precedessor, Gazit recommended that steps be taken to speed up the planning process in order to enable the planning needs of the Arab community to be met, but focused largely on ways to make enforcement of the laws against building outside the law more effective, such as shorter notice periods prior to demolition being carried out, tougher criminal penalties and the creation of a special police unit to carry out demolitions. The *Gazit Report* found that there were more than 22,000 cases of illegal building in Israel, excluding the south. It found that the phenomenon of illegal building existed in both Jewish and Arab sectors, but that the causes differed. Acknowledging the sentiment in the Arab population that the amount of land available for building legally was diminishing while the population was growing, the report confirmed that the lack of up-to-date zoning maps was causing problems.

Despite the findings of the Markovitz and Gazit reports identifying some of the problems underlying the proliferation of unlicensed buildings in the Arab sector, in line with the recommendations of both reports, the main policy tool used to address illegal construction in the Palestinian communities is punitive measures. The most extreme enforcement tool at the disposal of the planning authorities is the power to demolish construction in breach of the planning laws. Despite the fact that the courts have said it is an exceptional measure and not to be used without good reason, demolition is the measure preferred by the planning authorities. At their request, the courts have issued thousands of demolition orders, only a small proportion of which are carried out (Horowitz n.d.: 8). A report from 1998 indicated that in the Galilee alone, 12,000 demolition orders had been issued on unlicensed Arab building.[98] The issuing of so many demolition orders does not help to solve the underlying problem, and leaves the inhabitants in a state of uncertainty. At certain times, the number of actual demolitions has been stepped up. For instance, fifteen homes were demolished in Taibeh in November 1988 following the *Markovitz Report*, and there was an intensification of enforcement procedures in relation to the Palestinian unrecognized villages. In 1988, 462 unlicensed Palestinian houses were demolished, 62 per cent demolished by the owners after administrative or court orders, the remainder by planning authorities.[99] According to one Palestinian organization ten years later, 350 houses were demolished during 1998 (Mossowa 2001: 13). In 2001, demolitions had been stepped up to such an extent that a local human rights organization wrote to the Attorney General asking the government to stop applying a discriminatory policy of house demolition against Arab citizens.[100]

Demolitions are carried out ruthlessly, using a heavy police presence. The following account from an Arabic local newspaper is typical:

> 7am Monday morning, special forces of the police arrived at the houses of Mahmod Amon and Mahmod Taha without any prior notice and began the demolition. Amon was pinned to the ground by the police forces until they finished their job. Amon and Taha are living in very bad conditions. Amon is the father of four children who are living in

one small room. He tried very hard to get a building license, but was unsuccessful, so he decided to build a small house last May ... Khalil Assaf, attorney of both Taha and Amon, said: 'I was negotiating with the Israel Land Authority in order to convey title of the land to my clients when we were surprised with the demolition of the two houses, especially since the court was supposed to look into our request next November.'[101]

In the Jewish sector, unlicensed building also takes place on a large scale. However, unlike in the Arab sector, the authorities are prepared to look for options other than demolition. According to figures from the Ministry of the Interior in 1996, while 57 per cent of all unlicensed building was carried out by Palestinians, over 90 per cent of all demolitions were of Palestinian buildings.[102] An internal Minister of the Interior report found that only 20–25 per cent of all building was licensed in a wholly lawful manner; many buildings are legalized after the fact or built without or in deviation from a permit (Alexander et al. 1983: 138). One example of tolerance of breaches of the planning laws in the Jewish sector is the establishment of the *mitzpim*, the Jewish Agency's plan to establish some sixty tiny lookout posts throughout the Galilee. This project was approved and carried through in flagrant breach of the statutory planning procedures using a loophole in the law (Yiftachel 1992: 244–6). The *State Comptroller's Report 2000* looks at unlicensed building in the Jewish sector and finds that no steps have been taken to demolish such buildings but, on the contrary, measures are often taken to legalize them retroactively. For instance, a Committee to Examine Building for Non-agricultural Purposes in Moshavim, known as the Kadmon Committee, reported in August 1994 that some 4,000 illegal non-agricultural businesses were being run on 5,500 dunams of land in moshavs (semi-cooperative farms) around the country. Instead of enforcing the law, the government in May 1995 accepted the Committee's recommendation that such uses be legalized.[103]

The case of the Phoenicia factory already cited is another example of the unequal implementation of the planning laws in the two sectors. This was the glasswork factory for which plans were approved in 1992 even though the site was close to several Palestinian villages and would have emitted large quantities of poisonous sulphur dioxide that posed a threat to health, to flora and fauna, and to buildings and vehicles in several nearby Palestinian villages.[104] At an early stage in the legal proceedings the petitioners' representatives discovered that Phoenicia's developers had not obtained the required permit from the Environment

Ministry for constructing the factory, even though construction had been progressing for several months, making it effectively unlawful. Instead of applying the ample enforcement provisions in the Planning and Building Law, however, the Minister of the Interior simply obtained the approval of the Environment Minister for the plan to proceed. This contrasts sharply with the harsh approach taken by the planning authorities towards Arab illegal building.

In enforcing the planning laws as in other spheres, the influence of broader state policies towards the Palestinian community is apparent. So, for instance, enforcement mechanisms are used as one aspect of the policy to forcibly evict and relocate Palestinian communities (termed 'clusters of illegal buildings') in the Naqab and the north, in order to eradicate Palestinian unrecognized communities. The adoption of a discourse in which Palestinians are viewed as 'seizing' or 'encroaching on' land that is not rightfully theirs is prevalent in planning policy just as in other spheres.[105] The role played by planning enforcement in the political struggle for land is demonstrated by the difference in approach towards development within the built-up areas of the Arab communities on the one hand, and construction on land outside the boundaries of the Arab communities on the other. The planning authorities display relatively little interest in the former, which itself has negative consequences for the orderly development of the communities. On the other hand, there is intense interest in any construction by Palestinians outside the permitted boundaries of their communities.

Restrictions on access to housing for Palestinians in Israel

Israeli governments since 1948 have considered provision of housing to be among the foremost duties of the state. A mix of direct government projects and collaborations between the Ministries of Defence, Industry and Commerce, and Infrastructure and Housing, together with private corporations, local and international Zionist and Jewish national institutions and other non-state actors has produced construction on an enormous scale since 1948.[106] A panoply of incentives and subsidies in the form of loans, grants and rent subsidies are available. Housing consumes almost half the state's development budget and government has played a major role in planning and controlling housing activities.[107] The vast majority of housing inhabited by Jewish citizens of the state was initiated and constructed by or with the assistance of the state and/or Jewish national institutions, and is situated on state-owned land. The Jewish national institutions initiate projects such as rural settlement programmes for which they are allocated state land.[108]

When it comes to the Arab sector, however, the picture is rather different. Far fewer public resources are put into housing and development for the Arab communities, whether in all-Palestinian cities and villages or in Palestinian quarters of the so-called 'mixed cities' – Palestinian cities from before 1948 that now have a Jewish majority and a Palestinian minority. Most Palestinian housing is self-built, and on privately owned property. Until the mid-1970s there was no strategic planning for Palestinian housing at all.[109] Government-initiated public building projects within Arab localities are extremely rare. Since 1975, 337,000 living units have been built in public housing programmes, but fewer than 1,000 of these were in the Arab communities (Sikkuy 2001a: 16). Only 2.6 per cent of the Ministry of Infrastructure and Housing's development budget for 2002 was designated for the Palestinian communities.[110] National Plan Tama 35 included a plan to build 5,000 housing units in the Arab communities over four years, but this comprised only 0.5 per cent of all planned public housing construction in Israel.[111] Pressure created by the increase in population (3.1 per cent annual growth rate) and the high number of new households each year is not met by a corresponding increase in housing stock. No new localities have been created for Palestinians since the establishment of the state other than Bedouin concentration points, and few new housing opportunities have been created for Palestinians in the mixed cities or elsewhere. This means that the burden of absorbing the growing population falls on the established Arab towns and villages and on Arab quarters in the mixed cities.

Shortage of adequate housing is one of the major problems facing the Palestinian citizens of Israel today. Not only is there a serious shortage of housing units, but also a lack of infrastructure and services, a widespread problem of poor-quality housing and overcrowding. Major infrastructural inadequacies exist. In 1990, only eighteen Arab towns and villages had even begun projects for installing sewerage systems, and by no means all of these had been completed (Jaffa Research Centre 1990: 392). By 1998, 33 per cent of Arab localities in the Galilee and Triangle still lacked functioning sewerage systems, and 56 per cent of all households remained unconnected to a sewerage system.[112] The absence of sewerage systems causes considerable public health hazards, including contamination of wells and springs and of drinking water pipes.

Poor-quality housing is another problem, particularly in the 'mixed cities' (Jaffa, Haifa, Acre, Lod and Ramle) where Palestinians live mainly in separate all-Arab neighbourhoods, usually the old core of a formerly grand and thriving Palestinian city, in overcrowded conditions and neglected housing stock. The municipal authorities sometimes pursue a usually unwritten but openly espoused policy of encouraging the Palestinian populations to leave these areas. The Social Development Committee in Haifa has documented cases where Arab residents have been evacuated from buildings that had been allowed to fall into a dangerous state of disrepair, and subsequently demolished the buildings and built new housing for Jewish immigrants.[113] Similar policies have been documented in Acre and Jaffa. Government and municipal housing corporations that control the buildings have resisted requests by the inhabitants to carry out repairs, a situation that has allowed the buildings to deteriorate. A survey conducted by the Haifa municipality of accommodation in the Arab residential neighbourhood of Wadi Nisnas during the 1980s found that essential repairs and improvements were required and 44 per cent of the housing units were unfit for human habitation; a decade later the recommendations had still not been implemented.[114]

Palestinians in the mixed cities are also victims of discriminatory practices that exclude them from the housing market. In the city of Ramle, the Loram Corporation adopted an 'army veterans only' policy in relation to apartments it had built in the city. This condition had the effect of limiting purchasers to Jews, since most Arabs do not serve in the army. Bahjat Kahlil and Buthena Daoud, Palestinian residents of Ramle, appealed to the High Court to reverse the condition in the grounds that it discriminated against non-Jews. Only after the High Court agreed to hear the case did Loram alter its conditions of purchase and remove the veterans-only criterion.[115]

Palestinians are largely excluded from government urban renewal programmes aimed at developing infrastructure and services to under-developed communities. In January 2000, the National Committee of Arab Mayors petitioned the High Court, claiming that the implementation of the urban renewal programme had discriminated against Palestinian citizens of the state.[116] Since the establishment of the programme in 1977, fifty-six Jewish localities and ninety-nine Jewish neighbourhoods had benefited, compared with only four Arab villages and fourteen Arab neighbourhoods, despite the fact that the Palestinian communities experience the worst socio-economic conditions in the country.[117] In its decision of 12 December 2001, the High Court accepted the petition, acknowledged the need to set equitable criteria for the allocation of programme funds that should rely on appropriate considerations and relevant facts and reflect the purpose for which the money was intended, and the necessity of implementing the programme in the communities that needed it most. Yet in July

2002 the petitioners were forced to go to the High Court again when another government programme, 'Ofeq', aimed at improving areas with high unemployment rates and other poor socio-economic conditions, included only one Arab community among the eleven selected even though all twenty-five of the towns with the highest unemployment rates in the country are Arab.[118]

Almost all of the Palestinian communities also suffer from severe overcrowding. Table 7.4 demonstrates the contrast between housing density in the Arab and Jewish sectors. By international standards, the situation in the Palestinian population is poor: whereas in Western countries, the average housing density is 0.7 people per room and the acceptable limit is considered to be two persons per room, over 30 per cent of Palestinian citizens of Israel live in conditions of over two persons per room. Less than 5 per cent of Jewish citizens live in such conditions.

Despite increases in housing density and rapid urbanization in the Palestinian communities,[119] there has been relatively little development of high-rise apartment blocks. The common pattern is for families to build one- or two-storey buildings and later build more storeys on top as other family members require housing. In its report to the UN in 2001, commenting on illegal building, Israel acknowledges the need for more housing to be available to the Palestinian population, but appears to put the problem down to the lack of upward construction, concluding that 'there is a growing need for a move toward multi-story (high density) construction' and asserting that the size of the Palestinian communities 'cannot increase indefinitely' (State of Israel 2001: 100). Aside from the fact that the latter statement is disingenuous since the Palestinian communities have been allowed to grow so little since 1948 and are extremely dense, the assertion about the need for more high-rise construction is also misleading. While the lack of such construction is partly due to social and cultural traditions that favour lower-density housing, there is evidence of willingness in some parts of the Palestinian community to live in such housing if it becomes

TABLE 7.4 Housing density by population group in 2000

Number of persons per room	(–1)	(1–1.99)	(2–2.99)	(3+)
Arabs (% of pop.)	18.1	51.6	22.5	7.9
Jews (% of pop.)	51.0	44.4	4.2	0.5

Source: *Statistical Abstract of Israel* (2000: Tables 11.14 and 11.15).

available (Gonen and Khamaysi 1993: 21). But without the type of state assistance for urban construction that has occurred in the Jewish sector, this is unlikely to happen.

The 80,000 Palestinians living in communities not officially recognized by the government ('unrecognized' villages) experience the harshest living conditions.[120] Prohibited from building homes or carrying out other development of their communities, and having little or no access to the national electricity, water and road networks or to other services, they experience severe environmental distress and difficulty in obtaining fundamental necessities. Many live in tents or shacks and other non-permanent housing. The issue of the unrecognized villages will be looked at more closely in Chapter 8.

The major obstacles to Palestinian access to land and housing have already been described: large-scale land expropriation, reluctance to allocate state land for Arab use, and restrictive and discriminatory planning policies that arrest the natural growth of Palestinian communities. On top of these problems, Palestinian citizens find that their access to state schemes, which provide assistance for housing in the form of loans, grants, rent subsidies and public housing, denied or restricted. The state, via the Ministry of Housing, provides housing assistance through loans and grants for purchasing, building or repairing housing, rent subsidies, and provision of low-rental public housing owned by government housing corporations.[121] No statutory right to housing is recognized in Israel. Official criteria that determine who will receive assistance and at what levels are set by ministers. The criteria for allocating benefits are not based only on objective factors, such as socio-economic status. If they were, the Palestinians would be major beneficiaries, as their communities are among the poorest in the state. Instead, they are often based on criteria that have the effect of discriminating against Palestinian citizens.

Loans and grants Mortgages subsidized from public funds are provided for the acquisition or improvement of housing, or to build a home. Massive public investment has been poured into new towns and neighbourhoods intended for Jewish citizens, particularly for the absorption of new Jewish immigrants. The prices of publicly built housing are considerably lower than the market price. From the beginning of 1994 to July 1995, the Ministry of Housing marketed 58,000 properties: some at cost price, some under a 'build your own home' scheme, and others on a lottery system.[122] Those who take advantage of the 'build your own home' scheme, for instance, can save up to 89 per cent of the cost of their home.

Until 1992, the government's housing assistance programme was not regulated by legislation, but by undisclosed internal administrative procedures of the Ministry of Housing. The Housing Loans Law of 1992 brought statutory regulation to housing loans and grants for the first time. The law does not establish a 'right' to housing or to housing assistance, but provides that those who come within the Ministry's criteria for being in need of housing are entitled to housing loans. The Minister of Housing is given a broad authority to implement the law, including attaching additional conditions to loans and setting the levels of loans.

Governments claim to base rules for allocating loans and grants on objective criteria.[123] Entitlements to housing loans and grants are calculated by a points system, in which people are assessed on the basis of a range of factors such as marital status, age, number of children and disability. The regulations of 1992 divide localities in the country into groups according to type (development towns, cities, moshavs, settlements in the Occupied Territories, 'minority villages', etc.). The level of entitlement varies according to whether or not the person served in the army, is disabled, and other factors. The use of two conditions in particular has consistently excluded the Palestinian population: (i) completion of military service and (ii) place of residence. A criterion that has frequently been introduced is the completion of military service.[124] This automatically excludes most of the Palestinian population, who are not conscripted into the army. During the 1990s use of this condition was discredited as it became accepted that it constituted unlawful discrimination.[125] Nevertheless, the condition continues to appear and individuals are still forced to resort to the courts in order to persuade the relevant authorities to remove the military service criterion, as demonstrated by the case brought in relation to a public housing project against the Loram Corporation in Ramle in 2001.[126] Service in the army also continues to be a factor in assessing the level of assistance.

The second common factor determining governmental housing assistance is that benefits are sometimes made contingent on where one lives. For instance, some benefits such as low-interest mortgages and housing grants are given only in areas designated as national priority areas. Regulations issued to banks in January 1992 as a basis for calculating entitlements to loans and grants included only Nazareth of the Palestinian cities, and not a single Arab location was defined as a development area for the purpose of the loans and grants system. Small moshavs have higher entitlements than larger Arab localities nearby. Although it is a declared intention of the Housing Loans Law to target those most in need, the categorization is apparently not based on socio-economic grounds, at least so far as the Arab population is concerned (since on that basis the Arab population would be in the most preferred category).

A comparison of entitlements between an Arab family living in Barta'a and a Jewish family living in Katzir one kilometre away, each with three children, based on the tables, serves to illustrate the discrimination. If neither served in the army, their entitlements would be: NIS 63,600, of which NIS 20,000 is an outright grant, for the family of Barta'a, and NIS 80,000, of which NIS 26,100 is a grant, for the family of Katzir. If both did satisfy the military service criterion, the Barta'a family would be entitled to NIS 97,000, of which NIS 31,700 would be a grant, and the Katzir family to NIS 120,000, of which NIS 39,200 would be a grant. In the most likely scenario, that the family from Barta'a had not served in the army while that of Katzir had, the entitlements would be: NIS 63,600 (NIS 20,000 grant) for the Barta'a family, and NIS 120,000 (NIS 39,200 grant) for the Katzir family – an additional 100 per cent.

In 1992, the government announced a new 'Local Loans' scheme, according to which those in listed localities could obtain substantial additional loans, of which up to 80 per cent might be in the form of a grant. Brought in to cope with the housing crisis created by the influx of new immigrants, the list did not include any Arab localities other than Nazareth (where the grant available was less than in other localities).[127]

The Israeli State Comptroller in 1993 voiced strong criticism of such inequalities: 'An examination of the loan levels according to the Minister's Regulations shows a difference of between 10.6 per cent and 21.6 per cent in the level of loan received by different groups because of the supplemental loan for ex-soldiers ... From an examination of the loan levels according to the tables in the Circular it is apparent that the supplemental loan for those who served in the Israel Defence Forces (other than the disabled) compared to those who did not serve in the IDF increased the loan by 51.7 per cent and 51.9 per cent' (State Comptroller's Report 1993: 161). Furthermore, a comparison of levels of loans granted before the law and the regulations came into effect, based on the Ministry's internal regulations, showed that those who had served in the army received 50 per cent or more than those who had not. In their response to the charges in the State Comptroller's Report, the Ministries of Housing and Finance merely stated that the levels of assistance, whether granted under the 1992 law or otherwise, had been approved by the Knesset Finance Committee.

There are additional difficulties for the Arab sector in benefiting from housing loans. The regulations state that an applicant must register the house in his name and register a mortgage in favour of the bank. In the Arab sector, land is frequently registered in the name of a father or grandfather (rather than the applicant). Landowners are burdened by heavy taxes and often accumulate large debts. The costs involved in paying outstanding taxes and transferring the property into the applicant's name in order to be able to guarantee a mortgage and qualify for the loan may be prohibitive. Another barrier for Palestinians is the fact that housing projects are frequently organized by non-profit associations. The Housing Ministry and ILA collaborate with such associations and the community settlements established by the JA, offering land and concessions. The association sets its own criteria, which might include military service.[128] Such associations do not exist in the Palestinian communities.

There is also a lower take-up rate for assistance in the Arab sector. The State Comptroller in 1993 examined the number of couples taking part in the housing assistance programme, and found that relative to their proportion in the population, there was a lower take-up rate in the Arab population, despite the fact that there was a higher rate of eligibility (according to socio-economic status) than in any other population group. The State Comptroller found in 1993 that as little as one-third of those entitled under the housing assistance programme actually received assistance.[129]

The consistent pattern is that entitlements are influenced by dis-criminatory criteria as well as need. In addition, in certain policy areas the government uses the housing assistance programme as an additional tool for implementing unpopular policies such as moving Palestinians out of the mixed cities such as Acre and Lod, and concentrating Palestinian Bedouin and residents of the unrecognized communities in urban settle-ments. So, for example, special assistance is given for Bedouin building homes in the recognized townships in the Naqab.

Rent subsidies Rent subsidies are available for three years to young couples, for four years to new Jewish immigrants, and for an unlimited time to senior citizens. The main target of the subsidies is supposedly vulnerable groups in society. But once again Palestinians, at the bottom of all socio-economic indicators, are not prioritized. According to official figures, of families granted rent subsidies in 1999, 77.4 per cent were new Jewish immigrants.[130] The criteria for receiving such assistance initially included the stipulation that at least one family member had served in the army, police or prison service.[131] Only after the State Comptroller criticized this condition, on the basis that it excluded those, such as the Arab community and religious Jews, who did not serve in the army but were in need of the benefit, did the Housing Minister cancel it in January 1994. However, because the entitlements to subsidies are also based on the locality in which the house is situated, in the same categories as apply to housing loans, Palestinian communities have found that they are still often excluded from receiving the subsidy or receive lower subsidies. Only the threat of a legal challenge prompted the government in 1994 to modify somewhat the list of communities for which rent subsidies would be available.[132]

Despite changes made by the Ministry of Infrastructure and Housing following an appeal by the Association for Civil Rights in Israel regarding assistance towards rental costs, the problem of lack of rent subsidies to Palestinian citizens has continued. This is partly because there is no public construction of rental units in the Arab communities (for instance, whereas in the Jewish sector public construction companies such as Shikun Ovdim and Amidar are active, there are no such companies operating in the Palestinian sector), and partly because the idea of rental units, not part of traditional Palestinian society, has not yet become part of the make-up of the all-Palestinian communities, though there is no doubt that the need for it exists.

Public housing   Almost no publicly owned housing exists in the Arab sector. In the Jewish sector, the government owns housing and lets it on subsidized rents based on means-testing and the need to address those with particular needs including those living in overcrowded conditions. In 1998, the Public Housing (Rights of Acquisition) Law was enacted, giving residents of public housing the right to acquire their homes at a substantial discount (a reduction of up to 85 per cent of the market price), and to receive long-term loans to finance the payment. The law came into force from 1 January 2000 for a period of five years. With so little public housing available in the Arab sector, Palestinians have been largely unable to take advantage of this policy. And there is a further aspect of this law that particularly resonates for Palestinians. In so far as housing that existed before 1948 is affected, the sale into private hands of former Palestinian homes with no acknowledgement of the historic rights of the previous owners is a further blow.

The failure of legal protection for Palestinian rights in relation to planning and housing

The discriminatory policies and practices in relation to planning and housing that have been described here raise many questions about the status of the principles of equality and non-discrimination in Israeli law and the failure of the courts to protect those principles in relation to the Palestinian citizens of the state. These fundamental principles are also recognized and protected under international law, and Israel has come under severe criticism from the international bodies responsible for monitoring states' compliance with those rights. Because there is considerable overlap with the question of the so-called unrecognized Palestinian villages which will be considered in the following chapter and which also relate to the implementation of the planning laws, we will address these issues relating to protections offered by domestic and international law at the end of that chapter.

Notes

1. According to the *Statistical Abstract of Israel* (2000: Table 2.9), there are 126 Jewish urban localities and 949 Jewish rural localities in the state.

2. Of these some, like the city of Upper Nazareth (also known as Nazareth Elite, a Jewish city situated on the hill close to the Palestinian city of Nazareth), have in the last two decades had small Palestinian populations while others, such as the rural settlements established by the Jewish Agency, are exclusively for Jews (though see the case of Qa'dan in Chapter 6 that opens the question of the allocation of state land for the exclusive use of Jews).

3. According to the Statistical Abstract of Israel (2000: Table 2.7), 46.8 per cent of Arab citizens of the state live in the Northern District and just over 50 per cent of the residents of the Northern District are non-Jews. In the other districts, Palestinians are 25 per cent of the population in the Haifa District, 10 per cent in the Central District and 17 per cent in the Southern District.

4. A Master Plan for the Northern District, no. 2, Amendment 9, was commissioned by the Ministry of Planning in November 1990.

5. *Ha'aretz* (Hebrew daily newspaper), 14 October 2001.

6. These concerns, together with the fear that this would lead to a further reduction in the areas of jurisdiction allotted to the Palestinian communities, was voiced by Palestinian mayor Dr Hana Sweid, head of the local council of Eilabun, in *Al Ittihad* (Arabic daily newspaper), 19 October 2001.

7. For instance, during the Camp David negotiations of July 2000 between Israel and the Palestinian Authority, the Al-Khalsa area in the western Naqab was proposed for exchange between the two parties. The plan to settle Jews in that area now is clearly aimed at creating facts on the ground and placing obstacles before any such agreement.

8. Declaration of the Establishment of the State of Israel, *Official Gazette*, no. 1, 14 May 1948.

9. LSI, Vol. 19, p. 330, replacing the Town Planning Ordinance of 1936 introduced by the British Mandate administration.

10. Bar Horin Building Construction Ltd v. Nahariya Local Planning and Building Commission, HC case 178/74, PD 25(2), p. 757.

11. Summary of relevant provisions of the 1965 law.

12. Section 7(a) of the 1965 law. The six districts are: Jerusalem, Northern, Haifa, Central, Tel Aviv and Southern: Official Publications, 1957, p. 761. These districts have not changed other than the addition of annexed areas. For instance the Golan Heights were added to the Northern District in 1981. In addition there are two additional district commissions that deal with Jewish settlements in the West Bank and Gaza Strip.

13. An alternative plan submitted to the Ministry of the Interior by a community-based group representing the unrecognized villages, the Association of Forty, was rewarded with a degree of acknowledgement in National Planning Scheme Tama 31, which stated that the plan was being partially adopted by the Ministry of the Interior and that resources would be required for infrastructure in these communities. Another community-based organization, the Regional Council for the Unrecognized Villages of the Palestinian Bedouin in the Naqab, submitted its own plan, *Naqab Arabs 2020*, in 1999, proposing planning solutions for forty-five unrecognized Bedouin villages as an alternative to the Naqab plan Tama 4/14.

14. Amendment no. 43 to the 1965 law, section 3, allows interested parties to propose a plan for a planning area or part of it, and that plan will be considered in the same way as a plan initiated by a local planning and building commission. Previously a plan prepared by anyone other than the local planning and building commission or local council required approval by the Local Commission (Statutes, no. 1544, 24 August 1995, p. 450 [in Hebrew]).

15. This was commented upon by several Arab leaders and by urban planner Dr Hubert Law-Yone of the Architecture and Planning Department, the Technion, Haifa, in several interviews.

16. Once a local planning and building commission has decided to prepare a local outline or detailed plan, and when any plan is deposited, notice must be given in the *Official Gazette*, two daily newspapers and at the office of the commission (sections 77 and 89 of the 1965 Act). Once the plan is deposited, opposition may be filed by interested persons (section 100) and a public hearing may be held (section 107).

17. Amendment no. 37 to the 1965 Planning and Building Law (Statutes, no. 1456, 22 March 1994, p. 98 [in Hebrew]).

18. Amendment no. 43 to the 1965 law (Statutes, no. 1544, 24 August 1995, p. 450 [in Hebrew]).

19. In the UK, planning permission is conditional on the preparation of an environmental statement; Town and Country Planning (Assessment of Environmental Effects) Regulations 1988. A Directive of the European Economic Community, Directive 85/337/EEC of 27 June 1985, as amended by Directive 97/11/EC of 3 March 1997, sets out which development projects must be the subject of an environmental impact assessment, and the factors the assessment must look at. Directives are binding on all member states of the European Union.

20. Estimates produced by Con-Rep (the Consulting and Representing Environment Company) in July 1992; Hawkins (1995).

21. Section 29(b)(11) of the 1965 law.

22. Section 7(a) of the 1965 law.

23. Head of the Committee of Arab Mayors and Others v. Minister of the Interior and Others, HC 9472/00. The Court found that while appropriate representation of Arab residents of the district was one factor to be taken into account, it was not an overriding one in the case of the district commissions where the vast majority of seats on the commission were given over to government ministries and not community representatives. The fact that there were no Arab nominees among the government representatives was not a reason for the Court to intervene and order the relevant ministries to replace their chosen nominees with Arabs, the Court said, since the members were representing the ministries and not the interests of the community and certain expertise was required.

24. Section 19 of the 1965 law provides that seven members will be appointed by the Minister of the Interior from a list recommended by the local authorities of the area, ensuring so far as possible that all the areas are represented. Regarding representation on planning commissions of parties not represented on the local municipal council see: Yossi Dweik and Others v. Head of Kiryat Bialik Municipality, judgment of 8 August 2000, HC 5743/99, and Mor Shamgar v. Local Council of Ramat Hasharon and Others, Civil Appeal 2663/99.

25. Representatives of various government ministries attend meetings. They do not have a vote but can appeal against the commission's decisions.

26. See the website of Sikkuy <www.sikkuy.org.il>.

27. In 1995 there were just two Arab representatives on the commission, one for Rahat and one for Tel Sheva; interview with Mousa Abu Sahiban of the Rahat Municipality, March 1995.

28. Section 156 of the 1965 law and First Schedule, sections 1, 5 and 6. P.A.B. Services Ltd v. State of Israel, Appeal 30/86, PD 40(1), p. 249.

29. Dr Naftali v. Committee for the Protection of Agricultural Land, HC 113/68, PD 22(2), p. 270.

30. See below and Chapter 8.

31. Amendment no. 43 to the 1965 law means that local authorities, community groups, landowners and others can propose plans and they must be considered in the same way as plans drawn up by the local planning and building commission. Prior to this amendment any proposals had first to be adopted by the local commission.

32. An analysis of 1986 statistics aimed at discovering who initiated local outline plans in 120 Arab settlements found that they were almost always initiated by non-elected bodies such as the local planning and building commission, the ILA or the Housing Ministry, and in only 20.8 per cent of cases were they prepared by a local authority elected by the local community; Khamaysi (1990 82).

33. The same point was made by several representatives of Arab local authorities; for instance, interview with Majd El Krum engineer Mohammed Shibil, 17 October 1992.

34. See, for instance, clause 5 of the UK Royal Town Planning Institute's Code of Conduct, and similar measures in the USA and South Africa.

35. Although there is no statutory duty to allow public participation, in several recent judgments the High Court stressed the importance of participation by local communities in the planning process (see the cases cited in note 38, below).

36. In the UK, for instance, the right to make representations at the formative stage is an important principle of planning. The Town and Country Planning Act 1990 provides for public participation during the process of preparation of structural and local plans, and some local councils have created community councils as sounding boards of local opinion; sections 33 and 40, Town and Country Planning Act 1990. The planning authority must take steps to give adequate publicity so that people who may be expected to have an interest are made aware of their right to make representations; Town and Country Planning (Structure and Local Plan) Regulations 1982, reg. 5. The Jordanian Law of Cities, Villages and Buildings no. 79 of 1966, in force in the West Bank (though amended by Israeli military orders), mandated a process of consultation prior to the deposit of plans (Coon 1992: section 3.3.3). Most planning theories also emphasize the importance of public participation in decision-making in planning (Yiftachel 1992: 51).

37. A flaw in publication is considered a fundamental flaw which may lead to the cancellation of the plan, and the High Court has held that failure to comply with the requirement to publish in Arabic will constitute such a flaw: Hamma Hilef v. Northern District Planning and Building Commission and Others, HC 527/74, PD 29(2), p. 319.

38. Hashim Sawa'id and Others v. Local Planning and Building Commission of Misgav and Others, HC 7960/99, and Ismai'il Sawa'id and Another v. Local Planning and Building Commission of Misgav and Others, HC 6032/99, judgments handed down on 5 September 2001. The case is discussed in more detail in Chapter 8.

39. Page 11 of the Judgment.

40. Decision of 12 November 2001; *Adalah News Update*, 21 November 2001. On this basis, the Court quashed the demolition order issued against the mosque in Husseiniya, which like all the buildings in the village lacked a building permit. The government had agreed in 1995 to grant official recognition of Husseiniya but the planning process that would result in licensing of buildings had not yet been completed.

41. The High Court, rejecting a challenge to the erection of a relay station for radio broadcasting by the US government in the Naqab in accordance with a national plan, stated that the planning legislation envisaged that decisions reached by the National Planning and Building Board and approved by the government could not be challenged by submission of objections or by appeal; Central Arava Regional Council and Others v. National Board for Planning and Building and Others, HC 594/89, PD 44(1), pp. 558 and 564.

42. Section 100(1)(c) of the 1965 law allows for public or professional bodies with some public interest in the scheme to be listed by the Minister.

43. Tamra Local Council v. Appeals Sub-committee of the National Planning and Building Board, HC 38/76, PD 30(2), p. 631.

44. This is according to Sikkuy, which also says that the problems are most acute between the Arab local authorities and neighbouring regional councils; <www.sikkuy.org.il>.

45. The Minister retains wide powers to prevent or oblige municipal authorities to act, and exercises a strong supervisory function. Local government is governed by the Municipalities Ordinance and the Local Councils Ordinance but, under the Administration Ordinance, powers were transferred to the Israeli government, which in turn delegated its functions to the Minister of the Interior; *Official Gazette* 5, 1948, p. 22; see also Basic Law: The Government, s.31(a).

46. Land (Acquisition for Public Purposes) Ordinance, Palestine Gazette 1943, Suppl. 1, no. 1305, 44, section 20, as modified by section 190(a)(1) of the 1965 Law.

47. See 'Planning Bodies and Their Functions', pp. 203–4.

48. The Palestinian communities with city status are: Nazareth, Shafa'amr, Um El Fahem, Baqa Al-Gharbiya, Taibeh, Tira, Sakhnin and Tamra.

49. For example, Rahat, the largest of the Bedouin planned townships in the Naqab, was established in the early 1970s, had an appointed local council in 1980, but the first elections were held only in 1989.

50. See Kovetz Ha Takanot (KT) no. 5433 of 12 April 1992, p. 957.

51. Section 3, Municipality Ordinance (new version).

52. Rishon Lezion Municipality v. Ministry of the Interior, HC 94/74, PD 28(2), p. 711, at p. 715.

53. The announcements were made in KT no. 5484 of 8 December 1992, p. 145, and KT no. 5489 of 24 December 1992, p. 249. Irron was subsequently divided into two councils, Irron and Basmeh.

54. In February 2001 the Nazareth Municipality appealed to the High Court, asking for the area to be allocated to the jurisdiction of Nazareth.

55. See Sikkuy's website: <www.sikkuy.org.il/anglit/interior.htm>.

56. Misgav has jurisdiction over twenty-seven small Jewish communities, with a total in 2000 of fewer than 3,000 households, and six small Palestinian villages that have either been recently granted recognition or are still in the process of being recognized and further Palestinian inhabited areas that still have unrecognized status; website of the Misgav Regional Council: <www.misgav-region.muni.il>.

57. *Ha'aretz*, 7 May 1995, reporting on a presentation by urban planner Rassem Khamaysi at a conference at Tel Aviv University.

58. Sections 7 and 8, Order Regarding Municipalities, New Version, and Azur Local Council v. Minister of the Interior, HC 51/68, PD 22(2), p. 227.

59. KT no. 5342 of 21 March 1991, p. 751, no. 5454 of 1 July 1992, p. 1216.

60. Interview with Nazareth Deputy Mayor Suheil Fahoum, December 1994.

61. First petition HC 684/82; second petition HC 2657/90.

62. HC 6215/92.

63. Ghazi Abu Kaf and Others v. Minister of the Interior and the Local Council of Omer, HC 6672/00.

64. Yiftachel also makes the point that Eastern Jews control a smaller area than Ashkenazi Jews.

65. Ori Nir, 'The lost dreams of Sakhnin', *Ha'aretz*, 8 January 2001. Nir reports that following the violence of October 2000, the head of the Misgav Regional Council in a letter to the Minister of the Interior said he was suspending all discussions concerning allocation of land for neighbouring Arab localities, since he had 'no intention of holding discussions under pressure, terrorism and threats'.

66. Ibid.

67. Alexander et al. (1983) are extremely critical of the implementation of the Israeli statutory planning system.

68. This will be explored further in Chapter 8; the urban townships are inappropriately planned and their main purpose is to concentrate the Bedouin population on small areas of land and force them to give up their claims over land in the Naqab.

69. Sikkuy find that of eighty-two Arab municipalities, only twelve have approved plans in place, based on data from the Ministry of the Interior Planning Authority; <www.sikkuy.org.il>.

70. Document of the Ministry of Interior Planning Department dated 6 January 2000 appended to the Report of the Inter-Ministerial Committee to Examine Illegal Construction in the State of Israel (the *Gazit Report*), March 2000.

71. Gazit Concilium Investment and Development Co. Ltd v. Local Planning and Building Commission, HC 100/88, PD 43(1), p. 29.

72. Section 68 provides that where no approved local outline scheme exists, the relevant district commission may approve a detailed plan in any event.

73. Mahmoud Ali, Abed Rabo, Salman and Others v. District Planning and Building Commission and Others, HC 595/75, PD 30(3), pp. 337 and 344.

74. According to Sikkuy, while the so-called 'blue lines', which mark the area within which construction and development is permitted according to approved plans, make up 32 per cent of the areas of jurisdiction of the Palestinian local councils, as much as 82 per cent is taken up with actual construction. Website of Sikkuy: <www.sikkuy.org.il>.

75. Alexander et al. (1983: 156), refer to these as 'symptoms of system breakdown'.

76. The Planning and Building (Temporary Provisions) Law of 1990, Laws of the Knesset, 1990, p. 98 and Laws of the Knesset, 1991, p. 121 (in Hebrew). The law was renewed for a further year and then lapsed on 30 April 1994.

77. Maccabim communal settlement in Modi'in and Others v. Committee for Residential Construction in the Central District, High Court of Justice case 2683/92. The case related to three plans which together established the new town of Modi'in.

78. Arie Nesher cited in the *Jerusalem Post* (English-language daily newspaper), 20 September 1992.

79. Master Plan for the Northern District, no. 2, Amendment 9, completed in July 1992.

80. Analysis of the preliminary plan, issued in 1992, by the Committee for Planning in the Arab Sector, Shafa'amr, May 1997.

81. Adalah, 7 January 2002, Shafa'amr.

82. Master Plan for the Northern District, no. 2, Amendment 9, published in 1993.

83. Circulars 9 and 22 of 1980 of the Secretary of State for the Environment, issued under power of the Town and Country Planning Act.

84. Fourth Investments Ltd v. Bury Metropolitan Borough Council and the Secretary of State for the Environment, Queen's Bench Division, 1984, *Journal of Planning and Environmental Law* (1985), p. 185.

85. Though see Chapter 8 regarding the government's announcements of intention to permit a small number of agricultural communities in the Naqab for Bedouin.

86. Section 171, Town and Country Planning Act 1990.

87. Using agricultural land for non-agricultural purposes (as defined in the First Schedule to the 1965 law), without permission of the Committee for the Protection of Agricultural Land, constitutes a criminal offence. A change in the status of the land may be permitted but only after a significant change in circumstances; Local Commission of Savyon v. Committee for the Protection of Agricultural Land, HC 601/75, PD 31(1), p. 103.

88. State of Israel v. Issa, Criminal Appeal 578/78, PD 36(1), p. 723 at p. 725, and Pur v. State of Israel, Criminal Appeal 23/83, PD 38(1), p. 533 at p. 536.

89. Prishka v. State of Israel, Criminal Appeals, Haifa District Court, District Court Judgments 1, p. 367.

90. Local Planning and Building Commission for Tel Aviv v. Keren Mordecai and Others, Criminal Cases, Tel Aviv 4/87, Local Judgments 5750(b), p. 514.

91. J. Shamgar in Nataf Cooperative Settlement Organization v. State of Israel, PD 38(2), p. 558. Shamgar also said that the inflexibility of section 206 of the 1965 law was the result of the legislature's fear of perpetuating illegal building, and only a demolition order would serve to uphold the law.

92. An amendment of 1989 to sections 224–38 of the 1965 law, and an amendment of 1980 adding section 238A. A person issued with such an order may apply to the court for its cancellation. The court will only cancel the order if convinced that the construction was in fact legal or the demolition was not required for the purposes of avoiding a fait accompli. Hanania Peretz v. Chairman of the Local Planning and Building Commission, Appeal 273/86, PD (2), p. 445 and Avration Dwek and Others v. Mayor of Jerusalem and Others, Appeal 1/84, PD 38(1), p. 494.

93. Section 157A was added to the 1965 law. The Minister of Energy has issued directives exempting residents of certain areas from the need to obtain a licence for the purposes of connection to the electricty supply.

94. According to the *Gazit Report* of 2000, there are approximately 22,000 illegal buildings in central and northern Israel, of which 16,000 are in the Jewish sector and 6,000 in the Palestinian sector. There are also a further 24,000 illegal buildings in the south, most of which are in the Palestinian Bedouin unrecognized communities, and see Adalah 2001b: 37.

95. See, for instance, State of Israel (2001: 100).

96. Letter from Eliakim Rubenstein, Secretary to the Government, to the Abu Hussein Law Office, dated 25 October 1989.

97. Report of the Inter-Ministerial Committee to Examine Illegal Construction in the State of Israel, March 2000.

98. 'Build up, don't tear down', Editorial, *Ha'aretz* (English-language edition), 7 April 1998.

99. *Ha'aretz* (Hebrew daily newspaper), 4 April 1989.

100. Letter from Adalah to the Attorney General, 11 July 2001.

101. Extracts from *Al-Ittihad* and *Al-Sunnara* (Arabic newspapers) 7 August 2001, as translated and reported in *HRA Weekly Press Review*, 16 August 2001, Nazareth.

102. 'Build up, don't tear down', Editorial, *Ha'aretz* (English-language edition), 7 April 1998.

103. *Ha'aretz* (Hebrew daily newspaper), 5 May 1995.

104. See note 20 above, and Hawkins (1995).

105. See, for instance, State of Israel (2001: 100), which refers to Arabs 'seizing public lands' and building on them illegally.

106. A distinction should be made between public involvement in construction of housing that is then sold, often with substantial loans or grants, and housing that is owned by the state and leased to those who need it with subsidized rents. The latter is actually a rather small category in Israel.

107. *Israeli Equality Monitor*, no. 4, Adva Center (1995: 1).

108. According to the ILA (1993: 95), in 1991 the ILA allocated land for housing as follows: 11,511 units for public housing and to the Ministry of Housing, 5,307 for 'build your own home' projects and 15,617 to settlement institutions.

109. In 1975, a Development Plan for Minorities envisaged the creation of 18,700 new housing units.

110. Sikkuy <www.sikkuy.org.il>. Sikkuy also compare this allocation of development funding to the Arab sector, which totals 66.5 million shekels, and amounts to 104 shekels per resident, with the allocation to a single Jewish city, Modi'in, where the allocation for development of housing and infrastructure for 2002 amounted to a total of 252 million shekels, or 11,554 per resident.

111. Ibid.

112. Survey conducted in 1998 by the Galilee Society for Health Research and Services, Shafa'amr.

113. For instance, the German Colony neighbourhood of Haifa. Interview with Hussein Aghbarieh, Director of the Social Development Committee, Haifa, 21 November 1994.

114. Social Development Committee for the Arabs of Haifa, December 1994.

115. This case was reported in the local Arabic press: *Panorama* and *Sawt Al-Haqq wa Al-Hurriya*, 27 April 2001, *Al-Ittihad*, 20 May 2001 and *Panorama*, 29 June 2001.

116. The National Committee of Arab Mayors v. Minister of Housing and Building, HC 727/00.

117. *Adalah News Update*, 13 December 2001, 'Supreme Court orders government to provide Urban Renewal Program according to needs of Arab towns'.

118. The National Committee of Arab Mayors and Others v. the Directors' Committee for Fighting Unemployment in Settlements with High Unemployment Rates and Others, filed July 2002, Adalah, Shafa'amr.

119. Israeli official statistics define rural localities as those with a population of fewer than 2,000, regardless of density or dominant economic pursuit. According to the *Statistical Abstract of Israel* of 1998, only 8.5 per cent of the Arab population live in rural localities and the rest in urban localities. In 1961, the figure was 15.7 per cent.

120. The figure of 80,000 is estimated by community organizations representing the unrecognized villages including the Regional Council for the Unrecognized Villages of the Palestinian Bedouin in the Naqab and the Association of Forty. The phenomenon of the unrecognized Palestinian villages in Israel is examined in Chapter 8.

121. Amidar and six regional corporations: Halamish for Tel Aviv, Prazot for Jerusalem, Shikmona for Haifa, Afridar for Ashquelon, the Lod and Ramle Housing Corporation and Halad for Petah Tikva.

122. *Ha'aretz*, 2 July 1995.

123. See, for example, State of Israel (1998a: para. 488).

124. So, for example, the Discharged Soldiers Law 1984 provided that army veterans are eligible for government loans.

125. In 1970 a petition had been submitted to the Israeli High Court claiming that young couples who did not serve in the army were discriminated against by the Housing Ministry's assistance programme. In its response, the state announced changes in the programme: one of the criteria for setting the level of assistance was to be socio-economic status. However, a supplemental housing loan, of an additional 30 per cent or so of the base loan, would be given to families where at least one member served in the army. In 1993, and only as the result of a High Court petition issued on behalf of a Palestinian resident of Nahariya by the Association for Civil Rights in Israel, the Housing Ministry agreed that Palestinians are eligible for housing mortgages in development towns. Previously, only those who had served in the army were eligible with the exception of four Arab localities. According to Israel's report to the UN Human Rights Committee in 1998, the Attorney General viewed a veterans-only condition in determining who should be eligible for subsidized mortgages in development towns as impermissibly discriminatory, so the rule had been abolished (State of Israel 1998b: para. 850).

126. Two Palestinian residents of the mixed city of Ramle petitioned the

High Court in 2001, challenging military service criterion in a public housing project, and succeeded in persuading the project to widen its criteria; Adalah (2001b: 38).

127. Official public announcement in *Yediot Aharanot* (Hebrew daily newspaper), 27 March 1992.

128. For instance, 'Non-profit association initiates the building of 1,000 appartments for army veterans', *Ha'aretz*, 25 March 1995, and ILA Report 1993: 98–9 which describes land allocations for 8,000 units in 1991 to non-profit associations.

129. The take-up rate was only 32 per cent among Muslims and Christians and 43 per cent among Druze; State Comptroller's Report (1993).

130. Ministry of Housing Budget for rental assistance grants for 1999.

131. State Comptroller's Report (1993: 158); the criteria here are even wider than for housing loans, since they include not only those who have actually completed military service, but also family members of those who have served.

132. Subsidies for young couples were available only to towns and villages on a list that included only Nazareth of the Arab cities and villages, while in the Jewish sector not only the cities but also many other localities were eligible. The government claimed that the other Arab cities had been mistakenly classified as villages, and would from then on be included and that the question of adding other Arab localities would be considered. Subsequently, banks were instructed to give subsidies in the Arab cities of Um El Fahem, Taibeh, Tira and Shafa'amr in addition to Nazareth but other Arab localities remained excluded.

CHAPTER 8

The Phenomenon of the Palestinian 'Unrecognized Villages'

§ THE phenomenon of the 'unrecognized' Palestinian villages is one of the harshest and iniquitous outcomes of Israeli land and planning policies. As many as 7.5 per cent of Palestinian citizens of the country, around 80,000 people, live in such communities.[1] Israel has refused to grant them official recognition and effectively de-legalized them by declaring that they lie in areas not zoned for building. Like the 'present absentees' – those Palestinians who are 'absent' for the purposes of the Absentees' Property Law but are very much present in the state – the inhabitants of the unrecognized villages are a living anomaly: they exist, but are not marked on any official map or plan.

Until the 1990s, government policy was to eradicate the unrecognized villages altogether and to evict the inhabitants, assimilating them into already existing towns and villages or, in the case of the Bedouin, concentrating them in a few urban townships. In pursuing this policy Israel has literally tried to starve out the inhabitants of the villages, denying them access to mains electricity and water, to road networks and on-site education and health facilities. On top of the considerable hardships imposed by these policies, the villages endure additional measures designed to put pressure on them to leave. They are prohibited from developing infrastructure (such as paved roads and sewerage systems) and from constructing or repairing homes, and any buildings that do exist are subject to demolition at any time. Some people are forcibly evicted and, with the threat of eviction hanging over them, most live in a permanent state of insecurity. From the mid-1990s, governments began to show a willingness to recognize at least some of the villages, in response to intense pressure from local community groups and internationally. But progress has been slow and the government has so far been willing to recognize only the few largest of the villages. After decades of failure to treat these communities humanely and fairly, the majority are seeing only a slight improvement in their living conditions, and, most importantly, the same policies and legal framework that caused the problem remain largely in place.

The government has said that the people living in the unrecognized villages 'do not fit' its planning schemes,[2] and presents the issue as one of law and order, of simply enforcing the planning laws. But the question of the unrecognized villages is not merely about law and order; nor is it only about poverty, neglect and marginalization. It is an integral part of the ongoing denial of access to land that Palestinians have experienced in Israel since 1948. In many ways, it epitomizes all the various ways in which Israel denies Palestinians access to land. So, for instance, it is partly a result of internal displacement; some of the villages consist of Palestinian families displaced from their original villages during the war of 1948 who established themselves nearby when their homes were taken over by Israel.[3] It is also partly to do with the ongoing dispute over landownership. This is particularly clear in the Naqab where most of the unrecognized villages are situated. Here the situation is closely linked with the Bedouin's unresolved claims against the state over lands traditionally used and possessed by them. On the one hand, the government accuses the Bedouin of 'seizing', 'encroaching on' and 'spreading out over' state land, while the Bedouin see themselves as settling on land that is rightfully theirs but to which the State of Israel has long refused to recognize their rights. A population of around 70,000 Bedouin is resisting government attempts to expropriate their land and concentrate them in urban townships, which is the only legal option the government is offering them. In the Galilee, the issues are similar, and some of the land on which the unrecognized villages are situated is disputed land.

The question of the unrecognized villages is also about possession of land, and, in particular, the amount of land in the state that is taken up by Palestinian citizens. One aspect of this is the government's limitation on the number of Palestinian communities that are officially recognized. Since 1948, Israeli practice has been not to allow the number of Palestinian communities to increase; the 123 that now officially exist are hardly more than the 108 that survived the war, and the additional ones recognized are mainly concentration points for the Bedouin, which were established with the objective of reducing the amount of land they occupied. Government policy has been to concentrate the Bedouin in as few centres as possible. Whereas community groups identify at least forty-five separate communities in the Naqab, governments for decades were willing to recognize only seven, and recently only a handful more.[4] Another aspect of the government policy has been to restrict Palestinian localities to as little land as possible. The planned Bedouin townships all require that families live on small plots set close together, and do not allow a lower-density settlement pattern with each nuclear family some distance from the next in a style common in rural communities throughout the world. The phenomenon of the unrecognized villages is also a result of the planning policies described in the previous chapter that do not allow the Palestinian towns and villages enough land for natural expansion that would ensure that those who need housing are able to build legally. The Palestinian communities that survived the war of 1948 have had their land areas reduced drastically, and some of the unrecognized communities are actually satellite neighbourhoods of recognized communities that were excluded from official plans.

Finally, the question of the unrecognized villages is not only about the amount of land in the possession of Palestinians, but also where that land is situated, and here the political and security aspects of state policy have a bearing on the issue of the unrecognized villages. A common objective of district outline plans is to address the 'problems' of territorial continuity of the Arab villages.[5] Concentrations of Palestinians within the state are viewed as a threat. At the same time as small rural communities (*mitzpim*, or 'lookout posts') were being established for Jews in the Galilee in between the Arab villages, the authorities were busy trying to eradicate small rural unrecognized Palestinian communities that were in exactly the same areas.

The outcome of this mix of policy objectives, all connected to the desire to limit Palestinian access to land in the state, is that Israel simply decided to pretend that some of the smaller rural Palestinian communities that survived the war of 1948 were not there, and determined to eradicate others that appeared over the years as a result of the land and planning policies pursued by the state. While each unrecognized village has its own history, all are cohesive groupings. Some of the villages have been inhabited for centuries, others were estabished by internal refugees ejected from their homes following the war of 1948. All of those in the Naqab identify as Bedouin, while in the rest of the country, some but by no means all are of Bedouin origin. According to a survey conducted in 1988 of thirty-two of the villages in the north and centre, twenty-three were established prior to the establishment of the state, and only two were founded during the last twenty years (Association of Forty 1994). A common factor is that these groups consider themselves, and are considered by the wider Arab population, as communities. 'Community', like the word 'village', implies not only a place, but a group of people living together with a common interest in doing so. In both north and south, the villages consist of cohesive communities that are living and growing, with a low emigration rate and high birth rate. Even in the north, where most people are not organized along tribal lines, they tend to be common descendants of one family along a patrilineal line; close-knit communities with family ties and a common link to the territory and way of life they inhabit. They vary in size from tens to hundreds or even, in the Naqab, thousands of inhabitants. In other words, these are not transient or lawless individuals, but long-standing and well established communities.

The inability of the Palestinian unrecognized communities to achieve recognition through the statutory planning system has led to the development of alternative approaches in response to government policy. Their major strategy has been simply to remain where they are, refuse to move and do whatever they can to develop their communities. Some of the communities are relatively well developed, even when compared to 'recognized' Arab villages. Such development has been entirely the result of self-help programmes initiated by the inhabitants. Another strategy has been to prepare alternative plans and campaign for their acceptance. Since the early 1990s, several local community-based organizations have put forward professionally prepared plans backed by opinion surveys, field studies and other forms of consultation with the affected communities. Such plans related both to the centre and north of the country[6] and to the Naqab.[7]

The legal causes and consequences of 'unrecognized' status

The policy of not recognizing many rural Palestinian communities was made possible by the Planning and Building Law of 1965, which made all building outside approved outline schemes illegal.[8] The law distinguished between localities that are included in official plans, and are therefore 'recognized', and those that are not. The law also provided that outline planning schemes would designate land for certain purposes and that homes could be built only on land designated for residential use. Land declared to be agricultural land could not be used for residential or any other 'non-agricultural purpose' without the permission of a Committee for the Protection of Agricultural Land (see Chapter 7). The definition of 'non-agricultural purpose' is extremely narrow; any construction must be directly required for agricultural production, cultivation or raising livestock.[9] One consequence of this is that a farmer is not permitted to build a house on his farmland, and this has proved to be one way of keeping Palestinians living within essentially urban high-density towns and villages rather than on farm-land owned by them. Meanwhile, for Jews, planning accommodates the establishment of small rural settlements by altering the permitted use of sufficient land for residential use.

When implementing the Planning and Building Law after its enactment in 1965, Israeli planning authorities left the unrecognized villages out of all planning schemes. Instead, the authorities simply pretended they were not there and categorized the land as agricultural or forestland, on which it is illegal to build homes. The designation of land for certain uses and the establishment of 'new' settlements, including their location, type and size, are determined in the National Outline Scheme.[10] The refusal to legalize the villages is thus approved at the highest level.[11] As well as the villages finding themselves rendered illegal, individual buildings in the villages are also deemed illegal. A local planning and building commission will grant a building licence for construction only in conformity with an approved scheme, and any building work carried out without a licence or in breach of the terms of a licence is automatically illegal.[12]

It seems extraordinary that, in implementing the 1965 law, the planning authorities simply ignored the fact that many buildings already existed and that some of the villages were at varying stages of developing infrastructure such as roads, schools and services. Until the 1970s, although the communities were not incorporated in official plans, some building permits and services such as water were granted upon request. After this, government policy towards the unrecognized communities became increasingly restrictive. Services previously provided or permitted were withdrawn, no further building licences were granted, court demolition orders were sought and implemented, and a resettlement policy designed to force the inhabitants to relocate was systematically pursued. Legislation was enacted with the aim of making sure the unrecognized villages would no longer be connected to infrastructure networks. In 1981, an amendment (new section 157A) to the Planning and Building Law was enacted that prohibited the supply of electricity, water and telephone lines to buildings lacking a building licence.

The Markovitz Commission, appointed to look into illegal building in the Arab sector, considered the question of the unrecognized communities. In its *Report* released in 1986, the recommended solution for the 'illegal construction clusters' was their gradual phasing out. Some buildings were to be demolished immediately, while others were categorized as 'grey', which meant that all development was frozen pending a solution. The Markovitz recommendations put forward the legal framework for accelerated implementation of the relocation policy for the unrecognized villages. With regard to the Naqab, the *Markovitz*

Report stated: 'The enforcement of the Planning and Building Law in the Bedouin sector is closely tied to the policy of populating the … urban settlements.' After giving the resettlement policy a further four years for completion, the *Report* recommends demolition orders on the illegal buildings in the Naqab should be executed in 'an assertive and energetic policy', at which point, 'The Commission recommends preventing any failure to implement all the proceedings detailed in the Planning and Building Law' (Markovitz Commission 1986: 81).

Many of the recommendations of the *Markovitz Report* were implemented, and the monitoring and destruction of new development were more conscientiously carried out after 1986. Even some old buildings that pre-dated the 1965 law have been demolished. In a significant ruling, the High Court in 1994 ruled that older buildings could be demolished even where no person could be found to prosecute for illegal construction. This was the case of Sawa'id, which gave the green light for the courts to order the demolition of older buildings under section 205 of the Planning and Building Law.[13] The government also attempted to accelerate its relocation policy in response to Markovitz. Organizations representing the interests of the communities say that more and more pressure was applied on individual families and villages to reach agreement with the authorities. In tandem, there was an acceleration in planning other uses for the land in question, as evidenced by the new plans for the South and North Districts.

Bedouin unrecognized villages in the Naqab

Before 1948, both Bedouin and non-Bedouin Palestinians lived in the Naqab, but now virtually all Palestinian inhabitants of the Naqab are Bedouin.[14] The Bedouin were a semi-nomadic people who by 1948 were living in permanent settlements, even if some still moved seasonally with their herds. After 1948, the Palestinian Bedouin population that remained were all moved by the government into an area known as the *siyag*, a fertile area of the Naqab in which some tribes already lived. Constructing semi-permanent structures of cement block in addition to the traditional tents and huts, they arranged their communities following traditional settlement patterns with each tribe separate from the others and with nuclear family units spaced apart. After Israel began settlement of title operations in the area aimed at establishing ownership of the land, the Bedouin submitted thousands of claims, but Israel suspended consideration of the claims in 1976 when it decided to try instead to negotiate relocation and compensation.[15]

In national planning, the northern Naqab is considered to be an area of high development potential, and every year sees more intensive use of the land for human settlement and economic development – but only for Jews. In 2000, eleven urban and 105 rural localities were available for the Jewish population of the Naqab (Statistical Abstract of Israel 2000: Table 2.9). At the same time, the entire Palestinian Bedouin population – some 120,000 people, comprising 19 per cent of the population[16] – are expected to live in just seven urban townships (or a few more according to later announcements).[17] Even though moving to the planned townships is currently the sole legal option open to the Bedouin, to date, around half the Bedouin of the Naqab have still refused to move. Field surveys by local community-based organizations have established that there are at least 70,000 Bedouin living in forty-five unrecognized communities in the Naqab.[18] The vast majority of the structures in these communities are wooden huts, tents and animal sheds, and only a small minority are solidly constructed buildings.[19]

The Bedouin object to the relocation policy primarily because the government is linking it with their still unsettled land claims, forcing them to give up their land when they accept a plot in the townships. But there are also other objections. The relocation policy was developed and implemented without representation or any form of participation on the part of the Bedouin themselves. And the urban townships were planned without consideration for the structure of Bedouin society, culture and lifestyle. The plots within them are too small and close together for traditional patterns of settlement, and there is little or no opportunity to engage in traditional economic pursuits such as agriculture and herding. The townships are also severely underfunded and lack economic and social infrastructure and services. Unemployment in the townships is among the highest in the country. The establishment of infrastructure such as electricity and sewerage systems proceeds slowly.

Since the mid-1990s, a confusing and sometimes conflicting array of policy initiatives and official announcements have emerged. A Knesset Committee was appointed to investigate all aspects of the Bedouin community, and seek solutions, including the land issue. The government agreed to consider recognizing a further three to five townships as part of the plan for the development of Birsheba.[20] In 1999 the Comprehensive Programme for the Solution of the Problem of the Bedouin was published, the result of a study carried out with the support of Yossi Beilin, then Minister of Justice, recommending the recognition of seventeen villages and the installation of full services for the remainder as a first step. The *Gazit Report*, issued in March 2000, in general recommends that a solution be found for the unrecognized villages, either by recognizing them, or relocating the people to recognized communities through the ILA.[21] In July 2001, the government claimed to be dealing with the provision of basic utilities and services (water, electricity, education and health), to be working to settle land claims, to have halted demolitions and to be moving ahead with the planning and establishment of several new recognized settlements including one agricultural village (State of Israel 2001: 103–8). Yet in the very same period, reports were emanating from local human rights organizations of stepped-up demolitions, lack of progress on the planning front and an escalation in tension between the local community and the authorities.[22]

Israel has taken persistent action to cut the ties of the Bedouin Palestinians to their land, and the ILA and other government officials have not been shy to admit this. Pending a resolution of Bedouin land claims, the authorities are very careful about allowing the Bedouin to use disputed land. The Bedouin are also particularly vulnerable to eviction when they occupy such land. In general, the authorities have shown no qualms about uprooting once again those they forcibly removed from their land in the 1950s or later, and about employing draconian methods such as demolition of homes.

Government policy towards the Naqab Bedouin is influenced by deeply ingrained cultural attitudes. David Ben Gurion in 1963 made the following remarks:

> We should turn the Bedouin into urban workers, to work in industry, services, construction and agriculture. 88% of Israelis are not farmers. Let the Bedouin be among them. It will be a difficult transformation. It means the Bedouin will not live on his land and will have to do without his sheep. Instead he will be an urban dweller who will put his slippers on in the afternoon. His children will become used to seeing their father dressed in trousers, and not carrying a long knife and scratching his head for lice in public. They will go to school with their hair combed. It will be a revolution, but it could be brought about within two generations, not by being imposed but through government direction. If this occurs, the Bedouin way of life will disappear.[23]

Contemporary Israeli sociologist Ronen Shamir says that such attitudes stem from a basic view of the Bedouin as a people with an inferior culture who need to be dragged out of a historically backward age and into the modern day (Shamir: 525–46). Such a perception facilitates the view that the Bedouin are simply against a modern system of law that places a high value on certainty and logic. The Israeli courts, he says, also embrace this attitude, consistently dismissing the historical and cultural link between the Bedouin and their land, and endorsing state policies that aim to register Bedouin land in the name of the state and transfer the Bedouin to permanent planned settlements.

The strong sense that the Bedouin have of the importance of their link with land they consider to be theirs by right should not so easily be dismissed. Land is considered the core of the issue by the Palestinian Bedouin. In a survey of attitudes towards a proposed alternative plan for the Southern District, commissioned by the Association for Support and Defence of Bedouin Rights in Israel in 1990, it was found that attitudes towards land were the most important factor in shaping attitudes towards the plan (Association for Support and Defence of Bedouin Rights in Israel 1992: 26).

The refusal to establish agricultural villages for Bedouin One of the harshest and most iniquitous aspects of government policy towards the Bedouin in the Naqab has been the refusal to permit the recognition or establishment of agricultural villages, that is, communities that by their nature and layout are intended to allow farming, animal husbandry and a rural rather than urban lifestyle. Such communities suit the customs and traditions of the Bedouin better than an urban environment, and some of the Bedouin population would still prefer to live this way. Traditional agricultural pursuits remain important to the Bedouin Palestinians, both for their social-cultural and for their economic significance, particularly for those living outside the townships. Livestock rearing, for instance, is still a sole source of livelihood for some, and a source of supplemental income for others, while cultivation and herding together provide Bedouin families with significant income (Abu Rabia 1994: 1; Association for Support and Defence of Bedouin Rights in Israel 1990: 17–18). This income is particularly important given the precarious position of the Bedouin in the Israeli workforce and the high levels of unemployment in the Bedouin community. Agriculture is a preferred occupation for many: a survey carried out in 1992 showed that 77.8 per cent of the Bedouin prefer to live in a locality based on agriculture or shepherding; only 22 per cent said they preferred an urban locality (Association for Support and Defence of Bedouin Rights in Israel 1992: 26).

Master plans for the recognized localities in the Naqab do envisage agricultural quarters within the townships where residents will be permitted to raise sheep and engage in intensive agriculture that does not need much land.[24] In the township of Aroer, some residents were permitted to engage in intensive agriculture. However, the plots allocated were too small to be viable, water allocated was charged at a far higher rate than elsewhere, and the farmers have not been given proper guidance concerning what is for them an unfamiliar farming method (Association for Support and Defence of Bedouin Rights in Israel 1990: 69–70).[25]

Government policy discourages Bedouin engagement in agriculture in other ways also. The relevant authorities will lease land for short terms only, refuse to allocate sufficient water for irrigation, and harshly penalize agricultural practices carried out without permission, deploying the notorious paramilitary Green Patrol. Pastureland is strictly controlled: flocks must be registered and must not be moved outside tribal boundaries without permits, and compliance is closely monitored.

Leasing policy in relation to agricultural land is another tool used to restrict Bedouin possession of land and participation in agricultural pursuits. Since the establishment of the State of Israel, and their dispossession from their own lands, Bedouin Palestinians have been largely reliant on government allocations of land for cultivation and grazing purposes. However, there is insufficient land within the *siyag* to meet the needs of cultivation and pasture for all (there are around 400,000 dunams of cultivable land). In the 1960s, the ILC established conditions for granting land for agricultural purposes on a temporary basis to the Bedouin, limiting the amount of land per lessee and providing that grazing rights would be given to those with flocks for a season of ten months. A committee (with no Bedouin representatives) was set up to allocate land on this basis.[26] There is no transparency in the decision-making of the committee responsible for allocating leases; there are no representatives from the Bedouin community, no reasons are given, the criteria are not made known, the committee's discussions are not made public and no statistics are released. Conditions for leasing state land to Bedouin are published annually in the newspapers; they vary from year to year but tend to be restrictive and linked to the unresolved land disputes. In 1989, for instance, conditions 3 and 4 were: 'The age of the applicant is 50 years or above' and, 'The applicant does not hold any land for which he has filed a claim of ownership'.[27] Only short-term leases are ever granted, and never to those who claim the land; and the leasing of land is rotated so that no family is leased the same plot of land from year to year. These policies are designed to prevent the Bedouin Palestinians from forming ties to the land such as constructing buildings, planting trees and making improvements.

It would be perfectly possible to recognize the Bedouin communities while preserving a rural way of life for those who want it. While Bedouin populations exist in several Middle Eastern states and in most cases governments have initiated sedentarization programmes, solutions elsewhere are based on the premise that the Bedouin continue

to practise agriculture and animal husbandry, and it is only Israel that
has pursued a single-track urbanization process (Saban 1988: 32–4).
Freedom of occupation is one of the rights recognized in the Israeli
Basic Law: Human Dignity and Liberty of 1992. Section 3 provides:
'(E)very Israeli national or resident has the right to engage in any
occupation, profession or trade.' International law applicable to Israel
also protects this right.[28] According to the principle of equality, the
Bedouin should be permitted, like Jewish Israelis in the Naqab and the
rest of the country, to establish agricultural villages, which is a choice
desired by many in the community. Only in 1995 did the government
acknowledge that 'it cannot impose upon the entire Bedouin population
an urban solution which would be contrary to its wish and traditional
way of life' and announced that some agricultural settlements would
be planned (State of Israel 1998a: para. 472). However, by 2002 little
progress had been made towards this stated goal.

Planning that ignores the Bedouin population In October 1994, a new
master plan for the Southern District was deposited.[29] Although the
plan ignored the existence of Palestinian Bedouin settlements other
than the seven planned townships, its provisions directly impact as
many as half of those living in unrecognized villages.[30] No distinction
is made between land over which ownership is disputed and other
land, or between land on which Bedouin are settled and uninhabited
land. For instance, according to the plan, an industrial and commercial
area will be constructed on an area where some 3,000 Bedouin of the
Abu Kaf tribe live on their traditional lands. Land belonging to other
tribes is slated variously for forest or further industrial areas. From the
government's point of view, the unrecognized villages are temporary
settlements, and their inhabitants are on their way to moving into one
of the townships. So, for example, when the Ministry of the Interior
decided in March 2000 to confirm the enlargement of the area of
jurisdiction of the (Jewish) local council of Omer, it ignored the
presence of two Bedouin communities with a total of 6,000 inhabitants
on the land in question. The commission that had studied the matter
had failed to hear a single representative of the Bedouin communities,
and had recommended the annexation of the land to Omer, assuming
that the Bedouin were to be evacuated.[31] Once land on which they are
living becomes designated for development under an approved plan,
the Bedouin are under immediate threat of eviction. On occasion, they
have been evicted from land slated for development even where the
land was not subsequently used for over twenty years.[32]

It is reasonable for the Bedouin to ask why Palestinians should not be permitted to establish communities on sites that have been slated for development in the regional plan. When the ILA was negotiating with the Abu Ghardood sub-tribe in December 1994, having promised to allow them to establish an agricultural village, the Abu Ghardood proposed that they establish the village on one of the ten sites allocated to be new agricultural settlements in the new master plan for the Southern District. The ILA rejected this proposal. Palestinian local community groups have in recent years begun closely scrutinizing plans for the Naqab region that affect them, commissioning professional planners to advise them. One group has challenged the Southern District plan in the courts on the basis that it does not reflect the needs of the Bedouin population of the area.[33]

Unrecognized villages in the centre and north

The unrecognized Palestinian villages in the centre and north have more disparate histories than in the Naqab, where all the villages consist of Bedouin, and they also tend to be smaller; but they suffer from the same poor living conditions and lack of services.[34]

Specific policies have been developed in relation to those of the unrecognized villages in the centre and north that are Bedouin. The first government plan to concentrate the Galilee Bedouin in the late 1950s had the stated purpose to 'protect state land from being illegally seized, evict Bedouin from land they had taken, by moving them to planned permanent settlements' (Khamaysi 1990: 65). This attitude still endures, with government officials complaining that the Bedouin are living in homes built on agricultural land and, in some cases, on land claimed by the state. As in the Naqab, government policy has focused on lessening the geographical area the Bedouin inhabit, resettling them in the established Palestinian towns and villages or in sixteen recognized concentration points such as Wadi Salameh, which suffer problems similar to those of the townships established for Palestinian Bedouin in the Naqab. A new five-year plan designed to address the situation of some 3,000 Bedouin Palestinians in the north was announced in 1998, its objective to evacuate the people to concentration points and demolish their houses.[35] Those who agree to move will receive a plot of land on a forty-nine-year lease in one of the concentration points, and they will be paid compensation for being forced to demolish their homes.[36] Any land to which they lay claims of ownership must be given up and registered in the name of the state. A greater proportion of Bedouin in the north have moved into recognized localities than in the Naqab.

From 1965 until the early 1990s, the unrecognized villages in the centre and north lived in a constant state of uncertainty, unable to develop and receiving increasing scrutiny so that each time they tried to carry out improvements or new construction, demolition orders were issued by the planning authorities. The level of development in the villages varied quite considerably. Al-Arian in the Triangle was well developed; its modern houses had received building permits until 1976 and were connected to the water, telephone and electricity networks, the villagers had built their own road, and the land was the undisputed private property of the residents. Nevertheless, the *Markovitz Report* of 1986 recommended its eviction, and a plan submitted by the village was rejected in 1991 by the Haifa District Planning and Building Commission. Other villages had been less well developed. For instance, the village of Arab Naim in the Galilee had corrugated-iron huts and no connection to electricity or water networks, forcing the villagers to transport water to the village in tanks and causing a health hazard.

As a result of sustained lobbying by community-based groups, nine of the largest unrecognized villages in the centre and north of the country were recognized during the 1990s, including both Al-Arian and Arab Naim. In 1992, Yitzhak Rabin's Labour government agreed in principle to recognize some of the villages and to endeavour to incorporate others into other recognized villages. In December 1994, the government announced the decision to recognize four villages, a further four followed, and a ninth (Arab Naim) was added on 1 September 1998. Despite these agreements, however, progress towards approval of plans – without which no construction or development can start – has been painfully slow, and the process of recognition has been a battle at every stage.[37] The delays are caused partly by conflict between the villagers and the authorities regarding the amount of land to be included in the plan in each case. For instance, in the case of Arab Naim, the authorities attempted to impose a condition to the effect that the inhabitants agree to give up some of their land in exchange for recognition.[38] The process with regard to Kamaneh, recognized in 1995, was equally difficult. A zoning plan developed by the local planning authorities excluded two quarters of the village, an area known as Jalsi, home to some 100 people, and a western quarter with around 140 inhabitants. Residents of both applied to the High Court.[39] The state denied that the decision to give legal status to Kamaneh meant recognition of all quarters of the village, and maintained that factors such as the need to defend nature had been taken into account in leaving out parts of the village. However, the state had proposed a compromise whereby the homes left outside the plan could continue to be inhabited until their current owners died.

The High Court, in its judgment of 5 September 2001, rejected the state's compromise proposal as unreasonable and impractical. It said that Kamaneh was an organic village, that the intention had been to give recognition to the village as a whole, and that a planning solution must be found that included the two excluded quarters. While the Court did not address arguments raised by the applicants regarding the principle of equality and constitutional rights, it made some interesting comments that appeared to move towards the establishment of a duty to consult. Justice Matza ordered that the petitioners and all the residents of the two excluded quarters should be given the opportunity to present, within six months, proposals regarding the enlargement of the plan, and stated that during the planning process that would ensue in the district commission, these parties, and other interested parties such as representatives of the bordering areas, must be given a right of hearing.

In the meantime, while plans for the villages in the process of recognition are still pending, the villages remain in the same situation as before the decision to recognize them was announced. New building is illegal, and they cannot be connected to basic utilities and services or develop infrastructure.

The decision to recognize some but not all the villages was not based on any objective criteria. Approval of a new locality requires a national-level decision, followed by inclusion in district- and local-level plans. But there are no statutory criteria governing the recognition or establishment of localities. Policy is usually based on decisions of the various ministries and the ILC. Israeli governments have raised a variety of arguments against recognition of the communities, claiming the communities are too small and remote to be viable, and that the cost of providing them with services and facilities is too great. However, these arguments do not stand up to scrutiny and, if applied in the Jewish sector, would have prevented the establishment of hundreds of localities. For instance, if size is a factor, it is applied inconsistently. Over half of the unrecognized villages in the centre and north of the country surveyed in 1988 had over 100 inhabitants.[40] Meanwhile, Israeli official statistics show that in 1992 there were fifty-three recognized communities in Israel with fewer than 100 inhabitants, of which fifty-one are Jewish, and 706 with fewer than 500 inhabitants, of which 696 are Jewish.[41]

As regards cost, Arab community-based organizations have calculated that recognizing the villages on their present sites would cost no more than the government policy to break up the communities and settle the inhabitants elsewhere.[42] According to the *Markovitz Report* (1986:

12), construction outside the approved plans creates difficulties for the state in providing services as these would require large investment in infrastructure. Such services would, however, have to be provided to these citizens even if they relocated elsewhere. The communities themselves would expect to have to meet many of the costs of establishing services and infrastructure in any event after recognition. The villages have argued that it is possible to develop infrastructure and services on a regional level rather than to each small community, a model that has already been developed in the Jewish sector.[43] The government has proved willing to allow the provision of services to Jewish settlements that are equally small and remote. Indeed, road, water, electricity and telephone networks already frequently pass very close to unrecognized communities.

The government also claims that the land on which the communities are situated is not for residential use and is required for other purposes, but it has occurred not infrequently that this same land is included in plans for residential areas – for Jews. In other words, the planning authorities plan new Jewish localities in the same spot where they refused to recognize Palestinian communities. Khaled Nimer Sawa'id, a resident of the unrecognized village of Makhmanim, lived on a spot on Mount Kamon in the Galilee on which his family had lived for generations and on land owned by the family. A small Jewish locality, Mitzpe Makhmanim, had been established nearby and, in 1989, the planning authorities approved a plan that would expand the locality so as to encompass Sawa'id's land, which was designated for housing. A notice of confiscation of his land was published. Sawa'id applied for a licence to build there. In the course of correspondence with the Ministry of the Interior and the ILA, he was constantly told he must agree to accept a plot of land in one of the Arab villages in the area. Eventually, he was advised that the authorities were considering changing the status of the land in question back to agricultural land, presumably in order to avoid his application.

The unrecognized village of Ramya, also in the Galilee, provides another example of this phenomenon. Ramya is a community of some 100 persons inhabiting land they have owned and lived on since Palestine was part of the Ottoman Empire. Based on a declaration of expropriation of land dating from 1976 – of which the residents claim never to have received notice – the community received court eviction orders in 1991. The land was to be turned over to the nearby city of Karmiel for housing for new Jewish immigrants. A legal challenge to the High Court failed, but during 1995 negotiations resulted in an agreement whereby the villagers of Ramya were allocated 25 dunams of land nearby. By

1997, however, the city municipality continued to demand that the villagers evacuate their homes, but had still not allocated an alternative site in accordance with the agreement; meanwhile, the villagers found that their existing homes were surrounded by the construction of a new neighbourhood of the city, creating an unendurable environment (Arab Association for Human Rights 1998: 34).

While the agreement to recognize some of the unrecognized villages in the north and centre is to be welcomed, the process of recognition has proved difficult. Meanwhile, there has been little progress towards finding solutions for the remainder of the villages or providing services even on an interim basis. Nor has action been taken to tackle the underlying causes of the problem that lie in the implementation of the state's land and planning laws.

Enforcement policy towards the unrecognized villages

Over the years, as government efforts to eradicate the unrecognized communities intensified, so did the determination of the inhabitants to remain. According to the *Gazit Report* of 2000, there are an estimated 30,000 'illegal' buildings in Palestinian communities.[44] The vast majority of illegal dwellings in the Naqab consist of tents or corrugated-iron shacks rather than solid stone houses, whereas most of the buildings in the centre and north are solidly built structures.[45] All construction in the villages, whether of zinc or stone, is illegal. In the courts, offenders receive heavy fines, or the courts order demolition or prohibited uses of a building, and sometimes impose imprisonment. Many home-owners are forced to demolish their own homes. Since the late 1970s, thousands of court demolition orders have been issued. The Association for Support and Defence of Bedouin Rights in Israel estimated in its *Report on Legal Activities 1989–90* that between 80 and 90 per cent of the court hearings were carried out in a summary fashion and without the defendant being legally defended. When owners fail to carry out the demolition, selected demolitions are carried out. Periodically, the authorities demolish dwellings by force, usually without warning and giving little or no time for the inhabitants to remove household items, and with a large police and army presence.[46]

Following the Markovitz Commission's *Report* in 1986, which recommended an accelerated implementation of the relocation of the unrecognized villages and various measures to improve enforcement of the planning laws in relation to the villages, closer monitoring of new construction was instituted and the authorities cracked down upon violators, including renovations or repairs of existing buildings, which were immediately destroyed.[47] Demolitions have continued to take place on a particularly large scale in the Naqab. According to a survey carried out by the Association of Forty in 1997, between 1993 and the end of 1996, 2,040 homes in the Naqab Bedouin communities alone were demolished on the grounds that they lacked a permit (Arab Association for Human Rights 1998: 31). Demolitions throughout the country have been stepped up since 2001 with almost weekly reports of further homes demolished. Sometimes just one or two homes are destroyed, other times it is more: for instance, on 28 May 2002, fifty-two homes were destroyed in the unrecognized village of Al-'Araqib.[48]

While the government's long-term objective is to relocate all the Bedouin in recognized townships, the practice of evicting the unrecognized villages may be unconnected to any specific relocation plan. The result of this practice is that forced evictions sometimes take place, for instance to make way for development projects, even when no alternative is yet in place. For instance, in 1991, the government was trying to evict members of the Azazmeh tribe from land on which they had been living since being relocated there in the 1950s, even though the government itself had removed the tribe members from their traditional land and given them this land in its place and they had nowhere else to go. In August 1991, the Israeli High Court issued an order to prevent the government from evacuating the tribe, holding that it was not reasonable to remove them without providing an alternative.[49]

One of the key strategies adopted by the government to enforce its policies towards the unrecognized Palestinian communities has been the denial of basic infrastructure and services. In 1981, the 1965 law was amended so as to prevent the supply of electricity, water and telephone services to unlicensed buildings. Villages make whatever arrangements they can to make up for the lack of central supply, but a field survey of thirty-two unrecognized villages in the north conducted in 1988 by the Association of Forty revealed overcrowding and considerable environmental distress, and a critical lack of basic services. Testing showed drinking water in villages to be contaminated, and in an outbreak of hepatitis in 1989 in two villages, one child died and twenty-one contracted the disease. On-site health and education services have not been adequate. The Israeli government policy of depriving the unrecognized communities of water and other services was severely criticized by the International Water Tribunal in Holland in February 1992, in response to a case brought by local community groups. The international jury sitting in the case held that it was 'unable to countenance any governmental action which uses the denial of water as a means of enforcing zoning or planning'.[50] Following this decision, the Israeli government permitted the installation of a single water point for each village. In May 2001 several community-based organizations petitioned the Israeli High Court, demanding that seven unrecognized villages be supplied with water for drinking and domestic use. In the petition it was claimed that the single water point established for each village was far from the villagers' homes and inadequate, and that the refusal to allow connection to the water network denied the citizens who live in the communities the basic rights to life, dignity and equality.[51]

Community-based groups representing the unrecognized villages have consistently argued that the supply of basic services and amenities is the fundamental right of all citizens, and that the withholding of them should not be used as a form of punishment or inducement integrally connected with the government's policy to eradicate the villages and relocate the people. In addition to the case relating to water, community groups have successfully used these arguments in order to obtain decisions from the High Court ordering the relevant ministries to build six primary health care clinics in the unrecognized villages in the Naqab and to provide public transportation to others,[52] and to restore welfare services including social workers to the unrecognized villages in the Naqab after they had been suspended.[53] Important though these judgments have been in improving conditions in the villages and affirming the legal right of the communities to basic services and amenities, they represent only the tip of the iceberg, and the villages still suffer under harsh living conditions. Some communities are living in seriously hazardous environmental conditions. Members of the Azazme tribe living in the region of Ramat Hovav in the Naqab are suffering from respiratory and skin diseases resulting from emissions from a nearby factory. Their claims have not been officially investigated.

Another tool of enforcement is heavy-handed policing. A para-military force, the Green Patrol, assists the enforcement process. Established by Ariel Sharon in 1977 to protect state lands from 'tres-passers', the Green Patrol routinely ploughs up crops planted by Bedouin on land it considers illegally cultivated.[54] The force is known for its brutality. The *State Comptroller's Report* of 1980 criticized the Green Patrol for the use of physical coercion, confiscation of sheep and goats, destruction of crops, dismantling of tents and other such actions taken outside the law (Maddrell 1990). In the spring of 2002, the Israeli government sent out crop dusters with herbicides to destroy wheat crops planted by Bedouin without permission on disputed land.[55] The government claimed that the crops had been planted illegally on state-owned land but the operation caused health-related concerns, particularly since a school in the area had been sprayed, and outrage among the community.

The failure of legal protection for Palestinian rights in relation to planning and housing

In 1998, the United Nations Human Rights Committee, after considering reports from the State of Israel and from non-governmental organizations concerning Israel's compliance with the International Covenant on Civil and Political Rights, said: 'The Committee recommends that urgent steps be taken to overcome the considerable inequality and discrimination which remain in regard to land and housing' (United Nations Human Rights Committee 1998: para. 25).

The Israeli policies towards the Arab sector that relate to the implementation of the planning laws and the provision of housing assistance (described in this chapter and the previous one) reveal a pattern of systematic discrimination and a fundamental disregard for principles of equality and other fundamental rights including the right to human dignity. This situation must be seen as resulting directly from the emphasis that pervades all Israeli governments and government departments on the nature of Israel as a 'Jewish state'. Israel accords second-class status to non-Jews, ploughs resources into developing new communities and housing for Jews, uses land expropriated from Palestinians for establishing and expanding Jewish communities, goes to enormous lengths to restrict the amount of land taken up by Palestinian communities and tolerates the fact that 80,000 of its citizens live in unrecognized villages without access to water, electricity, sanitation, roads and other basic amenities.

But Israel also presents itself as a democratic state committed to the principles of equality and non-discrimination (see Chapter 2). In the international arena, it has also committed itself not only to respecting these principles, but also to the right to adequate housing.[56] The right to housing does not mean merely the right to shelter, but incorporates a wider right 'to live somewhere in security, peace and dignity'.[57] Some of the key elements of this right are legal security of tenure, availability of services, materials, facilities and infrastructure, affordability, habitability, accessibility, suitable location (allowing access to employment options and services) and cultural adequacy.

The United Nations Committee on Economic, Social and Cultural Rights has developed standards relating to the obligations and expectations of governments in relation to the right to adequate housing.[58] States are not necessarily expected to take a central role in the provision of housing; the extent of public sector housing will depend on the type of government and economy in the state concerned. However, any public housing sector that does exist must clearly observe the requirements of equality and non-discrimination. Although states are obliged to respect the right to adequate housing only 'to the maximum of its available resources', in Israel, which is a relatively developed country, there is simply no excuse for having tens of thousands of people living without their basic water, electricity, housing and other needs being met on a long-term basis, as is the case in the unrecognized villages. The requirement to *respect* and *protect* the right to adequate housing includes refraining from action that obstructs access to housing. This would include actions that arbitrarily deprive people of their own housing or prevent them from finding or building homes (Craven 1998: 331). The Committee has also shown concern about the availability of a variety of type of housing (ibid., p. 336). Here a link can be drawn with Article 12 of the ICCPR, which asserts the right for everyone lawfully within the state to 'liberty of movement and freedom to choose his residence'.[59] Israeli planning policies, particularly in relation to the Bedouin in the Naqab and other unrecognized villages, and the role of the Jewish national institutions, restrict the locations in which Palestinians are permitted to live and their choice of type of locality.

Equality and non-discrimination are a constant theme in the international human rights treaties, and the Committee on Economic, Social and Cultural Rights has adopted the view of other UN human rights bodies that it is the *effect* and not only the intent of a particular measure which is important (Craven 1998: 165). The Israeli High Court, guardian of these principles in the public sphere, has had a mixed record in protecting them in relation to planning and housing, including the unrecognized villages. Some useful principles have emerged from some of its more recent decisions. One is the decision of the High Court in December 2001 relating to the implementation of an urban renewal programme, in which the Court affirmed the importance of developing objective and equitable criteria for the disbursement of public funds.[60] The National Committee of Arab Mayors had petitioned the Court claiming that the implementation of the urban renewal programme had discriminated against Palestinian citizens because during more than twenty years of its existence, the programme had been applied to only four Arab villages and fourteen Arab neighbourhoods, as compared with fifty-six Jewish localities and ninety-nine Jewish neighbourhoods.[61] This was particularly iniquitous given that the Palestinian communities experience the worst socio-economic conditions in the country. In its judgment, the Court acknowledged the need to set equitable criteria for the allocation of funds, relying on appropriate considerations and relevant facts and reflecting the purpose for which the money was intended, and the necessity of implementing the programme in the communities that needed it most. This decision, if applied in other areas where public funds are allocated on a discretionary basis, could have significant implications for the Arab sector.

The right of communities affected by planning decisions to be consulted is another important principle that has been affirmed in two recent cases relating to unrecognized villages in the process of recognition. In September 2001 the High Court ordered that two areas of the village of Kamaneh that had been excluded from a development plan by the planning authorities must be included.[62] In its ruling, the Court added that the residents of those parts should be given the opportunity to submit their own proposals as to how the plan could be expanded so as to include them, and that the residents of the areas affected should be heard during the process, and stressed the importance of participation by the affected community in plan development. In another case relating to the village of Husseiniya, the Acre Magistrates' Court quashed a demolition order issued against a mosque on the grounds that the local planning and building commission should have consulted with the local committee of inhabitants before ordering the demolition of buildings within the community.[63]

Despite these limited possibilities, the courts are failing to protect Palestinian rights in a number of key areas. One notable failure is in relation to the practice of demolishing unlicensed construction. Although the courts have affirmed the general principle that demolition should be used only as an exceptional measure, and that there must be a good reason to implement it beyond the fact that the building was constructed illegally,[64] the courts have not yet followed through on this principle and questioned its use as a method of planning enforcement in the Palestinian sector other than in the Husseiniya decision. The courts have also failed to address satisfactorily the question of the chronic lack of representation of Palestinians on planning bodies. The High Court refused a request to order the government to nominate Palestinians to the planning commission for the Northern District, despite the fact that only two out of fifteen members of the commission were Palestinian although Palestinians made up more than half of the population in the district.[65] The Court was prepared only to find that appropriate representation of Arab residents of the district was one factor to be taken into account, and refused to intervene because most of the members of the commission were representing government ministries and not the interests of any particular community.

The role of the courts in relation to the situation of the unrecognized villages has been mixed. On the positive side are the decisions relating to consultation in the process of recognition of the villages of Kamaneh and Husseiniya, stepping in to prevent the eviction of the Azazmeh tribe from its land in the absence of an alternative place for them to go and several decisions recognizing the right of the unrecognized communities to basic services and infrastructure.[66] Other decisions have been positively unhelpful. In a decision of 1994 concerning fifteen buildings in the unrecognized villages of Um El-Sahali and Sarkis, for instance, the High Court gave the green light for the demolition of old buildings even in situations where no individual transgressor could be prosecuted for illegal building due to the limitation period having expired.[67] Lawyers representing the residents of these buildings feared that this decision could have serious implications, placing in danger many older buildings in unrecognized communities.

While these and other minor battles have been won in the courts, the courts have stopped short of attacking government policy relating to the unrecognized villages in general. Such major concessions as have been won, such as the agreement by the Rabin government in the mid-1990s to recognize some villages in the north, were won not in the courts but as a result of political pressure. In other words, the courts have shown themselves willing to take small steps in relation to questions raised by the unrecognized villages, but not bolder ones. Why, for instance, have the courts not challenged the government's decisions forcibly to evict established populations, without obliging the government to justify its actions and to demonstrate that there was no other way to achieve its objectives which would cause less harm to citizens and to established rights? Moving entire communities is a cause of upheaval and dislocation from traditional lifestyles and social, cultural as well as economic norms, and an affront to human dignity. In the case of the unrecognized Palestinian communities, however, it has been shown that there are apparently no reasons based on sound planning or other public policy considerations why these communities must be moved. Public authorities have a duty to act reasonably. In the Naqab, most of the communities were established following the government's relocation policies of the 1950s, and on sites to which they were moved by the Israeli authorities. No alternative was given at that time. In other words, these villages were established with the full knowledge and consent of the Israeli government. Yet twenty years later the government decides they must move again, this time to inhabit an even smaller area of land.

Forced eviction as a specific aspect of the right to adequate housing has been the subject of particular concern within the UN. In its General Comment 7 of 1997, the Committee on Economic, Social and Cultural Rights defined the term as follows: 'the permanent or temporary removal against their will of individuals, families and/or communities from the homes and/or land they occupy, without the provision of, and access to, appropriate forms of legal or other protection. The only exceptions to the prohibition on forced evictions are those carried out by force in accordance with the law and in conformity with the provisions of the International Human Rights Covenants' (UNCESCR 1997: para. 4).

The Committee notes that the practice of forced evictions is widespread, and that one of the situations in which it tends to occur is in connection with conflict over land rights, development and infrastructure projects. Drawing a link with the right to be protected against 'arbitrary or unlawful interference' with one's home in Article 17.1 of the ICCPR and the right to an effective remedy, the Committee emphasized the need for adequate legal protection from violation of this right. The existence of 'illegal' settlements or housing is one of the factors specifically identified by the UN monitoring Committee as one of the factors that should be used to measure compliance with the Covenant on Economic, Social and Cultural Rights.[68]

As regards the circumstances in which forced evictions may be justified, the Committee said: 'Forced evictions and house demolitions as a punitive measure are also inconsistent with the norms of the Covenant ... States parties shall ensure, prior to carrying out evictions, and particularly those involving large groups, that all feasible alternatives are explored in consultation with affected persons' (UNCESCR 1997: paras 13 and 14). Procedural protections required in relation to forced evictions identified by the Committee include: an opportunity for genuine consultation with those affected, adequate and reasonable prior notice, information on the proposed evictions and any alternative purpose for which the land or housing is to be used, provision of legal remedies (ibid., para. 16).

Forced evictions are taken so seriously by the UN that the practice has been declared by the Commission on Human Rights to constitute a gross violation of human rights. The Commission urged governments to 'provide immediate restitution, compensation and/or appropriate and sufficient alternative accommodation or land, consistent with their wishes and needs, to persons and communities which have been forcibly evicted, following mutually satisfactory negotiations with the affected persons or groups'.[69]

The Israeli policy of involuntarily relocating the unrecognized Palestinian villages in Israel is clearly in breach of these internationally accepted standards. Violations include the practice of carrying out random demolitions and evictions from the thousands of Arab homes rendered illegal, without exploring alternatives in consultation with the affected communities, and often without adequate procedural safeguards such as reasonable prior notice or information on the alternative purpose for which the land or housing is planned. These matters have been highlighted before the Committee, which has frequently criticized Israel.[70] The policy of removing even long-existing communities while planning brand-new settlements in their place that are exclusively for Jews not only violates the prohibition on discrimination that is contained in both international Covenants, but also fails the test of providing the procedural guarantees that the Covenants require and contravenes the prohibition on forced eviction which is considered to be one of the most serious violations of human rights.

The means Israel uses to bring about the forced evictions have also been criticized by international human rights monitoring bodies. In 1998, the UN Human Rights Committee deplored the practice of demolishing illegally constructed Arab homes, and said that it considered the demolitions that were taking place to 'conflict directly with the obligation of the State party to ensure without discrimination the right not to be subjected to arbitrary interference with one's home (art. 17), the freedom to choose one's residence (art. 12) and equality of all persons before the law and equal protection of the law (art. 26)' (UN Human Rights Committee 1998: para. 24). Another UN body, the Committee Against Torture, has said that Israeli policies on house demolitions 'may, in certain circumstances, amount to cruel, inhuman or degrading treatment or punishment' (UN Committee Against Tortutre 2001: para. 6[j]).

One feature of Israeli planning and housing policy has been the continuing separation of the Palestinian and Jewish communities. This raises the question of what role racial factors play in decision-making, as well as the lawfulness of taking into account such considerations. Practices that could be defined as as 'racial steering' or 'social engineering' – steering people to particular areas on the basis of their racial origin – are strictly outlawed, for instance, in the USA and the UK.[71] On the other hand, in the UK providing for special or unmet needs, such as housing schemes specifically for ethnic minorities to make up for inadequate provision, are permitted where they are intended not to segregate groups but to meet the needs of a distinct group of people (Handy 1993: 15). When the Israeli government plans and develops neighbourhoods specifically for Jews, and when it plans townships intended specifically for the Bedouin, is this racial steering, or affirmative action?

The Israeli High Court has confidently declared both policies to be legitimate. The case of Burkhan concerned a Palestinian former resident of the Old City of Jerusalem who had been evacuated when Israel took over the Old City in the 1967 war. He tried to apply for a new home when the area known as the Jewish Quarter was subsequently reconstructed. After old houses were renovated and new ones built in the quarter, offers were opened for leases 'to citizens and residents of Israel and to new immigrants' only. Burkhan, who was a Jordanian citizen, was turned down and petitioned the High Court. In his judgment, Judge Shamgar stressed that while the principle of non-discrimination was a basic principle in Israeli law, the point at issue was not discrimination in housing rights but the right of a state to reconstruct a quarter of the Old City, which was of historical and national value.[72] Similarly, in the case of Avitan v. ILA, in which a Jewish citizen challenged the allocation of plots of land at special low rates only to Palestinian Bedouin in the planned townships, the High Court rejected the petition. The Court said that the decision to give land to the Bedouin on favourable conditions was not discrimination on grounds of nationality because it was a policy aimed at catering to the special needs of the Bedouin as a community with a distinct ethnic and cultural character.[73]

However, the line between social steering and special measures is perhaps not so straightforward. In delivering judgment on the Burkhan case, Judge Cohn placed the emphasis in a different way to Judge Shamgar when he said, 'There is no illegal discrimination in preserving the existence of separate quarters for different religious communities', suggesting that a policy of segregation was in some cases justified. The question of the concentration policy towards the Palestinian Bedouin highlights the contradictions in the Israeli approach. All the indications are, as we have tried to show, that the main considerations taken into account by successive governments in their relocation strategy for the Bedouin are minimizing the area of land they use, discouraging them from rural pursuits that would involve the possession of large areas of land, restricting the spatial extent of the recognized communities and security considerations. In other words, the objective has not been to provide for their special unmet needs, or indeed to offer them any choice, but to force them to comply with a government policy that is so unpopular that half of the population prefers to live in appalling conditions rather than comply with it.[74] And when the Israeli government plans new settlements and neighbourhoods designed exclusively for Jews, while it is the Palestinians who are regularly at the bottom of all the socio-economic indicators but no new settlements or neighbourhoods are built for them, and when land is taken from Palestinians in order to build for Jews, is not the objective to promote the interests of one racial group at the expense of the other? Such policies surely amount to racial steering rather than positive discrimination or affirmative action, and to the subjugation of planning considerations to racial and ideological factors.[75] As such, they violate the strong prohibition on racial discrimination that exists in international law, to which Israel is committed.[76]

Why have the Israeli courts not intervened more often in order to uphold the principles of non-discrimination, equality and other fundamental rights such as the right to human dignity in relation to planning and housing? The answer lies partly in the fact that until recently there have been relatively few legal challenges brought by the community on these issues. A further reason lies in the nature of the powers given under law and the way in which the law has been interpreted by the courts. One obstacle to establishing a practice of discrimination as illegal in Israel is the general lack of statutory definition of criteria, of factors that must be taken into account and of specific and mandatory responsibilities on public authorities. Israeli legislation commonly gives wide discretionary powers in relation to land-use planning and related matters, unlike in the UK, for instance, where official circulars lay down factors that planning authorities must take into account, including some specifically targeted at protecting the interests of minorities.[77] In the absence of such guidelines, the Israeli courts have generally been reluctant to intervene in decisions of the planning authorities in order to protect Palestinian rights. For instance, when Kufr Yasif attempted to challenge the decision to reduce the local council's area of jurisdiction, the High Court was not willing to intervene in the exercise of discretion by the Minister. The Minister of the Interior, the Court said, had followed all the procedures provided in the law, and it was not the Court's role to look at the merits of the case.[78] In the absence of positive duties to take steps to promote equality, the general duty on public authorities in Israel not to discriminate is insufficient. An example of how housing rights can be framed so as to ensure the interests of different groups are taken into account in a way that is legally binding is the Indian Housing Rights Bill, developed through a process of consultation throughout the country by a coalition of organizations and individuals.[79] The bill sets out the rights of citizens and the corresponding duties of government, stressing the procedural aspects (such as steps that must be taken before any eviction may take place) and provides for democratic participation in housing matters by dwelling unions.

A further factor is the relatively weak status given to the principle of equality. While the principle has been recognized as having fundamental status in Israeli law for many years, it will not necessarily outweigh other considerations such as planning goals that compete with it. So, for instance, in the 1987 case of Poraz, the High Court said that public authorities must give 'reasonable weight' to the principle of equality and consider whether there are alternative ways of achieving the policy aim that is sought to be achieved.[80] The failure to include the principle of equality in the Basic Law: Human Dignity and Liberty enacted in 1992 meant that the opportunity was not taken further to enhance the status of this supposedly fundamental principle by entrenching it in constitutional legislation.

Notes

1. There are no official statistics on the number of unrecognized villages or their populations. The figure of around 80,000 is an estimate based on field studies carried out by community-based organizations, particularly the Regional Council for the Unrecognized Villages of the Palestinian Bedouin in the Naqab and the Association of Forty.

2. This phrase came from State of Israel (1998a: para. 463). These people, the report says, 'consistently refuse governmental aid proposals for resettling in appropriate locations'.

3. Ein Hod is one example of this category. In 1948, the inhabitants of this village, situated on the slopes of Mount Carmel near Haifa, were displaced and prevented from returning, so they settled nearby. Their original homes were taken over by the state and became an artists' colony.

4. The government indicated in 1998 its willingness to consider establishing a further four or five urban centres; see the *Initial and First Periodic Report of Israel on the Implementation of the International Covenant on Civil and Political Rights*, July 1998, para. 716. Subsequently the government announced the establishment of three more concentration points in the Naqab, Bet Felet, Mir'it and Bir Hayil. In April 2001 a further announcement was made by the planning authorities that three further recognized localities for the Bedouin would be established, Um Batin, Qasr il Sir and Wadi il Ghwein, and that these would be agricultural villages.

5. This objective was included, for instance, when a Master Plan for the Northern District, no. 2, Amendment 9, was commissioned by the Ministry of Planning in November 1990.

6. The Association of Forty, a community-based organization representing the unrecognized villages, submitted an alternative plan for the north and centre in 1992. It aimed to ascertain the aspirations of the communities and to show how they could be permitted to remain and develop where they were while adhering to sound planning considerations. They proposed that some would be recognized as independent villages while others would be amalgamated

to form new recognized entities that would receive services jointly, and the remainder would be joined to a neighbouring village or town. National Plan Tama 31 stated that the plan had been partially adopted. It was influential in bringing about the decision in 1995 to recognize some of the villages.

7. In 1990 the Association for Support and Defence of Bedouin Rights in Israel commissioned the preparation of a plan that aimed to present an alternative centred on the wishes of the Bedouin; it proposed a diversity of types of settlement designed to achieve a quality of life in harmony with the human and physical environment of the Bedouin. The plan proposed that the currently recognized townships be expanded to take in surrounding unrecognized villages and be developed to provide the opportunity for farming for those who wish it and industrial zones and other commercial enterprises to provide employment opportunities. The plan also proposed the recognition of thirteen other existing unrecognized settlements and two sheperds' villages and the inclusion of communities bordering established Jewish localities in their municipal boundaries. A survey of attitudes towards the plan found that 86.8 per cent of the Bedouin population support the plan; Association for Support and Defence of Bedouin Rights in Israel (1992: 10). From the late 1990s, a new group, the Regional Council for the Unrecognized Villages of the Palestinian Bedouin in the Naqab, took up the task of proposing planning solutions and engaging with the planning authorities in relation to those proposals, which included a plan 'Negev Arabs 2020', detailing solutions for the forty-five unrecognized villages.

8. LSI, Vol. 19, p. 330.

9. Section 7(b) of the First Schedule to the Planning and Building Law 1965.

10. Planning and Building Law 1965, sections 49(1) and (7).

11. The question of which planning and municipal authority has jurisdiction over the villages can nevertheless be important. A local planning and building commission may, for instance, apply for a change in use of land, submit plans and generally try to support moves towards recognition. Given the minimal representation and decision-making power of the Palestinian community, however, it is rare for the community to be able to influence policy decisions.

12. Sections 145(a) and (b) of the Planning and Building Law 1965.

13. Sawa'id v. Central Galilee Planning and Building Commission, Appeal 874/78 (see Chapter 7).

14. Prior to 1948 Birsheba was a thriving town inhabited by non-Bedouin Palestinians but they left or were driven out during the war. Most of the Bedouin also left: of 65,000–90,000 who lived in the area before 1948, only 11,000 remained after the war (Maddrell 1990: 6).

15. 3,220 claims relating to a total of 776,856 dunams were submitted by Bedouin in order to establish their rights; Association for Support and Defence of Bedouin Rights in Israel (1990: 19–20), and information compiled from official sources in 1979. This does not represent the full amount of land used by Bedouin before 1948, which is close to 2 million dunams.

16. Official statistics put the 'arab' population of the Naqab at 106,400,

making them around 17 per cent of the population. However, a general note in the Statistical Abstract says that the statistics regarding the Bedouin are incomplete. A Bedouin organization, the Regional Council for the Unrecognized Villages in the Naqab, estimates that the Bedouin population in the Naqab is around 120,000, making the Bedouin around 19 per cent.

17. See above, note 4, regarding the announced intention to establish three to five further recognized localities for the Bedouin, and the possibility of at least some agricultural communities.

18. The Regional Council for the Unrecognized Villages of the Palestinian Bedouin in the Naqab say that there are forty-five villages with the populations ranging from 600 to 4,000. The classification into distinct communities is not always easy due to the patterns of settlement. In 1994 the Association of Forty carried out a field survey and found thirty-six large localities and sixty-four small localities.

19. Esther Levinson, Town Planning Adviser, Association for Support and Defence of Bedouin Rights in Israel, in an interview in February 1993, said the Ministry of the Interior had announced in 1992 that the Bedouin had constructed 12,489 illegal buildings, only 1,853 of which were solid buildings. In May 2001, it was reported that officials in the Ministry of the Interior had informed the Minister that there were some 30,000 Bedouin illegal structures in the Naqab; Aliza Arbeli, 'Bedouin build 30,000 illegal structures, interior minister told', *Ha'aretz* (Hebrew daily newspaper), 4 May 2001.

20. Announced in Israel's Initial and First Periodic Report on the implementation of the UN Covenant on Civil and Political Rights, presented to the UN Human Rights Committee in July 1998, para. 716. This had not been followed up with specific details.

21. Report of the Inter-Ministerial Committee to Examine Illegal Construction in the State of Israel.

22. For example, Adalah wrote to the Attorney General on 11 July 2001 in response to the recently stepped-up policy of demolition of homes, including in the unrecognized communities in the Naqab.

23. 'Land policy and the problem of the Bedouin in Israel', *Ha'aretz*, 31 July 1963.

24. Interview with Esther Levinson, February 1993.

25. These observations are made with the proviso that a more in-depth study is needed in order to make an assessment of the situation; the information is based on complaints from the inhabitants of Aroer.

26. ILC Decisions 29 of August 1967 and 64 of 28 October 1968.

27. Announcement of the ILA in *Yediot Aharanot* (Hebrew daily newspaper), 12 June 1989.

28. ICESCR Art. 6. The Draft Declaration on the Rights of Indigenous Peoples, para. 19, also provides that indigenous peoples are to be allowed to engage in their traditional and other economic activities, including herding and cultivation, and must be accorded equal treatment in governmental agrarian programmes.

29. Amendment 14 to the Outline Plan of 1981, drawn up in order to implement National Outline Plan 31, a response to the large-scale immigration to Israel of Soviet Jews in the late 1980s and early 1990s. National Plan 31 envisages large-scale development of Birsheba which would become the fourth metropolitan area in the country.

30. The information in this and the following paragraph is provided by Esther Levinson, town planner and adviser to the Association for Support and Defence of Bedouin Rights in Israel, in interviews in December 1994 and March 1995.

31. Petition to the High Court by Ghazi Abu Kaf and others v. Minister of the Interior and the Local Council of Omer, HC 6672/00, in which the Bedouin villages of Um Bten and Al Makiman ask for the annexation to be cancelled.

32. The case of Ramat Beker, referred to in Chapter 6.

33. The Regional Council for Unrecognized Villages in the Naqab filed the petition in 2001. In response to the petition, the High Court ordered the Ministry of the Interior and planning bodies to draw up a plan taking into account the Bedouin communities and their alternative plan by October 2002.

34. Whereas in the Naqab some of the communities have a population of several thousands, a survey conducted in 1988 of thirty-two unrecognized villages in the north found that they varied in size from 28 to 650 inhabitants. A majority (twenty-three) already existed before 1948, and only two had been founded in the previous twenty years. The survey also found that these communities had a high birth rate and low emigration rate, suffered overcrowding and environmental stress, and lacked basic services such as water, electricity and access roads, schools and clinics. Survey conducted by the Association of Forty, a community-based organization which campaigns for the recognition of the unrecognized villages, Haifa, 1988.

35. Government Decision 4464 of 15 November 1998, cited in ILC Decision 864 of 3 May 1999 regarding compensation for evacuated land and property of Bedouin in the north.

36. ILC Decision 864. Incentives are given to Bedouin to encourage them to move, such as reduced payments for the land they are allocated; ILC Decision 864, and ILC Decision 860 of 3 May 1999.

37. By December 2001, according to information from the Association of Forty, plans had been approved for only three of the villages (Al-Arian, Domeidi and Khawalid); plans had been deposited but not approved for four others (Ras Il Naba', Husseinyeh, Kamaneh and Ein Hod), and in Kamaneh and Ein Hod only parts of the village had been included in the plan; and in the remaining two (Arab Naim and Hamira), plans were still being prepared.

38. 'Committee rejects conditions for recognition in exchange for giving up land', statement of the Association of Forty, 16 September 1998.

39. Hashim Sawa'id and Others v. Local Council of Misgav and Others, HC 7960/99 was brought by residents of Jalsi, and Ismai'il Sawa'id and Another v. Local Council of Misgav and Others, HC 6032/99 by residents of the Western Quarter.

40. Survey by the Association of Forty, Haifa, 1988.

41. *Statistical Abstract of Israel*, 1992; the 2000 *Statistical Abstract* does not include statistics on the number of localities with fewer than 2,000 inhabitants.

42. Master Plan for the Arab Unrecognized Villages in the Haifa and Northern Districts, Association of Forty, 1989.

43. A good example is the Misgav Regional Council, which provides services to twenty-six small rural Jewish settlements through an integrated programme including agriculture, industrial and service sectors in a rural setting; Faour (1991).

44. *Gazit Report* (2000). The *Report* finds that there are approximately 22,000 illegal buildings in central and northern Israel, of which 16,000 are in the Jewish sector and 6,000 in the Palestinian sector. There are also a further 24,000 illegal buildings in the south, most of which are in the Palestinian Bedouin unrecognized communities; Adalah (2001b: 37).

45. According to a survey carried out in 1995 by a community-based organization, whereas in the Naqab some 75 per cent are tents or corrugated-iron huts, and only 25 per cent are stone houses, in the north, 83.6 per cent are built of stone and cement. Survey by the Association of Forty, Haifa, 1994.

46. For instance, on 2 April 1998, half of the homes in the unrecognized village of Um El-Sahali near Shefa 'Amr were demolished by officials of the Planning and Building Commission accompanied by a large police force. Two days later, after the villagers and others started to rebuild the houses and a community protest was held, a large military force moved in and violently broke up the protest; Arab Association for Human Rights (1998: 30).

47. In the Naqab, official Ministry of the Interior statistics show that 507 Bedouin homes were demolished in the Naqab between June 1988 and May 1990; Itim news agency, 16 October 1990.

48. 'Border Police and Green Patrol destroy 52 homes in the Negev', press release of the Arab Association for Human Rights, Nazareth, 29 May 2002.

49. The Association for Support and Defence of Bedouin Rights, bi-monthly report for Sept.–Oct. 1991.

50. Decision of the International Water Tribunal in the case of the Galilee Society for Health Research and Services and the Follow-up Committee on Health in the Arab Sector v. Government of the State of Israel, Amsterdam, 19 February 1992.

51. Regional Council for the Unrecognized Villages in the Naqab and Others v. Minister of National Infrastructure and Others, HC 3586/01.

52. Adalah and Others v. Ministry of Health and Others, HC 7115/97. The order was made in March 1999, but the petitioners were forced to go back to the Court in 2000 to enforce it when the Ministry failed to implement the order. Subsequently the clinics were built.

53. Regional Council for the Unrecognized Villages in the Naqab and Others v. Minister of Labour and Social Welfare and Others, HC 5838/99. The services were restored and expanded after the Court accepted the state's proposals to do so in September 2000.

54. See for instance, the *Jerusalem Post* (English-language daily newspaper), 9 March 1994.

55. Press release of the Regional Council for the Unrecognized Villages of the Palestinian Bedouin in the Naqab, 15 February 2002.

56. A wide variety of international instruments address the right to adequate housing, for instance Article 25.1 of the UDHR, Article 5(e)(iii) of CERD, Article 14.2 of CEDAW, Article 27.3 of the CRC. The most comprehensive regime for the protection of this right is in the International Covenant on Economic, Social and Cultural Rights. Article 11.1 of the ICESCR provides: 'The States Parties to the present Covenant recognize the right of everyone to an adequate standard of living for himself and his family, including adequate food, clothing and housing, and to the continuous improvement of living conditions. The States Parties will take appropriate steps to ensure the realization of this right, recognizing to this effect the essential importance of international co-operation based on free consent.'

57. General Comment no. 4 of the Committee on Economic, Social and Cultural Rights, which monitors compliance with the ICESCR (1992).

58. Article 2.1 of the ICESCR provides: 'Each State Party to the present Covenant undertakes to take steps, individually and through international assistance and co-operation, especially economic and technical, to the maximum of its available resources, with a view to achieving progressively the full realization of the rights recognized in the present Covenant by all appropriate means, including particularly the adoption of legislative measures.' And see Leckie (1992: 63), and COHRE (1994: 65).

59. This right may only be restricted by law, and only as necessary to protect national security, public order, public health or morals or the rights and freedoms of others, and only in a manner consistent with other rights recognized in the Covenant.

60. The National Committee of Arab Mayors v. Minister of Housing and Building, HC 727/00.

61. 'Supreme Court orders government to provide Urban Renewal Program according to needs of Arab towns', Adalah News Update, 13 December 2001.

62. Hashim Sawa'id and Others v. Local Planning and Building Commission of Misgav and Others, HC 7960/99, and Ismai'il Sawa'id and Another v. Local Planning and Building Commission of Misgav and Others, HC 6032/99, judgments handed down on 5 September 2001.

63. Decision of 12 November 2001; Adalah News Update, 21 November 2001. On this basis, the Court quashed the demolition order issued against the mosque in Husseiniya, which like all the buildings in the village lacked a building permit. The government had agreed in 1995 to grant official recognition of Husseiniya but the planning process that would result in licensing of buildings had not yet been completed.

64. Local Planning and Building Commission for Tel Aviv v. Keren Mordecai and Others, Criminal Cases, Tel Aviv 4/87, Local Judgments 5750(b), p. 514.

65. Head of the Committee of Arab Mayors and Others v. Minister of the Interior and Others, HC 9472/00. See Chapter 7.

66. See in relation to the Azazmeh, the Association for Support and Defence of Bedouin Rights bi-monthly report for Sept.–Oct. 1991. Successful cases relating to the provision of services to unrecognized villages include Regional Council for the Unrecognized Villages in the Naqab and Others v. Minister of National Infrastructure and Others, HC 3586/01, regarding the connection of seven villages to the water network, Adalah and Others v. Ministry of Health and Others, HC 7115/97, regarding the building of health clinics and Regional Council for the Unrecognized Villages in the Naqab and Others v. Minister of Labour and Social Welfare and Others, HC 5838/99, regarding the appointment of social workers.

67. Sawa'id and Others v. Central Galilee Planning and Building Commission, HC 874/78. The High Court in October 1994 agreed that section 212 of the 1965 law could be used in cases of buildings constructed long ago, where the criminal proceedings against individuals concerned were barred by the limitation period. However, in Falah v. State of Israel, Criminal Appeal, Nazareth District Court case 224/91, the Court said the special power should be used with caution and mainly only where an illegal construction caused a hindrance to the public or interfered with the implementation of an approved plan, and it was not appropriate to implement it in this case where the applicant had been acquitted in court and the authorities had erred in failing to take enforcement action earlier.

68. Revised Guidelines Regarding the Form and Contents of States Reports to be submitted by States Parties under Articles 16 and 17 of the Covenant on Economic, Social and Cultural Rights, reproduced in COHRE (1993: 37).

69. Commission on Human Rights, Resolution 1993/77, Articles 1(b) and 3.

70. Oral Statement to the 51st Session of the UN Commission on Human Rights, Geneva, February 1995, by Miloon Kothari of the Habitat International Coalition.

71. In the UK, this is illegal if it arises from a definite act of the planning authorities; Handy (1993: 14). It would be illegal under s.1(2) Town and Country Planning Act 1990. In the USA, the landmark case of Brown v. Board of Education of Topeka, 347 US 485, 190/54, held that separate is inherently unequal.

72. Burkhan v. Corporation for Reconstruction and Development of the Jewish Quarter in the Old City of Jerusalem, Ltd, HC 114/78, PD 32(2) 800; the judgment is also summarized in English in *Israel Yearbook on Human Rights* (1990), p. 374.

73. HC 528/88, cited in Bankler (1991: 146).

74. Or, as Yokhai Bankler points out, if the aim of the policy is to sedentarize the Bedouin, why are they given no choice and only offered favourable conditions (or indeed, any possibility of settling legally) if they agree to settle in a particular place? (Bankler 1991: 154).

75. In the UK, as an additional safeguard against racial or other considerations influencing planning, the courts have stated that planning authorities must base their decisions on planning considerations rather than other considerations.

In Israel there is no such limitation and planning policies from the national level down are influenced by ideological and racial factors.

76. For instance, Israel is party to the International Convention on the Elimination of All Forms of Racial Discrimination of 1965; see Chapter 2.

77. For instance, the Welsh Office circular 53/88 (issued on 20 June 1991) obliged the planning authorities to 'consider the relationship of planning policies and proposals to social needs and problems including their likely impact on different groups in the population', including the interests of the Welsh language.

78. HC 684/82, HC 2657/90 and HC 6215/92.

79. 'The Housing Rights Bill', National Campaign for Housing Rights, Bombay, 1992.

80. Giving judgment, Judge Barak stated that the test as to whether or not a public authority had illegally discriminated was based on three elements: (1) the authority must show it had considered the harm to the principle of equality, (2) the authority must show it had balanced the competing considerations, and given reasonable weight to the principle of equality, (3) the authority had assessed the harm to the other, competing considerations, and concluded there was no other way to achieve the particular policy aim. Poraz v. Mayor of Tel Aviv, HC 953/87, discussed in Bankler (1991: 142).

CHAPTER 9

Conclusion

§ LAND lies at the heart of the 'Palestinian Question'. This is true not only because of its centrality in the negotiations that relate to the territories occupied by Israel since 1967; land is also central to the situation of the Palestinian refugees from 1948, whose right of return to their land in Israel has to be considered as part of any solution that is in accordance with international law.[1] But what is too often forgotten is that the question of land also lies at the heart of the nature of the state of Israel itself: the third major component of the Zionist–Palestinian conflict. The various means by which Israel has denied Palestinian citizens access to land within the state are the central theme of this study.

We have identified three main tools that are part of an exclusionary land regime. The first of these is dispossession. Prior to 1948 Palestinian Arabs owned or used the vast majority of the land in Palestine; this was no 'land without a people'. The undermining of Palestinian land rights really began when the area was placed under the Mandate of Britain, which had already, in the Balfour Declaration of 2 November 1917, committed itself to allowing the establishment of a Jewish homeland in Palestine. During the 1948 war, the land of 750,000 Palestinian refugees was seized and four-fifths of the Palestinian communities in the area that became Israel disappeared. Israeli governments subsequently stated that they regarded the solution to the Palestinian refugee problem as being solely in the Arab states; the refugees might have a right to compensation, but not return to their land. Israel took an equally uncompromising stance as regards Palestinians displaced internally, who were also prohibited from returning to their villages and homes even though they had become Israeli citizens. From 1948 onwards, the new state continued to seize Palestinian land using a variety of legislation. The surviving Palestinian communities within the state have lost as much as 70 per cent of their land to date.

A particularly harsh policy has been pursued against the Palestinian Bedouin of the Naqab. Israel forcibly evicted most of the Bedouin from their lands in the 1950s and has since been trying to relocate them in small and inappropriate urban townships, a solution rejected by the Bedouin. Meanwhile, the Bedouin land claims have still not been recognized or resolved. The state has played a waiting game, while applying pressure on the population to comply with its re-settlement policy and demanding that Bedouin surrender their land claims in exchange for moving into the townships. Forced off their land, prohibited from developing their communities yet not offered an acceptable alternative, many Bedouin prefer to suffer harsh conditions in 'permanently temporary' communities.

A second major tool for restricting Palestinian access to land has been the regime for the ownership and administration of non-private land. The land regime formalized in legislation of 1960 involved not so much 'nationalization' as 'Judaization' of land. All of the land that was owned by the state and the JNF was renamed 'Israel Lands', and now comprises around 94 per cent of all land in the state. This land may be leased for particular purposes, but not sold. Control and administration of Israel Lands was placed in the hands of a new and powerful public body, the ILA. Since it controls so much land immediately surrounding and even within the Palestinian communities, every Palestinian community is dependent on the ILA for land. Any land regime that keeps a very high proportion of land in non-private ownership and administered directly by the state is under a heavy burden to ensure equality of access to that land. But although as a public body it has a duty to treat all citizens equally, the ILA, dominated by representatives of the JNF, systematically discriminates against the Palestinian communities, and makes it extremely difficult for them to obtain access to land for agriculture, building and other development.

The third major tool for denying Palestinians access to land in Israel has been the system regulating land development and land-use planning. For Jews in Israel, positive planning is a dynamic and proactive if uncoordinated push to 'create facts', encouraging and initiating development even if this means breaking the law or creating special procedures (Alexander et al. 1983: 125). Palestinians, on the other hand, experience 'negative planning' that is passive, regulatory and reactive. Planning fails to take account of their needs and in some aspects actu-ally works to prevent development. Palestinians face obstacles whether they try to develop existing communities, establish new localities or move into predominantly Jewish areas. Planning authorities have not allowed the establishment of any new communities for Palestinians since 1948 other than those aimed at concentrating Bedouin. They have contained existing towns and villages, starving them of land and development to such an extent that they all face severe crises in housing and infrastructure. A particularly harsh policy has been pursued against the 'unrecognized villages', tens of Palestinian communities that Israeli governments and planning bodies have refused to include in planning processes and have labelled as illegal. Prohibited from developing as a punitive measure, these communities have little or no access to national water, electricity and other networks.

One issue that consistently arises throughout this study is the exclusion of Palestinians from bodies that take key decisions regarding access to land. Nor are Palestinians allowed anything more than a minimal degree of self-government even at the local level. There is a need for an Arab body that looks at the questions of planning and building across the whole Arab sector and acts as a single voice for the aspirations of the Palestinian communities. Such a body could also raise issues such as the need for different choices of types of community and patterns of migration and employment. Israel has discouraged the development of independent Palestinian institutions.

The combined force of these three policy tools of what constitutes a discriminatory Israeli land regime form an extremely powerful bar on Palestinian access to land in the state. The question of access to land in Israel goes to the core of the nature of Zionism and of the State of Israel, and of the relationship between Israel and the Palestinians within its borders. The Zionist movement that was created at the end of the nineteenth century set out to acquire land in Palestine and to settle it exclusively with Jews. Land, once acquired, was considered to be 'redeemed' for the Jewish people, and could be possessed and worked only by Jews. By the time the State of Israel was established in 1948, two separate land systems had already developed within the boundaries of Palestine. The 6 or 7 per cent of land in Jewish ownership was effectively closed to Palestinians, held by Zionist national institutions for the benefit of Jews only. The rest was still largely in the possession of the indigenous Palestinians.

More than fifty years after the establishment of Israel, the same situation still prevails – only now, the proportions are reversed. Today some 94 per cent of all land in the state is regarded as 'redeemed' land that is considered to be at the disposal of the Jewish people. This is known as 'Israel Lands'. Only the remaining 6 per cent can still be bought and sold, with around half of this in Palestinian ownership. Some 13 per cent of Israel Lands is owned by the JNF, which excludes Palestinians from using its land. Although the remainder is not subject to the same restrictions, it is managed in many respects as if it were also still in the ownership of the Zionist movement. As we have sought to demonstrate, all of the bodies that control the land regime – the JNF, the ILA, planning bodies, government ministries and officials – have consistently been driven by the ideological goals of Zionism.

A particularly problematic factor is the extensive role given to the JNF and the JA. Established as institutions of the early Zionist movement, these organizations were not disbanded after 1948 but were incorporated into the framework of the new state and given special statutory responsibilities relating to the development and ownership of land. But despite having been assigned what are in reality key public functions, these bodies have still been permitted to act as if they are private bodies and to exclude Palestinians entirely from their projects. The JNF, for instance, still regards itself as fulfilling the Zionist enterprise, as was clearly shown in the interview with the head of the JNF cited in Chapter 2.[2] Neither the state nor the courts, responsible for protecting the rights of all citizens, have stepped in to impose on them an obligation to respect the principle of equality. This surrendering of state functions to unaccountable bodies that act in the private interests of one category of citizens is unacceptable. These institutions, if they are to be allowed to retain their public functions in the state, must be required to change their policy as regards non-Jews. They should be required either to carry out their functions for the benefit of all citizens or to hand over their functions to the state. Legislation defining their role and functions should be amended so as to ensure that they are not permitted to perform their functions in a discriminatory manner. They should also be made subject to public law, in so far as they do retain public functions.

The narrative Israel presents of itself is as a state governed by rule of law, fundamental principles of equality and human rights; a state both Jewish and democratic.[3] When Israel defines itself (such as in Basic Laws) as the Jewish state, it presents a publicly acceptable face as a state in which Jews can find a home. But what is less easy in today's world, in which apartheid and discrimination are abhorred, is to justify a situation in which Israel retains its Zionist character, and which marginalizes the almost 20 per cent citizens of the state who are not Jews, purely on the basis of their ethnicity and nationality. In other words, it is not easy to justify an ethnic state that is not ready to tolerate the presence of other ethnic groups within its borders. Israel as a Jewish state deals with the Palestinians by ignoring their presence as an ethnic and national group. Aside from the indirect reference in the Declaration of the State to 'all inhabitants', and reference by exclusion in several pieces of legislation that refer to Jews only (such as the Law of Return), there is little recognition or acknowledgement of the indigenous Palestinians, whether individually or as a group, as having a status in the state. In official dealings, they tend to be referred to by their religious or other affiliation, as Druze, Bedouin, Muslims, Christians etc. At most, where the state is forced to refer to them collectively, the term 'non-Jews' tends to be used (such as in the annual Statistical Abstracts) or the generic word 'Arabs'. The implications as regards land are clear. Israel aims to deny the particular link that the Palestinians have with land in what is now Israel, and suggest that this is a disparate collection of groups with no particular identity that could settle anywhere in the Arab world. Access is denied in fact and conceptually.

The treatment of Palestinians in Israel that we have described is not a question of discrimination by private persons, or even of low-level officials, though these certainly occur. They are overwhelmingly instances where public and quasi-public bodies exercising public functions are consistently and systematically pursuing policies that restrict Palestinian access to land. One of the most remarkable aspects of the Israeli land policy is the extent to which government departments, planning bodies, the Israel Lands Administration, the Jewish national institutions and others charged with developing and implementing policies relating to land work with extraordinary singleness of purpose to pursue this objective.[4] Israel does not necessarily ignore the principle of legality: it makes sure to pass the laws it wants in order to achieve its objectives. And it constructs a framework of state and Zionist bodies to control and develop land that have built-in mechanisms aimed at carefully protecting them from having to treat non-Jews in the same way that they treat Jews.

This manipulation also occurs in an international context. Israel is bound by a wide range of international law principles that oblige the state to provide equal rights to its Palestinian citizens, including the principles of equality and non-discrimination. International law also obliges Israel to recognize the historical rights of the indigenous Palestinians to land and property within the state, including the refugees. Because Israel aspires to acceptance by the international community and wants to be viewed as a democratic state abiding by the rule of law, it seeks to justify its actions to the external world. Israeli officials prepare reports to international human rights bodies explaining how its policies and practices are in line with international standards and not discriminatory.

Given that Israel claims to be a state committed to rule of law (including international law), democracy, equality and non-discrimination, there are a number of institutions and mechanisms that ought to operate to safeguard these principles. Throughout this study we have sought to identify these domestic and international principles and have demonstrated how, far from protecting the land rights of the Palestinians, the legislature, ministries and other branches of the executive, and the courts, have operated with remarkable consistency to limit Palestinian access to land. The wide discretions granted under legislation and insufficient safeguards against discrimination have had a major impact on Palestinians.

We found that the entrenchment of certain rights, such as the right to property and to freedom of occupation, as constitutional principles since 1992 has had only limited positive impact.[5] Since the Basic Law does not affect the validity of legislation already in force, it leaves intact the main legislative framework used for expropriating Palestinian land, including the Absentees' Property Law. Basic Laws are, however, to be taken into account for the purposes of interpreting existing legislation, and have proved significant in a few cases before the High Court (see below).

The role of the Israeli High Court in protecting Palestinian land rights has been particularly disappointing. For more than fifty years it has been assigned the role of guardian of the rule of law in Israel,[6] and has been called upon to adjudicate on many of the crucial issues concerning Palestinian land rights. In the course of this study we have examined a large number of these decisions. Many cases have been linked to the process of expropriation and dispossession of Palestinian land; in these decisions, the Court has dealt blow after blow to Palestinian interests in land, and its role in securing the transfer of ownership and control of land to the state has been considerable. When confronted with these issues, the Court has tended largely to defer to the executive, though in certain areas it has played a more proactive role in facilitating the state goal of seizing Palestinian land. In cases relating to control of land use, the Court's record has been little better. Far from championing the rights to equality and non-discrimination for Palestinian citizens of the state in relation to land-use planning and access to state land, the Court has proved reluctant to intervene in decisions of the executive.

Significant gaps remain between the jurisprudence of the High Court and internationally accepted standards on questions such as the scope of discrimination.[7] The practices we have described reveal many violations of international law and human rights law, and Israel has in recent years come under heavy criticism from United Nations bodies responsible for monitoring states' compliance with human rights obligations they have committed themselves to. Yet the Israeli courts have rarely referred to these international standards even when they are pleaded before them.

The record of the High Court is not all negative, and particularly in recent years significant general principles have been established or reaffirmed by the High Court including the right of participation in the planning process, the ongoing link of the original owners of land following expropriation and the fact that the state may not discriminate in allocation of land.[8] But in each of the three examples given, the principle was stated in one specific case, or has been qualified or tentative. And these cases have yet to have a wider impact. Such decisions hardly scratch the surface of the exclusionary land regime in Israel. Palestinians have not been able to look to the High Court to deliver bold judgments touching on the Jewish nature of the state. Rather, the Court has worked in tandem with other organs of the state, the legislature and the executive, to preserve the dominance of Zionist interests and goals; and it has not had a pivotal role in such changes as have occurred in the status of Palestinians in Israel. Unlike the USA, where the Supreme Court played a key role in the 1950s and 1960s in confronting institutional racism, the Israeli High Court has not been willing to criticize or depart from the prevailing regime and, in particular, the nature of ethnic relations in the state (Saban 1996). The High Court has preferred to avoid taking bold decisions that threaten the established order and will go out of its way to turn the matter over to the legislature.[9] When forced to confront the question of the Jewish character of the state when it comes up against other principles it is bound to uphold, such as the principle of equality, the Court comes down clearly on the side of the former. For instance, in giving judgment in the case of Qa'dan, in which it held that the state cannot allocate land to a third party (the Jewish Agency) that uses it on a discriminatory basis, the Court affirmed that the Jewish state incorporates the right to equality. But the Court also said the JA has a historical mission in Israel and its work is not yet complete. The High Court has also, like the state itself, consistently refused to address issues relating to the Palestinian community as collective issues. Palestinians have based many petitions on a claim of national historical discrimination, but the Court has insisted on dealing with them as individual cases.[10]

Where does this lack of protection of their rights leave the Palestinian citizens of Israel? This population is now ghettoized in almost the same number of communities that they had more than fifty years ago, or in pockets within a few 'mixed' cities, which were Palestinian cities before 1948. Some 7.5 per cent still live in appalling conditions in communities that have not been formally recognized by the government, because the government wants them to move elsewhere. The last two decades have seen an increase in broader Israeli–Palestinian tension, including two Intifadas. This has coincided with a deepening of identity of Palestinian citizens as Palestinians, and the violence of October 2000, in which thirteen Palestinian citizens of Israel were killed in confrontations echoing the start of the Al Aqsa Intifada in the Occupied Territories, represents at least in part a spilling over of frustration at Israeli land policies. Since 1948, land expropriation has consistently been the leading source of popular protest against the government among the Palestinian citizens of Israel. At the same time, Israel has been even more concerned than before to place more emphasis on ethnicity and on the Jewish nature of the state. In the run-up to general elections in January 2003, the election committee responsible for regulating political parties and candidates disqualified two Arab parties and candidates on the basis that their goals and activities deny 'the existence of the state of Israel as a Jewish and democratic state'.[11] Calls from Israeli right-wingers for the expulsion of Palestinian citizens of the state, or for a population exchange, have become more vocal.[12]

Looking ahead, it is difficult to envisage a willingness on the part of Israel to resolve the many aspects of the Palestinian land question. A crucial question for Palestinians is what will be done to redress fifty years of violations. Even if new legislation and policies were effectively to guarantee Palestinian access to land today, what of all the land lost and all of the violations committed during all the years since 1948? Even the Israeli High Court has acknowledged that expropriation does not sever the link between a land and its owner. The Israeli attempts to do so by passing land from the Custodian of Absentees' Property to the Development Authority to the JNF, and now possibly to private Jewish owners, cannot magically make the historic rights of the Palestinian owners disappear. As Justice Dorner remarked in the case of Nusseibeh, compensation is not sufficient to deal with the harm done to property rights.

At the same time, the legal and practical machinery used to dispossess Palestinians of their land and to limit Palestinian access to land in the State of Israel remains fully intact in all fundamental aspects, and Palestinian citizens of the state remain all too aware that these same laws could be used again. They also see little political will to change the policies and practices that have consistently denied Palestinians access to land. Planning is now taking place that will determine how Israel will look in 2020. These plans involve exactly the same objectives to contain Palestinian development and promote Jewish development that characterized earlier plans. This cannot be done without further harming the rights of Palestinians. On a day-to-day level, a million Palestinians live as citizens of Israel, but find it increasingly difficult to gain access to the land they need to survive. Palestinians in Israel, like any other population, depend on access to land for housing and the natural growth of their communities, industry and agriculture, leisure and other activities. Yet their growing communities are increasingly finding themselves hemmed in on ever-decreasing amounts of land. If Israel is to evolve into a state that accepts basic international and human rights norms, it will have to prove itself willing to redress the wrongs of the past fifty years, modify its fundamental systems regarding land and allow equality of access to land to its Palestinian citizens. But such moves would be to contradict the basic character of the state as it is now. So long as it remains a Zionist and an ethnic state, committed to acquiring and using the land and other state resources for the benefit of Jews only to the exclusion of others, Israel will not be able to evolve in this way. The state cannot at one and the same time be both an ethnic state that relies on oppression, and a state for all its citizens based on principles of equality and democracy. Access to land is the core of the question.

Notes

1. According to Article V of the Declaration of Principles on Interim Self-Government Arrangements of 13 September 1993, the question of the Palestinian refugees is one of the issues to be covered in permanent status negotiations. For a discussion of the right of return in international law see Chapter 2. For a Palestinian perspective on how the right of return could be implemented, see for example Abu Sitta (2001), and for an Israeli viewpoint, Arzt (1997).

2. 'One hundred years of the JNF', interview with Shlomo Gravitz, head of the JNF Council, *Globes* (financial newspaper), 5 October 2001, p. 29 (in Hebrew), cited in detail in Chapter 2.

3. The Declaration of the Establishment of the State of Israel declares that Israel is 'the Jewish State' but also that the state will 'foster the development of the country for the benefit of all its inhabitants' and will 'ensure complete equality of social and political rights to all its inhabitants', *Official Gazette*, no. 1, 14 May 1948.

4. For example, the settlement of title process that took place in the 1950s and 1960s comprised a concerted effort by the legislature, the courts and the ILA; see Chapter 4 and Kedar (1999: 443).

5. The Basic Law: Human Dignity and Liberty, enacted by the Israeli Knesset in 1992, purports to bring about constitutional entrenchment of property rights in Israel. Article 3 provides: 'There shall be no violation of the property of a person.' The Basic Law was enacted by the Knesset on 17 March 1992 and is available in English on the Knesset website <www.knesset.gov.il>. Exceptions are provided for in Article 8 which provides that rights guaranteed under the Basic Law shall not be violated: 'except by a law befitting the values of the State of Israel, enacted for a proper purpose, and to an extent no greater than is required, or by regulation enacted by virtue of express authorization in such law'.

6. The Israeli High Court has two functions: it both acts as the highest Israeli Court of Appeal, ruling on appeals from the District Courts in civil and criminal cases, and, sitting as the High Court of Justice, hears petitions in constitutional and administrative law issues against any government body or agent.

7. Compare the case of Nazareth Committee for the Protection of Expropriated Land v. Minister of Finance, decided by the High Court in 1955, with more recent cases relating to discrimination in funding of religious cemeteries, discussed in Chapter 3.

8. The question of consultation was addressed in the cases of Hashim Sawa'id and Others v. Local Planning and Building Commission of Misgav and Others, HC 7960/99, and Ismai'il Sawa'id and Another v. Local Planning and Building Commission of Misgav and Others, HC 6032/99, judgments handed down on 5 September 2001. The Court ordered that the inhabitants of the unrecognized village of Kamaneh should be consulted by the planning authorities during the process of preparation of a plan for their community. The link of original owners with their land was affirmed in the Kersek case, involving a Jewish landowner whose land had been expropriated for public purposes. The High Court said that the effect of Basic Law: Human Dignity and Liberty in a case where the original reason for the expropriation no longer existed was that the land should be returned to the owner (Kersek and Others v. State of Israel, the ILA and Others, HC 2390/96, PD 55[2]). The third case, regarding discrimination in allocation of land, is the Qa'dan case, 'Adil Qa'dan v. ILA and Others, HC 6698/95, judgment of 8 March 2000, PD 54(1), 258.

9. So, for example, in the Kersek case, having found that practices relating to the Expropriation for Public Purposes Ordinance would contravene the Basic Law: Human Dignity and Liberty, the Court asked the legislature to address the issue.

10. For instance, the petitions brought by the legal advocacy group Adalah and many of those brought to the Court in the early years, such as the Nazareth and Makhul cases under the Public Purposes Ordinance.

11. The requests were submitted pursuant to section 7(a) of the Basic Law: The Knesset; *Adalah News Update*, 21 December 2002. One of the applications for disqualification was issued by the Attorney General who based his request on security and undisclosed information.

12. Israeli Tourism Minister Benny Elon of the far-right Moledet party called for 'transfer' of Palestinians; Ben Lynfield, 'Israeli expulsion idea gains steam', *Christian Science Monitor*, 6 February 2001. According to an opinion poll conducted by the Jaffee Center for Strategic Studies in February 2002, 31 per cent of Israel's Jewish citizens favour transferring Israeli Arabs out of the country, while 60 per cent favoured encouraging them to leave the country; 'More Israeli Jews favor transfer of Palestinians, Israeli Arabs – poll finds', *Ha'aretz* (English-language edition), 12 March 2002. In March 2002 Adalah, the Legal Center for Arab Minority Rights in Israel, wrote to the Minister of the Interior following newspaper reports that he had prepared a list of Arab citizens of Israel whose citizenship he plans to revoke on the basis that they pose a potential security threat; *Adalah News Update*, 20 February 2002.

Bibliography

Abu El Haija, M. (1994) 'National Plan: The Extreme and Intentional Disregard for the Arab Sector', paper presented at the Conference on Human Right in the Arab Sector, Nazareth (October).

Abu Kishk, B. (1963) *Survey of Arab Agriculture and Development Plan A*, Joint Development Centre, Ministry of Agriculture, Nazareth: Unit for Survey and Planning for the Minority Villages.

— (1981) 'Arab land and Israeli policy', *Journal of Palestine Studies*, vol. XI, no. 1, Autumn.

Abu-Rabia, A. (1994) *The Negev Bedouin and Livestock Rearing*, Oxford: Berg.

Abu Rayah, I. (1995) *The Arabs in the Regional Councils in Israel*, Israel: Givat Haviva Centre.

Abu Saad, I. and K. Fredrick (1993) *Social and Political Change in the Bedouin Arab Community in Israel During the Past Four Decades*, Hubert H. Humphrey Institute for Social Ecology, Ben-Gurion University of the Negev.

Abu Shakrah, S. (1994) *The Right to Adequate Housing as a Human Right An Argument for the Housing Rights Approach to the Global Housing Crisis*, Jerusalem: Palestine Human Rights Information Center.

Abu-Sitta, S. (1999) *Palestinian Right to Return, Sacred, Legal and Possible*, 2nd rev. edn, London: Palestinian Return Centre.

— (2000) *The Palestinian Nakba 1948, The Register of Depopulated Localities in Palestine*, London: Palestine Return Centre.

— (2001) *From Refugees to Citizens at Home*, London: Palestine Land Society and Palestinian Return Centre.

Adalah (The Legal Center for Arab Minority Rights in Israel) (1998) *Legal Violations of Arab Minority Rights in Israel* (March), Shafa'amr, Israel.

— (1999) *Adalah's Review*, vol. 1 (Autumn), Shafa'amr, Israel.

— (2000) *Adalah's Review*, vol. 2 (Autumn), Shafa'amr, Israel.

— (2001) *Institutionalised Discrimination against Palestinian Citizens of Israel, Adalah's Report to the World Conference against Racism, Racial Discrimination, Xenophobia and Related Intolerance, Durban, South Africa* (August/September), Shafa'amr, Israel.

Adva Center (1995) *Israeli Equality Monitor*, no. 4, Tel Aviv.

Albeck, P. (1985) in Land Use Research Institute, *The Negev :Lands from a Legal Point of View*, Report of the Legal Policy Discussion Group, vol. 24, Jerusalem (in Hebrew).

Alexander, E. R., R. Alterman and H. Law-Yone (1983) 'Evaluating Plan Implementation: The National Statutory Planning System in Israel', *Progress in Planning*, vol. 20, Part 2.

Al Haj, M. (1991) 'The Attitudes of the Palestinian Arab Citizens in Israel towards Soviet Jewish Immigration', *International Journal of Refugee Law*, vol. 3, no. 2, Oxford University Press, p. 250.

Al Haq (1986) *Planning in Whose Interest? Land Use Planning as a Strategy for Judaization*, Occasional Paper no. 4, Ramallah.

Alternative Information Center (1997) *News from Within*, vol. XIII, no. 6 (June), Jerusalem and Bethlehem.

Amnesty International (2001) *The Right to Return: The Case of the Palestinians*, Policy Statement, London: Amnesty International (March).

Anglo-American Committee of Inquiry (1946) *A Survey of Palestine*, prepared between December 1945 and January 1946.

Arab Association for Human Rights (1996) *Housing for All?*, Report of the Arab Coordinating Committee on Housing Rights in Israel to the UN Committee on Economic, Social and Cultural Rights, Nazareth (April).

— (1998) *The Palestinian Arab Minority in Israel: Economic, Social and Cultural Rights*, Nazareth.

Arzt, D. (1997) *Refugees into Citizens: Palestinians and the End of the Arab–Israeli Conflict*, New York: Council on Foreign Relations Press.

Association for Support and Defence of Bedouin Rights in Israel (1990) *Master Plan for the Bedouin Population in the Southern District*, Final Report.

— (1992) *Bedouins in the Negev: Attitudes and Aspirations*, Final Report, DIIMA Institute, Musmus, Israel.

Association of Forty (1994) *Field Study of the Unrecognized Villages in the North of Israel*, Haifa (in Arabic).

Attrash, A. (1994) 'Land and Industry in the Arab Sector in Israel', paper presented at the Conference on the Human Rights of the Palestinians in Israel, Nazareth (October).

Aukerman, M. (2000) 'Definitions and Justifications: Minority and Indigenous Rights in a Central/East European Context', *Human Rights Quarterly*, vol. 22, no. 1 (February), Johns Hopkins University Press.

Bachrach, P. and M. S. Baratz (1970) *Power and Poverty: Theory and Practice*, New York: Oxford University Press.

BADIL Resource Center (2001) *Palestinian Refugees and the Right of Return*, Brief no. 8, Bethlehem (January).

Baer, G. (1957) *Land Economics*, vol. 33, no. 3.

Bankler, Y. (1991) 'Discrimination in Housing', *Law Studies*, vol. 16, no. 1 (in Hebrew).

Barak, A. (1993) *Interpretation in Law, Vol. II, Statutory Interpretation*, Jerusalem: Aharon Nevo Publishing Limited (in Hebrew).

Ben David, Y. (1993) *Urbanisation of the Nomadic Bedouin Population of the Negev, 1967–1992*, Jerusalem: Jerusalem Institute for Israel Studies (in Hebrew).

— (1999) 'More about the conflict over Land between the Bedouin of the Negev and the State', *Karka* ('Land' journal), no. 44 (June) (in Hebrew).

Benvenisti, E. and E. Zamir (1995) 'Private Claims to Property Rights in the Future Israeli–Palestinian Settlement', *American Journal of International Law*, vol. 89.

Benyan, M. (2001) 'The Rights of Agriculturalists to State Land in the Land of Israel', paper presented at the first annual Israeli Bar Association meeting, Eilat (in Hebrew).

Brownlie, I. (1998) *Principles of Public International Law*, 5th edn, Oxford: Oxford University Press.

B'Tselem: The Israeli Information Center for Human Rights in the Occupied Territories (1995) *A Policy of Discrimination: Land Expropriation, Planning and Building in East Jerusalem*, Jerusalem.

Buchanan, S. W. (1997) 'A Conceptual History of the State Action Doctrine', *Houston Law Review*, vol. 34, no. 333, Texas.

Bunton, M. (2000) 'Demarcating the British Colonial State: Land Settlement in the Palestine Jiftlik Villages of Sajad and Qazuza', in R. Owen (ed.), *New Perspectives on Property and Land in the Middle East*, Cambridge, MA, and London: Harvard University Press.

Cano, J. (1992) *The Question of Land in the National Conflict between Jews and Arabs 1917–1990*, Israel: Poalim Library (in Hebrew).

Central Bureau of Statistics (2002) report dated 11 March 2002, cited in Arab Association for Human Rights, Nazareth, *Weekly Press Review*, no. 68 (12 March).

Chomsky, N. (1975) in U. Davis, A. Mack and N. Yuval-Davis (eds), *Israel and the Palestinians*, London: Ithaca Press.

COHRE (Centre on Housing Rights and Evictions) (1993) *Forced Evictions and Human Rights: A Manual for Action*, Netherlands.

— (1994) *Legal Provisions on Housing Rights*, Souces 4, COHRE booklet series (November).

Coon, A. (1992) *Town Planning under Military Occupation: An Examination of the Law and Practice of Town Planning in the Occupied West Bank*, Dartmouth, UK: Ashgate.

Craven, M. (1998) *The International Covenant on Economic Social and Cultural Rights*, Oxford: Clarendon Press.

Crawford, J. (ed.) (1992) *The Rights of Peoples*, Oxford: Clarendon Press.

Daes, E. (1999) *Special Rapporteur's Report on Indigenous People and their Relation to Land*, UN Doc E/CN.4/Sub.2/1999/18 (3 June).

Dakwar, J. (2000) 'On the Politics of Legal Formalism', *Adalah's Review*, vol. 2 (Autumn), Shafa'amr, Israel.

Daneels, I. (2001) *Palestinian Refugees and the Peace Process*, London: Oxfam and JMCC.

Davis, U. and W. Lehn (1978) '"And the Fund Still Lives": The Role of the Jewish National Fund in the Determination of Israel's Land Policies', *Journal of Palestine Studies*, vol. 7, no. 4.

Davis, U. and N. Mezvinsky (eds) (1975) *Documents from Israel 1967–73*, London: Ithaca Press.

Dorner, P. (1972) *Land Reform and Economic Development*, London: Penguin.

Dumper, M. (1994) *Islam and Israel*, Washington, DC: Institute for Palestine Studies.

Eide, A. (1993) 'Possible Ways and Means of Facilitating the Peaceful and Constructive Solution of Problems Involving Minorities', summarized in a report for the Minority Rights Group, *New Approaches to Minority Protection* (December).

El-Aref, A. (1974) *Bedouin Love, Law and Legend*, New York: AMS Press, originally published in Jerusalem in 1944.

Ethridge, M. (1949) Report of the American representative to the Palestine Conciliation Committee, to the US Secretary of State (28 March).

Falah, G. (1985) 'How Israel Controls the Bedouin', *Journal of Palestine Studies*, no. 54 (Winter).

— (1989a) 'Israeli State Policy toward Bedouin Sedentarization in the Negev', *Journal of Palestine Studies*, no. 70 (Winter).

— (1989b) 'Israeli "Judaization" Policy in Galilee and its Impact on Local Arab Urbanization', *Political Geography Quarterly*, vol. 8, no. 3 (July).

Faour, H. (1991) 'The Problem of Services in Unrecognised Villages; Husseinya, a Case Study', MA thesis, Clark University, USA and Settlement Studies Centre, Israel.

Galilee Society for Health Research and Services (1998) *Survey on Sewage Systems in the Arab Villages in Israel*, Shafa'amr.

Gavish, D. (1990) 'Land Settlement during the Mandatory period', in R. Kera (ed.), *The Redemption of the Land in Israel: Thought and Deed*, Jerusalem (in Hebrew).

— (1992) *Land and Map: The Surveying of Palestine 1920–1948*, Jerusalem: Yad Yetzhak Ben-Zvi publishers (in Hebrew).

Gazit Report (2000) Report of the Inter-Ministerial Committee to Examine Illegal Construction in the State of Israel (March) (in Hebrew).

Givati, H. (1981) *One Hundred Years of Settlement*, third edn, vol. 2, Israel: Hakibutz Hame Uchad Publishing House (in Hebrew).

Goadby, F. and M. Doukhan (1935) *The Land Law of Palestine*, Tel Aviv: Shoshany's Printing Co.

Goldenberg, A. (1987) 'Land Policies: The Rights of Municipal Lands', *Karka* ('Land' journal), nos 29–32, 1987 (in Hebrew).

Gonen, A. and R. Khamaysi (1993) *Towards a Policy of Urbanization Poles for the Arab Population in Israel*, Jerusalem: Floersheimer Institute for Policy Studies.

Gouldman, M. (1966) *Legal Aspects of Town Planning in Israel*, Jerusalem: Institute for Legislative Research and Comparative Law, Hebrew University Law Faculty.

Granott, A. (1952) *The Land System in Palestine*, London: Eyre and Spottiswoode.

— (1956) *Agrarian Reform and the Record of Israel*, London: Eyre and Spottiswoode.

Gross, A. (1998) 'The Politics of Rights in Israeli Constitutional Law', *Israel Studies*, vol. 3, no. 2, Indiana University Press.

Hadawi, S. (1963) *Palestine: Loss of a Heritage*, San Antonio: Naylor.

— (1988) *Palestinian Rights and Losses in 1948*, London: Saqi Books.

Haidar, A. (1990) *The Arab Population in the Israeli Economy*, Tel Aviv: International Center for Peace in the Middle East.

Halima, J. (1985) in Land Use Research Institute, *The Negev Lands from a Legal Point of View*, Report of the Legal Policy Discussion Group, vol. 24, Jerusalem (in Hebrew).

Handy, C. (1993) *Discrimination in Housing*, London: Sweet and Maxwell.

Harris, D. J., M. O'Boyle and C. Warbrick (1995) *Law of the European Convention on Human Rights*, London: Butterworths.

Hawkins, J. (1995) 'The Phoenicia Glass Factory', *Challenge*, vol. IV, no. 5, Jaffa: Hanitzotz Publishing.

Higgins, R. (1982) 'The Taking of Property by the State: Recent Developments in International Law', *Recueil des Cours*, vol. 176, Chapter V.

Hirschl, R. (2000) 'Negative Rights vs. Positive Entitlements: A Comparative Study of Judicial Interpretations of Rights in an Emerging Neo-liberal Economic Order', *Human Rights Quarterly*, vol. 22, no. 1 (February), p. 1060.

Hope Simpson, J. (1930) *Palestine: Report on Immigration, Land Settlement and Development*, commissioned by the British government.

Horowitz, Y. (regularly updated) *Enforcement of the Planning and Building Laws – Demolition Orders*, compilation of the Local Authorities (in Hebrew).

Israel Defence Forces (1994) 'The Emigration of the Arabs of Palestine in the Period 1/12/1947 to 1/6/1948', in B. Morris, *1948 and After*, Oxford: Oxford University Press.

ILA (Israel Lands Administration) (1969) *Report for the Years 1967–68*, Jerusalem (in Hebrew).

— (1993) *Report for the Year 1992*, no. 32 (April), Jerusalem (in Hebrew).

— (1997) *Report for the Year 1996*, no. 36 (April), Jerusalem (in Hebrew).

— (2000) *Report for the Year 2000*, selected extracts, <www.mmi.gov.il>.

— (2001) *Report for the Year 2000*, no. 40 (April), Jerusalem (in Hebrew).

Jaffa Research Centre (1990) *Arab Cities and Villages in Israel*, statistical abstract, Nazareth.

Jewish Agency Settlement Department (1987) *Preconditions, Criteria and Procedures for Acceptance of Applicants to Settlements*, Part III, *Documents on Absorption and Residence, Collection of Documents Regarding Settlement* (in Hebrew).

Jiryis, S. (1976) *The Arabs in Israel*, New York and London: Monthly Review Press.

— (1985) 'Settlers Law: Seizure of Palestinian Lands', *Palestine Yearbook of International Law*, vol. II.

Joint Parliamentary Middle East Councils Commission of Enquiry (2001) *Palestinian Refugees, Right of Return* (March), London.

Kalin, W. (2000) *Guiding Principles on Internal Displacement, Annotations*, Washington, DC: American Society of International Law and the Brookings Institution.

Kamen, C. (1991) *Little Common Ground: Arab Agriculture and Jewish Settlement in Palestine 1920–1948*, Pittsburgh: University of Pittsburgh Press.

Kanaana, S. (1992) *Still on Vacation!* Jerusalem: International Center for Palestinian Studies.

Kanaaneh, H., F. McKay and E. Sims (1995) 'A Human Rights Approach for Access to Clean Drinking Water: A Case Study', *Health and Human Rights*, vol. 1, no. 2.

Karsh, E. (1997) *Fabricating Israeli History: The 'New Historians'*, London: Frank Cass.

Kedar, A. (1999) 'Time of Majority, Time of Minority: Land, Nationality and the Prescription Laws in Israel' in Hanoch Dagan (ed.), *Land Law in Israel: Between Private and National*, Ramot Publishers, Tel Aviv University (in Hebrew).

— (2001a) 'The Legal Transformation of Ethnic Geography: Israeli Law and the Palestinian Landholder 1948–1967', *New York University Journal of International Law and Politics*, vol. 33, no. 4.

— (2001b) 'National Land for Whom? The Agriculture Lobby and Its Activities to Legalise the Rights of Agriculturalists on Land', paper presented at the first annual Israeli Bar Association meeting, Eilat (May) (in Hebrew).

Khalidi, W. (ed.) (1992) *All That Remains*, Washington, DC: Institute for Palestine Studies.

Khamaysi, R. (1990) *Planning and Housing Policy in the Arab Sector of Israel*, Tel Aviv: International Center for Peace in the Middle East.

Klein, C. (1987) *Israel as a Nation-State and the Problem of the Arab Minority: In Search of a Status*, Tel Aviv: International Center for Peace in the Middle East.

Kretzmer, D. (1990) *The Legal Status of the Arabs in Israel*, Boulder, CO: Westview Press.

Lahav, P (1993) 'Rights and Democracy', in Sprinzak and Diamond (eds) *Israeli Democracy under Stress*, Boulder, CO: Westview Press.

Land Use Research Institute (1986a) 'Land and Security as Reflected in Israel's Land Policy', *Land Policy Discussion Group*, vol. 27, Jerusalem (in Hebrew).

— (1986b) 'The Implications of Selling National Land', *Land Policy Discussion Group*, vol. 27, Jerusalem (in Hebrew).

Leaber, S. C. 'The Case of Agricultural Land: the Supreme Court Awaits the Government', *Karka* ('Land' journal), no. 51 (in Hebrew).

Leckie, S. (1992) *From Housing Needs to Housing Rights: An Analysis of the Right to Adequate Housing under International Human Rights Law*, London: International Institute for Environment and Development.

Lehn, W. (1974) 'The Jewish National Fund', *Journal of Palestine Studies*, vol. III, no. 4 (Summer).

Lehn, W. and U. Davis (1988) *The Jewish National Fund*, London: Kegan Paul International.

Lekhtman, M. (2001)'Whoever Does Not Like the Milgrom Report Will Find It within the Ronen Report', *Karka* ('Land' journal), no. 51 (April–May).

Lerner, N. (1987) 'Israel's International Obligations Concerning Minorities and Discrimination', in International Center for Peace in the Middle East, *Relations between Ethnic Majority and Minority*, Tel Aviv.

Lichfield, N. and H. Darin-Drabkin (1980) *Land Policy in Planning*, London: George Allen and Unwin.

Limburg (1987) *Limburg Principles on the Implementation of the ICESCR*, Note 27, UN Doc. E/CN.4/1987/17, Annex.

Lustick, I. (1980) *Arabs in the Jewish State: Israel's Control of a National Minority*, Austin: Texas University Press.

McNeil, K. (1989) *Common Law Aboriginal Title*, Oxford: Clarendon Press.

— (1997) 'The Meaning of Aboriginal Title', in M. Asch (ed.) *Aboriginal and Treaty Rights in Canada*, Vancouver, Canada: UBC Press.

Maddrell, P. (1990) *The Bedouin of the Negev*, London: Minority Rights Group Report, no. 81.

Markovitz Commission (1986) *Report on Illegal Building in the Arab Sector* (English trans. available on the website of the Association of Forty).

Masalha, N. (1992) *The Expulsion of the Palestinians*, Washington, DC: Institute for Palestine Studies.

Morris, B. (1987) *The Birth of the Palestinian Refugee Problem, 1947–1949*, Cambridge: Cambridge University Press.

— (1994) *1948 and After*, Oxford: Oxford University Press.

Mossawa (Equality Institute) (2001) *Report on the Social, Economic and Political Status of Arab Citizens of Israel* (Autumn), Haifa.

Nakkara, H. (1985) 'Israeli Land Seizure under Various Defence and Emergency Regulations', *Journal of Palestine Studies*, vol. XIV, no. 2 (Winter).

— (n.d.) Unpublished manuscript on the settlement of title in the Galilee and the Naqab.

Nardell, F. (1995) 'The Quantock Hounds and the Trojan Horse', *Public Law Journal* (Spring), London.

Neive, A. (2000) 'The JNF and the ILA, End of the Common Way', *Karka* ('Land' Journal), no. 50 (in Hebrew).

Oded, Y. (1964) 'Land Losses among Israel's Arab Villages', *New Outlook*, vol. 7.

Owen, R. (2000) 'Introduction', in R. Owen (ed.) *New Perspectives on Property and Land in the Middle East*, Cambridge, MA and London: Harvard University Press.

Peret, E. (1988) 'A Different State of Israel for the Year 2000', *Karka* ('Land' journal), no. 30 (in Hebrew).

Peretz, D. (1958) *Israel and the Palestinian Arabs*, Washington, DC: Middle East Institute.

— (1969) *The Palestine Arab Refugee Problem*, Santa Monica, CA: Rand Corporation.

Phorolis, S., A. Poznanski, A. Shmueli, A. Szskin and S. Zarhi (1979) *Rural–Urban Land Use Equilibrium*, Tel Aviv: Rural Planning and Development Authority, Ministry of Agriculture.

Plant, R. (1994) *Land Rights and Minorities*, London: Minority Rights Group.

Quigley, J. (1990) *Palestine and Israel*, Durham, NC: Duke University Press.

— (1997) 'Mass Displacement and the Individual Right of Return', *British Yearbook of International Law*.

— (1998) 'Displaced Palestinians and a Right of Return', *Harvard International Law Journal*, vol. 39, no. 1 (Winter).

Ratcliffe, J. (1976) *Land Policy*, London: Hutchinson.

Reade, R. (1987) *British Town and Country Planning*, Milton Keynes, UK: Open University Press.

Regional Council for the Unrecognized Villages of the Palestinian Bedouin in the Naqab (1999) *Negev Arabs 2020*, Birsheba.

Rekhes, R. (1977) *The Arabs of Israel and Land Expropriations in the Galilee*, Tel Aviv Surveys, University of Tel Aviv: Shiloh Institute.

Revital (1993) *Laws of Planning and Restriction*, Israel: Sadan (in Hebrew).

Ryan, J. (1973) 'Refugees within Israel', *Journal of Palestine Studies* (Summer).

Saban, I. (1988) 'The Indigenous Rights of the Israeli Bedouin of the Negev Region', unpublished LLM thesis, American University, Washington, DC.

— (1996) 'The Influence of the High Court on the Status of Arabs in Israel', *Law and Rule Journal*, no. 541, Haifa University Law Faculty (in Hebrew).

Schachter, O. (1983) 'Human Dignity as a Normative Concept', 77 *American Journal of International Law*, vol. 77, p. 848.

Shamir, R. (1999) 'The Bedouin in the Legal Sytem in Israel', *Land Law in Israel, Between Private and National*, Ramot Publishers, Tel Aviv University (in Hebrew).

Shanan, L. (1988) *Agricultural Settlements for the Bedouin Population, Policy Proposals*, Jerusalem Institute for Israel Research (in Hebrew), referred to in Association for Support and Defence of Bedouin Rights in Israel (1990) *Master Plan for the Bedouin Population in the Southern District*.

Shehadi R. (1993) *The Law of the Land*, Jerusalem: PASSIA.

Shetreet, S. (1988) 'Affirmative Action for Promoting Social Equality', *Israel Yearbook on Human Rights*, vol. 18.

Shmueli, A. (1983) 'Village Population of the Hilly Upper Galilee 1967–77', *Artzot Hagalil* ('Lands of the Galilee'), Jerusalem, Ministry of Defence (in Hebrew).

Sikkuy (The Association for the Advancement of Civil Equality) (2001a) *Equality and Absorption: The Arab Population in Israel 2000 and 2001* (June) (in Arabic).

— (2001b) *Report of Sikkuy-Misgav on the Equality and Integration of Arab Citizens 2000–2001* (September) (in Hebrew).

Smooha, S. (1999) *The Model of Ethnic Democracy: Characterisation, Cases and Comparisons*, conference proceedings, Conference on Multiculturalism and Democracy in Divided Societies, University of Haifa (March).

State Comptroller's Report (1990) *State Comptroller's Report*, no. 41, Jerusalem.

— (1993) *State Comptroller's Report*, no. 44, Jerusalem.

— (1994) *State Comptroller's Report*, no. 45, Jerusalem.

State of Israel (1998a) *Initial Report of Israel to the UN Committee on Economic Social and Cultural Rights*, UN Doc E/1990/5/Add.39(1) of 20 January.

— (1998b) *Initial report of Israel to the UN Human Rights Committee under the International Covenant on Civil and Political Rights*, UN doc. CCPR/C/81/Add.13 of 9 April.

— (2001) *Second Periodic Report to the Committee on Economic Social and Cultural Rights* (July), Ministry of Justice, Ministry of Foreign Affairs and Ministry of Labour and Social Affairs.

Statistical Abstract (2000) *Statistical Abstract of Israel 2000*, no. 51, Jerusalem: Central Bureau of Statistics.

Stein, K. (1984) *The Land Question in Palestine 1917–1939*, North Carolina: University of North Carolina Press.

Takkenberg, L. (1998) *The Status of Palestinian Refugees in International Law*, Oxford: Clarendon Press.

Thornberry, P. (1993) *The UN Declaration on the Rights of Persons Belonging to National or Ethnic, Religious and Linguistic Minorities: Background, Analysis and Observations*, London: Minority Rights Group.

Triggs, G. (1992) 'The Rights of "Peoples" and Individual Rights: Conflict or Harmony?' in J. Crawford (ed.), *The Rights of Peoples*, Oxford: Clarendon Press.

Tyler, W. P. N. (2001) *State Lands and Rural Development in Mandatory Palestine 1920–1948*, Brighton, UK: Sussex Academic Press.

Tzur, Z. (1972) *Land Status Law in Israel*, booklets 25–26 (in Hebrew).

— (1989) 'The Agrarian Problem and the National Ownership of Land', in *Karka* ('Land' journal), no. 31, Jerusalem (in Hebrew).

UN Committee against Torture (2001) Conclusions and Recommendations, Consideration of the Third Periodic Report of Israel, UN Doc CAT/C/XXVII/Concl.5 of 23 November.

UNCERD (UN Committee on the Elimination of Racial Discrimination) (1998) *Concluding Observations on the Combined Seventh, Eighth and Ninth Periodic Reports of Israel*, UN doc. CERD/C/304/Add.45.

UNCESR (UN Committee on Economic, Social and Cultural Rights) (1991) *General Comment no. 4, on the Right to Adequate Housing*, adopted on 12 December.

— (1997) *General Comment no. 7, 1997, on The Right to Adequate Housing, Forced Evictions*, UN Doc E/C.12/1997/4.

— (1998) *Concluding Observations on the Initial Report of Israel*, UN. doc. E/C.12/1/Add.27 of 4 December 1998.

UNHCR (UN High Commissioner for Refugees) (1985) *Executive Committee Conclusion no. 40*, XXXVI.

— (2002) *Refugees by Numbers*.

UN Human Rights Committee (1989) *General Comment 18*, UN doc CCPR/C/Rev.1/Add.1, 9 November.

— (1993) *General Comment 22*, adopted at the 48th session.

— (1994) *General Comment 23(5), on Article 27 of the ICCPR*, UN Doc CCPR/C/21/Rev.1/Add.5 of 26 April.

— (1998) *Concluding Observations on the Initial Report of Israel Under the ICCPR*, UN doc CCPR/C/79/Add.93 of 18 August.

— (1999) *General Comment no. 27, on Freedom of Movement*, UN Doc.CCPR/C/21/Rev.1/Add.9 of 2 November.

Vitkon, G. (1999) 'Reform of land policy: an assessment of the Ronen Report' *Karka* ('Land' journal), no. 44 (June), p. 35 (in Hebrew).

— (2001) 'Correct separation between the ILA and the JNF, *Karka* ('Land' journal), no. 51 (in Hebrew).

Wade, H. R. W. and C. F. Forsyth (1994) *Administrative Law*, 7th edn, Oxford: Clarendon Press.

Weisman, J. (1970) *The Land Law 1969: A Critical Analysis*, Jerusalem: Israel Law Review.

— (1972) *Principal Features of the Israeli Land Law 1969*, Jerusalem: Hebrew University, Faculty of Law.

— (1981) 'Israel lands', in *Mishpatim* (Law Journal), vol. 21, Jerusalem: Hebrew University (in Hebrew).

Weisman, J. (1987) 'Leaseholds Renewable in Perpetuity: A Miracle Medicine or Closing of Eyes?' *Karka* ('Land' journal), nos 29–32 (in Hebrew).

Yiftachel, O. (1992) *Planning a Mixed Region in Israel*, Aldershot, UK: Avebury.

— (1999a) 'Ethnocracy: The Politics of Judaizing Israel/Palestine', *Constellations*, vol. 6, no. 3, pp. 364–90.

— (1999b) 'Building of a Nation and the Division of Space in the Israeli Ethnocracy' in Hanoch Dagan (ed.), *Land Law in Israel: Between Private and Public*, Ramot Publishers, Tel Aviv University.

Zamir, Y. (1996) *Administrative Power*, vol. 1, Jerusalem: Nebo Publishing.

Zidani, S. (1990) 'Democratic Citizenship and the Arabs in Israel', *Qadaya*, no. 5 (August), Jerusalem (in Arabic).

Zorea, M. and A. Poznisky (1976) 'A New Assessment of Land Policy', *Karka* ('Land' journal), no. 12 (in Hebrew).

Index

Some titles of related interest from Zed Books

Palestine/Israel: Peace or Apartheid, Occupation, Terrorism and the Future

UPDATED EDITION

Marwan Bishara

'Offers penetrating insights into why the Oslo Accords have failed. The author outlines innovative suggestions for overcoming the impasse and ensuring a genuine coexistence between Palestinians and Israelis.' – Alain Gresh, Editor in Chief, *Le Monde Diplomatique*

hb ISBN 1 84277 272 4 £32.95 $55.00

pb ISBN 1 84277 273 2 £ 9.99 $17.50

Apartheid Israel: Possibilities for the Struggle Within

Uri Davis

'Basing his argument on the struggle to end apartheid in South Africa, Uri Davis presents the only sensible way forward in the present deadlock – a roadmap based on civil rights, human dignity and international justice. It has the moral strength to convince victimizers and victims alike that there is a valid alternative to the present Israeli system of discrimination and occupation.' – Ilan Pappé, historian and author of *The Making of the Arab–Israeli Conflict, 1947–1951* (London and New York, 1992).

hb ISBN 1 84277 338 0 £49.95 $75.00

pb ISBN 1 84277 339 9 £14.95 $22.50

The Challenge of Post-Zionism: Alternatives to Israeli Fundamentalist Politics

Edited by Ephraim Nimni

Contributors – including A'sad Ghanem, Uri Ram and Ilan Pappé – explore Post-Zionism's meanings, ambiguities and prospects, and place it in its political context. The book concludes with a fascinating assessment by Edward Said of the implications of this debate for a reconciliation between Israelis and Palestinians.

hb ISBN 1 85649 893 X £45.00 $65.00

pb ISBN 1 85649 894 8 £14.95 $25.00

Tinderbox: US Middle East Policy and the Roots of Terrorism

Stephen Zunes

'A careful, informed and perceptive reconstruction of major historical forces in the Middle East and the world power nexus in which it is enmeshed. A very useful handbook to the complexities of this disturbed and fateful region.' – Noam Chomsky

hb ISBN 1 84277 258 9 £36.95
pb ISBN 1 84277 259 7 £12.99

Syria: Neither Bread nor Freedom
Alan George

'A devastating critique of one-party rule and unchecked power, and a stirring vindication of Syria's courageous civil society movement.' – Rana Kabbani

'Before President Bush turns his liberating attentions to Syria, he would do well to read Alan George' – Julie Flint in the *Guardian*

hb ISBN 1 84277 212 0 £39.95 $65.00
pb ISBN 1 84277 213 9 £13.95 $22.50

The Absence of Peace: Understanding the Israeli–Palestinian Conflict
Nicholas Guyatt

I hope this lucid and well-informed study will be widely read, and will help bring about a redirection that is imperative if ominous prospects are to be averted, and some measure of peace and justice are to be achieved.' – Noam Chomsky

hb ISBN 1 85649 579 5 £37.95 $55.00
pb ISBN 1 85649 580 9 £13.95 $19.95

Refusenik! Israel's Soldiers of Conscience
Compiled and edited by Peretz Kidron

'Our greatest admiration must go to those brave Israeli soldiers who refuse to serve beyond the 1967 borders.... These soldiers, who are Jews, take seriously the principle put forward at the Nuremberg trials in 1945–46: namely, that a solder is not obliged to obey unjust orders – indeed, one has an obligation to disobey them.' – Susan Sontag, novelist, essayist and playwright

hb ISBN 1 84277 450 6 £36.95 $59.95
pb ISBN 1 84277 451 4 £12.95 $19.95

Rogue State: A Guide to the World's Only Superpower
UPDATED EDITION
William Blum

'Bill Blum came by his book title easily. He simply tested America by the same standards we use to judge other countries. The result is a bill of wrongs – an especially well-documented encyclopedia of malfeasance, mendacity and mayhem that has been hypocritically carried out in the name of democracy by those whose only true love was power.' – Sam Smith, Editor, *Progressive Review*, Washington, DC

hb ISBN 1 84277 220 1 £36.95
pb ISBN 1 84277 221 X £ 9.99

Killing Hope: US Military and CIA Interventions Since World War II
William Blum

'Far and away the best book on the topic.' – Noam Chomsky

'A valuable reference for anyone interested in the conduct of US foreign policy.' – *Choice*

'I enjoyed it immensely.' – Gore Vidal

'The single most useful summary of CIA history.' – John Stockwell, former CIA officer and author

hb ISBN 1 84277 368 2 £50.00
pb ISBN 1 84277 369 0 £12.99